OXFORD MONOGRAPHS IN
INTERNATIONAL LAW

General Editors: Professor Ian Brownlie CBE, QC, FBA
*Former Chichele Professor of Public International Law in the
University of Oxford and Member of the International Law Commission*, and
Professor Vaughan Lowe, *Chichele Professor of Public International Law in
the University of Oxford and Fellow of All Souls College, Oxford*

INTERNATIONAL HUMAN RIGHTS AND
ISLAMIC LAW

OXFORD MONOGRAPHS IN
INTERNATIONAL LAW

The aim of this series is to publish important and original
pieces of research on all aspects of international law. Topics
that are given particular prominence are those which, while of
interest to the academic lawyer, also have important bearing
on issues which touch upon the actual conduct of international
relations. Nonetheless, the series is wide in scope and includes
monographs on the history and philosophical foundations of
international law.

INTERNATIONAL HUMAN
RIGHTS AND ISLAMIC LAW

MASHOOD A. BADERIN

OXFORD

UNIVERSITY PRESS

OXFORD

UNIVERSITY PRESS

Great Clarendon Street, Oxford ox2 6DP

Oxford University Press is a department of the University of Oxford.
It furthers the University's objective of excellence in research, scholarship,
and education by publishing worldwide in

Oxford New York

Auckland Bangkok Buenos Aires Cape Town Chennai
Dar es Salaam Delhi Hong Kong Istanbul Karachi Kolkata
Kuala Lumpur Madrid Melbourne Mexico City Mumbai Nairobi
São Paulo Shanghai Taipei Tokyo Toronto

Oxford is a registered trade mark of Oxford University Press
in the UK and in certain other countries

Published in the United States
by Oxford University Press Inc., New York

© M. Baderin, 2003

The moral rights of the author have been asserted

Database right Oxford University Press (maker)

First published 2003

British Library Cataloguing in Publication Data

Data available

Library of Congress Cataloging in Publication Data

Data available

ISBN 0–19–926659–X

1 3 5 7 9 10 8 6 4 2

Typeset by Newgen Imaging Systems (P) Ltd., Chennai, India
Printed in Great Britain
on acid-free paper by
Biddles Ltd, Guildford and King's Lynn

General Editors' Preface

The need for international lawyers to pay attention to the diversity of cultures and legal traditions is more discussed than fulfilled. Dr Baderin's study addresses that need through a detailed and specific analysis of the relationship between international human rights law and Islamic law. His book will be of much interest both to those concerned with these specific matters and those more generally interested in the plurality of the foundations of contemporary international law.

IB
AVL

Dedication

To the memory of my beloved daughter Haolat 'Laitan.

Acknowledgements

My acknowledgements here are not a mere perfunctory ritual but a genuine expression of thanks to all those who offered me valued help during my PhD research and its subsequent publication in this book form. I thank the University of Nottingham and the UK Committee of Vice-Chancellors for the scholarship grants that funded my PhD studies. I thank my research supervisor, Professor David J. Harris, for his academic guidance during my research. I learnt a great deal from his academic excellence and fine qualities. I consider myself very privileged to have benefited from his academic expertise. I greatly appreciate his assistance and concern for my well-being throughout my academic pursuit at the University of Nottingham. I thank Professor Nigel White, Professor Stephen Livingstone, Dino Kritsiotis, Ms Maureen Welch Dolynskyj, Professor Dawood Noibi, Professor Robert McCorquodale, and Michael Anderson, for their help at different stages of my research and the publication of this book. I thank Ademola Abass and all fellow research students, with whom I interacted at the University of Nottingham, for such memorable camaraderie. Thanks to the staff of the University of Nottingham Library, especially for assisting with my many inter-library loan requests, and also to SOAS Library, London, Abul A'lâ Maudûdî Library of the Madni Trust in Nottingham, the Office of the UN High Commissioner for Human Rights, Geneva, the Office of the Organization of Islamic Conference (OIC), Geneva, and Dilwar Hussein of the Islamic Foundation, Leicester, for help with needed materials.

I thank John Louth, Gwen Booth, and Geraldine Mangley, all of the Oxford University Press, and Alison Morley for their co-operation at the publishing stage. I also thank the unanimous reviewers of the manuscript for their valuable comments. I thank Professor Ian Brownlie and Professor Vaughan Lowe for finding time to read the manuscript and for judging this work suitable for inclusion in the esteemed series, Oxford Monographs in International Law. I thank my best friend, Abdul Latif Abdulkadir and my uncle, Hassan O. Arogundade for their valued support throughout.

In some parts of this book I have developed upon some of my ideas and materials on the subject, which were first published elsewhere. Sections of Chapter 2, particularly, contain material from my previous articles: 'The Evolution of Islamic Law of Nations and the Modern International Order: Universal Peace through Mutuality and Cooperation', first published in *The American Journal of Islamic Social Sciences* (2000) Volume 17, No. 2, pp. 57–80; 'Establishing Areas of Common Ground between Islamic Law and International Human Rights', first published in *The International Journal of Human Rights* (2001) Volume 5, No. 2 pp.72–113; 'Dialogue Among

Civilisations as a Paradigm for Achieving Universalism in International Human Rights: A Case Study with Islamic Law', first published in *Asia-Pacific Journal on Human Rights and the Law* (2001) Volume 2, No. 2, pp.1–41; 'A Macroscopic Analysis of the Practice of Muslim State Parties to International Human Rights Treaties: Conflict or Congruence?', first published in *Human Rights Law Review* (2001) Volume 1, No. 2, pp.265–303. I thank the respective Journals for permission to reuse the relevant passages.

Finally, I thank and specially acknowledge the valuable support, love and co-operation of my wife, Hamdallah, and my children all the way through. I love you all from the bottom of my heart.

MAB
Bristol
June, 2003

Preface

This study was originally submitted as a PhD thesis to the School of Law, University of Nottingham, UK in July 2001. Since completion of the thesis, unfolding international events generally, and in relation to the Muslim world especially, have continued to impress me with the importance and relevance of this contribution to the international human rights/Islamic law discourse. During my review of the original thesis for publication I have been very well pleased with the comprehensive nature of the work and feel very rewarded and fulfilled for the time and effort put into it.

The book examines the important question of whether or not international human rights and Islamic law are compatible and whether Muslim States can comply with international human rights law while they still adhere to Islamic law. The traditional arguments on the subject are examined and responded to from both international human rights and Islamic legal perspectives. The book formulates a synthesis between two extremes and argues that although there are some differences of scope and application, that does not create a general state of dissonance between international human rights law and Islamic law. The book argues that the differences would be easier to address if the concept of human rights were positively established from within the themes of Islamic law rather than imposing it as a concept alien to Islamic law. To avoid a simplistic generalization of the arguments, each article of the International Covenant on Civil and Political Rights, and the International Covenant on Economic, Social and Cultural Rights, as well as relevant articles of the Convention on the Elimination of all Forms of Discrimination against Women are analysed in the light of Islamic law. The book theoretically engages international human rights law in dialogue with Islamic law, facilitating an evaluation of the human rights policy of modern Muslim States within the scope of that dialogue. The book concludes, *inter alia*, that it is possible to harmonize the differences between international human rights law and Islamic law through the adoption of the 'margin of appreciation' doctrine by international human rights treaty bodies and the utilization of the Islamic law doctrines of *'maqâsid al-sharî'ah'* (overall objective of *Sharî'ah*) and *'maslahah'* (welfare) by Muslim States in their interpretation and application of Islamic law respectively. The book asserts that Islamic law can serve as an important vehicle for the guarantee and enforcement of international human rights law in the Muslim world and puts forward some recommendations to that effect in the conclusion.

Contents

**CHAPTER 4: THE INTERNATIONAL COVENANT ON
ECONOMIC, SOCIAL, AND CULTURAL
RIGHTS (ICESCR) IN THE LIGHT OF
ISLAMIC LAW**

CHAPTER 5: CONCLUSION

Tables of Cases

Tables of Cases

PAKISTAN

UNITED STATES OF AMERICA

Tables of Treaties and Declarations

TREATIES

DECLARATIONS

1

Introduction

In today's world, the concept of human rights influences every aspect of international relations and cuts across every aspect of contemporary international law. It is an important international objective that permeates all the other purposes of the United Nations (UN).[1] Similarly, regional intergovernmental organizations also acknowledge the idea of human rights,[2] and different human rights non-governmental organizations consistently censure State acts for human rights violations.[3] The protection of human rights has thus become a powerful tool of internationalism that pierces the 'sacred' veil of State sovereignty for the sake of human dignity. The universality of human rights has been regularly reiterated since the adoption of the Universal Declaration of Human Rights (UDHR) by the General Assembly of the United Nations in 1948.[4]

Despite its popularity and universal acceptance however, opinions still differ considerably about the conceptual interpretation and scope of human rights. As observed by Weston, '(t)o say that there is widespread acceptance of the principle of human rights on the domestic and international plane is not to say that there is complete agreement about the nature of such rights or

---

[1] *See* Article 1 of the UN Charter (1945) 1 UNTS, p.xvi, on the Purpose and Principles of the UN. The UN Secretary General reiterated in his Statement to the 55th Session of the Commission on Human Rights in 1999 that human rights is 'at the heart of every aspect of our work and every article of our Charter' (i.e. the United Nations Charter). *See* UN Doc. SG/SM/99/91 of 7 April 1999, para.3.

[2] *See* e.g. Art. 3(h) of the Constitutive Act of the African Union (2000), Art. F(2) of the European Union Treaty (1992), Art. 3(l) of the Charter of the Organization of American States (1948), the Arab Charter on Human Rights (1994), and the Preamble of the Charter of the Organization of Islamic Conference (1972). There are also hundreds of Non-Governmental Organizations (NGOs) spread across the globe involved in the promotion of human rights all over the world.

[3] *See* e.g. Amnesty International UK website: http://www.amnesty.org.uk/amnesty/ [1/3/03]; Human Rights Watch website: http://www.hrw.org/ [1/3/03]; and Interights website: http://www.interights.org/ [1/3/03].

[4] Adopted by UN General Assembly Resolution 217A(III) of 10 December 1948. Both the Proclamation of Tehran [UN Doc. A/CON.32/41at31(1968)] after the 1st World Conference on Human Rights in Tehran in 1968 and the Vienna Declaration after the 2nd World Conference on Human Rights in Vienna in 1993 [UN Doc. A/CONF.157/23 of 12 July 1993] reiterated the universality of human rights.

their substantive scope'.[5] This has generated the paradox of universalism and cultural relativism in international human rights discourse.[6] The conceptual differences are neither meaningless nor trivial but emanate from the complexity and diversity of human society and civilization. Some scholars do argue that we need not address the conceptual differences anymore but rather focus on the problems of guaranteeing human rights and preventing their continued violations universally.[7] Such argument ignores the fact that the conceptual differences have major consequences for the practical universal observance of human rights. The drafters of the UDHR had correctly identified that 'a *common understanding* of these rights and freedoms is of the greatest importance for the(ir) full realization'.[8] This demands a continued attempt at harmonizing the different concepts, to achieve, despite the complexity and diversity of human society, a common universal understanding that ensures the full guarantee of human rights to every human being everywhere. This book is written with that aim. It constructs a dialogue between international human rights law and Islamic law to promote the realization of human rights within the context of the application of Islamic law in Muslim States.

Islam is one of the major civilizations of the world, and it is the fastest growing religion in the world today.[9] Many Member States of the UN are Muslim States that apply Islamic law either fully or partly as domestic law. Also, Islamic law influences, one way or another, the way of life of more than one billion Muslims globally.[10] While Muslim States participate in the international human rights objective of the UN, they do enter declarations and reservations on grounds of the *Sharî'ah* or Islamic law when they ratify international human

---

[5] Weston, B., 'Human Rights' in *New Encyclopaedia Britannica,* 15th Ed., Vol. 20, p.713 at p.714. *See also* Steiner, H.J., and Alston, P., *International Human Rights in Context, Law, Politics and Morals* (2nd Ed., 2000) p.324 at p.326.

[6] Thus it is argued herein that 'universality of' human rights differs from 'universalism in' human rights. *See* Ch. 2, para.2.3.3 below. *See also* e.g. Donnelly, J., *Universal Human Rights in Theory and Practice* (1989) (defends a universal conception of human rights, but argues also that the concept of human rights is purely Western and foreign to non-western cultures); Milne, A.J.M., *Human Rights and Human Diversity* (1986) (proposes that human rights are not the same everywhere and argues that the concept of human rights must not presuppose Western values and institutions); Mutua, M., 'The Ideology of Human Rights' (1996) 36 *Virginia Journal of International Law,* pp.589–657 (argues that even though the concept of human rights is not unique to European societies the philosophy of contemporary human rights is essentially European). *See* n.3 thereof for a list of literature on discussion of different philosophical perspectives of human rights. *See also* Renteln, A.D., *International Human Rights: Universalism versus Relativism* (1990) p.10 and literature cited there on the conceptual differences about human rights.

[7] *See* e.g. Bobbio, N., *The Age of Rights* (1996) pp.12–13.

[8] Emphasis added. *See* the 7th Preambular paragraph of the UDHR.

[9] *See* e.g. Freamon, B.K., 'Slavery, Freedom, and the Doctrine of Consensus in Islamic Jurisprudence' (1998) 11 *Harvard Human Rights Journal,* p.1 n.2 for a list of citations on the fast growth of Islam and importance of Islamic law in the world today.   [10] *ibid.*, n.5.

rights treaties.[11] Also, in their periodic reports to UN human rights treaty and Charter bodies, many Muslim States do refer to *Sharî'ah* or to Islamic law in their arguments.[12]

On the one hand, there is a general view, especially in the West,[13] that Islamic law is incompatible with the ideals of international human rights and that human rights are not realizable within the dispensation of Islamic law. On the other hand, there is also some pessimism, especially in the Muslim world, about the disposition of current international human rights principles and the objective of the UN in that regard. Due to the fact, *inter alia*, that human rights are best protected by States within their different cultures and domestic laws, the relevance of Islamic law to the effective application of international human rights law in the Muslim world cannot be overemphasized. As Muslim States[14] possess the sovereign right of applying Islamic law within their jurisdictions, the question of whether or not international human rights can be effectively protected within the application of Islamic law remains very important in the international human rights discourse.

Previous works on this subject have mostly emphasized some traditional interpretations of Islamic law and an exclusionist interpretation of international human rights law. This has obscured many commonalities that do exist between Islamic law and international human rights law and has continued to strengthen the theory of incompatibility between them. The incompatibility theory puts international human rights law at a sort of crossroads in Muslim States that apply Islamic law. Apart from much very general literature on this important subject, the more prominent works include An-Na'im's *Towards an Islamic Reformation*,[15] Mayer's *Islam and Human*

---

[11] *See* e.g. United Nations, *Multilateral Treaties Deposited with the Secretary General, Status as at 31/12/1999*, Vol.1, Part 1, Chapters I to XI.

[12] *See* Baderin, M.A., 'A Macroscopic Analysis of the Practice of Muslim State Parties to International Human Rights Treaties: Conflict or Congruence?' (2001) 1 *Human Rights Law Review*, No. 2, pp.265–303.

[13] Reference to 'the West' or 'Western' nations, culture or perspectives in human rights literature is not often specifically defined but connotes a generic reference to Western Europe and America. Traditionally, the notion of 'the West' in international relations did refer to the non-Communist States of Europe and North America.

[14] *See* text to n.32 to n.36 inclusive below on definition of Muslim State.

[15] An-Na'im, A.A., *Towards an Islamic Reformation, Civil Liberties, Human Rights, and International Law* (1990). Other works of An-Na'im on this subject include: 'The Position of Islamic States Regarding the Universal Declaration of Human Rights' in Baehr, P., *et al.* (eds.), *Innovation and Inspiration: Fifty Years of the Universal Declaration of Human Rights* (1999) pp.177–192; 'Human Rights in the Muslim World: Socio-Political Conditions and Scriptural Imperatives' (1990) 3 *Harvard Human Rights Journal*, pp.13–52; 'Toward an Islamic Hermeneutics for Human Rights' in An-Na'im, A.A., *et al.* (eds.), *Human Rights and Religious Values: An Uneasy Relationship?* (1995) pp.229–242; 'Islamic Law and Human Rights Today' (1996) *Interights Bulletin*, No.1, 3; 'Problems of Universal Cultural Legitimacy for Human Rights' in An-Na'im, A.A., and Deng, F.M. (eds.), *Human Rights in Africa: Cross-Cultural Perspectives* (1999) pp.331–367; 'Towards a Cross-Cultural Approach to Defining International Standards of Human Rights: The Meaning of Cruel, Inhuman or Degrading Treatment or Punishment' in

Rights[16] and Monshipouri's *Islamism, Secularism, and Human Rights in the Middle East.*[17] The approach in this book differs significantly from the one adopted in those previous works. The approach in most previous works has been generally monological, and reflects what Watson has described as the presumption that the current interpretations of international human rights law are impeccable with everything else being

An-Na'im, A.A. (ed.), *Human Rights in Cross-Cultural Perspectives* (1992) pp.19–43; 'Universality of Human Rights: An Islamic Perspective' in Ando, N. (ed.), *Japan and International Law: Past, Present and Future* (1999) pp.311–325. Professor An-Nai'm's work subjected traditional Islamic law to the jurisprudence of international human rights, disregarding any Islamic jurisprudential justifications. His main proposition is for an Islamic law reformation 'from within' to conform with international human rights principles through a reversed process of *'naskh'* (i.e. abrogation of certain verses of the Qur'an by others), whereby the application of some Medinan revelations of the Qur'an would be abandoned in favour of other Meccan revelations. Some writers on the subject have however questioned the practicality of that proposition. *See* e.g. Sachedina, A., 'Review of Abdullahi Ahmed An-Na'im, Toward an Islamic Reformation: Civil Liberties, Human Rights and International Law' (1993) 25 *International Journal of Middle East Studies*, pp.155–157; and Manzoor, P., 'Human Rights: Secular Transcendence or Cultural Imperialism?'(1994)15 *Muslim World Book Review,* No.1, p.3 at p.8.

[16] Mayer, A.E., *Islam and Human Rights, Tradition and Politics* (3rd Ed., 1999). Other works of Mayer on this subject include: 'Universal versus Islamic Human Rights: A Clash of Cultures or a Clash with a Construct?' (1994) 15 *Michigan Journal of International Law,* pp.306–404; 'Islam and the State' (1991) 12 *Cardozo Law Review*, pp.1015–1056; 'Current Muslim Thinking on Human Rights' in An-Nai'm, A.A., and Deng, F.M. (eds.), *Human Rights in Africa: Cross-Cultural Perspectives* (1999) p.131. The main thesis of Professor Mayer's work is that modern Islamic human rights schemes are dubious, in the sense that they borrow their substance from international human rights but use Islamic law to limit human rights applications. She relied mostly on traditional interpretations of the *Sharî'ah* and the practice in some Muslim countries based on those traditional interpretations, disregarding other legally valid alternative interpretations of the *Sharî'ah* in that regard. Although she referred to the fact that 'Islamic heritage offers many philosophical concepts, humanistic values, and moral principles that are well adapted for use in constructing human rights principles', she did not elaborate on those alternatives. One reviewer has thus observed that: 'As to the crucial task of comprehensively elaborating a methodologically sound and truly contemporary Islamic human rights teaching based on the pre-modern Islamic heritage, she has been wise to leave this to Muslim believers and to the internal doctrinal debate among them'. *See* Troll, C.W., 'Book Review of Islam and Human Rights: Traditions and Politics By Ann Elizabeth Mayer' (1992) 3 *Islam and Christian-Muslim Relations*, No.1, p.131 at p.133.

[17] Monshipouri, M., *Islamism, Secularism, and Human Rights in the Middle East* (1998). Other works of Monshipouri on this subject include: 'Islamic Thinking and the Internationalization of Human Rights' (1994) 84 *The Muslim World*, No.2–3, pp.217–239; 'The Muslim World Half a Century after the Universal Declaration of Human Rights: Progress and Obstacles' (1998) 16 *Netherlands Quarterly of Human Rights,* No.3, pp.287–314; Monshipouri, M., and Kukla, C.G., 'Islam, Democracy, and Human Rights: The Continuing Debate in the West' (1994) 3 *Middle East Policy,* No.2, pp.22–39. The central theme of Professor Monshipouri's work is that 'fusing secular and Islamic principles can effectively promote human dignity'. *See* Monshipouri, M., *Islamism, Secularism, and Human Rights in the Middle East* (this note, above) p.25. One reviewer has however observed that while 'he judges specific rules of Islamic law against conceptual values of secularism for compatibility [he] does not articulate the parallel essential values of Islam, let alone place specific secularist human rights norms against them for judgment'. *See* Quraishi, A., 'Book Review of Islamism, Secularism, and Human Rights in the Middle East By Mahmood Monshipouri' (2000) 22 *Human Rights Quarterly,* p.625 at p.628.

adjusted to maintain that assumption.[18] The argument has often been that when Muslim States ratify international human rights treaties they are bound by the international law rule that a State Party to a treaty 'may not invoke the provisions of its internal law as justification for its failure to perform a treaty'.[19] In practice however, Muslim States do not generally plead the *Sharî'ah* or Islamic law as justification for 'failure to perform' their international human rights obligations. They often argue not against the letter of the law but against some interpretation of international human rights law which, they contend, does not take Islamic values into consideration.[20]

The important question is how far can international human rights law be interpreted in the light of Islamic law and vice versa? In that regard, there is need for a synthesis between two extremes and provision of an alternative perspective to the relationship between international human rights law and Islamic law. Using evidence from Islamic jurisprudence and international human rights practice, this book challenges the argument that the observance of international human rights law is impossible within an Islamic legal dispensation. It theoretically engages international human rights practice in dialogue with Islamic jurisprudence. It develops a dialogical perspective to the issues. A dialogical approach demands a culture of tolerance and persuasion and the abandonment of a culture of parochialism, violence and rivalry. It requires capacity to listen, respect, accommodate and exchange.[21]

The importance of a dialogical approach for achieving '*a common understanding*'[22] of human rights is reflected in the conclusions adopted by the Council of Europe at the end of its inter-regional meeting organized in advance of the World Conference on Human Rights at Strasbourg in 1993, that:

We must go back to listening. More thought and effort must be given to enriching the human rights discourse by explicit reference to other non-Western religions and cultural traditions. By tracing the linkages between constitutional values on the one hand and the concepts, ideas and institutions which are central to Islam or the Hindu-Buddhist tradition or other traditions, the base of support for fundamental rights can be expanded and the claim to universality vindicated. The Western World has no monopoly or patent

---

[18] Watson, J.S., *Theory & Reality in the International Protection of Human Rights* (1999) p.15.

[19] Art. 27, Vienna Convention on the Law of Treaties (1969). *See* e.g. Mayer, *Islam and Human Rights* etc. (n.16 above) pp.10–12.   [20] *See* Baderin (n.12 above) at p.267.

[21] *See further* Baderin, M.A., 'Dialogue Among Civilisations as a Paradigm for Achieving Universalism in International Human Rights: A Case Study with Islamic Law' (2001) 2 *Asia-Pacific Journal on Human Rights and the Law*, No. 2, p.1 at pp.13–17.

[22] *See* n.8 above.

on basic human rights. We must embrace cultural diversity but not at the expense of universal minimum standards.[23]

Similarly, the 4th Principle of the Rome Declaration on Human Rights in Islam, issued after the World Symposium on Human Rights by the Muslim World League in February 2000, indicated the need to:

Encourage dialogue amongst cultures and civilisations in a manner that would contribute to a better understanding of human rights . . . [24]

Certainly there are some differences of scope between Islamic law and international human rights law but that does not create a general antithesis between the two. The differences can be meaningfully discussed and the noble ideals of international human rights realized in the Muslim world if the concept of international human rights can be convincingly established from within the themes of Islamic law rather than expressing it as a concept alien to Islamic law. This is premised on the fact that the positive means to promote any concept within a particular culture is through evidential support from within its legitimizing principles. Although Islamic law is not uniformly applied today in all Muslim States, yet Islamic principles and norms constitute a principal legitimizing factor for cultural-legal norms in most parts of the Muslim world. Also, since morality and substantive justice are important principles applicable to the philosophy of both Islamic law and international human rights law, the principle of justification need be accommodated in proposing practical harmonization of the conceptual differences between Islamic law and international human rights law. Thus, the jurisprudential arguments of Islamic jurists on relevant issues is herein analysed vis-à-vis the interpretations of modern international human rights law. Applying the justificatory principle, a paradigm shift is sought from traditional hardline interpretations of the *Sharî'ah* and also from exclusionist interpretations of international human rights law. The Islamic legal doctrine of *maslahah* (welfare)[25] and the European human rights 'margin of appreciation'[26] doctrine are explored in establishing the arguments herein.

---

[23] *See* Council of Europe Doc. CE/CMDH (93) 16, of 30 January 1993, at p.3. *See also* Robinson, M., 'Human Rights at the Dawn of the 21st Century' (1993) 15 *Human Rights Quarterly,* p.629 at p.632.

[24] *See* 4th Principle, Rome Declaration on Human Rights in Islam (2000).

[25] Kamali has observed that the Islamic law doctrine of *'maslahah'* can strike a balance between public expectations of government and its meaningful identification with Islam. *See* Kamali, M.H., 'Have We Neglected the Sharî'ah Doctrine of Maslahah?' (1988) 27 *Islamic Studies,* p.287 at p.288.

[26] According to Macdonald, the 'margin of appreciation' is more of a principle of justification under the European human rights regime. *See* Macdonald, R. St. J., 'The Margin of Appreciation' in Macdonald, R. St. J., *et al.* (eds.), *The European System for the Protection of Human Rights* (1993) p.83 at p.123.

After this introductory chapter, the conceptual issues are addressed in Chapter 2 setting out the general arguments regarding human rights and Islamic law. The approach adopted generally is different from the traditional 'end of history' approach usually followed, especially in the analysis of Islamic law. The possible and continued evolution of both international human rights law and Islamic law in directions that promote their harmonious coexistence in Muslim States to ensure the protection of individuals against the misuse of the apparatus of State is highlighted.

Chapters 3 and 4 are the main core presenting a comprehensive comparative legal analysis of the International Bill of Rights (i.e. International Covenant on Civil and Political Rights and International Covenant on Economic, Social and Cultural Rights) and Islamic law. The International Covenant on Civil and Political Rights (ICCPR)[27] and the International Covenant on Economic, Social and Cultural Rights (ICESCR)[28] are examined respectively in the light of Islamic law. The Covenants are analysed article by article to avoid a simplistic generalization of the issues. The practices of the Human Rights Committee and the Committee on Economic, Social, and Cultural Rights are respectively analysed in respect of the rights guaranteed under each of the two Covenants. Due to the topicality of the question of women's rights in the international human rights/Islamic law debate, necessary Articles of the Convention on the Elimination of All Forms of Discrimination Against Women (CEDAW)[29] are also referred to in the examination of women's rights under the two Covenants. The sources of Islamic law and juristic views from Islamic schools of jurisprudence are then examined on each aspect of the rights guaranteed under the two Covenants. Reference is also made to relevant provisions of the Cairo Declaration on Human Rights in Islam[30] as current codified Islamic human rights adopted by Muslim States under the auspices of the Organization of Islamic Conference in 1990.[31] The Islamic juristic views are analysed vis-à-vis liberal principles of international human rights law as interpreted by the UN Committees and vice versa. Using the justificatory principle discussed at the end of Chapter 2, an inclusive and accommodative approach is suggested, where necessary, to facilitate legitimate shifts from static hardline traditional

---

[27] Adopted by General Assembly Resolution 2200A (XXI) of 16 December 1966; 999 UNTS, p.171.
[28] Adopted by General Assembly Resolution 2200A (XXI) of 16 December 1966; 993 UNTS, p.3.
[29] Adopted by General Assembly Resolution 34/180 of 18 December 1979; 1249 UNTS, p.13.
[30] OIC, Cairo Declaration on Human Rights in Islam, of 5 August 1990. UN Doc. A/45/5/21797, p.199. *See* Annexe.
[31] Human rights obligations are principally placed upon States, thus the OIC Cairo Declaration on Human Rights in Islam, being a document adopted by Muslim States rather than by individuals or private non-governmental organizations, reflects a more authoritative document in relation to the human rights obligation of Muslim States.

Islamic jurisprudence and from exclusionist interpretations of international human rights law.

For purposes of clarity it is necessary to define the notion of 'Muslim States' as used in this book. The Muslim world is today divided into separate sovereign nation-states.[32] A few of these States have been specifically declared as Islamic Republics, some others indicate in their Constitutions that Islam is the religion of the State, while most are only identifiable as Muslim States on the basis of their predominant Muslim population and the allegiance of the people to Islam.[33] A different single criterion adopted in this book for defining modern Muslim States is membership of the Organization of Islamic Conference (OIC).[34] That all 57 Member States of the OIC are definable as Muslim States is supported by the first charter-objective of the Organization, which is the promotion of Islamic spiritual, ethical, social, and economic values among the Member States.[35] While the OIC Member States exist as independent sovereign States, they are theoretically linked by their Islamic heritage, traditions, and solidarity. As far as the application of Islamic law as State law is concerned, Esposito has observed that the majority of Muslim States today fall between the two poles of 'purist' Saudi Arabia and 'secular' Turkey.[36] Since this book is principally concerned with the enforcement of international human rights

---

[32]   For analysis of the evolution of the Muslim world into modern nation-states *see* e.g. Baderin, M.A., 'The Evolution of Islamic Law of Nations and the Modern International Order: Universal Peace through Mutuality and Co-operation' (2000) 17 *The American Journal of Islamic Social Sciences,* No.2, pp.57–80. *See also* Nasr, S.V.R., 'European Colonialism and the Emergence of Modern Muslim States' in Esposito, J.L. (ed.), *The Oxford History of Islam* (1999) pp.549–599; Khadduri, M., *The Islamic Law of Nations: Shaybani's Siyar* (1966) pp.19–20; and al-Ghunaimi, M.T., *The Muslim Conception of International Law and the Western Approach* (1968) pp.38–54.

[33]   Currently, 5 States are specifically designated as Islamic Republics, 15 States constitutionally declare Islam as the religion of the State and 46 States have majority Muslim populations.

[34]   The OIC, as of August 2002, has 57 Member and 3 Observer States. The Members States are: Islamic Emirate of Afghanistan; Republic of Albania; Algeria; Azerbaijan; Bahrain; Bangladesh; Republic of Benin; Brunei; Burkina Faso; Republic of Cameroon; Chad; Islamic Republic of Comoros; Republic of Côte d'Ivoire; Djibouti; Egypt; Gabon; Gambia; Guinea; Guinea-Bissau; Guyana; Indonesia; Islamic Republic of Iran; Iraq; Jordan; Kazakhstan; Kuwait; Kyrgyzstan; Lebanon; Libya; Malaysia; Republic of Maldives; Mali; Islamic Republic of Mauritania; Morocco; Mozambique; Niger; Nigeria; Oman; Islamic Republic of Pakistan; Palestine; Qatar; Kingdom of Saudi Arabia; Senegal; Sierra Leone; Somalia; Sudan; Surinam; Syria; Tajikistan; Togo; Tunisia; Turkey; Turkmenistan; Uganda; United Arab Emirates; Uzbekistan; and Yemen. The Observer States are: Republic of Bosnia and Herzegovina; Central African Republic; and Kingdom of Thailand. *See* the OIC Website: http://www.oic-un.org/about/members.htm [1/3/03]. Note: although Palestine is listed as a Member State on the OIC website, it is not yet considered as a State under international law.

[35]   *See* The Preamble and Article II (A) (1) of the OIC Charter, 914 UNTS, p.111. An updated version of the Charter is available at the OIC Permanent Mission to the United Nations in Geneva. *See also* Moinuddin, H., *The Charter of the Islamic Conference and Legal Framework of Economic Co-operation among its Member States* (1987) pp.10–11.

[36]   Esposito, J., 'Contemporary Islam: Reformation or Revolution?' in Esposito, J. (ed.), *The Oxford History of Islam* (1999) p.643 at pp.651–652.

within the application of Islamic law as State law, the emphasis on relevant Muslim State practice in that regard will be on those States that apply Islamic law fully or partly as State law.

The concluding Chapter 5 discusses necessary complementary and practical approaches to the theoretical discussions and arguments advanced in the preceding four chapters.

2

Human Rights[1] and Islamic Law[2]

2.1 BREAKING TRADITIONAL BARRIERS

Traditionally, a number of difficulties confront the discourse of human rights from an Islamic legal perspective. They are traditional barriers that must be broken to facilitate the dialogical approach adopted in this book.

On one hand is the domineering influence of the 'Western' perspective of human rights, which creates a tendency of always using 'Western' values as a yardstick in every human rights discourse.[3] While it is true that the impetus for the formulation of international human rights standards originated from the West, the same cannot be said of the whole concept of human rights, which is perceivable within different human civilizations.[4] Related to that, is the negative image of Islam in the West. Often, some of the criminal punishments under Islamic law and the political cum human rights situation in many parts of the Muslim world today are, *inter alia*, cited by some Western analysts as evidence of lack of provision for respect for human rights in

---

[1] For detailed analysis of the theory of human rights, *see, inter alia*, Cranston, M., *What Are Human Rights?* (1973); Rosenbaum, A. (ed.), *The Philosophy of Human Rights, International Perspectives* (1980); Shestack, J.J., 'The Jurisprudence of Human Rights' in Meron, T., (ed.), *Human Rights in International Law: Legal and Policy Issues* (1984) Vol.1, pp.69–113; Donnelly, J., *The Concept of Human Rights* (1985); Vincent, R.J., *Human Rights and International Relations* (1986); Donnelly, J., *Universal Human Rights in Theory and Practice* (1989); Winston, M.E. (ed.), *The Philosophy of Human Rights* (1989); Nino, C.S., *The Ethics of Human Rights* (1991); and Douzinas, C., *The End of Human Rights* (2000).

[2] For English language analysis of Islamic law and jurisprudence, *see, inter alia*, Ramadan, S., *Islamic Law: Its Scope and Equity* (1970); Qadri, A.A., *Islamic Jurisprudence in the Modern World* (1986); Philips, A.A.B., *The Evolution of Fiqh* (1988); Kamali, M.H., *Principles of Islamic Jurisprudence* (1991); Hallaq, W.B., *A History of Islamic Legal Theories* (1997); Nyazee, I.A.K., *Theories of Islamic Law* (n.d); and Nyazee, I.A.K., *Outlines of Islamic Jurisprudence* (2000).

[3] *See* e.g. Mayer, A.E., 'Current Muslim Thinking on Human Rights' in An-Na'im, A.A. and Deng, F.M. (eds.), *Human Rights In Africa, Cultural Perspectives* (1990) p.133 at p.148 (asserts that human rights 'are principles that were developed in Western culture' and suggests that Western culture should serve as the universal normative model for the content of international human rights law) and Tibi, B., 'The European Tradition of Human Rights and the Culture of Islam' in *ibid.*, p.104 at p.105. For opposing views *see* e.g. Said, M.E., 'Islam and Human Rights' (1997) *Rowaq Arabi*, January, p.11 at p.13; Manglapus, R., 'Human Rights are not a Western Discovery' (1978) 4 *Worldview*, pp.4–6; and Kushalani, Y., 'Human Rights in Asia and Africa' (1983) 4 *Human Rights Law Journal*, No.4, p.404.

[4] *See* e.g. Kushalani (n.3 above), and Smith, J. (ed.), *Human Rights: Chinese and Dutch Perspectives* (1996) for discussions on some different perceptions of the concept of human rights.

Islamic law.[5] This is part of what has been termed 'Islamophobia'[6] in the West, which adversely affects the view about human rights in Islam generally. In the academic realm there is also what Strawson has called the 'orientalist *problematique*' by which 'Islamic law is represented within Anglo-American scholarship as an essentially defective legal system',[7] especially with regards to international law.[8]

On the other hand is the obstacle of static hardline interpretations of the *Sharî'ah* and non-relative application of traditional Islamic jurisprudence on some aspects of inter-human relations. Islamic law or *Sharî'ah* are both sometimes vaguely advanced by some Muslim countries as an excuse for their poor human rights records without exhaustive elaboration of the position of Islamic law on the matter.

Due to the above difficulties, the concept of human rights under Islamic law has often been discussed from either a reproachful or a defensive angle, depending on the leanings of the discussant. Piscatori has frowned at the defensive approach of most Muslim writers in the international human rights discourse.[9] We need to determine however, whether the defensiveness is merely an apology in the face of genuine challenges posed by international human rights to Islamic law, or reasonable defence against criticisms of Islamic law for human rights situations in Muslim countries not necessarily justifiable even under the *Sharî'ah*. On one hand, it is undeniable that Western initiatives and modern challenges, which include the international human rights regime, have forced contemporary Muslim thinkers and intellectuals to propose strongly a review

[5] *See* Bannerman, P., *Islam in Perspective, A Guide to Islamic Society, Politics and Law* (1988) p.25. *See also* Robertson, B.A., 'Islam and Europe: An Enigma or a Myth?' (1994) 48 *Middle East Journal*, No.2, pp.288–307.

[6] *See* e.g. Tash, A.Q., 'Islamophobia in the West' (1996) *Washington Report on Middle East Affairs*, November/December p.28; *and* 'Islamophobia' in *BULLETIN*, *University of Sussex Newsletter*, 7 November 1997, p.16: http://www.sussex.ac.uk/press_office/bulletin/07nov97/item12.html [1/3/03].

[7] *See generally* Strawson, J., 'Encountering Islamic Law', *University of East London Law Department Research Publications Series*, No.1, p.1.

[8] Strawson, for instance, refers to Schacht's very well-known work, *Introduction to Islamic Law*, which omits the discussion of Islamic international law because of what Schacht described as 'its essentially theoretical and fictitious character and the intimate connection of the relevant institutions with the history of Islamic states . . .' (*see* Schacht, J., *Introduction to Islamic Law* (1964) p.112). It is difficult to imagine how international law can stand without an 'intimate connection of the relevant institutions' of the State. As to the excuse of 'its essentially theoretical and fictitious character', this was in 1964 when, even in Western discourses, public international law had its own cynics as to whether it was really law or not, but this never ostracized public international law from the law books. Such approaches to Islamic law were some of the barriers, *inter alia*, which shut out Islamic law from contemporary international law discourses. *See also generally* Said, E.W., *Orientalism, Western Conceptions of the Orient* (1978).

[9] *See* Piscatori, J.P., 'Human Rights in Islamic Political Culture' in Thompson, K., (ed.), *The Moral Imperatives of Human Rights: A World Survey* (1980) p.139 at pp.152–162; *see also* Manzoor, P., 'Humanity Rights as Human Duties' *Inquiry*, July 1987, p.34 at pp.37–38.

of some traditional Islamic jurisprudential views, especially in the area of international law and relations.[10] On the other hand, there have also been general erroneous reproaches of Islamic law for the sometimes appalling attitudes or actions of some governments in Muslim countries that are not justifiable even under the *Sharî'ah*. At the end of a Seminar on Human Rights in Islam held in Kuwait in 1980, jointly organized by the International Commission of Jurists, the University of Kuwait and the Union of Arab Lawyers, the conclusion, *inter alia*, was that:

> It is unfair to judge Islamic law (Shari'a) by the political systems which prevailed in various periods of Islamic history. It ought to be judged by the general principles which are derived from its sources . . . Regrettably enough, contemporary Islamic practices cannot be said to conform in many aspects with the true principles of Islam. Further, it is wrong to abuse Islam by seeking to justify certain political systems in the face of obvious contradictions between those systems and Islamic law.[11]

While the theoretic arguments concerning the conceptual foundations of human rights may be difficult to settle, the indisputable fact is that international human rights are today not a prerogative of a single nation. They are a universal affair that concern the dignity and well-being of every human being. However, there is yet to emerge what we may call a 'universal universalism' in international human rights. What exists now has been described as 'provincialism masquerading as universalism'.[12] While the flagrant abuse of human rights in Muslim States under the pretext of cultural differences is unacceptable, the role and influence of the Muslim world in achieving a peaceful coexistence within the international community does permit Muslim States to question a universalism 'within which Islamic law (generally) has no normative value and enjoys little prestige'.[13] Since human rights are best achieved through the domestic law of States, recognition of relevant Islamic law principles in that regard will enhance the realization of international human rights objectives in Muslim States that apply Islamic law fully or partly as State law.

Conversely, there is a need for the Muslim world also to acknowledge change as a necessary ingredient in law. The adaptability of the *Sharî'ah* must be positively utilized to enhance human rights in the Muslim world.[14] While Muslims must be true to their heritage, the noble ideals of international human rights

---

[10]   *See* e.g. AbuSulayman, A.A., *Towards an Islamic Theory of International Relations: New Directions for Islamic Methodology and Thought* (1993).

[11]   *See* International Commission of Jurisits, *Human Rights in Islam: Report of a Seminar held in Kuwait in December 1980* (1982) p.7.

[12]   *See* Strawson (above n.7) at p.2, and also Mutua, M.W., 'The Ideology of Human Rights' (1996) *Virginia Journal of International Law*, p.589 at pp.592–593.

[13]   *See* Mayer, A.E., *Islam and Human Rights, Tradition and Politics*, (3rd Ed., 1999) p.41.

[14]   *See* Yamani, A.Z., 'The Eternal Shari'a' (1979) 12 *New York University Journal of International Law and Politics*, p.205.

can shed new light on their interpretation of the *Sharî'ah*, their international relations and self-awareness within the legal limits of Islamic law.

2.2 ISLAMIC RESPONSES IN INTERNATIONAL HUMAN RIGHTS DISCOURSE

Halliday has identified at least four classes of Islamic responses to the international human rights debate. The first is that Islam is compatible with international human rights. The second is that true human rights can only be fully realized under Islamic law. The third is that the international human rights objective is an imperialist agenda that must be rejected, and the fourth is that Islam is incompatible with international human rights.[15] There is a fifth noteworthy response omitted by Halliday, which is that the international human rights objective has a hidden anti-religious agenda.[16] Viewed critically, most of these responses are Muslim reactions to what is often described as the double standards of countries at the helm of international human rights promotion. The responses reflect the entrapment of human rights between humanitarianism and international politics rather than actual disagreements with the concept of human rights in Islamic law. We will now evaluate these responses within the perimeter of Islamic law.

The view that Islam is compatible with human rights is the most sustainable within the principles of Islamic law. This is not merely by vaguely or apologetically reading the Western notion of human rights into Islamic principles. The sources and methods of Islamic law contain common principles of good government and human welfare that validate modern international human rights ideals. Respect for justice, protection of human life and dignity, are central principles inherent in the *Sharî'ah* which no differences of opinion can exclude. They are the overall purpose of the *Sharî'ah*, to which the Qur'an refers.

God commands justice, the doing of good, and liberality to kith and kin, and He forbids all shameful deeds, and injustice and rebellion: He instructs you, that you may receive admonition.[17]

The view that true human rights can only be fully realized under Islamic law is exclusionist and will be culpable of the same egoism of the criticized

[15] Halliday, F., 'Relativism and Universalism in Human Rights: The Case of the Islamic Middle East' in Beetham, D. (ed.), *Politics and Human Rights* (1995) p.152 at pp.154–155.

[16] *See* e.g. Mortimer, E., 'Islam and Human Rights' *Index on Censorship*, October, 1983, No.12, p.5.

[17] Q16:90. *See* Baderin, M.A., 'Establishing Areas of Common Ground between Islamic Law and International Human Rights' (2001) 5 *The International Journal of Human Rights*, No.2, pp.72–113, for further analysis of the compatibility between human rights and Islamic law.

exclusive Western perspective to human rights. Islam is not egocentric with respect to temporal matters but rather encourages co-operation (*ta'âwun*) for the attainment of the common good of humanity.[18] Islam encourages inter-action and sharing of perception. A Tradition of the Prophet Muhammad (PBUH)[19] advised Muslims to seek knowledge as far away as China, (a non-Muslim country) and in another Tradition he stated that wisdom is the lost property of a Muslim and he or she is most entitled to it wherever it may be found. All these point towards the recognition by Islam of possible comple-mentary permissible routes to the betterment of humanity in temporal matters. AbuSulayman has thus observed that: '[t]he Islamic call for social justice, human equality [equity], and submission to the divine will and directions of the Creator requires the deepest and sharpest sense of responsibility, as well as the *total absence of human arrogance and egoism, both in internal and external communication*'.[20]

The view that the international human rights regime is an imperialist agenda is not peculiar to the Islamic discourse on human rights. It is common in the human rights discourses of all developing nations.[21] This results from the fear of neo-colonialism, and is a psychological effect of the past colo-nial experience of most developing nations under Western imperialism. That fear is sometimes strengthened by the Western nations' insistence on defining human rights only in the Western perspective without consideration for the contribution and understanding of other cultures.

If we understand international human rights strictly as a universal human-itarian objective for the protection of individuals against the misuse of State authority and for the enhancement of human dignity, then the view that Islam is incompatible with it is very unsustainable. That is because the protection and enhancement of the dignity of human beings has always been a principle of Islamic political and legal theory. While there may be some areas of con-ceptual differences between Islamic law and international human rights law, this does not make them incompatible. It is sometimes also argued that human beings have no rights in Islamic law but only to submit to God's commands.[22] That is also misleading. While it is true that human beings are to submit to God's commands, this does not mean that they have no inherent rights under Islamic law. The principle of legality is a fundamental principle of Islamic law whereby all actions are permitted except those clearly prohibited by the

---

[18] *See* e.g. Q5:5 '... Co-operate with one another in good deeds and piety but not in sin and enmity'.

[19] The abbreviation PBUH which means 'Peace be Upon Him', will not be repeated in writing after this first occurrence but shall be implied as repeated after every occurrence of the Prophet's name throughout this book.   [20] AbuSulayman (above n.10) at p.54 (emphasis added).

[21] *See* e.g. Mutua (above n.12) at pp.589–657.

[22] *See* e.g. Rajaee, E., *Islamic Values and Worldview: Khomeyni on Man, the State and International Politics* (1983) pp.42–45.

Sharî'ah,[23] which means that human beings have inherent rights to everything except for things specifically prohibited. To hold that humans have no rights but only obligations to God expresses a principle of illegality, which makes life very restrictive and difficult. That will be inconsistent with the overall objective of the *Sharî'ah*, (i.e. *maqâsid al-Sharî'ah*), which is the promotion of human welfare as will be analysed later.[24]

Most Muslim proponents of the incompatibility view are not really opposed to the concept of human rights per se. Their position only reflects a disappointment with, and protest against, Western hegemony and thus against any ideology considered as championed by Western nations. They often refer to the 'double standards' of the West and the general disparity in reactions to human rights abuses under 'Islamic' and 'non-Islamic' regimes as evidence of lack of sincerity in the international human rights regime.[25] For instance one Egyptian critic, 'Ismat Sayf al-Dawla, has been quoted as denouncing the UDHR in the following words:

I must admit that I am not a supporter of the *Universal Declaration of Human Rights* that the United Nations Organisation issued on December 10, 1948. Our history of civilisation has taught us to be wary of big and noble words as the reality of our history has taught us how big words can be transformed into atrocious crimes. We cannot forget that the initiators of the *Declaration of Human Rights* and the plain French citizens are the same people who shortly afterwards, and before the ink of the *Declaration* had dried up, organised a campaign and sent their forces under the leadership of their favourite general, Napoleon, to Egypt. We must not forget either that the United Nations Organisation issued the *Universal Declaration of Human Rights* in the same year that it recognised the Zionist state that usurped Palestine and robbed its people of every right stipulated in the *Declaration*, including the right of life.[26]

According to Ridwan al-Sayyid, this position 'stems . . . from the contradiction between word and deed among Westerners despite the beauty and truth of the word'.[27] Huntington has also drawn attention to this protestation by observing that:

Non-westerners . . . do not hesitate to point to the gaps between Western principle and Western action. Hypocrisy, double standards, and 'but nots' are the price of universalist pretensions. Democracy is promoted but not if it brings Islamic fundamentalists to power; nonproliferation is preached for Iran and Iraq but not for Israel; . . . human

---

[23] *See* e.g. Ramadan (above n.2) at p.68. *See also* al-Shâtibî, A.I., *al-Muwâfaqât* (Arabic) (1997) Vol.2; Ibn al-Qayyim, *I'lâm al-Muwaqqi'în 'An Rabb al-'Alamîn* (Arabic) (1996) Vol.1, pp.71–72; and Nyazee, I.A.K., *Theories of Islamic Law* (n.d) pp.47–50, for a brief discussion of this principle of permissibility under Islamic law, as well as the opposing *Hanafî* view of the principle of illegality. [24] *See* para.2.4.5 below.

[25] For example, in nearly all human rights communiqués or resolutions adopted at every Islamic conference, the question of Palestine comes up as an issue of double standards in international relations and law.

[26] *See* Sayf al-Dawla, I., 'Islam and Human Rights: Controversy and Agreement' (1988) 9 *Minbar al-Hiwar* pp.33–39, cited in al-Sayyid, R., 'Contemporary Muslim Thought and Human Rights' (1995) 21 *Islamochristiana*, p.27 at p.28. [27] al-Sayyid (above n.26) at p.28.

rights are an issue with China but not with Saudi Arabia; . . . Double standards in practice are the unavoidable price of universal standards of principle.[28]

Finally, the view that the international human rights objective harbours a hidden anti-religious agenda also results from some suspicion among Muslims that, having separated the Church from the State in the Western world, the West intends the same for the Muslim world and through the 'crusade' of international human rights wants to discredit the Islamic faith with a new international ideology of humanism in its effort to remove religiosity totally from the world order. This, as it may seem, is not an opinion canvassed only by governments in Muslim States but even by individual Muslims whom international human rights are intended to protect.

This indicates the need for continuous education and practical demonstration of sincerity and genuine commitment to the humanitarian ideals of international human rights, especially by the 'big' States at the helm of human rights promotion. Bielefeldt has stressed in this regard that human rights 'do not pretend to serve as a transhistoric yardstick, for measuring cultures and religions generally (and) . . . are not, and should not be presented as, an international "civil religion" ' but should be presented as shedding 'new light on the self-perception of cultural and religious communities because, the principle of human dignity, which has roots in many cultures, serve as the foundation for human rights'.[29]

2.3 WHAT ARE HUMAN RIGHTS?

Human rights are the rights of humans. They are the rights of all human beings in full equality. We are entitled to them simply because we are human beings. They emanate from the 'inherent dignity of the human person'[30] and have been defined as 'those claims made by men, for themselves or on behalf of other men, supported by some theory which concentrates on the humanity of man, on man as a human being, a member of mankind . . .'.[31] These claims relate to standards of life, which every person has a right to expect from society as a human being. In the words of Umozurike:

Human rights are thus claims, which are invariably supported by ethics and which should be supported by law, made on society, especially on its official managers, by individuals or groups on the basis of their humanity. They apply regardless of race,

[28] Huntington, S.P., *The Clash of Civilizations and the Remaking of World Order*, (1996), p.184.
[29] *See* Bielefeldt, H., 'Muslim Voices in the Human Rights Debate' (1995) 17 *Human Rights Quarterly*, p.587 at p.616.
[30] *See* e.g. 2nd Preambular paragraphs of the ICESCR (1966) and ICCPR (1966) and 1st Preambular paragraph of the UDHR (1948).
[31] Dowrick, F.E. (ed.), *Human Rights: Problems, Perspectives and Texts* (1979) p.8.

colour, sex or other distinction and may not be withdrawn or denied by governments, people or individuals.[32]

Scholars have advanced different views concerning the origins of the human rights idea. While some authors assert that 'human rights are as old as people are', others hold that human rights should be listed as 'new business'.[33] A better perspective to considering the idea of human rights either as old or new business, is to conceive it as an evolutionary phenomenon that has matured over time through the different stages of human civilization and enlightenment. Lauren has thus observed that:

> The historical evolution of visions of international human rights that continues to this day started centuries ago with efforts attempting to address these difficult and universal questions. It began as soon as men and women abandoned nomadic existence and settled in organized societies, long before anyone had ever heard of the more recent expression 'human rights,' or before nation-states negotiated specific international treaties.[34]

2.3.1 Emergence of the international human rights regime[35]

Although the historical origins of human rights date back into ancient times and are often linked with the idea of natural rights, the First and Second World Wars and the periods between them played the antecedent roles for the emergence of the current international human rights regime.[36] The opprobrious and savage treatment of individuals and groups during the period, and the use of the apparatus of State to deal unwholesomely with human beings created international concerns for the general protection of human beings.

Concern for the protection of minority groups in Central and Eastern Europe after the First World War was the first attempt for an international human rights regime. Two human rights notions emerged in the process, namely the notion of individual rights and that of collective rights. The first was for the protection of the rights of individuals and the second for the protection of minorities.[37] Attempts at including human rights provisions in the Covenant of the League of Nations that was to be created were, however, unsuccessful.

---

[32] Umozurike, U.O., *The African Charter on Human and Peoples' Rights* (1997) p.5.

[33] *See* e.g. Cleveland, H., 'Introduction: the Chain Reaction of Human Rights' in Henkin, A.H. (ed.), *Human Dignity: The Internationalization of Human Rights* (1979) p.ix.

[34] Lauren, P.G., *The Evolution of International Human Rights, Visions Seen* (1998) p.5. *See also generally* Ishay, M.R. (ed.), *The Human Rights Reader: Major Political Essays, Speeches and Documents from the Bible to the Present* (1997).

[35] *See* e.g. Sohn, L.B., 'The New International Law: Protection of the Rights of Individuals Rather than States' (1982) 32 *American University Law Journal*, pp.1–64.

[36] *See* e.g. Weston, B., 'Human Rights' in *New Encyclopaedia Britannica*, 15th Ed.,Vol.20, p.713; Douzinas, C., *The End of Human Rights* (2000); Szabo, I., 'Historical Foundations of Human Rights and Subsequent Developments' in Vasak, K. (ed.), *The International Dimensions of Human Rights* (1982) Vol.1, p.11; Cassese, A., *Human Rights in a Changing World* (1990) pp.1–23. [37] *See* Szabo (above n.36) at p.21.

What emerged were separate minority protection treaties and State declarations guaranteeing the protection of the rights of minorities. The League of Nations however performed a supervisory role over the obligations created, which were considered of international concern.[38]

Private endeavours continued both within and outside the League of Nations for the realization of an international human rights regime. In 1929 the Institute of International Law, a private body of distinguished authorities on international law in Europe, the Americas and Asia, adopted the Declaration of the Rights of Man,[39] in which it considered it the duty of every State to recognize, *inter alia*, the equal rights of every individual to life, liberty, and property. The Institute also considered that every State had a duty to accord to everyone within its territory the full and entire protection of these rights without distinction as to nationality, sex, race, language, or religion. Although the Declaration was not a binding document, it contributed to the popularization of the idea of international human rights in the years immediately after its adoption. The Declaration also set a pace for a new relationship between the individual and the State under international law. Marshall Brown, an editor of the American Journal of International Law, in 1930 reflected the Declaration's significance in the then emerging international regime as follows:

> This declaration . . . states in bold and unequivocal terms the rights of human beings, 'without distinction of nationality, sex, race, language and religion,' to the equal right to life, liberty and property, together with all the subsidiary rights essential to the enjoyment of these fundamental rights. It aims not merely to assure to individuals their *international* rights, but it aims also to impose on all nations a standard of conduct towards all men, *including their own nationals*. It thus repudiates the classic doctrine that states alone are subjects of international law. Such a revolutionary document, while open to criticism in terminology and to the objection that it has not juridical value, cannot fail, however, to exert an influence on the evolution of international law. It marks a new era which is more concerned with the interests and rights of sovereign individuals than with the rights of sovereign states.[40]

The fascist atrocities during the Second World War further aroused the asperity of humanity and moved the world community to call for formal international measures aimed at ensuring the protection of human rights and achievement of world peace and security. The Allies determined even before the end of the war that an international commitment to the protection of human rights should be a part of the post Second World War settlement. Thus, in the preamble to the Charter of the United Nations Organization which emerged after the

[38] *See* e.g. Art. 12 of The Polish Minorities Treaty (1920). *See also* Cassese (above n.36) at pp.17–21; Weston (above n.36) at p.717; and Ezejiofor, G., *Protection of Human Rights Under Law* (1964) pp.38–50.

[39] *See* (1941) 35 *American Journal of International Law*, pp.662–665.

[40] *See* (1930) 24 *American Journal of International Law*, p.127.

war,[41] the Member States declared their determination '. . . to reaffirm faith in fundamental human rights, in the dignity and worth of the human person, in the equal rights of men and women and of nations large and small . . .'.[42] They also made it clear in Article 1(3) that one of the purposes of the UN was '(t)o achieve international co-operation in. . . promoting and encouraging respect for human rights and for fundamental freedoms for all without distinction as to race, sex, language, or religion . . .'.

The UN Member States also pledged themselves under Article 56 of the Charter 'to take joint and separate action in co-operation with the Organization for the achievement of the purposes stated in Article 55', which include 'universal respect for, and observation of, human and fundamental freedoms for all without distinction as to race, sex, language, or religion'. Although the Charter contains no provisions as to the contents of human rights, it signalled the dawn of the international human rights regime. It provided for the establishment of an Economic and Social Council (ECOSOC) whose functions included making 'recommendations for the purpose of promoting respect for, and observance of, human rights and fundamental freedoms for all'.[43] Henkin has succinctly described the development as follows:

The UN charter ushered in a new international law of human rights. The new law buried the old dogma that the individual is not a 'subject' of international politics and law and that a government's behaviour toward its own nationals is a matter of domestic, not international concern . . . It gave the individual a part in international politics and rights in international law, independently of his government. It also gave the individual protectors other than his government, indeed protectors and remedies against his government.[44]

The UDHR was the first UN document adopted containing a list of internationally recognized human rights.[45] It was adopted as a simple resolution of

---

[41] The UN Charter was adopted on 26 June 1945 and is regarded as 'the constitution of the organized world community after World War II' and is binding between all the Member States of the UN. *See* Ermacora, F., Nowak, M., and Tretter, H. (eds.), *International Human Rights: Documents and Introductory Notes* (1993) p.3.

[42] *See* Preamble to the UN Charter (1945) 1 UNTS, p.xvi.

[43] *See* Chapter X of the UN Charter.

[44] *See* Henkin, L. (ed.), *The International Bill of Rights: The Covenant on Civil and Political Rights* (1981) p.6.

[45] The rights covered by the UDHR are Life, liberty and security of person (Art. 3), Recognition as a person (Art. 6), Equality before the law (Art. 7), Effective legal remedies (Art. 8), Due process of law (Arts 9, 10 & 11), Freedom of movement (Art. 13), Asylum (Art. 14), Nationality (Art. 15), Marriage and family (Art. 16), Property (Art. 17), Freedom of thought, conscience and religion (Art. 18), Freedom of opinion and expression (Art. 19), Peaceful assembly and association (Art. 20), Participation in government (Art. 21), Social security (Art. 22), Work and equal pay for equal work (Art. 23), Rest and leisure (Art. 24), Adequate standard of living (Art. 25), Education (Art. 26), Cultural life (Art. 27), Prohibition of slavery or servitude (Art. 4), Prohibition of torture or cruel, inhuman or degrading treatment (Art. 5), Prohibition of arbitrary interference with privacy (Art. 12).

the General Assembly of the UN in 1948.[46] The rights in the UDHR were stated in very general terms and some of its principles are today considered to have become part of customary international law because they lead to rights accepted by States generally.[47] The UDHR has served as a framework not only for subsequent international human rights treaties but also for many national and regional human rights documents.[48]

In 1966, the International Covenant on Civil and Political Rights (ICCPR)[49] and the International Covenant on Economic, Social and Cultural Rights (ICESCR)[50] were adopted, and both entered into force in 1976.[51] The two Covenants together with the UDHR constitute the International Bill of Rights. The rights guaranteed under the two Covenants cover nearly all the basic values cherished by every civilized human society.[52] Apart from the International Bill of Rights, the UN has also adopted other ancillary international treaties and declarations on the rights of women, children, refugees, stateless persons, diplomatic agents, minorities, and the like. There are also specific international human rights treaties for the protection of the human person against atrocities such as genocide, racial discrimination, apartheid, slavery, forced labour, torture, etc.[53]

Regional organizations such as the Council of Europe, the Organization of American States, the Organization of African Unity,[54] and the League of Arab States have also adopted different regional human rights treaties in recognition of the noble ideals of international human rights. The basic regional human rights treaties are the European Convention for the Protection of Human Rights and Fundamental Freedoms (1950),[55] the European Social Charter (1961),[56] the American Convention on Human Rights (1969),[57] the African Charter on

---

[46] 10 December 1948, GAOR, 3rd Sess., Res.217A.

[47] *See* Lillich, R.B., 'The Growing Importance of Customary International Human Rights Law' (1995–96) 25 *Georgia Journal of International and Comparative Law*, Nos. 1 & 2, pp.1–30.

[48] *See* Hannum, H., 'The Status of the Universal Declaration of Human Rights in National and International Law' (1995–96) 25 *Georgia Journal of International and Comparative Law*, Nos. 1 & 2, pp.287–396.   [49] 999 UNTS, p.171.

[50] 993 UNTS, p.3.

[51] For the drafting history and long-standing contentious debate on the nature of civil and political rights and economic social and cultural rights, *see* e.g. Sohn, L.B., 'A Short History of United Nations Documents on Human Rights' in *United Nations and Human Rights* (1968); Szabo, I., 'Historical Foundations of Human Rights and Subsequent Developments' in Vasak, K., (ed.), *The International Dimensions of Human Rights* (1982) Vol.1.

[52] *See* Chen, L., *An Introduction to Contemporary International Law* (1989) pp.209–211.

[53] *See* UN Human Rights Treaty Website: http://www.unhchr.ch/html/intlinst.htm [1/3/03].

[54] The OAU has now been replaced by the African Union (AU); *see* Art. 28 of the Constitutive Act of the African Union which came into force on 26 May 2001.

[55] Adopted on 4 November 1950. E.T.S. No.005.

[56] Adopted on 18 October 1961. E.T.S. No.035.

[57] Adopted on 22 November 1969. O.A.S.T.S. No.36 at p.1.

Human and People's Rights (1981),[58] and the Arab Charter on Human Rights (1994).[59] Also of relevance is the Cairo Declaration on Human Rights in Islam adopted by the Organization of Islamic Conference in 1990.[60]

All the above international treaties and declarations on human rights confirm, as rightly observed by Henkin, the acceptance of the human rights idea by 'virtually all states and societies' of the contemporary world 'regardless of historical, cultural, ideological, economic or other differences'.[61]

2.3.2 Categorization of human rights

Human rights are today classified either by subject, object or 'generation'. Thus, we talk of civil and political rights distinct from economic, social and cultural rights, and of individual rights separate from collective or group rights. We also talk of first generation, second generation, and third generation rights.

The civil and political rights are often referred to as the 'first generation' rights.[62] They are the traditional rights relating to the liberty and justice that individuals are entitled to expect from the State. They are the favourites of Western States, some of whom considered them as the only true human rights.[63] The ICCPR contains the list of the internationally recognized civil and political rights. Apart from the right of self-determination, the civil and political rights are mostly individual rights, which every individual may demand of the State. In the past, these rights were sought through the channel of civil disobedience and revolution. Today, international human rights law provides the individual with legal channels for the demand and guarantee of these rights.[64]

Economic, social, and cultural rights are the so-called 'second generation' rights. They are mostly rights which States have to take positive action to promote. They may be called the sustenance or enjoyment rights, and are strongly advanced by socialist and developing nations.[65] The ICESCR contains a list of internationally recognized economic, social, and cultural rights. Despite their inevitability for the sustenance of human dignity, the economic, social, and cultural rights are often considered as 'utopian aspirations', non-legal and

[58] Adopted on 27 June 1981. OAU Doc.CAB/LEG/67/3 rev. 5; (1982) 21 *ILM* 58.

[59] Adopted 15 September 1994, but not yet in force. Reprinted in (1997) 18 *Human Rights Law Journal*, p.151. *See* Rishmawi, M., 'The Arab Charter on Human Rights: A Comment' (1996) 10 *Interights Bulletin*, No.1, pp.8–10 for an overview of the Arab Charter.

[60] Adopted on 5 August 1990. The Declaration was submitted by the OIC to the UN prior to the 2nd World Conference on Human Rights in Vienna as representing the view of the Muslim States on human rights in Islam. *See* UN Doc. A/CONF.157/PC/62/Add.18 (1993).

[61] *See* Henkin (above n. 44) at p.1.

[62] *See* e.g. Harris, D.J., *Cases and Materials on International Law* (5th Ed., 1998) p.625; Weston (above n.36) at p.715; and Sohn (above n.35) at p.32.

[63] *See* e.g. US position in UN Doc. A/40/C3/36, p.5 (1985) that economic, social, and cultural rights were 'societal goals' rather than human rights.

[64] *See* e.g. Optional Protocol 1 to the ICCPR (1966); 999 UNTS, p.171.

[65] *See* Harris (above n.62) Weston (above n.36); and Sohn (above n.35).

non-justiciable.[66] Shue however argues strongly that there is a basic or fundamental human right to subsistence which the economic, social, and cultural rights fulfil. He contends that justice and international law require the rich nations to share their abundant resources with the millions of human beings who are chronically malnourished all over the world.[67] Human rights would certainly be meaningless in a world where one part of humanity is in abundance but yet feels no obligation for another part of it in abject poverty. The notion of 'generations' of human rights can thus be misleading if not well addressed. For instance, it had for a long time distracted attention from the important role of the economic, social, and cultural rights in the enhancement of human dignity. Many scholars therefore reject this notion of 'generations'.[68] While the civil and political rights might have been pursued more vigorously in international law for political and ideological reasons, this does not mean that the economic, social, and cultural rights are less important.[69]

Supplementary to the so-called first and second 'generation' of rights mentioned above is also the notion of a 'third generation' of human rights. These are collective rights, not individual rights. They are described as solidarity rights based on solidarity between men. According to its major proponent, Karel Vasak, the 'third generation' human rights are born of the obvious brotherhood of men and their indispensable solidarity.[70] The right to development, right to peace, and right to a healthy and balanced environment are prominent on the list of the proposed third generation of human rights. This group of human rights also expresses aspirations for co-operation between developed affluent nations on one hand and developing poor nations of the world on the other, for the benefit of humanity. With the exception of treaties on environmental protection,

---

[66] *See* e.g. Cranston, M., *What Are Human Rights?* (1973) pp.9–17.

[67] *See generally*, Shue, H., *Basic Rights: Subsistence, Affluence and US Foreign Policy* (2nd Ed., 1996).

[68] *See* e.g. Eide, A., and Rosas, A., 'Economic, Social and Cultural Rights; A Universal Challenge', in Eide, A., *et al.*, (eds.), *Economic, Social and Cultural Rights: A Textbook* (1995) p.27.

[69] *See* Van Hoof, G.J.H., 'The Legal Nature of Economic, Social and Cultural Rights: A Rebuttal of Some Traditional Views' in Alston, P., and Tomasevski, K., (eds.), *The Right to Food* (1984) pp.97–110 (argues that it is wrong to construe a strict dichotomy of the two groups of rights, and suggests a more integrated approach that covers both sets of rights). For analyses of the long-standing and contentious debate on the relationship between civil and political rights, and economic, social, and cultural rights, *see* e.g. Vierdag, E.W., 'The Legal Nature of the Rights granted by the International Covenant on Economic, Social and Cultural Rights '(1978) 9 *Netherlands Yearbook of International Law*, p.69; Craven, M.C.R., *The International Covenant on Economic, Social and Cultural Rights: A Perspective on its Development* (1995) pp.8–16 and footnotes thereof; Vincent, R.J., *Human Rights and International Relations* (1986) pp.11–13; Donnelly, J., *Universal Human Rights in Theory and Practice* (1989) pp.28–45.

[70] *See* Vasak, K., 'For the Third Generation of Human Rights: The Rights of Solidarity', Inaugural Lecture to the 10th Study Session of the International Institute of Human Rights, Strasbourg, 2–27 July, 1979.

which are reflective of the right to a healthy and balanced environment, there is no UN international treaty yet on the 'third generation' of human rights.[71]

Although the categorization of human rights may serve the useful purpose of easy identification of particular rights, there is the need to emphasize the treatment of human rights as a totality. The UN General Assembly has thus stressed the fact that all human rights are indivisible and interdependent.[72] This will prevent a rigid compartmentalization of human rights and ensure a wholesome realization of the ideals of international human rights law.

2.3.3 Universalism in international human rights law

The question of universalism in international human rights law has been very intensely debated.[73] It is noted however that the 'universality of' human rights has often generally been confused with 'universalism in' human rights within the international human rights discourse. Although the two concepts are inter-related, each refers to a different aspect of the universalization of human rights. An appreciation of the distinction between the two concepts is very important for a realistic approach to the question of universalism in international human rights law.

'Universality of' human rights refers to the universal quality or global acceptance of the human rights idea as elaborated above, while 'universalism in' human rights relates to the interpretation and application of the human rights idea.[74] The universality of human rights has been achieved over the years since the adoption of the UDHR in 1948, and is evidenced by the fact that there is no State today that will unequivocally accept that it is a violator of human rights. Today, all nations and societies do generally acknowledge the human rights idea, thereby establishing its universality. However, universalism

---

[71] The UN General Assembly has however adopted the Declaration on the Right to Development at its 97th plenary meeting on 4 December 1986, and recognized in its preamble that 'development is a comprehensive economic, social, cultural and political process, which aims at the constant improvement of the well-being of the entire population and of all individuals on the basis of their active, free and meaningful participation in development and in the fair distribution of benefits resulting therefrom'. The right to development also continues to be a subject of discussion within the activities of the UN Commission for Human Rights. *See* e.g. the UN Secretary General's Report on Right to Development to the 55th Session of the UN General Assembly UN Doc. A/55/283 of 8 August 2000.

[72] *See* e.g. GA Res. 32/130 of 16 December 1977, and also paragraph 5 of the Declaration of the World Conference on Human Rights, Vienna 1993, UN Doc. A/CONF.157/23.

[73] *See* e.g. Symposium on 'Universalism and Cultural Relativism: Perspectives on the Human Rights Debate' (1997) *Human Rights at Harvard*, 5 April 1997, pp.9–38. *See also* Steiner, H.J., and Alston, P., *International Human Rights in Context, Law Politics Morals* (2nd Ed., 2000) p.366.

[74] Linguistically the suffix '-ity' denotes the quality, condition or degree of a phenomenon while the suffix '-ism' denotes its system, principle, result or practice. *See* e.g. Pearsall, J., and Trumble, B., (eds), *The Oxford English Reference Dictionary* (Oxford: Oxford University Press, 2nd Ed., 1996) p.746 and p.749.

in human rights has not been so achieved. Universalism connotes the existence of a common universal value consensus for the interpretation and application of international human rights law. The current lack of such universal consensus is evidenced by the fact that universalism continues to be a subject of debate within the international human rights objective of the UN.[75] Universalism is often confronted by the cultural relativist argument at every opportunity in the international human rights discourse. For example during the Vienna Conference on Human Rights, representatives of some African, Asian, and Muslim States challenged the present concept of universalism in international human rights as being West-centric and insensitive to non-Western cultures. Prior to the conference, a group of Asian States had adopted the Bangkok (Governmental) Declaration recognizing the contribution that can be made by Asian countries to the international human rights regime through their diverse but rich cultures and traditions.[76] An NGO coalition from the Asia Pacific region had also adopted the Bangkok NGO Declaration on Human Rights promoting the emergence of 'a new understanding of universalism encompassing the richness and wisdom of Asia pacific cultures'.[77] Muslim States that apply Islamic law also often advance similar arguments in respect of Islamic law.[78]

When the UDHR was adopted by the UN General Assembly in 1948 it was very clear from the outset that the human rights it guaranteed were intended to be universal. Apart from it being titled a 'Universal Declaration', the General Assembly proclaimed it as 'a common standard of achievement for all peoples and all nations'. The need to promote respect for the rights through national and international measures and to secure their universal and effective recognition and observance was also identified in the Declaration.[79] The UN was then constituted of only 58 Member States.[80] Although none of the

---

[75] *See* e.g. Ghai, Y., 'Human Rights and Governance: The Asia Debate' (1994) 15 *Australian Yearbook of International Law*, p.11. *See also generally* Renteln, A.D., *International Human Rights: Universalism Versus Relativism* (1990); Bauer, J.R., and Bell, D.A., (eds.), *The East Asian Challenge for Human Rights* (1999); and also Smith, J., (ed.), *Human Rights: Chinese and Dutch Perspectives* (1996).

[76] *See* 'Report of the Regional Meeting for Asia of the World Conference on Human Rights' (Bangkok, 29 March–2 April 1993), UN Doc. A/Conf.157/ASRM/8, Preambular paragraph 2.

[77] *See* 1st paragraph under *Challenges* in the Bangkok NGO Declaration on Human Rights. Reproduced in (1993) 14 *Human Rights Law Journal*, p.352.

[78] *See* e.g. the 1st Principle in the Rome Declaration on Human Rights in Islam (2000) and *generally* Baderin, M.A., 'A Macroscopic Analysis of the Practice of Muslim State Parties to International Human Rights Treaties: Conflict or Congruence?' (2001) 1 *Human Rights Law Review*, No. 2, pp.265–303.   [79] *See* paragraph 8 of the Preamble of the UDHR.

[80] Afghanistan, Argentina, Australia, Belgium, Bolivia, Brazil, Belarus, Canada, Chile, China, Colombia, Costa Rica, Cuba, Czechoslovakia, Denmark, Dominican Republic, Ecuador, Egypt, El Salvador, Ethiopia, France, Greece, Guatemala, Haiti, Honduras, Iceland, India, Iran, Iraq, Lebanon, Liberia, Luxembourg, Mexico, Myanmar, Netherlands, New Zealand, Nicaragua, Norway, Pakistan, Panama, Paraguay, Peru, Philippines, Poland, Russian Federation, Saudi Arabia, South Africa, Sweden, Syrian Arab Republic, Thailand, Turkey, Ukraine, United Kingdom of Great Britain and Northern Ireland, United States of America, Uruguay, Venezuela, Yemen, Yugoslavia.

Member States opposed the human rights idea or its universalization, eight of them (Byelorussian SSR, Czechoslovakia, Poland, Saudi Arabia, South Africa, USSR, Ukrainian SSR, and Yugoslavia) abstained from voting for the adoption of the Declaration due principally to interpretational differences on some of its provisions.[81] While the number of abstaining States may have seemed insignificant, it was no doubt a signal of the possible interpretational divergence ahead of the then emerging universal human rights initiative. Renteln has observed notably in this respect that all the eighteen drafts considered for the UDHR 'came from the democratic West and that all but two were in English'.[82] She concluded thus that '(t)he fact that there were no dissenting votes should not be taken to mean that complete value consensus had been achieved'.[83]

One of the earliest indications of the need for a universal value consensus and thus a multicultural approach to the then emerging international human rights initiative was given in 1947 by the American Anthropological Association in its memorandum submitted to the UN Commission on Human Rights charged with the drafting of the UDHR. The Association had stated, *inter alia*, that:

> Because of the great numbers of societies that are in intimate contact in the modern world, and because of the diversity of their ways of life, the primary task confronting those who would draw up a Declaration on the Rights of Man is thus, in essence, to resolve the following problem: How can the proposed Declaration be *applicable* to all human beings, and not be a statement of rights conceived only in terms of the values prevalent in the countries of Western Europe and America?... the problem is complicated by the fact that the Declaration must be of *world-wide applicability*. It must embrace and recognize the validity of many different ways of life. It will not be convincing to the Indonesian, the African, the Indian, the Chinese, if it lies on the same plane as like documents of an earlier period. The rights of Man in the Twentieth Century cannot be circumscribed by the standards of any single culture, or be dictated by the aspirations of any single people. Such a document will lead to frustration, not realization of the personalities of vast numbers of human beings.[84] (emphasis added)

The above observation was calling attention to universalism in human rights because it referred specifically to the 'world-wide (that is, universal) applicability' to the Declaration. The UN Commission seemed however to have

---

[81] In particular, Saudi Arabia had objected, *inter alia*, to the interpretation of the article on religious liberty (Art. 18) and the provision on equal rights in marriage (Art. 16). *See* UN Official Records, 3rd Committee, 3rd Session, 1948–49, Pt.120, cited in Little, D., Kelsay, J., and Sachedina, A., *Human Rights and the Conflict of Cultures* (1988) pp.33–52.

[82] Renteln (above n.75) at p.30; *See also* Tolley, H., *The UN Commission on Human Rights*, (1987) p.20.   [83] Renteln (above n.75) at p.30.

[84] *See* American Anthropological Association, 'Statement on Human Rights' (1947) 49 *American Anthropologist*, pp.539–543. *See also* the 1999 AAA Declaration on Anthropology and Human Rights available at: http://www.aaanet.org/committees/cfhr/ar95.htm [1/3/03] and Engle, K., 'From Skepticism to Embrace: Human Rights and the American Anthropological Association from 1947–1999' (2001) 23 *Human Rights Quarterly*, No.3, pp.536–559, for an analysis of the two statements.

concentrated more on the universality of human rights at that early stage and not necessarily on the means of identifying a universal value for achieving the rights guaranteed by the Declaration—that is, universalism in human rights. It is in the context of universalism (not universality) that many publicists, in retrospect, contend that were the UDHR to be readopted, it would perhaps be impossible to reach the same unanimity in today's fragmented world of more than 190 culture-conscious Member States of the UN.[85]

It is discernible however that emphasizing universalism by the UN Commission at that early stage in 1947 could have stalled the whole universal human rights initiative. Rather, the UDHR was drafted in very general terms to secure the support of all the States despite their different cultures. The seventh preambular paragraph to the Declaration however stated that 'a common understanding of these rights and freedoms is of the greatest importance for the full realization of this pledge'. But since the Declaration contained no ultimate interpretative organ, the interpretation of the rights declared was, more or less, left to the individual States, each interpreting the values within its cultural context. The controversy on universalism in human rights did not fully arise until human rights had established itself as a powerful catalyst in international relations championed strongly by Western States, and Western scholarship consequently projecting human rights as a strictly Western concept subject to complete West-oriented interpretations. This was met by counter arguments advocating a culturally relative interpretation of international human rights norms. Thus began the contending theories of universalism versus cultural relativism within the universal human rights objective of the UN, which has resulted in a sort of paradox.

2.3.4 The paradox of universalism and cultural relativism

The theory of universalism is that human rights are the same (or must be the same) everywhere, both in substance and application. Advocates of strict universalism assert that international human rights are exclusively universal. This theory is mostly advocated by Western States and scholars who present universalism in human rights through a strict Western liberal perspective. They reject any claims of cultural relativism and consider it as an unacceptable theory advocated to rationalize human rights violations. Scholars who argue that human rights were developed from Western culture also often argue that Western norms should always be the universal normative model for international human rights law.[86] Advocates of this exclusive concept of

---

[85] *See* e.g. An-Na'im, A.A., 'Universality of Human Rights: An Islamic Perspective' in Ando, N., (ed.), *Japan and International Law: Past, Present and Future* (1999) p.311 at pp.318–319.

[86] *See* e.g. D'Amato, A.A., *Collected Papers, International Law Studies* (1997) Vol.2, pp.139–40; and Mayer, E.A., 'Current Muslim Thinking on Human Rights' in An-Na'im, A.A.,

universalism usually seek support for their argument in the language of international human rights instruments, which normally state that 'every human being', 'everyone', or 'all persons' are entitled to human rights. While it is trite that the language of international human rights instruments generally supports the theory of universalism, present State practice hardly supports any suggestion that in adopting or ratifying international human rights instruments, non-Western State Parties were indicating an acceptance of a strict and exclusive Western perspective or interpretation of international human rights norms.[87] One may observe in this regard that Article 31(2) of the ICCPR, for instance, provided that in electing members of the Human Rights Committee 'consideration shall be given to equitable geographical distribution of membership and to the *representation of the different forms of civilization and of the principal legal systems*' of the State Parties (emphasis added). It is arguable that this recognizes the need for an inclusive and multi-civilizational approach in the interpretation of the Covenant.[88]

The theory of cultural relativism is thus advocated mostly by non-Western States and scholars who contend that human rights are not exclusively rooted in Western culture, but are inherent in human nature and based on morality. Thus human rights, they claim, cannot be interpreted without regard to the cultural differences of peoples. Advocates of cultural relativism assert that 'rights and rules about morality are encoded in and thus depend on cultural contexts'.[89] The theory emanates from the philosophy of the need to recognize the values set up by every society to guide its own life, the dignity inherent in every culture, and the need for tolerance of conventions though they may differ from one's own.[90] Cultural relativism is thus conditioned by a combination of historical, political, economic, social, cultural, and religious factors and not restricted only to indigenous cultural or traditional differences of people.

A critical evaluation of both theories reveals that, on the one hand, the theory of cultural relativism is prone to abuse and may be used to rationalize human rights violations by different regimes. It admits of pluralistic inputs, which, if not properly managed, can debase the efficacy of human rights. On the other hand, the current values projected for the interpretation of international human rights law by advocates of strict universalism have been criticized as

and Deng, F.M., (eds.), *Human Rights in Africa, Cultural Perspectives* (1990) p.131 at pp.147–148.

[87] *See* e.g. Baderin (above n.78).

[88] The same provision can be found in Art. 8 of the International Convention on the Elimination of All Forms of Racial Discrimination (1965) on the election of the members of CERD. Also Art. 9 of the Statute of the International Court of Justice (1945) provides for 'the representation of the main forms of civilization and of the principal legal systems of the world' in the election of its judges.

[89] *See* Steiner, H.J. and Alston, P., *International Human Rights in Context, Law Politics Morals* (2nd Ed., 2000) p.366.   [90] *See* Herskovits, M., *Man and His Works* (1950) p.76.

purely Western and not really universal.[91] The present theory of universalism is itself thus criticized as being culturally relative to Western values.[92] That is the paradox, whereby the controversy between universalism and cultural relativism actually portrays a situation of cultural relativisms.

To most of the former colonies, Western values are essentially being used as the universal repugnancy test for the interpretation of international human rights law in the same way colonial laws and customs were used in colonial periods to eliminate local laws.[93] The question has thus often been raised as to whether the theory of strict universalism in human rights is not another 'form of neocolonialism serving to strengthen the dominance of the West'.[94] The ideals of universalism in international human rights law need therefore to be advanced in a manner that escapes charges of cultural imperialism within non-Western societies.

A supposed coherent and homogeneous notion of a 'Western' human rights tradition is however also misleading and must therefore be embraced with caution. It is contestable whether there is, in fact, a complete homogenized legal interpretation of human rights among 'Western' States. For example, there is evidence from the practice and case law of both the European and Inter-American regional human rights mechanisms that 'Western' States do also differ in some cases on the scope of some human rights principles. While there is certainly a wide area of consensus in human rights traditions among 'Western' States, this does not in practice always translate into a single homogeneous 'Western' human rights approach in relation to universalism in international human rights law.

Universalism in international human rights law demands the evolution or identification of a universal consensus in the interpretation of human rights principles. This calls for a multicultural or cross-cultural approach to the interpretation and application of the international human rights principles in a manner that will not reduce its efficacy but lead to the realization of an inclusive theory of universalism. The American Anthropological Association had argued in its earlier quoted comment to the Human Rights Commission that international human rights should '. . . not be circumscribed by the stand-ards of any single culture, or be dictated by the aspirations of any single people'.[95] An-Na'im has also reiterated that: 'Any concept of human rights that is to be universally accepted and globally enforced demands equal respect

---

[91] *See* e.g. Mutua, M., 'The Ideology of Human Rights' (1996) 36 *Virginia Journal of International Law*, p.586 at pp.592–593.   [92] *ibid.*
[93] For e.g. *see* Obilade, O.A., *The Nigerian Legal System* (1979) and Park, A.E.W., *The Sources of Nigerian Law* (1963) for analyses of the application of the repugnancy principle in the Nigerian legal system. *See also* Allot, A.N., *New Essays in African Law* (1970).
[94] *See* Higgins, R., 'The Continuing Universality of the Universal Declaration' in Baehr, P., *et al.* (eds.) *Innovation and Inspiration: Fifty Years of the Universal Declaration of Human Rights* (1999) p.17 at p.19.
[95] *See* American Anthropological Association (1947) (above n. 84).

and mutual comprehension between rival cultures'.[96] That argument continues to be advanced today mostly by non-Western States. There is thus a need for an objective evaluation of what every civilization can contribute to universalism in international human rights law. Presumptions of cultural inferiority must be avoided and justifications on cultural differences must be examined and critically evaluated within the parameters of human dignity with a view to evolving an inclusive universalism in international human rights law.

Whatever definition or understanding we ascribe to human rights, the bottom line is the protection of human dignity. There is perhaps no civilization or philosophy in today's world that would not subscribe to that notion. Thus it may only be difficult, but not impossible to evolve a universally acceptable conception in that respect. There is need for sincere and justificatory cross-cultural evaluations of human dignity with a view to evolving international moral values which no repressive regime may find easy to circumvent in the business of State governance.

2.3.5 Relevance of Islamic law to universalism in international human rights law

The relevance of Islamic law in the quest for an inclusive universalism that will ensure the full realization of international human rights in the Muslim world is, in view of the number of Muslim States in the international legal order, quite obvious. This has often been practically demonstrated by references to Islamic law in the arguments and reports of Muslim States to UN charter and human rights treaty committees.[97] The general relevance of Islamic law in international law is also demonstrated by the existence of a 'Committee on Islamic Law and International Law' amongst the international committees of the International Law Association (ILA). Notably, the Committee for instance proposed in its report after the ILA London Conference in July 2000, 'to contribute to the advancement of International Law on asylum and refugees by incorporating some aspect of Islamic Law on asylum in International Law'.[98]

Mayer has however observed that there is a general indifference to the Islamic tradition within learned international human rights literature and that '[q]uestions of Islamic law are only occasionally mentioned in scholarly writing on international human rights—for the sake of comparison with international norms or to illustrate the problems of introducing international norms in areas of the developing world'.[99] Thus, while Islamic law is recognized as

---

[96] An-Na'im, A.A., 'What Do We Mean By Universal?' (1994) *Index on Censorship*, September/October, p.120. *See also* An-Na'im, A.A., 'Universality of Human Rights: An Islamic Perspective' in Ando, N., *Japan and International Law: Past, Present and Future* (1999) p.311 at pp.314–319.   [97] *See* Baderin (above n.78).

[98] *See* the ILA Internet Website at http://www.ila-hq.org/ [1/3/03].

[99] *See* Mayer, A.E., *Islam and Human Rights, Traditions and Politics* (3rd Ed., 1999) p.41.

a factor relevant to the introduction of international norms in Muslim areas of the developing world, legal scholarship on the subject has not been projected strongly enough to achieve effective harmonization of the differences in scope between Islamic law and international human rights law.

It is noteworthy however that the ILA adopted Resolution No. 6/2000 after the London Conference acknowledging that '... aspects of Islamic Law are protective of human rights' and requested its Committee on Islamic Law and International Law 'to continue its work on the contribution of Islamic Law to the development of International law by undertaking further studies, with a view of reporting on that work to the 70th conference to be held in New Delhi in 2002'.[100]

More than just establishing a religious and legal order, Islam is an institution of legitimacy in many States of the Muslim world. Many regimes in the Muslim world today seek their legitimacy through portraying an adherence to Islamic law and traditions. Thus any attempt to enforce international or universal norms within Muslim societies in oblivion of established Islamic law and traditions creates tension and reactions against the secular nature of the international regime no matter how humane or lofty such international norms may be. For example the Representative of the Islamic Republic of Iran, Said Raja'i-Khorasani at the 65th meeting of the Third Committee during the 39th Session of the UN General Assembly on 7 December 1984 had argued in defence of alleged violation of human rights by his country that the new political order in Iran was:

> in full accordance and harmony with the deepest moral and religious convictions of the people and therefore most representative of the traditional, cultural, moral and religious beliefs of Iranian society. It recognised no authority ... apart from Islamic law ... (therefore) conventions, declarations and resolutions or decisions of international organisations, which were contrary to Islam, had no validity in the Islamic Republic of Iran.[101]

Conversely, accommodation of Islamic law is also often seen in international human rights circles as accommodating a constraint on freedoms, liberties, and human rights generally. The assumption is that it is impossible to realize human rights within an Islamic legal dispensation. For example when one of the States in the Federal Republic of Nigeria promulgated a law in

---

[100] *See* above n.98.

[101] UN General Assembly, 39th Sess., Third Committee, 65th Mtg, 7 December 1984, A/C.3/39/SR.65. Note however that the Deputy Permanent Representative of Iran to the UN, Mr Ziaran, declared at the Third Committee of the 53rd Session of the General Assembly in November 1998 that: '(t)he government of the Islamic Republic of Iran is fully committed to the promotion of human rights'. This commitment, he further observed, 'is not out of political expediency rather it stems from the supreme teachings of Islam' and that 'the government of the Islamic Republic of Iran would extend its full co-operation to the human rights mechanisms' of the UN. *See* statement by H.E. Mr Bozorgmehr Ziaran at the Permanent Mission of the Islamic Republic of Iran to the UN Website: http://www.un.int/iran/statements/3ga/3ga53008.html [12/12/2000].

1999 for the full application of Islamic law within its jurisdiction[102] many human rights groups both within and outside the country expressed fears that such application of Islamic law would adversely constrain fundamental human rights and freedoms within the jurisdiction of the State.[103] Similar fears were expressed by human rights groups in 1998 when the government of Pakistan proposed a constitutional amendment Bill to its Parliament seeking to make the Qur'an and *Sunnah* the supreme law of Pakistan.[104] Such apprehension is believed to have also contributed to the abortion of the democratization process in Algeria in 1992 through a military takeover, when it appeared that the Islamic Salvation Front (FIS) would emerge victorious in the overall elections. According to Bassam Tibi: 'If the FIS were to come to power, the first measure it would have taken would have been to abolish the constitution and declare nizam al-islami [Islamic system of government based on the *sharî'ah*]'.[105]

While the political and legal philosophy of Islam may differ in certain respects from that of the secular international order, it does not necessarily mean a complete discord with the international human rights regime. Removing the traditional barriers of distrust and apathy would reveal that diversity is not synonymous to incompatibility. Mayer has observed that:

> The Islamic heritage offers many philosophical concepts, humanistic values, and moral principles that are well adapted for use in constructing human rights principles. Such values and principles abound even in the premodern Islamic intellectual heritage.[106]

It is those Islamic humanistic concepts and values of the *Sharî'ah* that need to be fully revived for the realization of international human rights within the application of Islamic law in Muslim States.

Judge Weeramantry formerly of the International Court of Justice had also observed in his penetrating work, *Justice Without Frontiers, Furthering Human Rights*, that although Locke, the founding father of Western human rights, never attended most of his lectures as a student at Oxford, 'he assiduously attended only the lectures of Professor Pococke, the professor

---

[102] *See* Shari'a Court of Appeal Law of Zamfara State of the Federal Republic of Nigeria; Zamfara State of Nigeria Law No.6 of 8 October 1999.

[103] Similar fears were raised in 1979 and 1989 during the debates on provisions for a Sharî'ah Court of Appeal in the Nigerian Constitution. *See generally* Basri, G., *Nigeria and Sharî'ah: Aspirations and Apprehensions* (1994).

[104] Constitution (15th Amendment) Act 1998. The Bill was passed by the National Assembly on 9 October 1998. But the Senate had not voted on it before it was suspended by the Musharraf regime that took power in October 1999. However, there is an Enforcement of Sharî'ah Act of 1991 already in force, Art. 3(1) of which provides that, 'The Sharî'ah, that is to say the Injunctions of Islam as laid down in the Holy Qur'an and Sunnah, shall be the supreme law of Pakistan'.

[105] Tibi, B., 'Islamic Law/Shari'a and Human Rights: International Law and International Relations' in Lindholm, T., and Vogt, K., (eds.), *Islamic Law Reform and Human Rights: Challenges and Rejoinders* (1993) p.75 at p.76.   [106] *See* Mayer (above n.99) at p.43.

of Arabic studies'. According to the learned judge: 'Those studies may well have referred to Arabic political theory including the idea of rights that no ruler could take away, subjection of the ruler to the law, and the notion of conditional rulership'. He concluded that: 'When Locke proclaimed his theory of inalienable rights and conditional rulership, this was new to the West, but could he not have had some glimmerings of this from his Arabic studies?'.[107]

The wide gap that still exists between the theory and reality of the universal protection of human rights[108] indicates that universalism in international human rights law is not yet a fait accompli. The evolution of international human rights has therefore not reached the end of its history yet. With the cognizance that international human rights law is aimed at the enhancement of human dignity and the promotion of human welfare, it is submitted that Islamic law rather than contradicting it, should be able to contribute to the realization of its ideals and also to the achievement of its universal observation, especially in the Muslim world. What is required, as observed by one writer, is an analysis 'from within by a Muslim intellectual who can engage in dialogue with the traditionally educated scholars of Islamic jurisprudence',[109] comparatively with international human rights law in a manner that facilitates better understanding and appreciation between the two legal regimes.

2.4 WHAT IS ISLAMIC LAW?

Traditionally, Islamic law is not strictly speaking monolithic. Its jurisprudence accommodates a pluralistic interpretation of its sources, which does produce differences in juristic opinions that can be quite significant in a comparative legal analysis. Afshari has thus argued that '(w)hen reference is made to "Islamic law", a host of diverse positions . . . comes into the picture'.[110]

The complexity of Islamic law does not however make it indeterminable. The differences of the jurists and schools of Islamic jurisprudence represent 'different manifestations of the same divine will' and are considered as 'a diversity within unity'.[111] This depicts recognition of the inescapable

---

[107] *See* Weeramantry, C.G., *Justice Without Frontiers: Furthering Human Rights* (1997) Vol.1, pp.139–140.

[108] *See generally*, Watson, J.S., *Theory & Reality in the International Protection of Human Rights* (1999) for a critical analysis of this.

[109] *See* Sachedina, A., 'Review of Abdullahi Ahmed An-Na'im, Toward an Islamic Reformation: Civil Liberties, Human Rights and International Law' (1993) 25 *International Journal of Middle East Studies*, pp.155–157.

[110] Afshari, R., 'An Essay on Islamic Cultural Relativism in the Discourse of Human Rights' (1994) 16 *Human Rights Quarterly*, p.235 at p.271; *See also* Lawyers Committee on Human Rights, *Islam and Justice* (1997) p.18 where Azziman also stated that when people talk about *Shari'ah* or Islamic law he really does not know what is meant.

[111] *See* Kamali, H.M., *Principles of Islamic Jurisprudence* (1991) p.169, and Hallaq (above n.2) at p.202.

pluralism that exists within human society. According to Breiner, Islam 'refuses the temptation to find unity only in uniformity, even in matters of law'.[112] The appreciation of differences, Breiner continued, is an 'important principle of Islamic law, one quite different from the assumptions of Roman law inherited throughout most of Europe'.[113] There is in fact an Islamic jurisprudential maxim that says: 'The blessing of the Muslim community lies in the jurists' differences of opinion'.[114]

Law is ultimately the product of its sources and methods, and Islamic law is not an exception to that fact. It is important therefore to distinguish between *Sharî'ah* as the source from which the law is derived and *Fiqh* as the method by which the law is derived and applied.[115]

2.4.1 Nature of Islamic law

There is often a traditional misconception about Islamic law being wholly divine and immutable. This usually arises from a non-distinction between the sources and methods of Islamic law. Distinguishing between *Sharî'ah* and *Fiqh* is very significant for a proper understanding of the nature of Islamic law. Although either of the terms '*Sharî'ah*' and '*Fiqh*' is often referred to as Islamic law, they are not technically synonymous.

Literally *Sharî'ah* means 'path to be followed' or 'right path'[116] while *Fiqh* means 'understanding'.[117] The former refers principally to the sources while the latter refers principally to the methods of Islamic law. In the strict legal sense *Sharî'ah* refers to the corpus of the revealed law as contained in the Qur'an and in the authentic Traditions (*Sunnah*) of the Prophet Muhammad. It differs in this sense from *Fiqh* because it (*Sharî'ah*) refers here to the primary sources

---

[112] Breiner, B., 'A Christian View of Human Rights in Islam' in Breiner, B., (ed.), *Two Papers on Sharî'ah* (1992) p.3.   [113] *ibid.*

[114] The maxim says: '*Rahmah al-Ummah fî Ikhtilâf al-A'immah*'. This indicates that the jurists' differences of opinion in the interpretation of legal sources on certain matters offer a broad and equally legal scope from which judges may appropriately choose the most compassionate and beneficial opinion from time to time in cases before them. It was on the basis of this that the Islamic legal principle of '*takhayyur*' or '*takhyîr*' (eclectic choice) was evolved and advocated to allow for unification or movement within the different schools of Islamic jurisprudence. *See* e.g. Coulson, N.J., *Conflicts and Tensions in Islamic Jurisprudence* (1969) pp.20–39 and Hallaq (above n.2) at p.210. A 15th century Islamic jurist, Abû Abdullah al-Dimashqî, wrote a jurisprudential book entitled '*Rahmah al-Ummah fî Ikhtilâf al-A'immah*' in which he listed the legal consensus and dissension of the classical Islamic jurists (republished by Dâr al-Kutub al-Ilmiyyah, Beirut, Lebanon (1995)).

[115] *See* e.g. Kamali, M.H., 'Law and Society: The Interplay of Revelation and Reason in the Shariah' in Esposito, J.L., *The Oxford History of Islam* (1999) p.107.

[116] *See* e.g. Doi, A.R., *Sharî'ah: The Islamic Law* (1984) p.2.

[117] In Q45:18 the word *Sharî'ah* is used as 'straight path' or 'right way'—'Then We put you on a right way (*Sharî'ah*) of the affairs, so follow it . . .' and the Prophet Muhammad used *Fiqh* in one of his sayings to mean 'understanding'—'*To whomsoever God wishes good, He gives the understanding (fiqh) of the faith*'. *Fiqh* is also used in the Qur'an to mean understanding. *See* e.g. Q9:87. *See also* Qadri (above n.2) at pp.15–17.

of the law, which is textually immutable. *Fiqh* on the other hand refers to methods of the law, that is, the understanding derived from, and the application of the *Sharî'ah*, which may change according to time and circumstances.[118] The significance of this distinction with respect to the Islamic law arguments advanced in this book are:

1. *Sharî'ah* as a source of Islamic law is divine in nature and thus immutable, while *Fiqh*, as the understanding, interpretation, and application of the *Sharî'ah*, is a human product that may change according to time and circumstances; and

2. *Sharî'ah* broadly covers the moral, legal, social, and spiritual aspects of the Muslims' life, while *Fiqh* mostly covers the legal or juridical aspect of the *Sharî'ah* as distinguished from the moral.[119]

Islamic law thus consists of two component parts: (i) immutable divine revelation termed *Sharî'ah* and (ii) human interpretation of the *Sharî'ah* termed *Fiqh*. 'Abd al 'Atî has correctly observed that 'confusion arises when the term *sharî'ah* is used uncritically to designate not only the divine law in its pure principal form, but also its human subsidiary sciences including *fiqh*'.[120] We will now examine the characteristics of these two component parts of Islamic law.

2.4.2 Sources of Islamic law—(Sharî'ah)[121]

The Qur'an and the *Sunnah* primarily constitute both formal and material sources of Islamic law. Their nature as formal sources of Islamic law emanates from their being divine and quasi-divine revelations respectively, which Muslims must religiously obey and follow. Their nature as material sources of Islamic law follows from the fact that they contain the corpus of the revealed law. The Qur'an is the principal source and is believed by Muslims to be the exact words of God revealed to the Prophet Muhammad over a period of approximately twenty-three years for the guidance of humanity.[122] It is

---

[118] *See* e.g. Ramadan (above n.2) at p.36 and Philips (above n.2) at pp.1–4.

[119] Note however as pointed out by Kamali that 'There is often . . . a relationship between strict compliance to a legal duty and the Islamic concept of moral excellence'. *See* Kamali, M.H., *Freedom of Expression in Islam*, (Revised Ed., 1997) p.27; and Kamali (above n.115) at p.109.   [120] 'Abd al 'Atî, H., *The Family Structure in Islam* (1977) p.14.

[121] The approach adopted here deviates from the traditional classification of the Qur'an, *Sunnah*, *Ijmâ'* and *Qiyâs* as main sources of Islamic law, a classification which Ramadan has rightly observed, 'is by no means a decisive or authoritative one'. *See* Ramadan (above n.2) at p.33. The approach here distinguishes the sources of the law (i.e. Qur'an and *Sunnah*) from the methods of the law (i.e. *Ijmâ' Qiyâs, Ijtihâd*, etc.) to avoid the confusion of the traditional misconception of the whole of Islamic law as being strictly divine and immutable.

[122] *See* e.g. Q26:192 which says: 'Verily this is a Revelation from the Lord of the Worlds' and Q45:2 which says: 'The revelation of The Book is from God, The Exalted in Power, Full of Wisdom'.

not strictly a constitutional code, but more specifically described by God as a book of guidance.[123] Out of its approximately 6,666 verses, which cover both the spiritual and temporal aspects of life, Muslim jurists estimate between 350 to 500 verses as containing legal elements,[124] while according to Coulson: 'No more than approximately eighty verses deal with legal topics in the strict sense of the term'.[125] This, conceivably, anticipates the application of some juridical principles to extend the few strictly legal verses to cover the dynamic and expansive nature of human life. However, those verses that may be viewed largely as moral rules also constitute the basis for every Islamic legal principle.[126]

The words of the Qur'an are, to Muslims, immutable and from it 'springs the very conception of legality'[127] in Islam. The Qur'an forms the foundation or the basic norm of Islamic law, the *grundnorm*, as Kelsen calls it. However, while legal texts are very significant as material sources in every legal system, their interpretation is what actually constitutes law at every point in time. The text of the Qur'an is divine, but its application has been through human interpretation since revelation. The Prophet Muhammad being the receiver of its revelation, was obviously in the best position to interpret the Qur'an during his lifetime, and he did so in his dual role as a Prophet and a judge. His elucidation of some verses of the Qur'an formed the initial basis of what came to be known as his *Sunnah* or Traditions.

The *Sunnah* as a source of law consists of the Prophet's lifetime sayings, deeds and tacit approvals on different issues, both spiritual and temporal. The *Sunnah* developed from the need for elucidation, by the Prophet, of some Qur'anic verses, supply of details to some general provisions of the Qur'an and instructions on some other aspects of life not expressly covered by Qur'anic texts. Thus Imâm al-Shâfi'î, the eponym of the *Shâfi'î* school of Islamic jurisprudence[128] had stated that:

the *Sunnah* of the Prophet is of three types: first is the *Sunnah* which prescribes the like of what God has revealed in His Book; next is the *Sunnah* which explains the general principles of the Qur'an and clarifies the will of God; and last is the *Sunnah* where the Messenger of God has ruled on matters on which nothing can be found in the Book of God.[129]

---

[123] *See* e.g. Q2:2 which says: 'This is the Book; In it is guidance sure, without doubt, to those who fear God'. [124] *See* Kamali (above n.2) at pp.19–20 and p.41 n.19.

[125] Coulson, N.J., *A History of Islamic Law* (1964) p.12.

[126] Although law and morals are not fully merged in Islamic law, they are also not strictly separated as understood in the theory of positivism in Western legal philosophy. *See* Kamali (above n.119) at p.27. [127] *See* Ramadan (above n.2) at pp.42–43.

[128] The development of the Schools of Islamic Jurisprudence is explained below. *See* para.2.4.3 below.

[129] Shâfi'î, M., *al-Risâlah* (1983) pp.52–53. English translation cited in Kamali (above n.2) at p.63.

The role of the *Sunnah* as a source of law is supported in the Qur'an itself.[130] The Qur'an and the *Sunnah* thus formed the only sources of law from the Prophet's lifetime. Ramadan has therefore observed that 'the structure of Islamic Law—the *Sharî'ah*—was completed during the lifetime of the Prophet, in the Qur'an and the *Sunnah*'.[131] An illustrative evidence of the Qur'an and *Sunnah* being sources of Islamic law from the time of the Prophet Muhammad is the well-known Tradition in which the Prophet was reported to have asked one of his companions named Mu'âdh ibn Jabal, when he deployed the latter as a judge to Yemen, as to what would be his source of law in deciding cases. Mu'âdh replied: 'I will judge with what is in the book of God (Qur'an)'. The Prophet then asked: 'And if you do not find a clue in the book of God?'. Mu'âdh answered: 'Then with the *Sunnah* of the Messenger of God'. The Prophet asked again: 'And if you do not find a clue in that?'. Mu'âdh replied: 'I will exercise my own legal reasoning'.[132] The Prophet was reported as being perfectly satisfied with these answers by Mu'âdh, which signified an approval by the Prophet.

The general rule on the application of the Qur'an and *Sunnah* as main sources of Islamic law is that in case of any irresolvable conflict between a verse of the Qur'an and a reported *Sunnah*, the former prevails, because of its indubitable authenticity in Islamic law.[133]

While Muslims believe generally that the *Sunnah* also has elements of divine inspiration, they appreciate that not every reported Tradition is authentic. The political differences between the fourth Caliph, Ali and Mu'âwiyah in the middle of the first century of Islam, which led to the emergence of factions among the Muslims, led to the emergence of fabricated statements and distorted Traditions attributed to the Prophet.[134] A conscientious and critical technique of authenticating the *Sunnah* was thus developed which eventually culminated in the emergence of the six recognized and authentic books of *Sunnah* of the *Sunnî* School in the third century of Islam.[135]

In applying a *Sunnah*, the two main questions that need to be answered are whether the *Sunnah* is authentic and if so whether it is obligatory. The first

---

[130] See e.g. Q3:31 and Q33:21.   [131] Ramadan (above n.2) at p.36.

[132] See e.g. Abû Dâwûd, *Sunan Abû Dâwûd*, Trans. A. Hasan, (1984), Vol. III, p.1019, Hadîth No.3585. Mu'âdh is reported in this Tradition to have used the words '*ajtahidu râ'îy*' meaning 'I will exert my own reasoning'. The noun *ijtihâd*' meaning exertion was later adopted to indicate 'legal reasoning' as a legal method of Islamic law.

[133] See Kamali (above n.2) at p.59.   [134] *ibid.*, pp.65–68.

[135] The six authentic *Sunni* books of the collections of the Prophet's Traditions are those by al-Bukhâri (d. 870AD), Muslim (d. 875AD), Abû Dâwûd (d. 888AD), al-Tirmidhî (d. 892AD), al-Nasâ'î (d. 915AD) and Ibn Mâjah (d. 886AD). Muslims are divided into the two main groups of *Sunnî* and *Shî'ah*. The *Sunnî* are the majority while the *Shî'ah* constitute about 10 per cent of the world Muslim population. The *Shî'ah* group developed from a schism among the Muslims during the Caliphate of Ali. The *Shî'ah* also have their own different collections of the Prophet's Traditions, such as *al-Kâfî* by Abû Ja'far al-Kulaynî al-Râzî (d. 939AD) and *al-Istibsâr* by Abû Ja'far al-Tûsî (d. 971AD).

question is basically a question of fact that is usually considered on the basis of the evidence adduced to support it in accordance with laid down criteria for the verification of Prophetic Traditions. The second question is a question of law depending, *inter alia*, on the context and language of the particular Tradition.

2.4.3 Methods of Islamic law—(Fiqh)

The passage of time and the expansion of Islam after the demise of the Prophet brought many new cases that were not directly covered by the Qur'anic texts or the Prophetic Traditions. On the authority, *inter alia*, of the Tradition of Mu'âdh ibn Jabal quoted earlier above, the concept of *ijtihâd* (legal reasoning) was developed as a method of Islamic law from which later emerged the legal methods of *Ijmâ'* (juristic consensus) and *Qiyâs* (legal analogy) as well as doctrines such as *Istihsân* (juristic preference), *Istislâh* or *Maslahah* (welfare), *'Urf* (custom), *Darûrah* (necessity), through which the formal sources could be extended to cover new developments of life. These methods, which are usually considered as secondary or subsidiary sources of Islamic law, were products of human reasoning, an indication of the recognition of human reasoning in the Islamic legal process from the earliest period of Islam. The methods were applied to new cases not expressly covered by Qur'anic texts or the *Sunnah*, and also facilitated the adequate interpretation and application of those two sources to suit the different and changing circumstances of human life. Thus, while the revealed sources of Islamic law (that is, *Sharî'ah*) was completed with the demise of the Prophet, the evolved methods of Islamic law were to be the vehicle by which the jurists would transport the *Sharî'ah* into the future. In the words of Qadri, 'the jurists are emphatic in saying that though God has given us a revelation He also gave us brains to understand it; and He did not intend to be understood without careful and prolonged study'.[136] The careful and prolonged study helps to prevent misapplication of the methods.

With the expansion of Islam and its establishment within different cultures outside Arabia, about 500 schools of legal reasoning developed in the early years but most of them disappeared and others merged by the beginning of the third century of Islam. Four *Sunnî*[137] schools of jurisprudence survive up to the present times. They are the *Hanafî* School (prevails in Turkey, Syria, Lebanon, Jordan, India, Pakistan, Afghanistan, Iraq, and Libya), the *Mâlikî* School (prevails in North Africa, West Africa, and Kuwait), the *Shâfi'î* School (prevails in Southern Egypt, Southern Arabia, East Africa, Indonesia, and Malaysia) and the *Hanbalî* School (prevails in Saudi Arabia and Qatar). Other schools of jurisprudence also emerged from within the *Shî'ah*. The major ones being the *Ithnâ 'Asharî* or Twelvers (prevails in Iran and Southern Iraq), the

---

[136] Qadri (above n.2) at p.199.   [137] *See* above n.135.

Zaydî (followed in Yemen), the *Ismâ'ilî* (followed in India) and the *Ibâdî* (followed in Oman and parts of North Africa).[138]

All the schools of Islamic jurisprudence generally recognize the Qur'an and *Sunnah* as the primary sources of Islamic law. The differences of opinion on particular matters result from their different interpretations of some Qur'anic verses and Prophetic Traditions. The different views of jurists on certain matters reflected their sensitivity to the different cultures of the different provinces within which the schools of jurisprudence flourished.[139] To control the divergence in interpretation of the sources and also to regulate the legal process, the jurisprudence of the established schools on both the aspects of worship *(ibâdât)* and inter-human relations *(mu'âmalât)* compiled in form of legal treatises became accepted as the established material sources of Islamic law. By the tenth century it was thought that the established schools of jurisprudence had fully exhausted all the possible questions of law and that the necessary material sources of Islamic law were fully formed. The utilization of the doctrine of independent legal reasoning *(ijtihâd)* consequently diminished and this led, by the thirteenth century, to what was termed as 'closing the gate of legal reasoning *(ijtihâd)* and opening that of legal conformism *(taqlîd)*'. Islamic law thus became restricted largely to the application of the legal findings of the jurists as recorded in the legal treatises of the established schools of jurisprudence dating back to the tenth century.[140] Muslims thus became restricted to conform to or follow the rulings of any one of the schools of jurisprudence but were not generally allowed to exercise independent legal reasoning on any matter. This brought a halt, or at least a slowdown, to the dynamism that had been injected into Islamic law from its inception, and that, according to Iqbal, 'reduced the Law of Islam practically to a state of immobility'.[141] Although many contemporary scholars have challenged the notion of the closing of the gate of *ijtihâd*,[142] the legal conformism *(taqlîd)* of following the rulings of the jurists of the very early period of Islam continues to this day. The jurisprudence *(fiqh)* of the established schools found in their treatises dating from the tenth century are today held as the corpus of Islamic law and portrayed as the immutable *Sharî'ah*. In respect to which Ramadan has rightly observed that:

the invariable basic rules of Islamic Law are only those prescribed in the *Sharî'ah* (Qur'an and *Sunnah*), which are few and limited. Whereas all juridical works during

---

[138] *See* e.g. Makdisi, G., *The Rise of Colleges: Institutions of Learning in Islam and the West* (1981) p.2; Kamali (above n.115) at pp.112–114; and Coulson (above n.114) at p.24.

[139] *See generally* Daura, A., 'A Brief Account of the Development of the Four Sunni Schools of Law and Some Recent Developments' (1968) 2 *Journal of Islamic and Comparative Law*, p.1.   [140] *See* e.g. Kamali (above n. 115) at pp.114–115.

[141] Iqbal, M., *The Reconstruction of Religious Thought in Islam* (1951) p.148.

[142] *See* e.g. Hallaq, W., 'Was the Gate of Ijtihâd Closed?' in Hallaq, W., (ed.), *Law and Legal Theory in Classical and Medieval Islam* (1995) pp.3–41.

more than thirteen centuries are very rich and indispensable, they must always be subordinated to the *Sharî'ah* and open to reconsideration . . .[143]

While legal conformism (*taqlîd*) is not in itself an undesirable practice, it must be distinguished from blind conservatism that does not allow for a reflective and contextual application of classical precedents. It is a necessary methodology of Islamic law, especially for lay persons not qualified in the science of Islamic jurisprudence. Nyazee has observed that legal conformism *(taqlîd)* 'as distinguished from blind conservatism, . . . is a legal method for ensuring that judges who are not fully qualified *mujtahids* may be able to decide cases in the light of precedents laid down by independent jurists'.[144] That neither places unnecessary restrictions on the development of new theories of interpretation nor prevents qualified judges or jurists from exercising their own independent *ijtihâd* when necessary. Nyazee has further observed that Islamic jurists do 'maintain that if a person has the necessary ability, it is binding upon him to follow his own opinion. . . . The only requirement is that he must declare his principles of interpretation so that other jurists should be able to judge his competence'.[145]

2.4.4 *Spiritual and temporal aspects of Islamic law*

As already observed above, the provisions of the *Sharî'ah* broadly cover all aspects of human life. However, through the methods of Islamic law the jurists have categorized Islamic law into two broad spheres. The first sphere embodies spiritual rulings regulating religious observance and acts of worship. This is generally referred to as *ibâdât* and concerns the direct relationship between an individual and God. The second sphere embodies temporal laws regulating inter-human relations and the temporal affairs of this world. This is generally referred to as *mu'âmalât* and generally promotes the realization of the common good *(ma'rûf)* of humanity. While the jurisprudence on the spiritual aspects is considered to be fully settled and mostly unchanging, the same is not true of the temporal aspects. It is in the sphere of temporal affairs that the arrest in the dynamism of Islamic jurisprudence is greatly felt. The traditional jurisprudence *(fiqh)* of the established schools on some aspects of inter-human relations has been overtaken by the dynamic nature of human life and thus created some lacunae that must be revisited in Islamic legal and political thought.[146]

The need to rejuvenate the methods of Islamic law to generate a more encompassing and realistic jurisprudence to meet contemporary challenges became

---

[143] Ramadan (above n.2) at p.36.

[144] Nyazee, I.A.K., (Trans.), *The Distinguished Jurist's Primer, Bidâyat al-Mujtahid wa Nihâyat al-Muqtasid by Ibn Rushd* (2000) Vol. 1, p.xxxv.

[145] *ibid.*; *see also* al-Ghazâlî, A.M., *al-Mustasfâ fî 'Ilm al-Usûl* (Arabic) (1996) p.368.

[146] *See* Hallaq (above n.2) at pp.209–210.

evident from the nineteenth century with the intimate interaction between the East and the West. That urge continues today. The advancements and developments of modern life have affected inter-human relations in many ways which Islamic law needs to address from contemporary perspectives. The challenges of international human rights law is one of such developments. Due to the erroneous impression that the traditional opinions of the established schools of Islamic jurisprudence were totally immutable, Muslims were hesitant in formally accepting the need for a reappraisal of the methods of Islamic law and of the established views of its early great jurists. Nevertheless, Islamic legal scholarship aimed at a formal, adequate and cohesive reappraisal of the methodology of Islamic law in the light of contemporary challenges has been going on since the late nineteenth century with general contributions from many Muslim thinkers and intellectuals.[147] However, the stagnation from the thirteenth century continues to eclipse the great legacy of the earliest Islamic jurists that developed Islamic law into a most dynamic legal system from which even the West was a borrower in the Middle Ages.[148]

2.4.5 Scope and purpose of Islamic law

Today, Islamic law continues to be formally applied in many parts of the Muslim world as we had it interpreted by the classical *Sunnî* schools of Islamic jurisprudence with regards to the *Sunnî* Muslims and the classical *Shî'ah* schools with regards to *Shî'ah* Muslims. A static and immoderate application of some of the traditional interpretations of the *Sharî'ah* can however constrain the scope of Islamic law for present times. Research shows that the earliest Islamic jurists had utilized the methods of Islamic law within the scope of the *Sharî'ah* in an evolutionary and constructive manner that prevented any unwarranted circumscription upon humans living during their times. Such evolutionary and constructive application is more relevant today than before.

Taking cognizance of the object and purpose of the *Sharî'ah* (*maqâsid al-sharî'ah*), which has been identified as promotion of human welfare and prevention of harm (*maslahah*),[149] is an important holistic approach for realizing the proper and benevolent scope of Islamic law. In his discussion of al-Shâtibî's theory of the object and purpose of the *Sharî'ah* (*maqâsid al-sharî'ah*), Hallaq emphasizes, *inter alia*, al-Shâtibî's view that 'the original intention of God in revealing the law (is) to protect the interests of man (both

---

[147] *See* e.g. Kerr, M., *Islamic Reform: The Political and Legal Theories of Muhammad 'Abduh and Rashîd Ridâ* (1966); Donohue, J.J., and Esposito, J.L. (eds.), *Islam in Transition: Muslim Perspectives* (1982); Hallaq (above n.2) at pp.207–254; Kamali (above n.115) at pp.116–118.

[148] *See* e.g. Makdisi (above n.138) at pp.290–291.

[149] *See* e.g. al-Shâtibî, A.I., *al-Muwâfaqât* (Arabic) (1997), Vol. 2; and Masud, M.K., *Shatibi's Philosophy of Islamic law* (1995) p.151.

mundane and religious)'.[150] God says in the Qur'an, 'To each among you have We prescribed a Law (*shir'ah*) and an Open Way (*minhâj*)', that is, an approach for its application.[151] The *maqâsid* approach of interpreting and applying the *Sharî'ah* is thus recognized as guaranteeing the full equity of Islamic law.

In his analysis of the scope and equity of Islamic law, Ramadan identified six important characteristics of Islamic law deducible from a thorough study of the Qur'an, the *Sunnah* and the works of classical Islamic jurists. They are as follows:

1. The formal sources of Islamic law, namely the Qur'an and *Sunnah* 'are basically inclined towards establishing general rules without indulging in much detail'. This makes room for a wider application of the legal sources through the legal methods for the best benefit of humanity.
2. Qur'anic 'texts were directly meant to deal with actual events [and] Presupposition was basically excluded from' the legislative philosophy of Islamic law. This characteristic, Ramadan observes, is a method of realism which 'is apt to minimize the definite limitations imposed on human dealings', which in essence makes things easier for humanity.
3. 'As a rule, everything that is not prohibited is permissible.' In explaining this rule Ramadan rightly observed that: 'Islamic Law was not meant to paralyze people so that they might not move unless allowed to. Man on the contrary, is repeatedly called upon by the Qur'an to consider the whole universe as a Divine grace meant for him, and to exhaust all his means of wisdom and energy to get the best out of it'.
4. 'Even in the field of prohibition, the Qur'an sometimes used a method which could gradually meet a growing readiness in the society where the revealed enjoinments were to be implemented.' This is the so-called principle of gradualism (*tadrîj*) by which legislation was gradually upgraded in view of societal circumstances. Thus social circumstances are not overlooked in the development of the law.
5. 'All that the Qur'an and the Sunnah have prohibited becomes permissible whenever a pressing necessity arises.' This is based on the doctrine of necessity (*darûrah*) by which all Islamic jurists generally agree that 'necessity renders the prohibited permissible'.
6. 'The door is wide-open to the adoption of anything of utility, of whatever origin, so long as it does not go against the texts of the Qur'an and the Sunnah.'[152]

---

[150] *See* Hallaq (above n.2) at 181 and pp.180–187 for discussion of al-Shâtibî's theory of the *Maqâsid al-Sharî'ah* generally. [151] Q5:48.

[152] *See* Ramadan (above n.2) at pp.64–73. *See also* al-Shâtibî (above n.149); Ibn al-Qayyim, *I'lâm al-Muwaqqi'în 'An Rabb al-'Alamîn* (Arabic) (1996), Vol.1, pp.71–72; Ridâ, R., *Yusr al-Islam Wa Usûl al-Tashrî' al-Amm* (1956) pp.24–28; and Khallâf, A.W., *Masâdir al-Tashrî' al-Islâmî Fîmâ lâ Nass Fîh* (1955) p.131ff.

Apart from many other Qur'anic verses and Prophetic Traditions in support of the above characteristics of Islamic law, the following Qur'anic verse succinctly summarizes the benevolent nature of Islamic law.

... For he commands them what is just and forbids them what is evil; he allows them as lawful what is good and prohibits them from what is bad. He releases them from their heavy burdens and from the yokes that are upon them.[153]

Thus, the overall objective and purpose of the *Sharî'ah* is the promotion of human welfare and prevention of harm *(maslahah)*, which must always be kept in mind in both its interpretation and application as Islamic law.

2.4.6 Promotion of human welfare and prevention of harm—(Maslahah)

Among the different doctrines and principles established by the founding jurists for an intelligible application of Islamic law, *maslahah* is considered as the most viable means of bringing the ideals of Islam closer to realization for all time. Kamali has observed that:

The doctrine of *maslahah* is broad enough to encompass within its fold a variety of objectives, both idealist and pragmatic, to nurture the standards of good government, and to help develop the much needed public confidence in the authority of statutory legislation in Muslim societies. The doctrine of *maslahah* can strike balance between the highly idealistic levels of expectation from the government on the part of the public and the efforts of the latter to identify more meaningfully with Islam.[154]

The doctrine was originally introduced by Imâm Mâlik, the eponym of the *Mâlikî* school of Islamic jurisprudence, and later developed further by jurists such as al-Ghazâlî and al-Tûfî of the *Shâfi'î* and *Hanbalî* schools respectively. The fourteenth century Mâlikî jurist, Abû Ishâq al-Shâtibî further developed the concept as a 'basis of rationality and extendibility of Islamic law to changing circumstances (and also) as a fundamental principle for the universality and certainty of Islamic law'.[155] It is an expedient doctrine of Islamic law acknowledged today by Islamic legalists as containing 'the seeds of the future of the *Sharî'ah* and its viability as a living force in society'.[156]

The term *maslahah* literally means 'benefit' or 'welfare' and is generally used under Mâlikî jurisprudence, in a narrower sense, to express the principle of 'public benefit' or 'public welfare' and often qualified as *'maslahah mursalah'* (literally meaning 'released benefit') when such benefit is not tied down to

---

[153] Q7:157.
[154] Kamali, M.H., 'Have We Neglected the Sharî'ah-Law Doctrine of Maslahah?' (1988) 27 *Islamic Studies*, No.4, pp.287–288. *See also* Khallâf (above n.152) at pp.70–80.
[155] *See* Masud (above n.149) at p.viii.
[156] Kamali (above n.154) at p.288.

specific textual authority but based on consideration of collective well-being. *Maslahah* has in that sense often been understood to connote *'maslahah al-'ummah'*, that is, the benefit or welfare of the Muslim community as a whole. However, the utilization of *maslalah* to achieve collective/communal benefit or welfare does not necessarily preclude its broader application to protect the rights and welfare of individuals. The general concept of *maslahah* also accommodates what may be called *'maslahah shakhsiyyah'*, that is, individual benefit or welfare, to ensure the protection of human rights.

While human rights specifically aim at protecting the rights of individuals, the ultimate aim is equally to guarantee the benefit and welfare of human beings as a whole wherever they may be. Protecting the welfare of individuals does ultimately ensure communal/public welfare and vice versa. This makes the doctrine of *maslahah* very relevant in the discussion of human rights under Islamic law.

In relating *maslahah* to the overall objective of the *Sharî'ah (maqâsid al-sharî'ah)*, al-Shâtibî, building on al-Ghazâlî's theory, has advanced a three hierarchical classification for the determination of its scope. On the first and highest level are those benefits considered as indispensable benefits *(darûriyyât)*, consisting of what has been described as the five universals,[157] namely: protection of life, religion, intellect, family, and property. Due to their indispensability they must not only be promoted but also protected. Some contemporary Muslim scholars equate these with fundamental rights *(al-huqûq al-fitriyyah)*.[158] On the second level are those considered as necessary benefits *(hâjiyyât)*. These are supplementary to the first category and consist of those benefits the neglect of which may cause hardship to life, but the upholding of which does not lead to the collapse of society. They ensure accommodation of the necessary changes in life within the law and thereby make life tolerable. The third level are those considered as improvement benefits *(tahsîniyyât)* and consist of those things that improve and embellish life generally and thereby enhance the character of the *Sharî'ah* generally.[159]

Against the background of the nature and evolution of Islamic law established above, the doctrine of *maslahah* is thus advocated in this study as a veritable Islamic legal doctrine for the realization of international human rights within the dispensation of Islamic law. This is based on the understanding earlier expounded that international human rights has a universal humanitarian objective for the protection of individuals against the misuse of

---

[157] *See* Hallaq (above n.2) at p.168.

[158] *See* e.g. Kamali, M.H., 'Fundamental Rights of the Individual: An Analysis of Haqq (Rights) in Islamic Law' (1993) 10 *American Journal of Islamic Social Sciences*. No.3, p.340 at p.362.

[159] *See* Hallaq (above n.2) at p.168ff; and Nyazee (above n.2) at p.212ff for discussions of al-Ghazâlî and al-Shâtibî's approaches to *maslahah* and *maqâsid al-sharî'ah* in detail. *See also* Kamali (above n.2) at pp.267–282; Masud (above n.149) at pp.127–164; and al-Shâtibî (above n.149).

State authority and for the enhancement of human dignity.[160] We will rely on the doctrine of *maslahah* within the ample scope of the *Sharî'ah* in deriving legal benefits and averting hardship to the human person, as endorsed by the Qur'anic verse that: 'He [God] has not imposed any hardships upon you [humans] in religion'.[161]

This utilization of *maslahah* in relation to the *maqâsid al-sharî'ah* will accommodate the principle of *takhayyur* (eclectic choice),[162] to facilitate movement within the principal schools of Islamic jurisprudence as well as consideration of the views of individual Islamic jurists to support alternative arguments advanced on topical issues in this book.

Interpretations of the *Sharî'ah* in the Muslim world today may be classified into the main divisions of 'traditionalist' and 'evolutionist'. The 'traditionalists' are those who see value in a tenacious adherence to the classical interpretations of the *Sharî'ah* as laid down from the tenth century in the legal treatises of the established schools of Islamic jurisprudence. They are sometimes also referred to as 'conservatives' or 'hardliners' due to their often strict 'back looking' adherence to the classical legal treatises and 'non-forward looking' application of the classical opinions of the founding jurists of Islamic law. The 'evolutionists' are those who, while identifying with the classical jurisprudence and methods of Islamic law, seek to make it relevant to contemporary times. They believe in the continual evolution of Islamic law and argue that if the *Sharî'ah* must really cope meaningfully with modern developments and be applicable for all time, then such modern developments must be taken into consideration in the interpretation of the *Sharî'ah*. They are also referred to as Islamic liberals or moderates. They adopt a 'back and forward looking' approach in their interpretations of the *Sharî'ah* and a contextual application of classical Islamic jurisprudence. The scope of harmonization between Islamic law and international human rights law depends largely upon whether a hardline or moderate approach is adopted in the interpretation of the *Sharî'ah* and the application of classical Islamic jurisprudence. The expediency of each approach will be discerned in our comparative analyses of the ICCPR and ICESCR with Islamic law in the following chapters.

2.5 THE JUSTIFICATORY PRINCIPLE

Despite the fact that human rights is now viewed more in the context of legal positivism due to the embodiment of its contents in Bills and Treaties for specificity, this does not displace morality and substantive justice as very important factors of human rights philosophy. The strongest arguments for the universality of human rights are still hinged on moral arguments and the

---

[160] *See* text to n.29 above.   [161] Q22:78.   [162] (Also *Takhyîr*), see above n.114.

need for substantive justice in human relationships. This involves the question of values and beliefs, which do change over time and space. Unlike most of the previous works on this subject, this book will thus examine relevant justificatory or jurisprudential arguments in relation to the values attached to specific human rights from both the international human rights and Islamic law perspectives. This will facilitate an in-depth understanding of the areas of differences and provide a basis for the practical harmonization of the conceptual differences between international human rights and Islamic law principles.

Generally, human rights is viewed in Western nations as a product of Western liberalism, which advocates values such as freedom, liberty, individualism, and tolerance. In many Muslim nations however, Western liberalism is considered as very permissive and capable of corrupting the moral values of society as prescribed by the *Sharī'ah*. Conceiving liberalism and human rights as notions of total liberty and freedom of the individual to do whatever he pleases is however wrong because that will contradict the basic foundations of political and legal authority. By their nature, both law and political authority constitute some limitation upon the freedom and liberties of individuals. Perhaps, the correct perception is as stated by Locke that '. . . Liberty is to be free from restraint and violence from others, which cannot be, where there is no law: . . . Freedom is not, as we are told, A Liberty for every Man to do what he lists'.[163] Under what has been described as the 'fundamental liberal principle' there only exists a kind of presumption in favour of liberty, which places the burden of proof on anyone who contends for any restriction on it.[164] Thus the power of the State to interfere in the actions of individuals is not completely ousted under liberal theory or within human rights but only curtailed to its legitimate necessity. The necessity of control by the political authority through law is recognized, but any limitations they impose upon individual liberties and freedoms must be justifiable in accordance with the law and not be arbitrary. The justificatory principle thus establishes that restrictions upon the rights of individuals must be clearly determinable and justifiable under the law in order not to violate their freedom, liberties and fundamental human rights.

Under Islamic law the political authority owes a duty not only to the people but to God not to violate the freedom and liberties of the ruled without justification. The justificatory principle finds support from the fact that even in the Qur'an, a justifying clause usually accompanies nearly every prohibition concerning human relations *(Mu'āmalāt)*. The parameter of justification within Islamic law is thus often found within the Qur'an itself. While the text of the

---

[163] Locke, J., *Two Treatises of Government*, ed. P. Laslett (1967) p.324.

[164] *See* e.g. Gaus, G.F., *Justificatory Liberalism: An Essay on Epistemology and Political Theory* (1996) pp.162–166; and *generally* Gaus, G.F., *Value and Justification: The Foundations of Liberal Theory* (1990).

Qur'an is not subject to amendment, its provisions may thus be interpreted in the light of societal changes and the relevant justificatory principle within the holistic values of the *Sharî'ah* in a manner that ensures that there is no devi-ation from its divine basis. It is with respect to this that an Islamic legal maxim states that '*tatagayyar al-ahkâm bi tagayur al-zamân*' meaning that legal rul-ings may change with the change in time.[165] This applies mostly to matters concerning human interactions. Examples of this can be found in the practices of Muslim jurists of all ages. It is this approach that Islamic evolutionists tend to adopt in their interpretations of Islamic legal texts. This facilitates the inter-pretation of the Islamic legal texts to accommodate the dynamic changes in human life. When the justifications attaching to certain legal provisions change then the legal rule may also change. The same principle applies to the docu-mented juristic views of the early Islamic jurists, which must be considered in the light of their justifications. An example may be cited on the Northern Nigerian[166] case of *Tela Rijiyan Dorawa v. Hassan Daudu*[167] which involved a land dispute between one Dorawa, a Christian and one Daudu, a Muslim. The parties appeared before an Upper Area Court in Sokoto, each calling a witness in evidence. Dorawa called another Christian, John, as his witness while Daudu called another Muslim, Hausa, as his own witness. The Upper Area Court after reviewing the evidence before it, rejected the testimony of John because he was a Christian on grounds that the evidence of a non-Muslim was not acceptable under Islamic law. Judgment was thus entered in favour of Hassan Daudu. Dorawa appealed to the Sokoto High Court. The learned High Court judge, himself a Muslim, in consultation with the then Grand Kadi of Sokoto State,[168] allowed the appeal and overturned the ruling of the Upper Area Court. The High Court relied on the Islamic legal principle of *takhayyur* (eclectic choice) which allows reliance on the opinions of other Islamic schools of jurisprudence, and also cited Islamic legal literature to illustrate that the tra-ditional reason for the disqualification of the testimony of non-Muslims by classical Islamic jurists was the fear of their being unjust due to their lack of Islamic belief, and that their evidence was acceptable when there is no such fear or in case of necessity. The Court was said to have 'regarded the condition of Nigeria today being a country with large Muslims, Christian and animist communities, living side by side and transacting business with each other, as

---

[165] *See* e.g. Al-Ghunaimi, M.T. *Durûs fî Usûl al-Qânûn al-Wada'î* (Arabic) (1961) p.150, cited in Al-Ghunaimi, M.T., *The Muslim Conception of International Law and the Western Approach* (1968) p.101.

[166] Nigeria has a multi-religious population with Muslims in the majority, and it operates a pluralized legal system consisting of English common law, Islamic law, and customary law.

[167] [1975] Northern Nigerian Law Report, 87.

[168] The Grand Kadi of a State in Nigeria is the most senior Islamic law judge within the state's judiciary. He is the head of the Sharî'ah Court of Appeal of the State.

satisfying the necessity' making the evidence of a non-Muslim admissible in Islamic law.[169]

In our comparative analysis of the ICCPR and ICESCR in the light of Islamic law in the next two chapters, the justificatory principle will be utilized, where necessary, in arguing a paradigm shift from traditional hardline interpretations of Islamic law and also from exclusionist interpretations of international human rights law that do not consider Islamic normative values at all.

---

[169] *See* Hon. Justice Mohammed, U., 'Shariah and the Western Common Law: A Comparative Analysis', in Abdul-Rahmon, M.O., *Thoughts in Islamic Law and Ethics* (1992) p.16 at p.25.

3

The International Covenant on Civil and Political Rights (ICCPR) in the Light of Islamic Law

3.1 INTRODUCTION

The ICCPR represents the positive international law guarantee of civil and political rights under the international human rights objective of the UN. It entered into force on 23 March 1976 and has, as of December 2002, been ratified by 149 States, including 41 of the 57 Member States of the Organization of Islamic Conference (OIC).[1]

This chapter examines the provisions of the ICCPR in the light of Islamic law to determine their scope of compatibility. Each substantive right under the ICCPR is analysed, followed by an Islamic law perspective of each right. On one hand, we refer to the jurisprudence of the Human Rights Committee (HRC) and other scholarly expositions to throw light on the ICCPR as currently interpreted under international human rights law. On the other hand, we also refer to the main sources of Islamic law, namely the Qur'an and *Sunnah*, as well as Islamic juristic views for an Islamic perspective of the rights guaranteed under the ICCPR. The practices of relevant Muslim States are also cited for necessary illustration,[2] while the OIC Cairo Declaration on Human Rights in Islam is cited as current codified Islamic human rights standards recognized by Muslim States.

Although this chapter is specifically on the ICCPR, reference is made to necessary articles of the Convention on the Elimination of all Forms of Discrimination Against Women (CEDAW)[3] in the analysis of the rights of women under the Covenant due to its topicality in the international human rights cum Islamic law debate.

---

[1] *See* the Status of Ratification of the ICCPR at the UN Human Rights Treaty Website at: http://www.unhchr.ch/html/menu3/b/a_ccpr.htm [1/3/03].

[2] *See also* Baderin, M.A., 'A Macroscopic Analysis of the Practice of Muslim State Parties to International Human Rights Treaties: Conflict or Congruence?' (2001) 1 *Human Rights Law Review*, No. 2, pp.265–303.

[3] 1249 UNTS, p.13. Adopted 18 November 1979, entered into force on 3 September 1981 and has, as of December 2002, been ratified by 47 of the 57 Member States of the OIC.

3.2 THE RIGHTS GUARANTEED UNDER THE ICCPR

The ICCPR guarantees twenty-four substantive civil and political rights. They are:

Article 1 The right of self-determination.
Article 3 Equality of rights between men and women.
Article 6 The right to life.
Article 7 Freedom from torture or cruel, inhuman or degrading treatment and punishment.
Article 8 Freedom from slavery, servitude and forced labour.
Article 9 The right to liberty and security of person.
Article 10 The right to a humane incarceration system.
Article 11 Freedom from imprisonment for contractual obligation.
Article 12 The right to liberty of movement and choice of residence.
Article 13 Freedom of aliens from arbitrary expulsion.
Article 14 The right to fair hearing and due process of law.
Article 15 Freedom from retroactive criminal law.
Article 16 The right to recognition as a person before the law.
Article 17 The right to privacy.
Article 18 The right to freedom of thought, conscience and religion.
Article 19 The right to freedom of opinion and expression.
Article 20 The prohibition of propaganda for war and incitement to hatred.
Article 21 The right of peaceful assembly.
Article 22 The right to freedom of association.
Article 23 The right to marry and found a family.
Article 24 The rights of the child.
Article 25 Political rights.
Article 26 The right to equality before the law.
Article 27 The rights of ethnic, religious, or linguistic minorities.

The above list of rights as contained in the ICCPR should, prima facie, raise no problems in the light of Islamic law. They theoretically reflect humane ideals that are compatible with the general teachings of Islam. But, as is the case with all legal provisions, it is the interpretation of those rights that determine their scope. Being an international treaty, the ICCPR is subject to the general rules of interpretation of treaties under the Vienna Convention on the Law of Treaties.[4] Basically, the Vienna Convention provides that an international treaty 'shall be interpreted in good faith and in accordance with the ordinary meaning to be given to the terms of the treaty in their context and in light of

---

[4] *See* e.g. *Alberta Union v. Canada*, Communication No. 118/1998, Human Rights Committee, UN. Doc. CCPR/C/OP/1 at 34 (1984), para.6.3.

its object and purpose'.[5] Before proceeding to examine the substantive rights as listed above, we will first identify the object and purpose of the Covenant and also analyse the obligation of the State Parties as provided under Article 2 of the Covenant.

3.3 THE OBJECT AND PURPOSE OF THE ICCPR

Legally, the object and purpose serves as a parameter of interpretation that prevents the destruction of the essence of the substantive provisions of a treaty.[6] The HRC has broadly outlined the object and purpose of the ICCPR as follows:

> ... The object and purpose of the Covenant is to create legally binding standards for human rights by defining certain civil and political rights and placing them in a framework of obligations which are legally binding for those States which ratify; and to provide an efficacious supervisory machinery for the obligations undertaken.[7]

It follows from the above statement that the object and purpose of the ICCPR is to guarantee the civil and political rights of individuals from States. To realize that objective, the HRC was established under the Covenant as the supervisory machinery for the obligations undertaken by the State Parties. The preamble of the ICCPR also declares the purpose and aspirations that motivated the adoption of the Covenant.[8] It refers to the inherent dignity of the human person as the bedrock of human rights and also recognizes the 'equal and inalienable rights of all members of the human family' as the 'foundation of freedom, justice and peace in the world'. Through the enforcement of the ICCPR the State Parties aspire towards the enhancement of human dignity by fostering an ideal human community that guarantees freedom from fear and want; civil and political freedoms that lead to justice, and peace and general well-being of all human beings.[9]

From an Islamic perspective, the above objectives of the ICCPR are commensurate with the general provisions and ultimate objective of the *Sharî'ah*

---

[5] *See* Art. 31 of the Vienna Convention on the Law of Treaties (1969), 1155 UNTS, p.331. *See also* Nowak, M., *Commentary on the UN Covenant on Civil and Political Rights* (1993) p.xxiii for a brief analysis of the rules governing the interpretation of the ICCPR provisions.

[6] *See* e.g. Buergenthal, T., 'To Respect and to Ensure: State Obligations and Permissible Derogations' in Henkin, L., (ed.), *The International Bill of Rights, The Covenant on Civil and Political Rights* (1981) p.72 at p.90.

[7] *See* General Comment 24, para.7. The HRC General Comments are accessible through the Committee's website at: http://www.unhchr.ch/tbs/doc.nsf [1/3/03].

[8] *See* UN Doc. A/2929 *Annotation of the Draft International Covenants on Human Rights prepared by the Secretary General* (1955) pp.32–36.

[9] *See* Pechota, V., 'The Development of the Covenant on Civil and Political Rights' in Henkin (above n.6) at pp.32–33.

as already established in Chapter 2.[10] The OIC Cairo Declaration on Human Rights in Islam reiterates a similar aspiration in its preamble by declaring the wish of Muslim States 'to contribute to the efforts of mankind to assert human rights, to protect man from exploitation and persecution, and to affirm his freedom and right to a dignified life in accordance with the Islamic Shari'ah'.[11] It also states that the fundamental rights and universal freedoms are an integral part of Islam and are binding divine commandments which no one has the right to suspend, violate or ignore.[12] While the reference to Islamic *Sharî'ah* and to 'binding divine commandments' in the Cairo Declaration reaffirms a theocentric approach to human rights under Islamic law as distinguished from the anthropocentric approach under the ICCPR, that does not impede the shared noble objective of protecting and enhancing human dignity under both international human rights law and Islamic law.[13]

3.4 OBLIGATIONS OF STATES PARTIES UNDER THE ICCPR

Article 2

1. Each State Party to the present Covenant undertakes to respect and to ensure to all individuals within its territory and subject to its jurisdiction the rights recognized in the present Covenant, without distinction of any kind, such as race, colour, sex, language, religion, political or other opinion, national or social origin, property, birth or other status.
2. Where not already provided for by existing legislative or other measures, each State Party to the present Covenant undertakes to take the necessary steps, in accordance with its constitutional processes and with the provisions of the present Covenant, to adopt such legislative or other measures as may be necessary to give effect to the rights recognized in the present Covenant.
3. Each State Party to the present Covenant undertakes:
   (a) To ensure that any person whose rights or freedoms as herein recognized are violated shall have an effective remedy, notwithstanding that the violation has been committed by persons acting in an official capacity;
   (b) To ensure that any person claiming such a remedy shall have his right thereto determined by competent judicial, administrative or legislative authorities, or by any other competent authority provided for by the legal system of the State, and to develop the possibilities of judicial remedy;
   (c) To ensure that the competent authorities shall enforce such remedies when granted.

---

[10] We identified in Chapter 2 above that the ultimate objective of the *Sharî'ah* (namely, *maqâsid al-Sharî'ah*) is to realize the well-being of human beings. *See* para.2.4.5 above.

[11] *See* para.2 of the preamble of the Cairo Declaration on Human Rights in Islam (1990) UN. Doc. A/CONF.157/PC/62/Add.18(1993). [12] *See ibid.*, para.4.

[13] For an analysis of the theocentric and anthropocentric perspectives to human rights *see* Baderin M.A., 'Dialogue Among Civilizations as a Paradigm for Achieving Universalism in International Human Rights: A Case Study with Islamic Law' (2001) 2 *Asia-Pacific Journal on Human Rights and the Law*, No. 2, p.1 at pp.22–29.

Does Islamic law restrict Muslim States in any way from fulfilling these oblig-ations? Under Article 2(1), the States Parties undertake 'to respect' and 'to ensure' the effective and appropriate national implementation of all the rights guaranteed under the covenant 'without distinction of any kind'. The duty 'to respect' is a negative obligation on the part of the State not to violate the rights while the duty 'to ensure' is a positive obligation to take necessary steps to enable the enjoyment of the rights. An important aspect of this pos-itive obligation is the enactment, where not already provided, of necessary domestic legislation by each State Party to ensure the guaranteed rights.[14] Under Islamic law, the legislative power of the State is not totally unlimited. It is theoretically proscribed by the philosophy that God is the ultimate legislator who has prescribed what is lawful and what is unlawful through revelation in the Qur'an. According to Justice Iqbal:

> The legislature in an Islamic state has a restricted role; technically speaking, its authority is delegated and can be exercised only within the limits prescribed by the Qur'an and Sunnah. ... Generally speaking, there are three possible spheres for legislative activity in a Muslim national state:
>
> (1) to enforce laws which have specifically been laid down in the Qur'an and *Sunnah*;
> (2) to bring all existing laws in conformity with the Qur'an and *Sunnah*; and
> (3) to make laws as subordinate legislation which do not violate the Qur'an and *Sunnah*.[15]

Islamic jurists generally consider any State legislation that makes lawful what God has prohibited in the Qur'an or prohibits what God has made lawful in the Qur'an as exceeding the limits of human legislation allowed under Islamic law.[16] For instance, during the consideration of Sudan's second peri-odic report on the ICCPR, the Sudanese representatives stated, *inter alia*, before the HRC that:

> The Sudanese parliament had decided against abolition of the death penalty. The jurisprudential argument for its continued existence was that the death penalty was mandatory for certain offences under Islamic law.[17]

This general rule does not however mean that Muslim States are precluded from undertaking legislation at all. Today all Muslim States do legislate on

---

[14] Art. 2(2) ICCPR.

[15] *See* Justice Iqbal, J., 'The Concept of State in Islam' in Ahmad, M. (ed.), *State, Politics and Islam* (1986) p.37 at pp.49–50. This is, for example, evidenced in practice by the provision in the Constitution of the Islamic Republic of Pakistan that 'No law shall be enacted which is repugnant to the injunctions of Islam as laid down in the Holy Qur'an and Sunna ... and existing law shall be brought into conformity with such injunctions'.

[16] *See* e.g. al-Qaradawi, Y., *The Lawful and the Prohibited in Islam* (1984) p.18.

[17] *See* Human Rights Committee Summary Record of the 1629th Meeting: Sudan. 31 October 19, 1997. UN Doc. CCPR/C/SR.1629, para.15.

various aspects of life and State policy as required by the needs of time. While conscious of the general rule of non-violation of the *Sharî'ah* in enacting subsidiary legislation, many Muslim States often rely on Islamic legal principles such as *siyâsah shar'iyyah* (legitimate governmental policy), *ḍarûrah* (necessity), and *maslahah* (welfare) in necessary instances to legislate for the realization of human welfare and State policy. A combination of these facilitating principles of Islamic law together with some margin of appreciation under international human rights law are necessary paradigms, as will be analysed in the following sections, to ensure the positive realization of the rights guaranteed under the ICCPR within an Islamic legal dispensation.

The undertaking under Article 2(1) to respect and ensure all the rights guaranteed 'without distinction of any kind, such as race, colour, sex, language, religion, political or other opinion, national or social origin, property, birth or other status' is of utmost importance. It reiterates the principle of equality and non-discrimination in the enjoyment of human rights. After analysing the preparatory works on the Covenants, Ramcharan concluded that both the terms 'distinction' and 'discrimination' as used in the ICCPR and ICESCR 'exclude only arbitrary or unjust distinction or discrimination'.[18] Islamic law also generally prohibits arbitrary or unjust discrimination, but there is notable tension in respect of distinction on grounds of sex and religion vis-à-vis international human rights law, which will be examined under the relevant substantive Articles below.

Under Article 2(3), States undertake to provide effective domestic remedies against violations of the rights guaranteed under the Covenant and to ensure that such remedies when granted, shall be enforced by the competent authorities. This accommodates judicial, political, and administrative remedies in respect of human rights violations, but Nowak has observed notably that the intendment of Article 2(3)(b) is to place priority on judicial remedies.[19] This places the primary obligation of effectively protecting human rights on States Parties and is substantiated by the provision in Article 5(2) of the First Optional Protocol (OP1)[20] to the ICCPR that the HRC 'shall not consider any communication from an individual unless it has ascertained that . . . (t)he individual has exhausted all available domestic remedies'. In *R.T. v. France* the HRC observed that the reference to 'all available remedies' in Article 5(2) of the OP1 'clearly refers in the first place to judicial remedies'.[21]

There is nothing under Islamic law that inhibits Muslim States from fulfilling this obligation to provide effective domestic remedies in case of the violation of the rights of individuals guaranteed under the Covenant. Islamic law does

---

[18] *See* Ramcharan, B.G., 'Equality and Non-discrimination' in Henkin (above n.6) at pp.258–259.　　　　　　　　　　　　　　　　　　　[19] Nowak (above n.5) at p.59.
[20] 999 UNTS, p.171.
[21] *R. T. [name deleted] v. France*, Communication No. 262/1987 (30 March 1989), UN Doc. Supp. No. 40 (A/44/40) at p.277 (1989) para.7.4.

also prescribe for remedies in the form of compensation for violation of a person's right, payable by the injurer, be it an individual or the State.[22]

3.5 THE RIGHT OF SELF-DETERMINATION

Article 1

1. All peoples have the right of self-determination. By virtue of that right they freely determine their political status and freely pursue their economic, social and cultural development.
2. All peoples may, for their own ends, freely dispose of their natural wealth and resources without prejudice to any obligations arising out of international economic co-operation, based upon the principle of mutual benefit, and international law. In no case may a people be deprived of its own means of subsistence.
3. The States Parties to the present Covenant, including those having responsibility for the administration of Non-Self-Governing and Trust Territories, shall promote the realization of the right of self-determination, and shall respect that right, in conformity with the provisions of the Charter of the United Nations.

Both the ICCPR and ICESCR contain this common Article 1 on the right of self-determination. Although it is a right of peoples rather than of individuals,[23] its importance and relationship to the realization of individual human rights has been expressed by the HRC as follows:

The right of self-determination is of particular importance because its realization is an essential condition for the effective guarantee and observance of individual human rights and for the promotion and strengthening of those rights. It is for that reason that States set forth the right of self-determination in a provision of positive law in both Covenants and placed this provision as article 1 apart from and before all of the other rights in the two Covenants.[24]

The fact that two Muslim States, Afghanistan and Saudi Arabia, championed, in 1950, the proposal that culminated in Article 1 on the right of self-determination after an earlier initiative by the USSR had failed,[25] suggests that the right is not in conflict with Islamic law. This right was originally

---

[22] *See* e.g. Qadri, A.A., *Islamic Jurisprudence in the Modern World* (1986) pp.341–358.

[23] In *Lubicon Lake Band v. Canada* the HRC observed that: 'the author, as an individual, could not claim under the Optional Protocol to be a victim of a violation of the right of self-determination enshrined in article 1 of the Covenant, which deals with rights conferred upon peoples, as such'. *See* para.13.3, Communication No. 167/1984 (26 March 1990), UN Doc. Supp. No. 40 (A/45/40) at p.1 (1990). *See also* Joseph, S., Schultz, J., and Castan, M., *The International Covenant on Civil and Political Rights, Cases, Materials, and Commentary* (2000) pp.106–107.

[24] General Comment 12, para.1. Many of the countries that participated in the drafting of the Covenant had also expressed similar views on the importance of the right of self-determination to the realization of all other individual human rights. *See* Cassese, A., 'The Self-Determination of Peoples' in Henkin (above n.6) at p.101.   [25] *ibid.*, p.92.

conceived and utilized as an instrument of decolonization that accelerated the independence of most colonies. It essentially guaranteed the right of people to determine freely their own political status and independence and to pursue their economic, social and cultural development.[26]

The scope of the right was subsequently broadened and divided into external self-determination and internal self-determination.[27] The concept of external self-determination covers the prohibition of alien or colonial subjugation, both politically and economically, and is considered to be a peremptory norm of international law.[28] Internal self-determination is the right of 'peoples', within a given State, to internal political and economic autonomy, that is, 'the right to choose the form of their political and economic future'.[29] Sometimes in the exercise of this right a 'people' within an existing sovereign State may choose the path of independence which could lead to the creation of a separate State from an existing one. This usually arises as a consequence of the substantive State's denial of the fundamental rights of the 'people' claiming such autonomy.[30] This has enormous political problems with respect to State sovereignty and may lead to violations of other human rights especially when invoked as a minority right within an existing State. During the deliberating stage of the Covenant, most of the developing nations had opposed the extension of the right of self-determination beyond colonial situations for the fear of it conferring alleged rights of secession on minorities.[31] Harris has pointed out notably in this regard that the right of self-determination 'does not extend to claims for independence by minority groups in a non-colonial context'.[32]

---

[26] *See* Art. 1(1) of the ICCPR *and* the 4th Principle in the GA Declaration on Principles of International Law Concerning Friendly Relations and Co-operation Among States in Accordance with the Charter of the United Nations 1970, GA Res. 2625 (XXV) of 24 October 1970.

[27] *See* Cassese (above n.24) at p.96ff; Kiss, A., 'The People's Right to Self-Determination' (1986) 7 *Human Rights Law Journal* p.165 at p.170ff; and Nowak (above n.5) at pp.6–25; Higgins, R., *Problems and Process, International Law and How to Use It* (1994) pp.111–128. *See also* Principle VIII of the Helsenki Final Act 1 adopted on 1 August 1975 by the Conference on Security and Co-operation in Europe (CSCE) which, by virtue of the right of self-determination, recognizes the right of all peoples 'to determine, when and as they wish, their internal and external political status, without external interference . . .'.

[28] *See* e.g. Cassese (above n.24) at p.111; Dinstein, Y., 'Collective Human Rights of Peoples and Minorities' (1976) 25 *International and Comparative Law Quarterly*, p.102 at p.106; Kiss (above n.27) at p.174; Gros Espiell, H., *The Right to Self-Determination, Implementation of United Nations Resolutions, Study of the Special Rapporteur of the Sub-Commission on Prevention of Discrimination and Protection of Minorities* (1980) UN Doc. E/CN.4/Sub.2/405/Rev.1, p.11ff and p.40.

[29] *See* Higgins (above n.27) at p.118. *See also* McCorquodale, R., 'Self-determination: A Human Rights Approach' (1994) 43 *International and Comparative Law Quarterly*, p.857 at p.864. [30] *See* Higgins (above n.27) at p.124.

[31] *See* Cassese (above n.24) at p.93.

[32] *See* Harris, D.J., *Cases and Materials on International Law*, (5th Ed., 1998) p.113. *See also* Higgins (above n.27) at p.124, and McCorquodale, R., 'The Right of Self-determination' in Harris, D. J., and Joseph, S. (eds.), *The International Convention on Civil and Political Rights and United Kingdom Law* (1995) p.91 at p.104.

This is corroborated by the UN Committee on the Elimination of Racial Discrimination (CERD) in its General Recommendation No. 21 on the right of self-determination that:

> ... in accordance with the Declaration of the General Assembly on Friendly Relations, none of the Committee's actions shall be construed as authorizing or encouraging any action which would dismember or impair, totally or in part, the territorial integrity or political unity of sovereign and independent states conducting themselves in compliance with the principle of equal rights and self-determination of peoples and possessing a government representing the whole people belonging to the territory without distinction as to race, creed or colour. In the view of the Committee international law has not recognized a general right of peoples to unilaterally declare secession from a state. In this respect, the Committee follows the views expressed in the Agenda for Peace (paras. 17 et seq.), namely that a fragmentation of States may be detrimental to the protection of human rights as well as to the preservation of peace and security. This does not, however, exclude the possibility of arrangements reached by free agreements of all parties concerned.[33]

The former UN Secretary General, Boutros Ghali, also observed in his 'Agenda for Peace' that: 'If every ethnic, religious or linguistic group claimed Statehood, there would be no limit to fragmentation, and peace, security and economic well-being for all would become ever more difficult to achieve. One requirement for solutions to these problems lies in commitment to human rights.'[34] The tendency for invoking the right of self-determination towards independence or secession by minorities is often triggered by oppression or gross denial of their civil and political rights within a State. Thus, wherever the rights guaranteed under the Covenant are respected and ensured by the State to all without discrimination, the right of internal self-determination would have been fulfilled and any agitation for independence on grounds of self-determination becomes untenable. That is the human rights approach to self-determination.

Apart from its significance as a civil and political right, the right of self-determination also has an important link with economic, social, and cultural development. This is evidenced by its repetition in the ICESCR and also in Article 1(2) of the Declaration on the Right to Development.[35] Nowak has observed in that regard that '(s)elf-determination and development are closely associated', and has pointed out that 'the continually spiralling difference

---

[33] *See* para.6., Committee on the Elimination of Racial Discrimination, General Recommendation XXI on Self-determination, UN Doc. CERD/48/Misc. 7/Rev. 3 (1996). *See also* Art. 8 of UN Declaration on the Rights of Persons Belonging to National or Ethnic, Religious and Linguistic Minorities (1992) GA Res. 47/135.

[34] *See* 'An Agenda for Peace—Preventive Diplomacy, Peacemaking and Peace-keeping': UN Doc. A/47/277–S/24111 of 17 June 1992.

[35] GA Res. 41/128 of 1986. *See also* General Comment 12, para.5 for the HRC's comment on the economic content of the right of self-determination.

between over-and under-development and the current debt crisis in the countries of the Third World show that most peoples of the South are still far removed from true self-determination'.[36] It is in the context of this last statement and against colonization that developing nations generally and Muslim States specifically tend to view and advocate the right of self-determination.

The right of external self-determination against colonization and subjugation can be fully justified within the general context of *Sharî'ah* prohibitions of oppression and subjugation of peoples. In that regard, Article 11(b) of the OIC Cairo Declaration on Human Rights in Islam provides that:

Colonialism of all types being one of the most evil forms of enslavement is totally prohibited. Peoples suffering from colonialism have the full right to freedom and self-determination. It is the duty of all States and peoples to support the struggle of colonized peoples for the liquidation of all forms of colonialism and occupation, and all States and peoples have the right to preserve their independent identity and exercise control over their wealth and natural resources.

Apart from colonial contexts, Muslim States strongly abhor the invocation of the right of self-determination by minority groups as a basis for independence or secession. The classical Islamic politico-legal notion of a single Islamic political empire that transcends ethnic, tribal, racial, or territorial distinctions disfavours any claim to secession on the basis of the right to self-determination within the Islamic State. Hashmi has observed that Muslim States tend to 'condone only the self-determination of Muslims living within states with a non-Muslim majority' and consider as illegitimate '[c]laims of self-determination advanced by Muslim minorities within existing Muslim states, especially when pressed to the point of secession'.[37] In agreement with the requirements for internal self-determination, a Muslim State has a duty under Islamic law to deal equitably with all peoples within its jurisdiction and to guarantee the fundamental human rights of everyone so that the need for the minorities' advocating secession may not arise. Where such claim arises in a Muslim State, it would suggest the ruling authority's failure to discharge its human rights obligations in respect of such minorities and would in that case have to discharge the obligations rather than for the minorities to secede. This is in consonance with the human rights approach to self-determination which ensures the fundamental rights of everyone within a State rather than accommodating secession that often leads to graver human rights violations. CERD had observed in its General Recommendation 21 that governments should be sensitive towards the right of minority groups 'to lead lives of dignity, to preserve their culture, to share equitably in the

---

[36] *See* Nowak (above n.5) at p.8.
[37] *See* Hashmi, S.H., 'Self-Determination and Secession in Islamic Thought', in Sellers, M. (ed.), *The New World Order, Sovereignty, Human Rights and the Self-determination of Peoples* (1996) p.117.

fruits of national growth, and to play their part in the government of the country of which its members are citizens'.[38] The pertinent question of whether or not non-Muslim minority citizens of a Muslim State can, as of right, take part in the governance of the State, will be examined under Article 25 below.[39]

3.6 EQUALITY OF RIGHTS BETWEEN MEN AND WOMEN

Article 3

The States Parties to the present Covenant undertake to ensure the equal right of men and women to the enjoyment of all civil and political rights set forth in the present Covenant.

Equality and non-discrimination are very fundamental principles of human rights. Both principles are usually taken as equivalent to each other. They indicate a positive and negative means of ensuring an important component of justice, namely impartiality, and have been described as 'the most fundamental of the rights of man' and 'the starting point of all other liberties'.[40] It had also long been noted that 'inequality of rights has been the cause of all the disturbances, insurrections and civil wars that ever happened'.[41] It was the root cause of colonization and slavery, and it continues to be the cause of many inhuman treatments that exist in human society today. From the context of international human rights law, the principle of equality is based on the recognition that '(a)ll human beings are born free and equal in dignity and rights'.[42] Thus, human rights are supposed to be egalitarian in nature and to be enjoyed by all human beings in full equality. The principle of non-discrimination is an extension of that, whereby the enjoyment of human rights shall be '*without distinction of any kind*, such as race, colour, sex, language, religion, political or other opinion, national or social origin, property, birth or other status'.[43]

Apart from the general rule of equality and non-discrimination established within international human rights law,[44] Articles 2(1), 3, and 26 expressly guarantee equality and prohibit non-discrimination under the ICCPR. Reference has already been made above to Article 2(1) under the obligation of States

---

[38] *See* CERD General Recommendation 21 (above n.33) at para.5.

[39] *See* para.3.26 below.

[40] *See* Justice Tanaka in the *South West Africa Cases* [1966] ICJ Reports, p.304. *See also* Bayefsky, A.F., 'The Principle of Equality or Non-Discrimination in International Law' (1990) 11 *Human Rights Law Journal*, p.1.

[41] Paine, T., *Works* (ed.) Mendun, J.P., (1878) cited in McKean, W., *Equality and Discrimination under International Law* (1983) p.2.   [42] *See* Art. 1 UDHR.

[43] *See* Art. 2 UDHR, and Art. 2(1) ICCPR (emphasis added).

[44] *See* Ramcharan (above n.18) at p.246.

Parties 'to respect and to ensure . . . the rights recognized in the . . . Covenant' without discrimination.[45] The grounds of discrimination under Articles 2(1) and 26 are general and identical, namely 'race, colour, sex, language, religion, political or other opinion, national or social origin, property, birth or other status'. Article 3 thus seems superfluous because it only emphasizes the prohibition of discrimination on grounds of sex by guaranteeing equality of rights between men and women.[46] The HRC has however restated Article 3's 'important impact . . . on the enjoyment by women of the human rights protected under the Covenant'.[47] This is due to the culture of discrimination that has existed from time immemorial against women in all societies and which has placed women in positions of disadvantage in many spheres of civil and political rights.

Articles 2(1) and 3 are basically of an accessory character to ensure the equal enjoyment of the rights guaranteed under the Covenant, while Article 26 is of a general character. The Committee has observed however that the positive obligation of States 'to ensure' under Article 3 'may have an inevitable impact on legislation or administrative measures specifically designed to regulate matters other than those dealt with in the Covenant but which may adversely affect rights recognized in the Covenant'.[48] We will address Article 3 now on equality of rights between men and women under the Covenant and address Article 26 later in respect of equality and non-discrimination generally.

The HRC has issued General Comment 28 to update its former General Comment 4 on Article 3 in which it re-emphasized the need for ensuring the equality of rights between men and women and stated that 'State parties should take account of the factors which impede the equal enjoyment of women and men of each right specified in the Covenant'.[49] The Committee further observed that:

Inequality in the enjoyment of rights by women throughout the world is deeply embedded in tradition, history and culture, including religious attitudes . . . States parties should ensure that traditional, historical, religious or cultural attitudes are not used to justify violations of women's right to equality before the law and to equal enjoyment of all Covenant rights. States parties should furnish appropriate information on those aspects of tradition, history, cultural practices and religious attitudes which jeopardise, or may jeopardise, compliance with article 3, and indicate what measures they have taken or intend to take to overcome such factors.[50]

The obligation under Article 3 is understood to require both measures of protection and affirmative action for women through legislation, enlightenment and education to effect the positive and equal enjoyment of the rights between

---

[45] *See* para.3.4 above.
[46] *See* e.g. Joseph, S., and Lord Lester, 'Obligations of Non-Discrimination' in Harris and Joseph (above n.32) at p.565.   [47] General Comment 28, para.1.
[48] General Comment 4, para.3.   [49] *See* General Comment 28, para.6.
[50] *ibid.*, para.5.

men and women under the Covenant.[51] This derives from the concept that total elimination of discrimination against women and the achievement of total equality between the genders form an important aspect of international human rights law.[52]

Islamic law also recognizes equality of men and women as human beings but does not advocate absolute equality of roles between them, especially in the family relationship. Article 6 of the OIC Cairo Declaration on Human Rights in Islam states that:

(a) Woman is equal to man in human dignity and has rights to enjoy as well as duties to perform; she has her own civil entity and financial independence, and the right to retain her name and lineage.
(b) The husband is responsible for the support and welfare of the family.

Mayer has argued that the guarantee of equality 'in human dignity' under the OIC Cairo Declaration falls short of the guarantee of equality to the enjoyment of all civil and political rights under the ICCPR.[53] That will be true with a narrow interpretation of human dignity. A broad interpretation of human dignity will, of course, imply the enjoyment of all rights incidental to human dignity. The OIC Cairo Declaration has not, in any case, been subjected to any judicial or quasi-judicial interpretation to ascertain the scope of its provisions. The HRC has however observed that: 'Equality during marriage implies that husband and wife should participate equally in responsibility and authority within the family'.[54] The provision in Article 6(b) of the OIC Cairo Declaration above seems to foreclose women's right of equality in responsibility within the family under Islamic law.

While the wife is not debarred from providing support and welfare for the family under Islamic law, it is the husband that is legally bound to do so, as will be further expatiated under family rights in Article 23 below. Equality of women is recognized in Islam on the principle of 'equal but not equivalent'. Although males and females are regarded as equal, that may not imply equivalence or a total identity in roles, especially within the family.[55] Muhammad Qutb has observed that while the demand for equality between man and woman as human beings is both natural and reasonable, this should not extend to a transformation of roles and functions.[56] This creates instances of differentiation in gender roles under Islamic law that may amount to discrimination by

[51] *See* Nowak (above n.5) at pp.66–68.
[52] *See* e.g. the Convention on the Elimination of all Forms of Discrimination Against Women (1979), 1249 UNTS, p.13; and Nowak (above n.5) at p.66.
[53] *See* e.g. Mayer, A.E., *Islam and Human Rights* (1999) p.120 and Mayer, A.E., 'Universal versus Islamic Human Rights: A Clash of Cultures or a Clash with a Construct?' (1994) 15 *Michigan Journal of International Law*, p.306 at p.330.
[54] General Comment 28, para.25.
[55] *See* e.g. al-Faruqi, I.R., and al-Faruqi, L.L., *The Cultural Atlas of Islam* (1986) p.150.
[56] *See* Qutb, M., *Islam the Misunderstood Religion* (1978) p.129.

the threshold of international human rights law. Although the UN annotations on the draft of Article 3 on equal rights of men and women recorded an appreciation of the drafters that '[i]t was difficult to share the assumption that legal systems and traditions could be overridden, that conditions which were inherent in the nature and growth of families and organized societies could be immediately changed, or that articles of faith and religion could be altered, merely by treaty legislations',[57] the HRC now seems convinced that 'in the light of the experience it has gathered in its activities over the last 20 years',[58] it intends to push through a universal standard of complete gender equality under the Covenant aimed at changing traditional, cultural, and religious attitudes that subordinate women universally.

Muslim scholars argue that Islamic law had, over fourteen centuries ago, addressed the problem of gender discrimination and established the woman's position as a dignified human being sharing equal rights with her male counterpart in almost all spheres of life.[59] However, due to factors such as patriarchal conservatism, illiteracy, and poverty, women in most parts of the Muslim world still suffer one form of gender discrimination or the other. Mayer has observed that 'the most extensive conflicts between past interpretations of Islamic requirements and international human rights norms lie in the area of women's rights' and that 'conservative interpretations of the requirements of Islamic law' may result in many disadvantages for women, especially in the enjoyment of civil and political rights.[60]

Apart from the prohibition of discrimination on grounds of sex in nearly all international human rights instruments, the Convention on the Elimination of all Forms of Discrimination Against Women[61] specifically advocates equality for women and prohibits all forms of discrimination against them. It is noteworthy however that even Muslim countries, such as Tunisia, considered today as having adopted a most liberal approach in their interpretation of Islamic law,[62] entered reservations to the Women's Convention.[63] This may

---

[57] *See* UN Doc. A/2929 (above n.8) at p.62; *see also* Ramcharan (above n.18) at p.253ff.

[58] *See* General Comment 28, para.1.

[59] *See generally* e.g. Doi, A.R., *Woman in Sharî'ah* (1989); El-Bahnassawi, S., *Woman between Islam and World Legislations* (1985); and Al-Faruqi, L., *Women, Muslim Society and Islam* (1988). *See also* Chaudry, Z., 'The Myth of Misogyny: A Re-analysis of Women's Inheritance in Islamic Law'(1997) 61 *Albany Law Review*, 511 at pp.512–515.

[60] *See* Mayer (above n.53) at pp.323 and 329 (*see particularly* n.49 at 323).

[61] Above n.3.

[62] The CEDAW Committee had described Tunisia 'as a shining example for other (Muslim) countries, because of its progressive and programmative interpretation of Islam'. *See* UN Doc. A/50/38, para.222.

[63] *See* UN Human Rights Treaty Database at http://www.unhchr.ch/html/menu3/b/e1cedaw.htm [1/3/03]. *See also* Cook, R., 'Reservations to the Convention on the Elimination of All Forms of Discrimination Against Women' (1990) 30 *Virginia Journal of International Law*, p.643 at p.688.

not be unconnected with the revolutionary approach of the Women's Convention. It aims at '*a change in the traditional role of men as well as the role of women in society and in family* and at achieving *full equality between men and women*'.[64] Muslim States tend to be cautious in that regard because both the society and family are very important institutions in Islam. The family and societal structures of Muslim societies are based on principles prescribed by the religion, reinforced by the law, and cherished by the individuals. Some family rights and obligations are not considered as entirely private family affairs but of concern to society.[65] No impetuous change in these two institutions, that is, family and society, can thus occur in Muslim States without prompting serious debates on its Islamic legality. Authorities in Muslim States would thus be cautious to prevent total erosion of Islamic norms, which could in turn undermine their own Islamic credibility from within. Even individuals, either because of sincere religious conviction or for fear of societal reproach, are often very cautious in flouting Islamic norms without valid Islamic evidence. It is important to observe however that some of the specific CEDAW reservations by some Muslim States, such as to Article 7 (elimination of discrimination against women in political and public life), Article 9 (equal rights of men and women to acquire, change, or retain their nationality) and Article 15 (equality before the law, in civil matters and in choice of residence and domicile) are on grounds of national laws and not on grounds of Islamic law per se. The specific reservations on grounds of Islamic law or *Sharî'ah* are mostly those in respect of Article 2 and Article 16 of the Convention relating specifically to marriage and family matters.

Unlike its former General Comment 4, the HRC has offered a broader view on equality of rights between men and women in its General Comment 28. It interpreted Article 3 in the context of almost all the other substantive articles of the Covenant, which obviously raises issue with Islamic law in the following paragraphs of General Comment 28.

13: States parties should provide information on any specific regulation of clothing to be worn by women in public. The Committee stresses that such regulations may involve a violation of a number of rights guaranteed by the covenant, such as article 26, on non-discrimination; article 7, if corporal punishment is imposed in order to enforce such a regulation; article 9, when failure to comply with the regulation is punished by arrest; article 12, if liberty of movement is subject to such a constraint; article 17, which guarantees all persons the right to privacy without arbitrary or unlawful interference; articles 18 and 19, when women are subjected to clothing requirements that are not in keeping with their religion or their self-expression; and, lastly, article 27, when the clothing requirements conflict with the culture to which the woman can lay a claim.

---

[64] *See* 14th Preambular paragraph of CEDAW (above n.3) (emphasis added).
[65] *See generally* 'Abd al 'Atî, H., *The Family Structure in Islam* (1977).

14: With regards to article 9 States parties should provide information on any laws or practices which may deprive women of their liberty on an arbitrary or unequal basis, such as by confinement within the house.[66]

...

16: As regards article 12, States parties should provide information on any legal provision or any practice which restricts women's right to freedom of movement as, for example, the exercise of marital powers over the wife or parental powers over adult daughters, legal or de facto requirements which prevent women from travelling such as the requirement of consent of a third party to the issuance of a passport or other type of travel documents to an adult woman. States parties should also report on measures taken to eliminate such laws and practices and to protect women against them, including reference to available domestic remedies.[67]

...

18: States should inform the Committee...whether women may give evidence as witnesses on the same terms as men...[68]

...

24: ...the right to choose one's spouse may be restricted by laws or practices that prevent the marriage of a woman of a particular religion with a man who professes no religion or a different religion. States should provide information on these laws and practices and on the measures taken to abolish the laws and eradicate the practices...It should also be noted that equality of treatment with regard to the right to marry implies that polygamy is incompatible with this principle. Polygamy violates the dignity of women. It is an inadmissible discrimination against women. Consequently, it should be definitely abolished wherever it continues to exist.[69]

25: ...Equality during marriage implies that husband and wife should participate equally in responsibility and authority within the family.[70]

26: States must also ensure equality in regard to the dissolution of marriage...The grounds for divorce and annulment should be the same for men and women...Women should also have equal inheritance rights to those of men when the dissolution of marriage is caused by the death of one of the spouses.[71]

27: In giving effect to recognition of the family in the context of article 23, it is important to accept the concept of the various forms of family, including unmarried couples and their children...[72]

The Committee had already expressed concern on some of the above issues in its concluding observations on the reports of some Muslim States. In its concluding observations on the Islamic Republic of Iran in 1993 the Committee had observed that 'the punishment and harassment of women who do not conform with a strict dress code; the need for women to obtain their husband's permission to leave home; their exclusion from the magistracy; discriminatory treatment in respect of the payment of compensation to the

[66] This is discussed at para.3.10 below.   [67] This is discussed at para.3.13 below.
[68] This is discussed at para.3.15 below.
[69] This is discussed at paras.3.24.1 and 3.24.2 below.
[70] This is discussed at paras.3.24.3 and 3.24.4 below.
[71] This is discussed at para.3.24 below.
[72] This is discussed under paras.3.24 and 4.10 below.

families of murder victims, depending on the victim's gender and in respect of the inheritance rights of women; prohibition against the practice of sports in public; and segregation from men in public transportation' were incompatible with Article 3 of the ICCPR.[73] Also on Sudan in 1997 the Committee expressed concern at the 'official enforcement of strict dress requirements for women in public places, under the guise of public order and morality, and at inhuman punishment imposed for breaches of such requirements, [and that] [r]estrictions on the liberty of women under the Personal Status of Muslims Act, 1992 are matters of concern under articles 3, 9 and 12 of the Covenant'.[74]

The general regulation on women's clothing under Islamic law will be examined here, while each of the other issues raised in the quoted paragraphs of General Comment 28 above will be addressed under the relevant articles of the ICCPR cited. Under Islamic law, clothing is generally for the enhancement of human dignity. It serves as cover for private parts, adornment, and protection against atmospheric hazards.[75] Due to the prohibition of adultery and fornication under Islamic law, both men and women are required to dress modestly and not to expose sensuous parts of their body seductively in public. Specifically, the Qur'an directs women to 'draw their veils over their bosoms' and not to publicly display their beauty 'except for what must ordinarily appear'.[76] Opinions differ regarding the exception 'what must ordinarily appear', resulting in a division of juristic views as to the extent of women's covering in Islamic law.[77] While the *Shâfi'î* and the *Hanbalî* schools of Islamic jurisprudence generally hold that women must veil up their whole person in public, away from the view of strangers, the *Hanafî* and *Mâlikî* schools of jurisprudence generally allow exposure of the face, the hands up to the wrists and the feet up to the ankles.[78] Many contemporary Muslim thinkers and jurists have disagreed with the view on complete veiling of women.[79]

---

[73] Concluding Observations on Islamic Republic of Iran (1993) UN Doc. CCPR/C/79/Add.25., para.13.

[74] Concluding Observations on Sudan (1997) UN. Doc. CCPR/C/79/Add.85, para.22.

[75] *See* e.g. Q7:26—'Oh Children of Adam! We have bestowed raiment upon you to cover your Shame, as well as to be an adornment to you, but the raiment of righteousness . . . is the best.' and Q16:81—' . . . He made you garments to protect you from heat . . .'. *See further* right to clothing under Art. 11 of the ICESCR in the next chapter.   [76] *See* Q24:30–31.

[77] *See* e.g. Ali, S.S., 'Women's Rights in Islam: Towards a Theoretical Framework' (1997–98) *Yearbook of Islamic and Middle Eastern Law*, Vol. 4., p.117 and references cited there in respect of the differences of opinion with regards to the veiling of women in Islam.

[78] For further specifics *see* e.g. Darwish, M.H., *Fasl al-Khitâb fi Mas'alah al-Hijâb wa al-Niqâb* (Arabic) (1987) p.51; Al-Zuhayli, W., *Al-Fiqh Al-Islami wa-Adillatuh* (Arabic) (1997) Vol.1, pp.743–754; al-Jazîrî, A.R., *al-Fiqh ala Madhâhib al-'Arba'ah* (Arabic) (1996) Vol.1, p.184. *See also* Stowasser, B.F., *Women in the Qur'an, Traditions, and Interpretation* (1994) pp.93–94.

[79] *See* e.g. Rahman, F., *Status of Women in the Qur'an* in Nashat., G., (ed.), *Women and Revolution in Iran* (1983). *See also* the judgment of the Pakistan Federal Shariat Court in *Ansar Burney v. Federation of Pakistan* [1983] PLD (FSC), p.73 at p.75ff.

In response to a question on the regulation of women's dress by Muslim States during consideration of Iran's report by the ESCR Committee, the Iranian representatives stated that the 'Islamic Republic of Iran followed Islamic principles with regard to dress' and that the clothing worn by women in Iran reflected the requirements of Islam.[80] The Iranian representatives further argued that 'every society had a social code in that respect with limits which could not be exceeded' and in that regard the 'dress code in force in the Islamic Republic of Iran differed from the code prevailing in other societies and the real issue was to what extent a woman had the right to take off her veil, a subject that would involve a philosophical debate'.[81]

On one hand, Muslim women in most parts of the world today voluntarily follow the view that allows exposure of the face, hands, and feet, without hindrance to their daily life and careers. Nicole and Hugh Pole have observed in that regard that: 'Contrary to perceptions in the West, . . . women who often wear a long Islamic coat as well as a headscarf, are not always uneducated peasants submitting to tradition. Some are well educated professional women, who have made a conscious choice to embrace religion'.[82] On the other hand, some Muslim States do enforce the rule that women must veil up completely in public, sometimes with threats of corporal punishment for non-compliance. This restricts the liberty of women in many ways and sometimes confines them to the four walls of their homes.[83] From a jurisprudential perspective, it is arguable that the imposition by a Muslim State of complete veiling does essentially deny Muslim women the right voluntarily to follow equally legitimate views that permit the unveiling of the face, hands, and feet under Islamic law.

While Islam was the first to liberate women more than fourteen hundred years ago from the inhuman conditions they were in, it is hypocritical if men on one hand acquire and enjoy many rights and liberties of today's world, often through constructive and evolutionary interpretations of the *Sharī'ah*, but on the other hand consider the rights and liberties of women to be stagnated upon the juristic views of the classical schools of Islamic law. The Prophet Muhammad had stated that women are full sisters of men which is an expression of equality.[84] Women are therefore equally entitled to the rights and liberties of today's world, subject to respect for the principles of public morality as applicable to both men and women under Islamic law.[85] Rather

---

[80] *See* ESCR Committee, UN Doc. E/C.12/1993/SR.8 (1993) at para.54.

[81] *ibid.*, at paras.58 and 60.

[82] Pope, N., and Pope, H., *Turkey Unveiled: Ataturk and After* (1997) p.328.

[83] *See* Levitt, M.A., 'The Taliban, Islam and Women's Rights in the Muslim World' (1998) 22 *The Fletcher Forum*, p.113.

[84] *See* Yammani, M., 'Muslim Women and Human Rights: The New Generation' (paper delivered at the Cairo Conference on Democracy and the Rule of Law, December 1997) p.2.

[85] *See* e.g. Qutb, M., *Islam the Misunderstood Religion* (1978) pp.118–164.

than the State imposing the strict view of total veiling and thereby foreclosing the other moderate view, the better approach is to allow Muslim women to be able to choose voluntarily between the two legitimate Islamic jurisprudential views as analysed above. That will in practice strike a balance between the rights of women under Islamic law and international human rights law on the issue of dress regulation.

3.7 THE RIGHT TO LIFE

Article 6

1. Every human being has the inherent right to life. This right shall be protected by law. No one shall be arbitrarily deprived of his life.
2. In countries which have not abolished the death penalty, sentence of death may be imposed only for the most serious crimes in accordance with the law in force at the time of the commission of the crime and not contrary to the provisions of the present Covenant and to the Convention on the Prevention and Punishment of the Crime of Genocide. This penalty can only be carried out pursuant to a final judgement rendered by a competent court.
3. When deprivation of life constitutes the crime of genocide, it is understood that nothing in this article shall authorize any State Party to the present Covenant to derogate in any way from any obligation assumed under the provisions of the Convention on the Prevention and Punishment of the Crime of Genocide.
4. Anyone sentenced to death shall have the right to seek pardon or commutation of the sentence. Amnesty, pardon or commutation of the sentence of death may be granted in all cases.
5. Sentence of death shall not be imposed for crimes committed by persons below eighteen years of age and shall not be carried out on pregnant women.
6. Nothing in this article shall be invoked to delay or to prevent the abolition of capital punishment by any State Party to the present Covenant.

Life is mankind's most valuable asset from which all other human possibilities arise. There is thus agreement on the fact that the right to life is the supreme and most fundamental human right without which all other human rights will be meaningless.[86] Many scholars are of the view that right to life is *jus cogens* under international law.[87] It is a non-derogable right under the

---

[86] *See* e.g. General Comments 6 and 14. *See also* Nowak (above n.5) at p.104; Ramcharan, B.G., 'The Right to Life' (1983) *Netherlands International Law Review*, p.297 at pp.311–314; Dinstein, Y., 'The Right to Life, Physical Integrity and Liberty' in Henkin (above n.6) at p.114. *See also* Art. 1 Universal Islamic Declaration of Human Rights 1981; Chaudhry, M.S., *Islam's Charter of Fundamental Rights and Civil Liberties* (1995) p.9; al-Ghazali, M., *Huqûq al-Insân Bayn T'âlîm al-Islâm wa I'lân al-Umam al-Mutahidah* (Arabic) (1993) p.245; Doi, A.R., *Sharî'ah: The Islamic Law* (1984) p.229.

[87] *See* Ramcharan (above n.86) at pp.307, 308, 311ff; Higgins, R., 'Derogations under Human Rights Treaties' (1976/77) 48 *British Yearbook of International Law*, p.281 at p.282 and further references therewith.

ICCPR,[88] and the HRC has stated that '[i]t is a right which should not be interpreted narrowly'.[89]

Article 6(1) provides for the sanctity of human life and it imposes a positive obligation on the State to protect life and a negative obligation not to take life arbitrarily. Apart from the duty to prohibit and punish criminal homicide as a means of protecting the right to life, the HRC has interpreted the scope of the State's obligation under Article 6(1) to include, *inter alia*, 'the supreme duty to prevent wars, acts of genocide and other acts of mass violence causing arbitrary loss of life';[90] the duty 'to take all possible measures to reduce infant mortality and increase life expectancy, especially in adopting measures to eliminate malnutrition and epidemics';[91] the prohibition of 'production, testing, possession, deployment and use of nuclear weapons';[92] and also making efforts to 'strengthen international peace and security'.[93]

The right to life under the Covenant is however non-absolute. Article 6(1) only prohibits the arbitrary deprivation of life. While the term 'arbitrarily' is not defined by the Covenant, it generally connotes that the deprivation of life by the State is strictly limited.[94] It must be in full accordance with due process of law and strictly proportionate on the facts. The State must also prevent arbitrary killing by its security forces and law enforcement agents.[95]

Both the substantive provision and general interpretation of Article 6(1) are in concordance with Islamic law. There are many verses of the Qur'an and Traditions of the Prophet Muhammad that acknowledge the sanctity of human life, enjoin its protection and prohibit its arbitrary deprivation. The *Sharî'ah* provisions on the sanctity and protection of human life are so fundamental and emphatic that they cannot be denied. The following Qur'anic verses are examples in that respect.

... Take not life which God has made sacred, except by way of justice and law; thus does He (God) command you that you may learn wisdom.[96]

---

[88] *See* Art. 4(2).   [89] General Comment 6, para.1.

[90] General Comment 6, para.2.

[91] General Comment 6, para.5; cf. Dinstein (above n.86) at pp.115–116 for the view that the right to life is a civil right safeguarding against arbitrary killing and does not include issues such as guarantee against death from lack of medical attention or reduction of infant mortality. Nowak argues differently that such restrictive interpretation is due to 'an improper merging of the second and third sentences in Art. 6(1)'. *See* Nowak (above n.5) at p.106 n.16.

[92] General Comment 14, para.4. This opinion of the HRC created some controversy on the part of many States such as USA, UK etc.

[93] *See* General Comment 6, paras.2 and 5 and General Comment 14.

[94] *See* UN Doc. A/2929 (above n.8) p.83, para.3, where it is stated that the term 'arbitrarily' was explained to mean both 'illegally' and 'unjustly' during the drafting.

[95] *See* Joseph, Schultz, and Castan (above n.23) at p.108ff; and General Comment 6, para.3. *See also* the cases of *Suarez de Guerrero v. Colombia*, Communication No. R.11/45 (5 February 1979), UN Doc. Supp. No. 40 (A/37/40) at p.137 (1982); and *Rickly Burrell v. Jamaica*, Communication No. 546/1993, UN Doc. CCPR/C/53/D/546/1993 (1996).

[96] Q6:151.

Nor take life—which God has made sacred—except for just cause. And if anyone is slain wrongfully, We have given his heir authority (to demand *Qisâs* [retribution] or to forgive): but let him not exceed bounds in the matter of taking life: for he is helped (by the Law).[97]

... if anyone slew a person—unless it be for murder or for spreading mischief in the land—it would be as if he slew humanity as a whole: and if anyone saved a life, it would be as if he saved humanity as a whole.[98]

The above verses apply to the State as much as to individuals. Also in his oft-quoted sermon given at the end of his farewell pilgrimage, the Prophet Muhammad is reported to have declared, *inter alia*, that: 'Verily your lives and properties are sacred to one another till you meet your Lord on the Day of Resurrection'. In another Tradition he is also reported to have warned that: 'The first offences to be judged by God between mankind on the judgement day will be unlawful taking of lives'.[99]

Based on the above injunctions, Islamic jurists are unanimous on the sacredness of human life and that there is an obligation on the ruling authority of the State to protect the right to life of every individual.[100] The protection of life in Islamic law also includes the prohibition of suicide, thus shutting out the notion of a 'right to die' under Islamic law.[101] Article 2 of the OIC Cairo Declaration on Human Rights in Islam thus provides that:

(a) Life is a God-given gift and the right to life is guaranteed to every human being. It is the duty of individuals, societies and states to protect this right from any violation, and it is prohibited to take away life except for a Sharî'ah prescribed reason.
(b) It is forbidden to resort to such means as may result in the genocidal annihilation of mankind.
(c) The preservation of human life throughout the term of time willed by God is a duty prescribed by Sharî'ah.
(d) Safety from bodily harm is a guaranteed right. It is the duty of the state to safeguard it and it is prohibited to breach it without a Sharia-prescribed reason.'

The '*Sharî'ah* prescribed reason' proviso on the right to life in the Cairo Declaration is in respect of crimes attracting the death penalty under Islamic law, which must be strictly in accordance with the due process of law. This is reflected in the two provisions 'except by way of justice and law' and 'except for just cause' in the Qur'anic verses on the sanctity and protection of human life cited above.[102]

---

[97] Q17:33.   [98] Q5:32.

[99] Reported by al-Bukhâri and Muslim. *See* al-Jazîrî, A.R., *Kitâb al-Fiqh Alâ al-Madhâhib al-'Arba'ah* (Arabic) (1997) Vol. 5, p.218.

[100] *See* e.g. *ibid.*, pp.214–223; and al-Ghazali (above n.86) at p.245.

[101] *See* e.g. Ahmed, B.D., and Umri, J., 'Suicide and Euthanasia: Islamic Viewpoint' in Mahmood, T., *et al.* (eds.), *Criminal Law in Islam and the Muslim World* (1996) pp.164–177.

[102] *See* above n.96 and n.97.

This brings us to the exception to the right to life under the ICCPR in respect of the death penalty. Although Article 6(1) does not prohibit the death penalty, Article 6(2) to 6(6) places some restrictions on its imposition. Five specific restrictions on the death penalty may be identified from the provisions of Article 6(2) to 6(6).

The first is that the death penalty may not be imposed except only for the most serious crimes and in accordance with the law in force at the time of the commission of the crime.[103] Thus, while Article 6 does not abolish the death penalty, it restricts its imposition to the 'most serious crimes' and the HRC has stated the need for States Parties to review their criminal laws to that effect.[104] The term 'most serious crimes' is however not defined in the Covenant. During the drafting of this provision of the Covenant, the phrase 'most serious crimes' 'was criticized as lacking precision, since the concept of "serious crimes" differed from one country to another'.[105] The HRC has however observed that this expression 'must be read restrictively to mean that the death penalty should be a quite exceptional measure'.[106] The Committee has concluded that 'robbery,[107] traffic in toxic dangerous wastes,[108] abetting suicide, drug-related offences, property offences,[109] multiple evasion of military service,[110] apostasy, committing a third homosexual act, embezzlement by officials, theft by force,[111] crimes of an economic nature, adultery, corruption, and "crimes that do not result in the loss of life" '[112] are all not most serious crimes. Thus, according to Joseph, Schultz, and Castan 'it appears that only intentional killings or attempted killings, or the intentional infliction of grievous bodily harm, may permissibly attract the death penalty under Article 6(2)'.[113]

Under traditional Islamic law the death penalty is prescribed basically for the offences of murder, adultery, apostasy, and armed/highway robbery. The views of the HRC above puts all these offences, except murder, outside the Committee's definition of 'most serious crimes' under the Covenant. The argument of Muslim jurists and scholars is that the manner and circumstances in which the stated offences must be committed to attract

---

[103] Art. 6(2).   [104] *See* General Comment 6, para.6.

[105] *See* UN Doc. A/2929 (above n.8) at p.84, para.6; *See also* Dinstein (above n.86) at p.116.   [106] General Comment 6, para.7.

[107] Concluding Observations on Republic of Korea (1992) UN Doc. A/47/40, 122–4, para.9.

[108] Concluding Observations on Cameroon (1994) UN Doc. CCPR/C/79/Add.33, para.9.

[109] Concluding Observations on Sri Lanka (1996) UN Doc. CCPR/C/79/Add.56, para.14.

[110] Concluding Observations on Iraq (1997) UN Doc. CCPR/79/Add.56, para.11.

[111] Concluding Observations on Sudan (1997) UN Doc. CCPR/C/79/Add.85, para.8.

[112] Concluding Observations on the Islamic Republic of Iran (1995) UN Doc. CCPR/C/79/Add.25, para.8. *See* Joseph, Schultz and Castan (above n.23) at p.120.

[113] *See* Joseph, Schultz and Castan (above n.23) at p.120.

the death penalty makes them very serious offences under Islamic law.[114] Murder attracts the death penalty on retaliatory grounds of life for life. Armed/highway robbery attracts the death penalty where it results in the death of the victim. Adultery basically requires the unanimous eyewitness evidence of four, sane, Muslim adult male witnesses to the sexual act. For apostasy to attract the death penalty, many Islamic scholars now define it in the context of sedition or treason against the State, and not merely as apostasy *simpliciter*.[115]

The HRC has also observed that the provisions of Article 6(2) and 6(6) suggest the desirability of abolishing the death penalty under international law.[116] There is however no unanimity amongst the States of the world yet on the abolition of the death penalty. While some States are considered as 'abolitionist States' others are considered as 'non-abolitionist States' in respect of the death penalty. Muslim States generally belong to the group of 'non-abolitionist States'. Apart from the Republic of Azerbaijan, and recently Turkey[117] no other Muslim State has abolished the death penalty or become a Party to the Second Optional Protocol (OP2) to the ICCPR adopted in 1989 specifically aimed at abolishing the death penalty.[118] Since the Qur'an specifically prescribes the death penalty as punishment for certain crimes, Islamic jurists would consider any direct legislation against its legality as being outside the scope of human legislation under the *Sharî'ah*.[119]

Islamic jurists often cite the Qur'anic verse which says: 'In the law of *qisâs* [retribution] there is [saving of] life for you, O people of understanding; that you may restrain yourselves',[120] to argue that the death penalty for murder is itself a deterrent and a legal protection for the right to life and thus it will impugn the right to life to abolish it.[121] Most Muslim States who apply Islamic criminal law only try to avoid the death penalty through either procedural or commutative provisions available within the *Sharî'ah* instead of direct prohibition of it. Islamic law demands strict evidential requirements for capital offences. A strict compliance with the evidential requirements of Islamic law would often lead, for instance, to payment of blood money for murder, and

---

[114] *See* e.g. al-Jazîrî (above n.99) at Vol.5.

[115] *See* para.3.19.1 for further elaboration on this point.

[116] General Comment 6, para.6. *See also* Robertson, A.H., 'The United Nations Covenant on Civil and Political Rights and The European Convention on Human Rights' (1968–69) 43 *British Yearbook of International Law*, p.21 at p.31.

[117] Turkey abolished the death penalty in peace time in August 2002.

[118] Azerbaijan acceded to the OP2 on 22 January 1999. *See* UN Doc. A/RES/44/128.

[119] *See* e.g. Reference to the Sudanese Parliament on abolition of the death penalty at text to n.17 above. *See also* 'Uthmân, M.F., *Huqûq al-Insân Bayn al-Sharî'ah al-Islâmiyyah wa al-Fikr al-Qânûnî al-Garbî* (Arabic) (1982) pp.67–68.   [120] Q2:179.

[121] *See* e.g. 'Uthmân (above n.119) at p.68; and Ibn Rushd al-Qurtubî, M., *Bidâyah al-Mujtahid wa Nihâyah al-Muqtasid* (Arabic) (10th Ed., 1988), Vol.2, p.400. *See also* the English translation by Nyazee, I.A.K., *The Distinguished Jurist's Primer—Bidâyat al-Mujtahid wa Nihâyat al-Muqtasid* (2000) Vol.II, p.484.

discretionary *(ta'zîr)* punishments for the other capital offences in place of effecting the death penalty. In the case of murder, the *Sharî'ah* allows for the alternative payment of blood money by the offender to the heirs of the victim in lieu of the death penalty. Thus Sudan stated during consideration of its second periodic report on the ICCPR that: '... since 1973 ... execution had been avoided in cases involving the death sentence, either because the higher court or the President had not confirmed the sentence or because blood money—the *diya* had been paid' instead.[122] The Prophet Muhammad is also reported to have recommended that the death penalty should be avoided as much as possible.[123]

The second restriction on the death penalty under Article 6 is that no deprivation of life must be contrary to the provisions of the Covenant, thus for instance a fair hearing must be guaranteed,[124] there must be no discrimination in capital punishment[125] and the methods of execution must not amount to torture or to cruel, inhuman, or degrading punishment.[126] Also, deprivation of life must not be contrary to the Convention on the Prevention and Punishment of Genocide,[127] thus judicially imposed death sentences that may constitute genocide (as did the Nazi tribunals) are prohibited.[128]

Islamic law does also emphasize fair hearing, especially in capital offence cases as will be further elaborated under Article 14 below. The classical Islamic jurists differed however on the question of discrimination in capital punishment. Imâm al-Shâfi'î, Ahmad, al-Thawrî and others held the view that a Muslim offender will not be executed for the murder of a non-Believer. They based their view on a Tradition in which the Prophet is reported to have said that: 'A Believer is not to be executed for a non-Believer'. Imâm Mâlik held a similar view but with the added proviso that if the murder is treacherous (brutal) and especially for the purpose of taking property (*Qatl al-ghîlah*) then the Muslim offender will be executed.[129] Abû Hanîfah and his disciples however made no such religious discrimination for capital punishment. They held the view that a Muslim offender will be executed for the murder of a non-believer and vice versa.[130] The position of Abû Hanîfah and his disciples was based on the lack of a Qur'anic basis for such discrimination and the specific Qur'anic reference to the rule of 'life for life' in one verse.[131] They argued that the other jurists had interpreted the Prophet's Tradition they relied upon out of context to arrive at their view.

---

[122] *See* HRC Summary Record of the 1628th Meeting: Sudan; UN Doc. CCPR/C/SR.1628 of 02 October 1998, para.15.   [123] *See* e.g. Al-Zuhayli (above n.78) at Vol.7, p.5307.

[124] Pursuant to Art. 14 ICCPR.   [125] Pursuant to Art. 2(1) and Art. 26 ICCPR.

[126] Pursuant to Art. 7 ICCPR.   [127] Art. 6(2) and (3).

[128] *See* Nowak (above n.5) at p.108 and pp.116–117.

[129] *See* al-Jazîrî (above n.99) at Vol. 5, pp.244–245 and Ibn Rushd al-Qurtubî (above n.121) at Vol. 2, p.399, also Nyazee (above n.121) at p.483.

[130] *See* Ibn Rushd al-Qurtubî (above n.121) and Nyazee (above n.121). *See also* Al-Zuhayli (above n.78) at Vol.7, p.5671.   [131] Q5:45.

The *Hanafî* jurists further contended that since Islamic law does not discriminate between Muslims and non-Muslims in the punishment for theft and other offences, the same rule must apply in the case of murder. The *Hanafîs* further supported their position with another Tradition in which the Prophet Muhammad was reported to have ordered the execution of a Muslim offender for killing a non-Muslim. The other jurists however contended that this was a special case and an exception to the general rule.[132] The *Hanafî* view is more consistent with other Traditions of the Prophet on equality of human beings and also compatible with the principle of non-discrimination under the Covenant.[133]

The prohibition of genocidal capital punishment under the Covenant is also in full concordance with the sanctity of life under Islamic law. Article 2(b) of the OIC Cairo Declaration on Human Rights in Islam provides that: 'It is forbidden to resort to such means as may result in the genocidal annihilation of mankind'.

The third restriction is that the death penalty can only be carried out pursuant to a final judgment rendered by a competent court.[134] This proviso also aims at preventing the arbitrary deprivation of life and ensures justice as well as compliance with due process of law. This is in full agreement with the principle of justice under Islamic criminal law.[135] As earlier stated above, the Qur'an states clearly that: '... Take not life which God has made sacred, *except by way of justice and law;* thus does He [God] command you that you may learn wisdom'.[136] Islamic law differentiates the judgment *(qaḍâ')* of a competent court from a legal opinion *(fatwâ)* given by a jurisconsult *(muftî)*on a particular issue. A final and executable judgment *(qaḍâ')* can only be given by a competent judge *(qâḍî)* after the full consideration of a case in accordance with due process of the law. A *fatwâ*, on the other hand, is only a legal opinion given by a *muftî* (jurisconsult), which is neither legally binding nor executable.[137] On matters of public law, only competent judges may consult a *muftî* for a legal opinion to help them reach a legal decision on matters before the court. Thus under Islamic law, a *muftî* has no legal competence to give a binding *fatwâ* imposing the death penalty or any other punishment for any offence without the case first being tried by a competent court and

[132] *See* al-Jazîrî (above n.99) at Vol. 5, p.246 and Ibn Rushd al-Qurtubî (above n.121) Vol.2, p.399.

[133] *See also* El-Awa, M.S., *Punishment in Islamic Law* (1982) pp.78–80, especially p.79 where the author also observed that the *Hanafî* view 'is harmonious with the general spirit of Islamic law rather than the explanation of the majority'.   [134] Art. 6(2).

[135] *See generally* e.g. Awad, A.M., 'The Rights of the Accused under Islamic Criminal Procedure' in Bassiouni, M.C., (ed.), *The Islamic Criminal Justice* (1982) pp.91–107.

[136] Q6:151 (emphasis added).

[137] *See* e.g. al-Maqdisî, B.A.R., *al-'Udah Sharh al-'Umdah* (Arabic) (5th Ed., 1997) p.601.

affording the accused person opportunity to defend himself in accordance with the law.[138]

The fourth restriction is that anyone sentenced to death shall be entitled to seek pardon or commutation of sentence and may be granted amnesty, pardon, or commutation of sentence.[139] The entitlement to pardon, commutation of sentence, or grant of amnesty arises only after a final judgment and conviction by the highest court. It relates to the execution of the sentence after a fair trial and due process of law. The power normally lies with the Head of State. It is a prerogative act of clemency and thus subject to other non-legal and non-judicial considerations. It stands as a last resort by which a death penalty may be avoided, whereby the Heads of State in countries that still implement the death penalty may within their power avoid the execution of death sentences.

Based on Qur'anic verses that recommend and extol the act of pardoning the wrongdoer,[140] Islamic law also recognizes the principle of amnesty. Under Islamic law amnesty may be granted by the Ruler under the principle of *haqq al-'afw 'an al-'uqûbah* (that is, the right to pardon from punishment). The State may pardon any *ta'zîr* punishment provided that the victim's right is not undermined. According to the *Hanafî* school, *hudûd* punishments cannot be pardoned by the State because it is the 'right of God'. The other schools however hold that only the *hudûd* punishment for *zinâ* and theft may not be pardoned by the State after the court is seized of the case. Their argument in the case of *zinâ* is that the difficulty of proving *zinâ* through eyewitnesses is enough mitigation on the crime requiring no additional amnesty if an offender could be so heinous to commit the offence in the broad glare of four male witnesses.[141] Based on the Qur'anic provision on homicide, some Islamic jurists consider remission as the better alternative to the death penalty for homicide cases.[142] While the right to commute the death penalty in homicide cases *(qisâs)* for blood money *(diyah)* lies principally with the victim's heirs, the State may encourage such amnesty on the part of the heirs. It was reported in one Tradition that whenever a case of *Qisâs* was brought before the Prophet Muhammad, he recommended pardon.[143]

The fifth restriction is that the death penalty shall not be imposed for crimes committed by persons below eighteen years of age and shall not be carried out on pregnant women.[144] By this restriction the Covenant totally prohibits the

---

[138] *See* e.g. Kamali, M.H., *Freedom of Expression in Islam* (1997) pp.296–297 for views of Islamic scholars and institutions on this point in relation to the death *fatwâ* issued by the late Ayâtullah Khomeini, against Salman Rushdie.   [139] Art. 6(4).

[140] *See* e.g. Q2:178; Q3:134; Q5:45.

[141] *See* al-Jazîrî (above n.99) at Vol.5, pp.224–227.

[142] *See* Al-Zuhayli (above n.78) at Vol.7, p.5689.   [143] *ibid.*

[144] Art. 6(5).

sentencing of juveniles less than eighteen years old to death for any crime what-soever, including the 'most serious crimes'. In the case of pregnant women, they may be sentenced to death for the 'most serious crimes', but the sentence shall not be carried out until after the delivery of the pregnancy. Both cases are a consequence of appreciating the innocence of childhood.

The execution of the death penalty against pregnant women is also pro-hibited under Islamic law. The same exemption extends even to a woman breast-feeding a child until the child is weaned. A child will also not be liable to death penalty under Islamic law based on a Tradition in which the Prophet Muhammad stated, *inter alia*, that a child is free from responsibility until he attains maturity.[145] The only difference is that it is possible for a child to attain maturity before the age of eighteen years under traditional Islamic jurisprudence.

Finally, the HRC has observed in relation to the right of women to life under Article 6 that:

> When reporting on the right to life protected by Article 6 . . . States parties should give information on any measures taken by the State to help women prevent unwanted preg-nancies, and to ensure that they do not have to undertake life-threatening clandestine abortions.[146]

Similarly, the Committee has expressed in many of its concluding observa-tions of States' reports on the ICCPR that 'criminalization of abortion leads to unsafe abortions which account for a high rate of maternal mortality'.[147] The Committee has not also interpreted the right to life to include that of the unborn child, leading Joseph, Schultz, and Castan to conclude that '[c]ertainly, HRC comments have indicated that the *prohibition* of abortion is more likely to breach the ICCPR than the *permissibility* of abortion'.[148]

While Islamic law does not prohibit the prevention of pregnancy[149] it pro-hibits abortion except for valid reasons such as where continuance of the pregnancy endangers the mother's life.[150] Contrary to this Islamic law posi-tion, the CEDAW Committee in its response to the debate of what amounts to an 'unwanted pregnancy', emphasized freedom of choice for women.[151] Muslim States are anti-abortion States and would obviously consider abortion based on the freedom of choice by a pregnant mother as violating the right to life of the unborn child, which is prohibited under Islamic law. The anti-abortionist moral argument for the unborn child is simply that being 'unwanted'

---

[145] *See* al-Jazîrî (above n.99) at Vol.5, p.269.   [146] General Comment 28, para.10.

[147] *See* e.g. Concluding Observations on Cameroon (1999) UN Doc. CCPR/C/79/Add.116, para.13. *See also* Joseph, Schultz, and Castan (above n.23) at pp.135–137.

[148] *ibid.*, pp.474–475.

[149] Muslim jurists however hold divergent views on reasons and methods of prevention. *See* e.g. Musallam, B.F., *Sex and Society in Islam* (1986); and Omran, A. R., *Family Planning in the Legacy of Islam* (1992).   [150] *See* e.g. Omran (above n.149) at pp.8–9.

[151] *See* Joseph, Schultz and Castan (above n.23) at p.137.

is no justification to be denied the right to life. Rather than advocating abortion on grounds of women's rights, the better human rights approach that can be reconcilable with Islamic law is the obligation of States to provide adequate social help for both the mother carrying an 'unwanted pregnancy' and for the 'unwanted baby' after it is born.[152]

3.8 PROHIBITION OF TORTURE OR CRUEL, INHUMAN OR DEGRADING TREATMENT OR PUNISHMENT

Article 7

No one shall be subjected to torture or to cruel, inhuman or degrading treatment or punishment. In particular, no one shall be subjected without his free consent to medical or scientific experimentation.

The prohibition of torture is quite well established and is considered as a peremptory norm of international law.[153] The ICCPR does not define torture, but Article 1(1) of the Convention against Torture and Other Cruel, Inhuman or Degrading Treatment or Punishment (CAT)[154] contains a widely accepted definition of torture which provides that:

For the purposes of this Convention [i.e. CAT], the term 'torture' means any act by which severe pain or suffering, whether physical or mental, is intentionally inflicted on a person for such purposes as obtaining from him or a third person information or a confession, punishing him for an act he or a third person has committed or is suspected of having committed, or intimidating or coercing him or a third person, or for any reason based on discrimination of any kind, when such pain or suffering is inflicted by or at the instigation of or with the consent or acquiescence of a public official or other person acting in an official capacity. It does not include pain or suffering arising only from, inherent in or incidental to lawful sanctions.

Torture is usually distinguished from 'cruel, inhuman or degrading treatment and punishment' on intent, severity, and intensity of pain or suffering. In *Ireland v. UK*, the European Court of Human Rights observed that the term 'torture' attaches 'a special stigma to deliberate inhuman treatment causing very serious and cruel suffering'.[155] Also in *Tyrer v. UK*,[156] the same court held that the intensity of suffering justifying the use of the term 'inhuman'

---

[152] *See* further under rights of the child in Art. 24 below.

[153] *See* e.g. American Law Institute, *Restatement (Third) of Foreign Relations Law*, para.702; and O'Boyle, M., 'Torture and Emergency Powers under the European Convention on Human Rights: Ireland v. The United Kingdom' (1977) 71 *American Journal of International Law*, p.674 at pp.687–688.

[154] 1465 UNTS, p.85. *See also* Art. 7(2)(E) of the Statute of the International Criminal Court. UN Doc. A/CONF.183/9 of 17 July 1998.

[155] [1978] ECHRR, Series A, No. 3, para.167.

[156] [1978] ECHRR, Series A, No. 28, para.30.

is higher than in what may be described as 'degrading'. Inhuman relates to pain and suffering while degrading relates to humiliation. Thus there is some presumed 'scale of aggravation in suffering which commences with degradation, mounts to inhumanity and ultimately attains the level of torture'.[157] Also cruel treatment is presumed to lie 'somewhere between inhuman conduct and torture'.[158] Thus even though a particular act may escape being categorized as torture, it may still amount to either cruel, inhuman, or degrading treatment which are all prohibited under the Covenant. The underlying aim of the provision is 'to protect both the dignity and the physical and mental integrity of the individual'.[159]

The prohibition of subjecting anyone to medical or scientific experimentation without his or her free consent under Article 7, 'was intended as a response to the atrocities such as committed in concentration camps during World War II'[160] and thus excludes '[n]ormal medical treatment in the interest of the patient's health'.[161]

Based on the dignified nature of the human person under the *Sharî'ah,* there is no conflict under Islamic law with the general prohibition of torture or cruel, inhuman, or degrading treatment or the prohibition of subjecting a human being to scientific experimentation without consent.[162] There are many verses of the Qur'an and Traditions of the Prophet that enjoin compassion and prohibit cruelty and oppression even to animals. Bassiouni has observed that the Qur'an warns against persecution of human beings in two hundred and ninety-nine places.[163] The Prophet Muhammad was also reported to have warned against torture saying that: 'God will torture, in the hereafter, those who torture people in this life'.[164] And when he entrusted anyone with the affairs of the State the Prophet would instruct him thus: 'Give glad tidings and do not terrorise, give ease and do not molest the people'. Following this humane principle of the *Sharî'ah*, Caliph Umar ibn Abdul Azîz[165] was reported to have stated, in reply to a request of one of his governors who sought permission to torture those who refused to pay tax due to the public treasury, as follows:

I wonder at your asking permission from me to torture people as though I am a shelter for you from God's wrath, and as if my satisfaction will save you from God's anger. Upon receiving this letter of mine accept what is given to you or let him give an

---

[157] *See* Dinstein (above n.86) at pp.123–124; *See also* General Comment 7, para.2.
[158] *ibid.* [159] *See* General Comment 7, para.1, and General Comment 20, para.2.
[160] *See* UN Doc. A/2929, p.87, para.14. [161] *See* Nowak (above n.5) at p.139.
[162] *See* al-Saleh, O.A., 'The Rights of the Individual to Personal Security in Islam' in Bassiouni, M.C. (ed.), *The Islamic Criminal Justice System* (1982) p.72.
[163] Bassiouni, M.C., 'Sources of Islamic Law, and the Protection of Human Rights in the Islamic Criminal Justice System', in Bassiouni (above n.162) at p.19.
[164] *See* al-Saleh (above n.162).
[165] He ruled under the Umayyad Caliphate between 717–720CE.

oath. By God, it is better that they should face God with their offenses than I should have to meet God for torturing them.[166]

Muslim jurists thus generally agree that torture or cruel and inhuman treatment or punishment is prohibited during the interrogation of offenders.[167] Article 20 of the OIC Cairo Declaration on Human Rights in Islam thus provides that:

It is not permitted to subject (an individual) to physical or psychological torture or to any form of humiliation, cruelty or indignity. Nor is it permitted to subject an individual to medical or scientific experimentation without his consent or at the risk of his health or of his life. Nor is it permitted to promulgate emergency laws that would provide executive authority for such actions.

The severity of some criminal punishments under Islamic law has however been brought into issue within international human rights discourse. Bannerman has observed for example that 'it would be foolish to deny that in Western eyes today, amputations, executions, stoning, and corporal punishment are brutal',[168] and according to Mayer 'laws imposing penalties like amputations, cross amputations, and crucifixions would seem to be in obvious violation of Article 7 (of the ICCPR)'.[169] The UN Special Rapporteur on Sudan had in his February 1994 Report also criticized the application of the Islamic law punishments in the Sudan as violating the prohibition of cruel, inhuman, and degrading punishment under international law. Likewise, the HRC has observed in its consideration of the report of some Muslim States that punishments under Islamic law such as amputation, flogging, and stoning are incompatible with Article 7 of the ICCPR.[170] Some Muslim States have consistently objected to those criticisms.[171] Sudan for example has argued that this was 'an unwarranted interpretation of the international human rights instruments since they excluded from such category all punishments provided for in national legislation'.[172] Due to its topical nature in relation to international human rights law, it is important to examine the issue of Islamic criminal punishments in more detail.

---

[166] *See* al-Saleh (above n.162) at p.72.   [167] *ibid.*

[168] Bannerman, P., *Islam in Perspective* (1988) p.26; *See also* Dudley, J., 'Human Rights Practices in the Arab States: The Modern Impact of Shari'a Values' (1982) 12 *GA Journal of International and Comparative Law*, p.55 at p.74.

[169] *See* Mayer, A.E., 'A Critique of An-Na'im's Assessment of Islamic Criminal Justice' in Lindholm, T., and Vogt, K. (eds.), *Islamic law Reform and Human Rights: Challenges and Rejoinders* (1993) p.37 at p.47.

[170] *See* e.g. Concluding Observations on Sudan (1997) UN Doc. CCPR/C/79/Add.85, para.9; Concluding Observations on Libya (1994) UN Doc. CCPR/C/79/Add.45, para.9; Concluding Observations on Islamic Republic of Iran (1993) UN Doc. CCPR/C/79/Add.25, para.11.

[171] *See* Baderin (above n.2) at pp.288–293.

[172] *See* UN Doc. E/CN.4/1994/122. *See* also Sudan's contentions in that regard before the HRC in UN Doc. CCPR/C/SR.1628 (1998).

Criminal justice is an important aspect of public law. It is distributed by the State to maintain both public and private security within the State. The criminal jurisdiction of a State is thus generally not restricted to its nationals only but may extend also to foreign nationals who violate its laws. Normally, the determination of what constitutes criminal offences in a particular State and the prescription of sanctions and punishments for them are not the concern of international law but are within the discretion and sovereign authority of individual States. Although there are certain offences common to all civilized nations of the world, the punishments prescribed for them may differ in each State. While sovereign States have the autonomy of prescribing punishments for offences within their jurisdiction, international human rights law under the prohibition of torture also prohibits 'cruel, inhuman or degrading' punishments.[173] International human rights instruments do not however define 'cruel, inhuman, or degrading punishment'. It must be noted also that in defining torture, the CAT excluded 'pain or suffering arising from, inherent in or incidental to lawful sanctions'.[174]

The HRC has however observed in its General Comment 20 to Article 7 of the ICCPR that the prohibition of cruel, inhuman, or degrading punishment 'must extend to corporal punishment, including excessive chastisement ordered as punishment for a crime...'.[175] This means that criminal sanctions of a State Party that may not amount to torture, due to the exclusion of lawful sanctions from that definition by the Torture Convention, could still be considered by the HRC as amounting to 'cruel, inhuman or degrading' punishment under Article 7 of the ICCPR if it involves corporal punishment and excessive chastisement.[176] This could be problematic because of the lack of a universal agreement on what punishments may be deemed 'cruel, inhuman or degrading'. While it is not impossible, sociological factors may actually make a universal standard of criminal punishment quite difficult to achieve.[177]

3.8.1 Islamic criminal punishments and international human rights law

Islamic law prescribes fixed punishments called *hudûd* for certain offences, retributive punishments called *qisâs* for other offences and discretionary punishments called *ta'zîr* for certain others. The *qisâs* and *ta'zîr* are variable

---

[173] *See* also Art. 5 UDHR (1948) and Art. 16 of the CAT (1984) 1465 UNTS, p.85.

[174] *See* Art. 1 Convention Against Torture (1984) (above n.154).

[175] *See* UN Doc. HRI\GEN\1\Rev.1 at 30 (1994), para.5.

[176] *See* An-Na'im, A.A., 'Towards a Cross-Cultural Approach to Defining International Standards of Human Rights: The Meaning of Cruel, Inhuman, or Degrading Treatment or Punishment', in An-Na'im, A.A. (ed.), *Human Rights in Cross-Cultural Perspectives: A Quest For Consensus* (1992) p.19 at p.29.

[177] *See ibid.*, at p.32 for an illustration of the difficulty that may be encountered in the effort to find a universal standard of criminal punishment.

punishments and within the discretion of the victim of the offence (or the heirs) and the judge (or State) respectively. A Muslim State's conformity to an international standard of punishment in crimes that attract *qisâs* or *ta'zîr* punishments under Islamic law therefore depends on the political will and other international considerations of a particular State. The tension with international human rights law is essentially in respect of the *hudûd* punishments which are fixed and invariable as long as the crime is fully established as provided by Islamic law.[178]

The *hudûd* punishments are generally prescribed for six offences under traditional Islamic law. They are: amputation of a hand for theft *(sariqah)*;[179] death, crucifixion, cross-amputation of the hand and foot or banishment for rebellion or armed robbery *(hirâbah)*;[180] stoning to death for adultery and one hundred lashes for fornication *(zinâ)*;[181] eighty lashes for false accusation of unchastity *(qadhf)*;[182] death for apostasy *(riddah)*; and forty or eighty lashes for intoxication *(sharb al-khamr)*.[183] While there is consensus among Islamic jurists on the first four punishments, there are some differences about the offences of intoxication and apostasy. The majority of jurists concede that intoxication is a *hadd*-type offence while others consider it as *ta'zîr*-type. Also the punishment for intoxication is based on *Sunnah,* but while the *Hanafî, Hanbalî* and *Mâlikî* schools hold that the number of lashes for intoxication is eighty, Imâm al-Shâfi'î, and a few other jurists held it to be forty lashes. Some

---

[178] *See* e.g. El-Awa, M.S., *Punishment in Islamic Law* (1982) p.1.

[179] *See* Q5:38 which says: 'As to the thief, male or female, cut off his or her hand: a punishment by way of example, from God, for their crime . . .'.

[180] This punishment is based on Q5:33 which says: 'The punishment of those who wage war against God and His Messenger, and strive with might and main for mischief through the land is: execution, or crucifixion, or the cutting off of hands and feet from opposite sides, or exile from the land . . .'.

[181] Q24:2 says: 'The woman and the man guilty of zinâ, flog each of them with a hundred stripes; Let no compassion move you in their case, in a matter prescribed by God if you believe in God and the last day . . .'. While Muslim jurists agree that the term *zinâ* covers both adultery and fornication, the punishment prescribed here is applied only to unmarried persons (fornication) while according to the *Sunnah* the punishment for adultery in the case of married persons (adultery) is stoning to death *(rajm)*. While all the orthodox schools of Islamic jurisprudence uphold the punishment of stoning for adultery based on the *Sunnah*, the *Mu'tazilah* and *Khawârij* sects opposed the punishment on grounds that it has no existing Qur'anic evidence. *See* al-Jazîrî, A.R., *Kitâb al-Fiqh alâ al-Madhâhib al-'Arba'ah*(Arabic) (7th Ed., 1986) Vol.5, p.69. The death penalty by stoning for adultery under traditional Islamic law has also been quite topical. *See* e.g. the Pakistan Federal Shariat Court cases of *Hazoor Bakhsh v. Federation of Pakistan* (1981) 31 PLD (FSC) 145 and *Federation of Pakistan v. Hazoor Bakhsh and Others* (1983) 35 PLD (FSC) 255. *See also* Rizvi, S.A.H., *et al.*, 'Adultery and Fornication in Islamic Criminal Law: A Debate' in Mahmood, T., *et al.* (eds.), *Criminal Law in Islam and the Muslim World* (1996) pp.223–241 for a debate on the punishment of *zinâ* under Islamic law, and Maududi, A.A., *Towards Understanding the Qur'an: English version of Tafhîm al-Qur'ân* (1998) Vol. VII, pp.149–179 for a detailed discourse on the nature and punishment of adultery/fornication under Islamic law.

[182] Q24:4 says: 'And those who launch a charge against chaste women and produce not four witnesses (to support their allegations) flog them with eighty stripes . . .'.

[183] *See* e.g. Safwat, S.M., 'Offences and Penalties in Islamic Law' (1982) 26 *Islamic Quarterly*, p.169.

contemporary Muslim scholars and jurists also argue that apostasy *simpliciter* is not a *hadd*-type offence and is not punishable with death on its own except when it involves acts of rebellion against the State.[184]

From the perspective of international human rights law, Mayer has argued that these *hudûd* punishments are inconsistent 'with modern penological principles and modern human rights norms'.[185] There is also the argument that most Muslims who advocate the implementation of the *hudûd* punishments in Muslim countries are themselves quite ambivalent about them because of the severity of the punishments.[186] While Muslim jurists and scholars may not subscribe to the categorization of the *hudûd* punishments as 'cruel and inhuman', both classical and contemporary scholars of Islamic law do not deny the harshness of the punishments. Their justification however is that the harshness of the *hudûd* punishments are meant to, and actually do, serve as a deterrent to the offences for which they are prescribed. Muslim jurists have further argued that the standard of proof for all the *hudûd* offences under Islamic law is very arduous. They must be proved beyond any atom of doubt based on the Tradition of the Prophet in which he said: 'Avert the *hudûd* punishment in case of doubt . . . for error in clemency is better than error in imposing punishment',[187] which often makes the implementation of the punishments rare. Commenting on adultery and fornication *(zinâ)*for instance, Shalabî pointed out that the proof required makes the punishment for *zinâ* applicable only to those who committed the offence openly without any consideration for public morality at all, and in a manner that is almost impossible and intolerable in any civilized society.[188]

In a similar vein during a Conference in Riyadh, Saudi Arabia in 1972 on 'Moslem Doctrine and Human Rights' between delegates of the Saudi Arabian Ministry of Justice and delegates from the Council of Europe,[189] a member of the Saudi Arabian delegate Dr Al-Dawalibi observed as follows:

> I have been in this country (Saudi Arabia) for seven years . . . and I never saw, or heard of, any amputation of the hand for stealing. This is because crime is extremely rare. So, all that remains of that punishment is its harshness, which has made it possible for all to live in perfect security and tranquillity, and for those who are tempted to steal, to keep their hands whole. Formerly, when these regions were ruled by the French-inspired Penal Code, under the Ottoman Empire, pilgrims travelling between the two Holy Cities—Mecca and Medina, could not feel secure for their purse or their life, unless they had a strong escort. But when this country became the Saudi Kingdom, the Koranic Law was enforced, crime immediately disappeared. A traveller, then, could

---

[184] *See* Section on apostasy at para.3.19.1 below.

[185] *See* Mayer (above n.169) at p.37.

[186] *See generally, ibid.*, pp.37–60 and Bannerman, P., *Islam in Perspective* (1988) p.26.

[187] *See* e.g. Al-Zuhayli, *Al-Fiqh al-Islâmî wa-Adillatuh* (Arabic) (1997) Vol.7, p.5307.

[188] Shalabî, M.M., *al-Fiqh al-Islâmiyy Bayn al-Mithâliyyah al-Wâqi'iyyah* (Arabic) (1960) p.201.

[189] Comprising Prof. Sean MacBride, former President of Council of Europe, Prof. Karel Vasak, Prof. Henri Laoust and Maitre Jean-Louis Aujol.

journey, not only between the Holy Cities, but even from Al-Dahran on the Gulf to Jeddah on the Red Sea, and traverse a distance of more than one thousand and five hundred kilometers across the desert all alone in his private car, without harbouring any fear or worry about his life or property, be it worth millions of dollars, and be he a complete foreigner.[190]

Another delegate also stated that:

In this manner, in the Kingdom of Saudi Arabia, where Islamic Law is enforced, state money is transferred from one town to another, from one bank to another, in an ordinary car, without any escort or protection, but the car driver. Tell me, Gentlemen: in any of your Western States, would you be ready to transfer money from one bank to another, in any of your capitals, without the protection of a strong police force and the necessary number of armoured cars?[191]

The HRC has however ruled out any limitation or justification in respect of Article 7.[192] The European Human Rights Court has also held under Article 3 of the European Convention in *Tyrer v. UK* that: 'A punishment does not lose its degrading character just because it is . . . an effective deterrent or aid to crime control'.[193] The HRC has further observed that Article 7 must be read in conjunction with Article 2 of the Covenant to the effect that a State Party is under an obligation specifically to abrogate any law considered incompatible with Article 7 of the Covenant.[194]

Confidence in the deterrent nature of the *hudûd* punishments is just one of its influencing factors within Muslim societies. The most influencing factor however is the divine weight of the *hudûd* punishments since they are injunctions of the *Sharî'ah*. El-Awa has pointed out that while the considerations of social utility form the basis of the theories of punishment in Western penal systems, 'in Islamic law the theory of punishment is based on the belief in the divine revelation contained in the Qur'an and the Sunna of Prophet Muhammad'.[195] The *hudûd* punishments are thus classified as the rights of God *(huqûq Allah)*. They are prescribed as punishment for violating divine injunctions that protect public interest and are therefore not remissible. Al-Mâwardî had pointed out that the *hudûd* are 'deterrent punishments prescribed by God to prevent

---

[190] *See* Ministry of Justice (ed.), *Conference of Riyad on Moslem Doctrine and Human Rights in Islam (March 23, 1972)* p.8. Saudi Embassy News Website: at http://www.saudiembassy.net/press_release/hr-72.html [1/3/03].

[191] *ibid. See also* Mourad, F.A., and al-Sa'aty, H., 'Impact of Islamic Penal Law on Crime Situation in Saudi Arabia: Findings of A Research Study' in Mahmood, T., *et al.* (ed.), *Criminal Law in Islam and the Muslim World* (1996) pp.340–374 for an empirical comparative study on the crime situation in Saudi Arabia. [192]General Comment 20, para.3.

[193] Above n.156 at para.31.

[194] General Comment 20, para.14. *See also* para.3.4 above on legislative obligations of State Parties under the Covenant and the limitation of Muslim States in that regard under Islamic law. [195] El-Awa (above n.178) at p.xi.

Men from committing what He forbade . . . '.[196] For the above reasons Muslim
jurists hold that their severity cannot be questioned.[197]

While the need to punish those guilty of crimes is appreciated under international human rights law, the contention has been that offenders and criminals
are still human beings and must therefore be treated with some dignity. Thus the
punishment for crimes must not be excessively severe, degrading, or inhuman
but rather aim at reforming the offender. While Muslims are under a religious
obligation to believe in the divine nature of the *hudûd* punishments and not
question its severity, the same cannot be said of non-Muslims. Since criminal
punishments are generally not restricted to Muslims alone within the Muslim
State it becomes necessary to examine the principles of the Islamic criminal
punishments outside the scope of strict divine penology.

From a pragmatic perspective, the factors that are usually considered in the
prescription of punishments for crimes are: the interests of the society, that of
the victim, and that of the offender. Thus, penological policy is usually based
on the theories of deterrence, retribution, and reform. Although there may be
some overlapping, basically deterrence may be viewed as serving the interest
of society, retribution that of the victim, and reform that of the offender. There
could indeed be a difficulty in defining a balance between these interests in
the prescription of punishments for particular offences. For instance, while
a generality of opinion in a particular society may reveal that a particular
punishment is too severe for a particular offence, the opinion of victims of that
offence in the same society, depending on their ordeals, might reveal that no
punishment is too severe for perpetrators of such offences. It may be argued
too that offenders are products of the society, so it is their reform that must be
given priority in the determination of a penal policy.

Against this background, El-Awa has pointed out that the *hudûd* punishment
'cares very little for the criminal and his reform, and concentrates on preventing
the commission of offences'.[198] That is, it gives priority to the interest of society, by wanting to prevent, *ab initio*, the occurrence of the *hadd*-type offences
through a deterrent and retributive approach. This suggests that Islamic law
aims at an ideal society. But if, despite the deterrent nature of the severe
punishments, the offences still occur, there would then arise the question of
whether or not the society has played a contributory role for the commitment
of the offence. Thus, even in the enforcement of the *hudûd*, the rule also is that
there must exist an ideal Islamic society. Where it can be reasonably proved
that the offender was a product of the society's sociological problems then his

---

[196] *See* al-Mâwardî, A., *al-Ahkâm al-Sultâniyyah* (Arabic) (1386AH). *See also* the English
translation by Yate, A., *The Laws of Islamic Governance* (1996).
[197] *See generally*, e.g. Ibn Qayyim al-Jawziyyah, *I'lâm al-Muwaqqi'în 'An Rabb al-'Alamîn*
(Arabic) (1996) and Abû Zahrah, S.M., *al-Jarîmah wa al-'Uqûbah fî al-Fiqh al-Islâmî* (Arabic)
(n.d.).
[198] El-Awa (above n.178) at pp.23–35 and p.134.

interest must be taken into consideration and the *hudûd* punishments may be mitigated. There is evidence that the Prophet suspended the enforcement of the *hadd* punishment for theft during war, and the second Caliph, Umar, suspended its enforcement at a time of widespread famine in Medina.[199] El-Awa also referred to the account of Abû Yûsuf, the great eighth century *Hanafî* jurist, in his famous work *Kitâb al-Kharâj*,[200] to indicate that circumstances could make it necessary to relax or suspend the enforcement of the *hudûd* punishment by the ruling authority.[201] It could be argued therefore that, while to Muslims the prescription of the *hudûd* punishment is not questionable, its application by the State is however not in isolation of other sociological factors within the State. The determination of the enabling or inhibiting sociological factors for the application of the *hudûd* punishment is, as shown by the examples above, left to the discretion of the State to be exercised in good faith and the best interest of society and the populace (*maslahah*).

While the *hudûd* punishment is deterrent in nature for the public interest, the *ta'zîr* punishments, due to the wide authority that the State has in its prescription, provide means for punishments that aim for the criminal's reform. The *qisâs* punishments complete the cycle by taking the interest of the victim into consideration in the enforcement of retributive punishments.[202] It could be argued therefore that the three tiers of punishment under Islamic law are interpretable pragmatically to accommodate modern penological principles depending on the political and humanitarian will of the ruling authority.

Against the foregoing background, the conflict between criminal punishments under Islamic law and the prohibition of cruel, inhuman, and degrading punishments under international human rights law can be addressed from two dimensions. The first dimension concerns the punishment of non-*hudûd* offences. Since the State has discretion under Islamic law to impose less harsh punishments for non-*hudûd* offences, Muslim States can thus effectively exercise that discretion in cognizance of their international human rights law obligations, and directly proscribe their non-*hudûd* punishments that violate the prohibition of cruel, inhuman, and degrading punishments. It must be observed however that apart from religious factors, developing nations, for many reasons that include resource limitations, do often prefer an effectively deterrent, 'harsh' criminal punishment over a 'humane' reformative one even where the legislative authority lies completely within the prerogative of the State.

---

[199] *See* e.g. Abû Zahrah, M., *Usûl al-Fiqh* (Arabic) (1958) pp.222–228; Ibn Qayyim al-Jawziyyah, *I'lâm al-Muwaqqi'în* (Arabic) (1996) Vol.1, p.185. *See also* Kamali, M.H., *Principles of Islamic Jurisprudence* (1991) p.247 and p.270.

[200] Abû Yûsuf, Y., *Kitâb al-Kharâj* (Arabic) (1352A.H.) pp.149–152.

[201] El-Awa (above n.178) at p.137. *See also* Qutb, M., *Islam the Misunderstood Religion* (1978) pp.165–171.

[202] The victim (or his heir) in *Qisâs* cases has a mediating role in the punishment of the offender.

The second dimension concerns the *hudûd* offences, which are specifically prescribed by direct injunctions of the Qur'an. An-Na'im has observed in respect of the *hudûd* punishments that 'in all Muslim societies, the possibility of human judgment regarding the appropriateness or cruelty of a punishment decreed by God is simply out of the question', and that '[n]either Islamic re-interpretation nor cross-cultural dialogue is likely to lead to the[ir] *total abolition ... as a matter of Islamic law*'.[203] Questioning the *hudûd* punishments is considered as questioning the divine wisdom underlying them and impugning the divinity of the Qur'an and the theocentric nature of Islamic law. From an Islamic legal perspective the conflict may however be addressed indirectly through procedural means. Islamic legalists concede the fact that it is lawful to utilize procedural devices to avert the (*hudûd*) penalty without impugning the Law, the Prophet having advised that one should avert the *hudûd* punishment in case of doubt because error in clemency is better than error in imposing punishment.[204] Chief Justice Afzal Zullah (as he then was) of the Pakistan Supreme Court had thus observed in *The State v. Ghulam Ali*[205] that:

an uncontroverted principle of Hudood [is] that not only the maximum benefit of every reasonable doubt will be extended to the accused, but also ... effort is to be made not to inflict the Hadd so long [as] it can be avoided by all legitimate and established means.[206]

Thus even though Muslim States cannot, for the divine weight, directly proscribe the *hudûd* punishments, they can regulate its application through legally valid procedural devices under Islamic law.[207] One way adopted, for example, by the Islamic Republic of Pakistan to get around this difficulty is through strict adherence to procedural and evidential requirements for those Qur'anic offences. This often results in the application of *ta'zîr* (discretionary) punishments due to the difficulty of satisfying the required valid evidence for the enforcement of the *hudûd* punishments.[208] Mayer has however raised the question that 'if one attempts such a compromise, how does one go about defending it against fundamentalist critics, who are likely to accuse one of failing to take divine commands seriously?'[209] That question highlights the susceptibility of the issue, but can be addressed through internal dialogue within Muslim States and among Muslim jurists. It is establishable by reference to classical Islamic jurisprudence that averting

---

[203] *See* An-Na'im (above n.176) at pp.35–36 (emphasis added).

[204] *See* e.g. Al-Zuhayli, *Al-Fiqh al-Islâmî wa-Adillatuh* (Arabic) (1997) Vol.7, p.5307.

[205] (1986) 38 PLD (S.Ct) 741.   [206] *ibid.*, at p.759.

[207] For an analysis of the practice in Libya *see* Mahmood, T., 'Legal System of Modern Libya: Enforcement of Islamic Penal Laws' in Mahmood, T., *et al.* (eds.), *Criminal Law in Islam and the Muslim World* (1996) pp.375–388 and Mayer, A.E., 'Libyan Legislation in Defense of Arabo-Islamic Sexual Mores', in Mahmood, *ibid.*, pp.389–421.

[208] *See* e.g. Mehdi, R., *The Islamization of Law in Pakistan* (1994) p.115.

[209] *See* Mayer (above n.169) at p.47.

hudûd punishments through procedural means does not amount to impugning divine commands. Such aversion does not necessarily mean that there would be no punishment at all, but that through adherence to strict and lawful procedural rules of Islamic law *ta'zîr* punishments are applied instead of the *hudûd* punishments for difficulty of proof, as highlighted by Chief Justice Zullah above.

Although the obligations of States parties under international human rights instruments often require direct legislation abolishing punishments considered cruel, inhuman, and degrading, such direct legislation can divest a ruling authority of its Islamic legitimacy in many parts of the Muslim world today. While most Muslim States do not currently apply the *hudûd* punishments they also do not have legislation specifically prohibiting the punishments. The reverence of Qur'anic injunctions by Muslims thus puts at a crossroads the Human Rights Committee's demand on Muslim States to abolish the *hudûd* punishments directly. With the current resurgence and restoration of Islamic law in many Muslim States, it is more feasible to seek for reconciliation between the *hudûd* punishments and the prohibition of cruel, inhuman, and degrading punishments under international human rights law indirectly through legal procedural shields available within Islamic law.

3.9 FREEDOM FROM SLAVERY, SERVITUDE AND FORCED LABOUR

Article 8

1. No one shall be held in slavery; slavery and the slave-trade in all their forms shall be prohibited.
2. No one shall be held in servitude.
3. (a) No one shall be required to perform forced or compulsory labour;
   (b) Paragraph 3 (a) shall not be held to preclude, in countries where imprisonment with hard labour may be imposed as a punishment for a crime, the performance of hard labour in pursuance of sentence to such punishment by a competent court;
   (c) For the purpose of this paragraph the term 'forced or compulsory labour' shall not include:
      (i) Any work or service, not referred to in subparagraph (b), normally required of a person who is under detention in consequence of a lawful order of a court, or of a person during conditional release from such detention;
      (ii) Any service of a military character and, in countries where conscientious objection is recognized, any national service required by law of conscientious objectors;

(iii) Any service exacted in cases of emergency or calamity threatening the life or well-being of the community;

(iv) Any work or service which forms part of normal civil obligations.

Article 8 is aimed at protecting individuals from the most deplorable and degrading exploitation by fellow beings. The prohibition of slavery, slave trade and servitude is total, without exception and is non-derogable under Article 4(1) of the Covenant irrespective of whether or not the victim has consented to slavery or bondage.[210] The prohibition of slavery qualifies as an established norm of customary international law.[211] The prohibition of forced or compulsory labour is however subject to five exceptions under the Covenant, viz, (i) the performance of hard labour in pursuance of a sentence imposed by a competent court, (ii) any other work or service required of a person in lawful detention or during conditional release from such detention, (iii) any service of a military character or national service required by law for conscientious objectors to military service, (iv) any service exacted in cases of emergency or calamity threatening the life or well-being of the community, and (v) any work or service which forms part of normal civil obligation.[212] Apart from the traditional forms of slavery, servitude, and forced labour, other forms of modern slavery such as traffic in women for prostitution, exploitation of children, debt bondage, and exploitation of migrant workers have also been condemned in a UN Report on Slavery published in 1984.[213]

Slavery was widely practised in most parts of the world, including Arabia, before the advent of Islam in the seventh century. Despite the heinous nature of the institution it was a big source of labour and income in both the East and West. Slaves were treated in a most inhuman and undignified fashion. No philosophy that promoted the concept of human dignity could have reasonably been insensitive to the plight of slaves in those periods. Thus in the spirit of reformation, both the Qur'an and *Sunnah* greatly encouraged and recommended the manumission and humane treatment of slaves.[214] The Prophet and his companions also set many examples in the liberation of slaves.[215] Although there is no direct injunction on its abolition, the *Sharî'ah* also contains no direct provisions that authorizes or supports slavery. There is consensus among Islamic jurists that freeing slaves is a recommended act, indeed it is the first of the options prescribed in the Qur'an as expiation for certain sins.[216] While some scholars

---

[210] *See* Nowak (above n.5) at p.143ff; also Dinstein (above n.86) at pp.126–128.

[211] *See* e.g. American Law Institute, *Restatement (Third) of Foreign Relations Law*, para.702.

[212] *See* Art. 8(3)(b) and (c) of ICCPR. *See also* Nowak (above n.5) at pp.149–157.

[213] *See* Whitaker, B., Report on Slavery, UN Doc E/CN.4/Sub.2/1982/20/Rev.1, UN Sales No. E.84.XIV.1, p.10; *see also* the UN Convention for the Suppression of the Traffic in Persons and of the Exploitation of the Prostitution of Others (1949).

[214] *See* e.g. Q2:177; Q4:92; Q9:60; Q24:33; Q58:3; Q90:13.

[215] *See* e.g. Maududi, A.A., *Human Rights in Islam* (1993) p.20.

[216] *See* e.g. Q4:92 and Q58:3.

view that those steps pointed towards abolition, and slavery should therefore be considered as abolished today under Islamic law,[217] some others submit the contrary. For instance, while Tabandeh acknowledged those humane steps taken by Islam towards slaves, he still argued that 'should the legal condition for the enslavement of anyone be proven... Islam would be bound to recognise such slavery as legal, even though recommending the freeing of the person...'.[218] An-Na'im has rightly argued against that opinion, but, on the other hand, also queried the continual existence of rules on slavery in the traditional books of Islamic jurisprudence and asserted that this is a fundamental human rights issue for Muslims until slavery is specifically abolished in Islamic law.[219]

It is clear to see, however, that the rules in the traditional books of Islamic jurisprudence do not sanction or advocate slavery, they are mostly in respect of manumission and other ameliorating rules on the treatment of slaves. Those rules regulating the affairs of slaves found in traditional Islamic jurisprudence must thus be viewed inter-temporally. The problem of slavery could not have been solved radically in isolation of the prevailing social circumstances of that period. While Islam had, on one hand, endured the practice due to social factors of that period, it simultaneously promoted its gradual abolition on the other. Today most Muslim countries have ratified international instruments abolishing slavery or slavery-like practices, and no Muslim country will formally admit the practice of slavery. There is thus general consensus in Muslim States today against slavery. This can be adopted into a legal consensus *(ijmâ')* on its abolition in Islamic law. *Ijmâ'* (legal consensus) constitutes a strong 'source' of law in the absence of a direct text of the Qur'an or the *Sunnah* on any issue. It is appreciated that traditionally, *ijmâ'* was restricted to the consensus of the legists *(mujtahidûn),* meaning traditional Islamic theologians,[220] but that view is considered too restrictive for contemporary needs because contemporary international law and policy-making involve complex techniques and considerations beyond such restrictive consensus.[221] There can be no higher consensus on the abolition of slavery than this State practice of all Muslim States, none of which will officially sanction the practice of slavery today within its jurisdiction. This is strengthened by the fact that slavery contradicts the great emphasis laid by Islam on serving God alone. All human beings are referred to as servants or slaves *(ibâd)* of God and can thus not be the slaves of other human beings at the same time. Thus, the doctrine of

---

[217] *See* e.g. Malekian, F., *The Concept of Islamic International Criminal Law: A Comparative Study* (1994) pp.83–89; and Al-Zuhaylî (above n.78) at Vol.3, pp.2019–2020.
[218] Tabandeh, S., *Muslim Commentary on the Universal Declaration of Human Rights* (1970) p.27. [219] An-Na'im, A.A., *Towards An Islamic Reformation* (1990) pp.172–175.
[220] *See al-Âmidî, S.A., al-Ihkâm fî Usûl al-Ahkâm* (Arabic) (1402AH), Vol.1, p.196 and p.226, *see also* Kamali (above n.199) at pp.168–194, particularly p.173.
[221] *See* AbuSulayman, A.A., *Towards an Islamic Theory of International Relations: New Directions for Islamic Methodology and Thought* (1993) p.86.

the overall objective of the *Sharî'ah* (*maqâsid al-Sharî'ah*) strongly supports the consensus on the total abolition of slavery under Islamic law.[222]

The fact that most modern Muslim States are States Parties to the international conventions prohibiting slavery and slave trade indicates the general consensus of Muslims on the compatibility of the prohibition of slavery with the principles of Islamic law. This is further buttressed by Article 11(a) of the OIC Cairo Declaration on Human Rights in Islam, which provides that:

> Human beings are born free, and no one has the right to enslave, humiliate, oppress or exploit them, and there can be no subjugation but to God the Most-High.

3.10 THE RIGHT TO LIBERTY AND SECURITY OF PERSON

Article 9

1. Everyone has the right to liberty and security of person. No one shall be subjected to arbitrary arrest or detention. No one shall be deprived of his liberty except on such grounds and in accordance with such procedure as are established by law.
2. Anyone who is arrested shall be informed, at the time of arrest, of the reasons for his arrest and shall be promptly informed of any charges against him.
3. Anyone arrested or detained on a criminal charge shall be brought promptly before a judge or other officer authorized by law to exercise judicial power and shall be entitled to trial within a reasonable time or to release. It shall not be the general rule that persons awaiting trial shall be detained in custody, but release may be subject to guarantees to appear for trial, at any other stage of the judicial proceedings, and, should occasion arise, for execution of the judgement.
4. Anyone who is deprived of his liberty by arrest or detention shall be entitled to take proceedings before a court, in order that that court may decide without delay on the lawfulness of his detention and order his release if the detention is not lawful.
5. Anyone who has been the victim of unlawful arrest or detention shall have an enforceable right to compensation.

The right to liberty and security of person is perhaps next only to the right to life. The State may however deprive a person of his liberty only in accordance with the due process of law. Article 9(1) is thus aimed, on one hand, at preventing the arbitrary and unlawful deprivation of the liberty of individuals by the State, and, on the other hand, providing for the positive obligation of the State to ensure the security of all persons within its jurisdiction. Article 9(2) to 9(5) provides the necessary procedural guarantees to ensure that liberty is only deprived according to law.[223] Although the deprivation of liberty is more often

---

[222] *See generally*, Freamon, B.K. 'Slavery, Freedom, and the Doctrine of Consensus in Islamic Jurisprudence' (1998) 11 *Harvard Human Rights Journal*, p.1; and also Hassan, R., 'On Human Rights and the Qur'anic Perspective' in Swidler, A. (ed.), *Human Rights in Religious Traditions* (1982) p.51 at pp.58–59.

[223] For comprehensive illustration of the procedural guarantees under Article 9(2)–9(5) *see* Joseph, Schultz and Castan (above n.23) at p.291.

associated with criminal offences and imprisonment, the HRC has stated that Article 9(1) extends the prohibition of arbitrary deprivation of liberty to cases of 'mental illness, vagrancy, drug addiction, educational purposes, immigration control, etc'.[224] Thus, it has indicated that deprivation of liberty for these purposes must also be in accordance with law to ensure that the inherent liberty of the human person is fully secured from violation except for justifiable and necessary reasons.

In *Katombe Tshishimbi v. Zaire*[225] the HRC also observed that the right to security under Article 9 must not be limited only to situations of formal deprivation of liberty but extends to threats to the personal security of non-detained persons within a State's jurisdiction.[226] Thus, the right to security 'applies to persons in and out of detention'.[227]

The right to personal liberty and security is also fully sanctioned under Islamic law.[228] It is the duty of the State to ensure it. The State cannot violate the personal liberty and security of anyone without justification. There is evidence for this from the practice of the Prophet Muhammad as reported in a Tradition by Abû Dâwûd. Some persons were arrested during the Prophet's time in Medina on suspicion. While the Prophet was giving a sermon in the mosque a man stood up and asked: 'O Prophet of God! Why have my neighbours been arrested and detained?' The Prophet kept quiet, expecting the officer in charge of the arrests and detention who was present in the mosque, to give an explanation. The complainant asked the question a second and a third time, and when there was no answer from the officer in charge, the Prophet ordered that the detained persons be released since their arrest and detention could not be justified.[229] This incident accommodates the modern constitutional law remedy of habeas corpus guaranteed under Article 9(4). There is therefore no conflict between Islamic law and the important procedural guarantees to ensure liberty and security of the individual under Article 9(2) to 9(5). For example, scholars representing all schools of Islamic jurisprudence unanimously agreed during the Pakistan Constitutional debate of 1953 that the right of habeas corpus was in consonance with Islamic law and that the *Sharî'ah* fully recognizes the right of the individual to be able to move the highest court for redress against any unlawful detention.[230]

---

[224] *See* General Comment 8, para.1.
[225] Communication No. 542/1993, UN Doc. CCPR/C/53/D/542/1993(1996), para.5.4.
[226] *See also Delgado Páez v. Colombia,* Communication No. 195/1985 (12 July 1990), UN Doc. Supp. No. 40, para.5.5 (A/45/40) at 43 (1990).
[227] *See* Joseph, Schultz and Castan (above n.23) at p.207.
[228] *See* e.g. al-Saleh (above n.162) at pp.55–90.
[229] *See* Maududi, A.A., *Human Rights in Islam* (1993) p.26.
[230] *See* Maududi, A.A., *The Islamic Law and Constitution* (1997) pp.338–340.

Islamic jurists are thus agreed that a person cannot be deprived of his liberty without a legally valid justification.[231] Abû Yûsuf, the great eighth century *Hanafî* jurist, in his famous work *Kitâb al-Kharâj*, had instructed the Caliph Harûn al-Rashîd to order all governors in the provinces to investigate into the affairs of prisoners daily. They should punish those guilty of a charge and release them forthwith and release immediately those who are not charged with any specific offence.[232] The OIC Cairo Declaration on Human Rights in Islam thus provides, *inter alia*, in Article 18(a) that: 'Everyone shall have a right to live in security for himself, his religion, his dependants, his honour and his property', and in Article 20 that: 'It is not permitted without legitimate reason to arrest an individual, or restrict his freedom, to exile or to punish him'.

In the context of international human rights standards this must certainly accommodate the right to be tried within a reasonable time, right to bail, and right to compensation for illegal detentions as provided under Article 9 of the ICCPR.

In its General Comment 28, the HRC observed that laws and practices which 'deprive women of their liberty on an arbitrary or unequal basis, such as by confinement within the house' may violate Article 9.[233] It is sometimes alleged that Islamic law requires the confinement of women within the house. Many Muslim scholars and jurists refute this. According to El-Bahnassawi:

A Muslim woman was not doomed to be a crippled member in the society, with the sole task of welcoming her husband at his arrival and bidding him farewell at his departure. Stories reported from the early days of Islam demonstrated that women, immunized by their deep faith and chastity, had performed similar work as men . . . The Muslim society did not object to woman's work in many fields. Needless to say, the Prophet did not deny woman's active participation in social life and, in some instances, beside man, as in military operations aimed at defending the religion of Islam.[234]

This is supportable by the fact that the Qur'an had earlier prescribed confinement within the house as punishment for women who committed illegal sexual intercourse (sexual lewdness) under Islamic law.[235] If women were generally required to be confined within the house, its prescription as punishment would have then been meaningless.

3.11 THE RIGHT TO A HUMANE INCARCERATION SYSTEM

Article 10

1. All persons deprived of their liberty shall be treated with humanity and with respect for the inherent dignity of the human person.

---

[231] *See* e.g. Ibn Qayyim al-Jawziyyah., *Al-Turuq al-Hukmiyyah fî al-Siyâsah al-Shar'iyyah* (Arabic) (1961) p.103 and Ibn Hazm, A.A., *al-Muhallâ*, (Arabic) (n.d.) Vol.11, p.141.
[232] *See* e.g. Ali, A.A. (Trans.), *Kitab-ul-Kharaj* (1979) p.303.
[233] General Comment 28, para.14.   [234] El-Bahnassawi (above n.59) at p.64.
[235] Q4:15.

2. (a) Accused persons shall, save in exceptional circumstances, be segregated from convicted persons and shall be subject to separate treatment appropriate to their status as unconvicted persons;
   (b) Accused juvenile persons shall be separated from adults and brought as speedily as possible for adjudication.
3. The penitentiary system shall comprise treatment of prisoners the essential aim of which shall be their reformation and social rehabilitation. Juvenile offenders shall be segregated from adults and be accorded treatment appropriate to their age and legal status.

Public interest and the right to security of others may sometimes demand that certain persons be incarcerated in accordance with law as indicated in Article 9 above. Article 10 ensures that any such incarcerated person is still 'treated with humanity and with respect for the inherent dignity of the human person'.[236] The usual association of incarcerations with criminal offences and imprisonment mentioned above is portrayed here also by the references to 'accused persons' and 'treatment of prisoners' in Article 10(2) and 10(3). The HRC has pointed out that the right to humane treatment during incarceration is not restricted only to prisons but also includes 'for example, hospitals (particularly psychiatric hospitals), detention camps or correctional institutions' etc.[237] Incarcerated persons shall not be tortured or subjected to inhuman treatment and their living conditions must also be humane.

The presumption of innocence until conviction is protected by the provision in Article 10(2)(a) for the segregation of accused persons from convicted persons. Due to the vulnerability of juveniles, Article 10(2)(b) also provides for their separation from adults during incarceration. There is an obligation also on the State to ensure that the penitentiary system aims essentially for the reform and social rehabilitation of prisoners.

Under Islamic law, imprisonment of offenders falls within *ta'zîr* (discretionary) punishments. It is known as *habs* and could either be a preventive confinement pending investigation *(habs ihtiyâtî)*, imprisonment upon conviction for an offence, or even have a wider meaning of general deprivation of personal liberty.[238] The humane treatment of such incarcerated persons is generally covered by the rules of *asîr* (that is, captive in the custody of the State) under Islamic law. The humane treatment of captives and prisoners is found mentioned in the Qur'an.[239] Yusuf Ali observed in his commentary that in those times 'when captives of war had to earn their own food, . . . [and] prisoners . . . often starved unless food was provided for them by private friends or from their own earnings', the Qur'an declared the feeding, for God's sake, of prisoners, *inter alia*, as a means of gaining paradise in the hereafter.[240] The Prophet Muhammad is also reported to have ordered in respect of the prisoners

---

[236] Art. 10(1).
[237] *See* General Comment 9, para.1 and General Comment 21, para.2.
[238] *See* e.g. Awad (above n.135) at p.102.   [239] Q76:8.
[240] *See generally* Q76:5–22 and Commentary note 5839 to Q76:8 in Ali, A.Y., *The Meaning of the Holy Qur'ân* (1992) p.1572.

of war taken by the Muslims at the Battle of Badr as follows: 'Take heed of the admonition to treat prisoners fairly'.[241]

The Muslim jurists are agreed that since a prisoner is in the custody of the State, it is responsible for his feeding, clothing, medical care, and other essential needs. The prisoner's right to the integrity of his person, body, mind, and honour must be respected. Married prisoners are also entitled to periodic conjugal visitations.[242] Ali ibn Abî Tâlib, the fourth Caliph after the Prophet, was reported to make surprise visits to prisons to ensure the humane treatment of the inmates and to hear their complaints.[243] There are also numerous Traditions of the Prophet ordering the humane treatment and kindness of both the physically and mentally sick, whether or not under incarceration. Abû Yûsuf had stated in his *Kitâb al-Kharâj* that:

> all the Caliphs used to bestow upon the prisoners what would sustain them as regards their food and other goods and their clothing in winter and summer. The first one to do this was Ali b. Abi Talib in Iraq, then Mu'awiya did that in Syria then the rest of the Caliphs followed the practice after him.[244]

The OIC Cairo Declaration on Human Rights in Islam does not however contain any specific provision for a humane incarceration system.

3.12 FREEDOM FROM IMPRISONMENT FOR CONTRACTUAL OBLIGATION

Article 11

No one shall be imprisoned merely on the ground of inability to fulfil a contractual obligation.

Article 11 prohibits detention for liability arising from contractual obligations. There was agreement during the drafting that 'the article should cover any contractual obligations, namely, the payment of debts, performance of services or the delivery of goods'.[245] This indicates that

---

[241] *See* Tabarî, *History I*, pp.1337–1338 cited in Hamidullah, M., *Muslim Conduct of State* (Revised 7th Ed., 1977) p.214, para.441.

[242] The Saudi Arabian government is reported to apply this principle by allowing conjugal visitations to married prisoners of both sexes. *See* Al-Alfi, A.A., 'Punishment in Islamic Criminal Law', in Bassiouni, M.C. (ed.), *The Islamic Criminal Justice* (1982) p.227 at pp.235–236. *See also* Document issued by Saudi Arabian Ministry of Foreign Affairs on *Protection of Human Rights in Criminal Procedure and in the Organization of the Judicial System (2000)*. Section III: The Post-Trial Stage, para.7(a) and (b). Available Online at Saudi Embassy News Website: http://www.saudiembassy.net/press_release/hr-judicial-1-menu.html [1/3/03].

[243] *See* Al-Alfi (above n.242) at pp.235–236.

[244] *See* Ali, A.A. (Trans.) *Kitab-ul-Kharaj* (1979) p.301.

[245] UN Doc.A/2929, (above n.8) at p.106, para.46.

such liabilities are not considered as constituting a crime. The freedom from imprisonment does not however extend to criminal offences related to the liability, such as criminal conviction for fraud or embezzlement of public funds. The provision also applies only in cases of 'inability [of the debtor] to fulfil' such obligation and does not cover a refusal to fulfil contractual obligations nor fraudulent and negligent bankruptcy.[246]

Islamic law does not also consider the inability to fulfil contractual obligations as permitting imprisonment or any other punishment. Although the *Sharî'ah* strongly advocates the fulfilment of all obligations, 'O you who believe! Fulfil [all] obligations',[247] yet the obligee shall have respite for the obligor in case of inability of the latter to fulfil his contractual obligation. The obligee is even encouraged to write off the debt in case of total inability of the obligor to repay it. The Qur'an 2:280 provides that: 'If the debtor is in difficulty, grant him time till it is easy for him to repay, but if you remit it by way of charity, that is best for you if you only knew'. The Prophet Muhammad is also reported to have stated that: 'Whoever gives respite to a debtor or grants him remission, God will save him from the difficulties of the Resurrection Day'.[248] To indicate that the rule applies only in cases of inability of the debtor, the Prophet further stated that 'Delay by a solvent debtor to settle his debt is an act of oppression [against the creditor]'.[249]

The OIC Cairo Declaration on Human Rights in Islam does not provide specifically for this right.

3.13 THE RIGHT TO FREEDOM OF MOVEMENT AND CHOICE OF RESIDENCE

Article 12

1. Everyone lawfully within the territory of a State shall, within that territory, have the right to liberty of movement and freedom to choose his residence.
2. Everyone shall be free to leave any country, including his own.
3. The above-mentioned rights shall not be subject to any restrictions except those which are provided by law, are necessary to protect national security, public order (*ordre public*), public health or morals or the rights and freedoms of others, and are consistent with the other rights recognized in the present Covenant.
4. No one shall be arbitrarily deprived of the right to enter his own country.

---

[246] *See* Nowak (above n.5) at p.193ff.   [247] Q5:1.

[248] Reported by Muslim. *See* Karim, F., *Al-Hadis, An English Translation and Commentary of Mishkat-ul-Masabih with Arabic Text* (1994) Vol.2, p.206, Hadith No. 3.

[249] Reported by al-Bukhâri and Muslim. *See* Karim (above n.248) at p.207, Hadith No. 6.

Freedom of movement is an important human right and a cardinal element of right to personal liberty. It is thus vital for the enjoyment of other human rights. Article 12 guarantees both internal and external freedom of movement and choice of residence for those 'lawfully within the territory of a State'. The HRC has therefore observed that the provision 'does not recognize the right of aliens to enter or reside in the territory of a State party. It is, in principle, a matter for the State to decide who it will admit to its territory'.[250] The right is also subjected to limitations provided by law necessary to protect national security, public order, public health, morals, rights, and freedoms of others consistent with the Covenant.[251] Article 12(4) prohibits the arbitrary deprivation of the right to enter one's own country. Although the right to enter one's own country is not subjected to the limitations in Article 12(3), there seem nevertheless to be some implied limitations in the wordings of Article 12(4) itself. Article 12(4) prohibits only 'arbitrary' deprivation of the right to enter one's own country. Nowak has pointed out that based on the *travaux préparatoires* this limitation must be strictly interpreted 'to relate exclusively to cases of *lawful exile as punishment* for a crime'.[252] Jagerskoild has however argued that perhaps exile as punishment for a crime 'is now prohibited under customary international law, and it may even be *jus cogens*'.[253] This finds support in the HRC's Concluding Observation on the Dominican Republic that 'punishment by exile is not compatible with the Covenant'.[254] Also in *Charles Stewart v. Canada* the Committee observed that the obligation of a State under Article 12(4) to allow entry of a person into his own country also prohibited deporting a person from his own country.[255]

Freedom of movement and choice of settlement is recognized in Islamic law on the basis of the Qur'anic provision that: 'It is He [God] Who has made the earth tractable for you [mankind], so traverse through its tracts and enjoy of the sustenance which He [God] furnishes; but unto Him is the Resur-rection'.[256] The Qur'an even indicates that people who refused to emigrate from persecution and died in sin would be confronted with the question on Judgment Day that: 'Was not the earth of God spacious enough for you to emigrate therein?'[257] There are also numerous verses of the Qur'an that charge human beings to traverse the earth to appreciate the majesty and benevolence of God.[258]

---

[250] General Comment 15, para.5. *See also Charles Stewart v. Canada,* Communication No. 538/1993, Human Rights Committee, UN Doc. CCPR/C/58/D/538/1996 (16 December 1996) para.12.5 and 12.6; and *Canepa v. Canada,* Communication No. 558/1993, Human Rights Committee, UN Doc. CCPR/C/59/D/558/1993 (20 June 1997) para.11.3.

[251] Art. 12(3). *See also* Jagerskoild, S., 'Freedom of Movement', in Henkin (above n.6) at 174, and Nowak (above n.5) at p.206ff.   [252] *See* Nowak (above n.5) p.219.

[253] *See* Jagerskoild (above n.251) at p.181.

[254] Concluding Observations on Dominican Republic (1993) UN Doc. CCPR/C/790/Add.18, para.6. *See also* Concluding Observations on Islamic Republic of Iran (1993) UN Doc. CCPR/C/79/Add.25, para.14.   [255] (Above n.250) at para.12.2.

[256] Q67:15.   [257] Q4:97.   [258] *See* e.g. Q6:11; 27:69; 29:20; 30:42.

This right to freedom of movement and choice of settlement is reported to have been demonstrated by the fourth Caliph, Ali ibn Abî Tâlib, even in the face of the difficult political crisis with Mu'âwiyyah during his reign. Ali was advised then to prevent the movement of some people who were crossing from Medina to Syria to join Mu'âwiyyah who was then contending the leadership of the Islamic Empire with the Caliph. Caliph Ali declined to prevent the movement on grounds that the people had a God-given right of movement over the land, which the Caliph could not revoke without justification. He is reported to have even assured the Dissenters *(Khawârij)* that they might live wherever they wished within the Islamic Empire as long as they did not indulge in bloodshed and acts of oppression.[259] Article 12 of the OIC Cairo Declaration on Human Rights in Islam thus provides that:

> Every man shall have the right, within the framework of *Shari'ah*, to free movement and to select his place of residence whether inside or outside his country . . .

However, with regards to the right of women to freedom of movement under Article 12, the HRC has alluded to the requirements in some Muslim States that a male relative must accompany women on a journey.[260] This requirement is based on a Tradition of the Prophet Muhammad that 'No woman shall make journey covering the distance of a day and night except accompanied by a male relative *(Mahram)*'.[261] In a relative Tradition a man was reported to have then asked the Prophet for counsel saying that he had enrolled to take part in an expedition but his wife also intended to travel for pilgrimage. The Prophet instructed the man to abandon his expedition and follow his wife for her pilgrimage.[262] The latter Tradition explains that rather than being a restriction on the right of women to freedom of movement, the requirement was a security right to which women were entitled to ensure their safety on long journeys in those times.

Contemporary Islamic scholars have thus opined that where there is no fear for safety, a woman may travel alone without any violation of Islamic law. Kamali has observed in that regard as follows:

> . . . Another example of ongoing reinterpretation is the scholarly contribution of the Egyptian scholar Yusuf al-Qaradawi, who validated air travel by women unaccompanied by male relatives. According to the rules of fiqh that were formulated in premodern times, women were not permitted to travel alone. Al-Qaradawi based his conclusion on the analysis that the initial ruling was intended to ensure women's physical and moral safety, and that modern air travel fulfills this requirement. He further supported

---

[259] *See* Tabandeh, S., *A Muslim Commentary on the Universal Declaration of Human Rights* (1970) p.33 and Chaudhry (above n.86) at p.21.

[260] *See* e.g. HRC Summary Record of the 1628th Meeting: Sudan, UN Doc. CCPR/C/SR.1628 of 02/02/98, para.49. *See also* General Comment 28, para.16.

[261] Reported by al-Bukhâri and Muslim, *see* e.g. Karim (above n.248) at Vol.3, p.572, Hadith No. 11.

[262] Reported by al-Bukhâri and Muslim, *see* e.g. Karim (above n.248) at Vol.3, p.571, Hadith No. 9.

this view with an analysis of the relevant hadiths on the subject and arrived at a ruling better suited to contemporary conditions.[263]

3.14 FREEDOM OF ALIENS FROM ARBITRARY EXPULSION

Article 13

An alien lawfully in the territory of a State Party to the present Covenant may be expelled therefrom only in pursuance of a decision reached in accordance with law and shall, except where compelling reasons of national security otherwise require, be allowed to submit the reasons against his expulsion and to have his case reviewed by, and be represented for the purpose before the competent authority or a person or persons especially designated by the competent authority.

As is clear from the above provision, the guarantee here is not absolute but only protects legal aliens from arbitrary expulsion and also sets out some procedural guarantees that must be fulfilled in case of expulsion, except where national security requires otherwise.[264] The provision does not apply to the expulsion of illegal immigrants.

This provision is in full consonance with Islamic law. Hamidullah quotes al-Shaybânî on the rights of aliens to enjoy protection and justice within the Islamic State as follows:

It is a principle [of Muslim law] that the sovereign of the Muslims has the obligation to protect foreigners coming with permission as long as they are in our [Muslims] territory, and to do justice to them—this in the same way as he has an obligation regarding non-Muslim subjects. [265]

In the above statement, al-Shaybânî also referred specifically to 'foreigners coming with permission' (that is, legal immigrants). This was essentially in reference to the *Musta'min*, that is, non-Muslim aliens who entered the Islamic State with permission granted either by a Muslim citizen or by the State authority itself.

It must be noted however that even the right of those coming without permission (namely, illegal immigrants) to be heard and treated in accordance with the rule of law is equally recognized under Islamic law. Under classical Islamic law of Nations, aliens who entered the Muslim State secretly or without permission could be considered as enemy aliens or spies if they could not prove otherwise. In his *Kitâb al-Kharâj*, the great eighth century Islamic jurist Abû Yûsuf,[266] was asked 'about a man belonging to the enemy who comes out of

---

[263] *See* Kamali, M.H., 'Law and Society: the Interplay of Revelation and Reason in the Shariah' in Esposito, J.L. (ed.), *The Oxford History of Islam* (1999) p.107 at p.118.

[264] *See* General Comment 15, para.9 and 10. *See also* Joseph, Schultz and Castan (above n.23) pp.268–276.   [265] Hamidullah (above n.241) at p.133, para.249.

[266] *See* para.3.15.5 below.

his country intending to enter the country of Islam and passes by an armed party of Muslims on the way and he is captured and says: I have come out and I intend to enter the country of Islam in order to seek security for my own self and my family and my children, or he says: I am a messenger. Will his statement be accepted or not? What treatment with him will be advisable?'[267] Abû Yûsuf answered saying: 'If this enemy passes by the armed garrison and passes them secretly, then it will not be true and his word will not be accepted. But if he does not secretly pass by them, then he will be held true and his statement will be accepted'.[268] The important point here is that even such enemy aliens had a right to be heard and to prove otherwise under Islamic law.

Article 12 of the OIC Cairo Declaration on Human Rights in Islam however only recognizes the right of residence outside one's own country but failed to provide specifically for the right of aliens not to be arbitrarily expelled.

3.15 THE RIGHT TO FAIR HEARING AND DUE PROCESS OF LAW

Article 14

The right to fair hearing and due process of law is aimed at guaranteeing equity and fair play in the administration of justice. It protects the individual especially against abuse of the criminal process by the State or its agents. The real import-ance of Article 14, which is the longest of the substantive provisions of the ICCPR, lies in the fact that the realization of all human rights often depends on the proper administration of justice through equitable procedural guarantees.

The procedural guarantees under Article 14 apply not only in criminal tri-als but also in matters concerning the determination of 'rights and obligations in a suit at law'. The HRC has observed that '[l]aws and practices dealing with these matters vary widely from State to State'.[269] Nowak has poin-ted out that the provisions in Article 14 are based on Anglo-American (and Civil Law) *'liberal principles of separation of powers and the independence of the judiciary* vis-à-vis the executive'.[270] If it is perceived however, as stated by the HRC that '[a]ll of these provisions [in Article 14] are aimed at ensuring the proper administration of justice'[271] and not at imposing the Anglo-American or Civil Law systems, then it will be easier to interpret the provisions of Article 14 in relation to other systems such as the Islamic legal system.[272]

---

[267] *See* Ali, A.A., *Kitab-ul-Kharaj*, English translation (1979) p.382. [268] *Ibid.*
[269] *See* General Comment 13, para.2. [270] *See* Nowak (above n.5) at p.237.
[271] *See* General Comment 13, para.1.
[272] It is important to note that Islamic law is a complete legal system with specific judicial administration, having rules, procedures, courts, and specialized judicial personnel apart from the clergy. *See* e.g. Azad, G.M., *Judicial System of Islam* (1987) and below n.274.

Under Islamic law the issue of fair trial and due process, being procedural, is covered by the methods rather than by the sources of Islamic law.[273] The *Sharî'ah,* per se, mainly covers the substantive aspects of Islamic law while the procedural aspects fall within the realms of *fiqh* as formulated by the jurists. While the Qur'an and *Sunnah* may specify the crime, prescribe punishments, and enjoin substantive justice, they do not often give details of procedural matters such as arrest, detention, investigation, prosecution, hearing, judicial review, etc. The *Sharî'ah* mainly emphasizes substantive justice, leaving the procedure of its realization for the State authority to decide in accordance with the best interests of society.[274]

Drawing from the Prophet's practice and that of the rightly guided Caliphs, the early Muslim jurists endeavoured to lay down judicial procedures which they believed would facilitate the realization of substantive justice as prescribed by the *Sharî'ah.* The judicial procedures as found in the works of the classical jurists were not rigid but were adjusted in practice under the doctrine of *siyâsah shar'iyyah,* especially during the Abassid Caliphate. Muslim scholars fully agree that the particularities of the Islamic judicial system are not inflexible, but leave room for necessary refinement as the needs of substantive justice demand from time to time.[275] Thus, although the judicial procedures found in the works of classical Islamic jurists may not *expressis verbis* contain the list of guarantees provided in Article 14 of the ICCPR, it is not difficult to establish those guarantees within the *Sharî'ah* and the principles of Islamic administration of justice laid down by the jurists. Tabandeh had pointed out that all the six Articles relating to fair trial and due process of law under the Universal Declaration of Human Rights[276] 'conform fully to Islamic law, which has long dealt with all the points they raise under its perfect social regulations'.[277]

Due to the complexity of the provisions of Article 14 we shall examine the paragraphs one after the other and analyse the procedural rights they guarantee within the principles of Islamic law.

---

[273] *See* above para.2.4.1 on the nature of Islamic law.

[274] For classical analysis of the development of the Islamic judicial procedure, *see* e.g. Ibn Khaldûn, *al-Muqaddimah,* Vol.2, pp.35–37; Ibn Qayyim al-Jawziyyah, *al-Turuq al-Hukmiyyah fî al-Siyâsah al-Shar'iyyah* (Arabic) (1953) p.218ff and al-Mâwardî, *al-Ahkâm as-Sultâniyyah,* trans. Yate, A., (1996) pp.69–73. *See also* contemporary analysis on the subject by Awad (above n.135) at pp.91–92; Al-Alwani, T.J., 'Judiciary and Rights of the Accused in Islamic Criminal Law', in Mahmood, T., *et al.,* (eds.), *Criminal Law in Islam and the Muslim World* (1996) pp.256–263; Mahmood, T., 'Criminal Procedure at the Shari'ah Law as Seen by Modern Scholars: A Review', in Mahmood, T., *et al.,* p.292ff; *and generally* Lippman, M., *et al.,* (eds.), *Islamic Criminal Law and Procedure: An Introduction* (1988).

[275] *See* Al-Alwani (above n.274).   [276]i.e. Articles 6, 7, 8, 9, 10, and 11.

[277] *See* Tabandeh (above n.259) at p.28.

3.15.1 Equality of parties before the courts

Article 14(1)

All persons shall be equal before the courts and tribunals. In the determination of any criminal charge against him, or of his rights and obligations in a suit at law, everyone shall be entitled to a fair and public hearing by a competent, independent and impartial tribunal established by law. The press and the public may be excluded from all or part of a trial for reasons of morals, public order *(ordre public)* or national security in a democratic society, or when the interest of the private lives of the parties so requires, or to the extent strictly necessary in the opinion of the court in special circumstances where publicity would prejudice the interests of justice; but any judgement rendered in a criminal case or in a suit at law shall be made public except where the interest of juvenile persons otherwise requires or the proceedings concern matrimonial disputes or the guardianship of children.

The important rights guaranteed here are (i) equality of parties before the courts in both criminal and civil proceedings and (ii) fair and public hearing by legally competent tribunals. The HRC observed in *Bahamonde v. Equatorial Guinea*[278] that 'the notion of equality before the courts and tribunals encompasses the very access to the courts and that a situation in which an individual's attempts to seize the competent jurisdictions of his/her grievances are systematically frustrated runs counter to the guarantees of article 14, paragraph 1'.[279] The Committee has also observed that States Parties must ensure that courts 'are independent, impartial and competent, in particular with regard to the manner in which judges are appointed, the qualifications for appointment, and the duration of their terms of office; the conditions governing promotion, transfer and cessation of their functions'.[280] These guarantees are in full consonance with the provisions of the *Sharî'ah* as analysed below.

Regarding the question of equality of parties in both criminal and civil proceedings, the Qur'anic injunctions on justice are always laden with the idea of equality and fairness. For example:

O you who believe! Be maintainers of justice, bearers of witness for God's sake, even though it be against your own selves, your parents, or your near relatives, and whether it be against [the] rich or [the] poor . . .[281]

O you who believe! Be upright for God, bearers of witness with justice; and let not the hatred of a people swerve you to act inequitably. Act equitably, for that is nearer to piety . . .[282]

. . . And when you judge between people judge with equity; certainly God counsels you excellently, and God hears and sees [all things][283]

God commands [the doing of] justice and fairness . . . and prohibits indecencies and injustice . . .[284]

[278] Communication No. 468/1991, UN Doc. CCPR/C/49/D/468/1991 (1993).

[279] *ibid.*, para.9.4.   [280] General Comment 13, para.3.   [281] Q4:135.

[282] Q5:8.   [283] Q4:58.   [284] Q16:90.

Doing justice is considered under Islamic law as a duty to God from which emanates the rights to equality and fairness for all human beings without regard to status, race, gender, or religion. The Qur'an says:

O Mankind! Be mindful of your duty to your Lord who created you all from a single soul and from it created its mate and from the two of them spread out a multitude of men and women. Be careful of your duty toward God, through Whom you claim [your rights from one another] . . . and God is ever-watchful over you all.[285]

The expression 'O Mankind!', with which the above verse begins, is an important indicator of non-regard to status, race, gender, or religion in the claiming of rights and the doing of justice, with which the verse ends. The notion that 'the Crown or the King can do no wrong' has never existed in Islamic legal theory. The Prophet himself and the righteous Caliphs after him demonstrated the principle of equality before the courts and tribunals both in words and deeds. An illustrative example of this was in a case brought by a commoner called Ubay ibn Ka'b against the Caliph Umar ibn al-Khatâb during the latter's rule as second Caliph of the Islamic Empire. The case was before Zayd ibn Thâbit. When Caliph Umar entered the courtroom to defend the suit brought against him by the commoner, Zayd (the judge) stood up as a sign of respect for Caliph Umar. For doing that, the Caliph rebuked Zayd saying: 'that is your first injustice to the other party in this case'. After the hearing, Ubay could not adduce enough evidence to establish his claim against the Caliph, but requested, in accordance with the prescribed rules of evidence under Islamic law, that the Caliph must take an oath to sustain his denial of the claim. Zayd, again out of respect for the Caliph, requested Ubay to spare Umar from that formality since, he believed, the Caliph could not be lying. Caliph Umar frowned at this favouritism and said to Zayd, 'If an ordinary man and Umar are not equal before you, then you are not fit to be a judge'.[286] Al-Mâwardî also cited another instance in which Caliph Umar sent a message to one of the judges during his reign ordering him as follows: 'Make people equal before you in your dispensation of justice, so that no noble may look forward to your favouritism and no commoner may despair of your justice'.[287] There is thus a consensus among Muslim jurists that it is obligatory on a judge to maintain equality among the parties before him in every case.[288]

In its General Comment 28, the HRC raised the point of women giving evidence as witnesses 'on the same terms as men' under Article 14. This brings the evidential capacity of women under Islamic law into issue as a matter concerning the equal right to fair hearing.

---

[285] Q4:1.

[286] *See* e.g. Hussain, S.S., 'Human Rights in Islam: Principles and Precedents' (1983) 1 *Islamic and Contemporary Law Quarterly,* p.103 at pp.121–126 and Maududi (above n.229) at pp.21–22 and 31–32 for further illustrations.   [287] al-Mâwardî (above n.196) at p.76.

[288] *See* e.g. Ibn Rushd al-Qurtubî (above n.121) at Vol.2, p.472 (chapter on 'How to dispense justice'). *See also* Nyazee (above n.121) at p.568, para.57.5.

The rules of evidence under Islamic law require in some cases the evidence of two men or alternatively, one man and two women (that is, two women replacing one man). This is based on Qur'an 2:282 which provides, *inter alia,* that:

O you who believe! When you contract a debt for a fixed period, write it down. . . . And get two witnesses out of your own men, and if there are not two men [available] then a man and two women, such as you agree for witnesses, so that if one of them [two women] errs, the other can remind her . . .[289]

It will be observed that the above verse substitutes the evidence of one man with that of two women and thus raises a question on equality and non-discrimination on grounds of sex under international human rights law. Although this provision has traditionally been imposed generally upon all test-amentary evidences under Islamic law, Muslim scholars have argued that it does not apply in all cases but is restricted only to testimony in business trans-actions, civil debts, and contracts. They have contended that rather than being discriminatory, the provision is mainly precautionary, because such transac-tions being then seldom assumed by women, they ordinarily lacked experience in the intricacies involved and were more likely to err in the presentation of evidence in that respect. Therefore the reason for requesting two women in the place of one man here was that 'if one of them errs' in the presentation of issues 'the other can remind her'.[290] One observes that in all other provisions concerning the procurement of evidence other than in business or financial transactions, the Qur'an does not discern between the male and the female. For evidence in divorce cases, for example, the Qur'anic provision is that:

. . . When you divorce women . . . either take them back on equitable terms or part with them on equitable terms; and take for witnesses *two persons* from among you endued with justice . . .[291] (emphasis added).

Also for evidence in bequest matters the Qur'anic provision is:

Oh you who believe! When death approaches any of you, [take] witnesses among yourselves when making bequests—*two just persons* of your own . . .[292] (emphasis added).

And in evidence for fornication/adultery the Qur'anic provision is that:

And those of your women who commit lewdness [illegal sexual intercourse], take the evidence of *four witnesses* from amongst you against them . . .[293] (emphasis added).

---

[289] Q2:282 touches basically on financial transactions and obligations.
[290] *See* e.g. El-Bahnassawi (above n.59) at pp.130–131.   [291] Q65:1–2.
[292] Q5:106.
[293] Q4:15. This rule of evidence applies vice versa for men who commit the same offence.

In all these other cases, generic terms 'two just persons' (*dha wâ adlin*) or 'witnesses' *(shuhadâ')* are used without any differentiation of gender as was adopted in the first case. It can therefore be argued that the transposing of the provision concerning commercial transactions upon all other types of test-amentary evidence arose from the traditional position of women in society, not from a direct Qur'anic text. In the same way there is consensus among the jurists that female evidence alone is admissible in cases where men lack adequate knowledge or where it is impossible for men to have knowledge except women.[294] El-Bahnassawi thus concluded that:

> It should be borne in mind that Islam attributed this differentiation between the sexes to their respective natural dispositions, though it had acknowledged their creation from the same origin and essence. It is not indicative of woman's inferiority but touches directly on people's interests and the safeguarding of Justice. Should the law treat the testimony of a woman—as she is [was?] inexperienced in business and commercial fields—equal to that of a man, it would be detrimental to the cause of justice and the interests of the contracting parties. Woman, it is clear, shall not draw any gain or advantage therefrom.[295]

While generally conceding to the principle of equality, Islamic law also takes specific social needs that may arise in certain contexts into consideration.[296] The greatest desire is that of doing substantive justice. The Qur'anic pre-scription for two women in place of one man thus occurs only in business transactions in which women used not to have the same experience as men. This would then raise the question that, since women now partake in business transactions and many women have acquired professional experience com-mensurate to that of men in commerce, can the rule of two women witnesses in place of one man be suspended where no miscarriage of justice will be incurred? The argument of desire to do substantive justice can sway Muslim States that adopt a liberal interpretation of the *Sharî'ah* to leave out this rule on grounds of necessity or in the interest of justice as demonstrated in the case of *Ansar Burney v. Federation of Pakistan*[297] where the Pakistani Federal Shariat Court referred to possible instances of a single female witness. States that maintain a hardline traditional approach may however not be swayed by the same argument and will be in breach of Article 14(1) as interpreted by the HRC.

On the issue of public trials, Islamic law requires that all trials must be in public except for reasons of state security or protection of public order or morality. This is evident from the fact that traditionally, the mosques, which were the most obvious public places within the Islamic Empire, served as the

---

[294] *See* e.g. Al-Jazâirî, A.J., *Minhâj al-Muslim* (Arabic) (8th Edn., 1976) p.467; and Al-Zuhayli (above n.78) at Vol.8., pp.6045–6046. *See also* Qadri (above n.22) at p.505 and El-Bahnassawi (above n.59) at p.132.	[295] Bahnassawi (above n.59) at p. 132.
[296] *See* Hallaq, W.B., *A History of Islamic Legal Theories* (1997) p.184.	[297] Above n.79.

courtrooms. Thus a complete resort to closed criminal trials not only violates international human rights rules of fair trial, but is also a departure from the ordinary fair trial rules of Islamic criminal justice. Also, regarding the need for legally competent tribunals, Islamic law prescribes specific conditions and qualifications for the appointment of judges, and only competent and duly appointed judges can give binding judgments.[298]

The guarantees in Article 14(1) are thus generally compatible with Islamic law. This is substantiated by Article 19 of the OIC Cairo Declaration on Human Rights in Islam, which provides that: '(a) All individuals are equal before the law, without distinction between ruler and ruled; (b) The right to resort to justice is guaranteed to everyone'.

3.15.2 Right to be presumed innocent until proved guilty

Article 14(2)

Everyone charged with a criminal offence shall have the right to be presumed innocent until proved guilty according to law.

Islamic law fully recognizes this right. The presumption of the defendant's innocence is an important principle depicted in various rules of evidence under Islamic law. Basically, every human being is considered to be inherently immaculate.[299] Thus, by the Islamic legal principle of *istishâb* (presumption of continuity)[300] an accused person is considered innocent until the contrary is proved.

Generally, the Qur'an enjoins Muslims to ascertain the truth of every allegation to avoid wrongfully harming innocent persons.[301] This is more specifically demonstrated through the general rule of Islamic evidence, which provides that the onus of proof lies on the claimant or complainant. For instance, the Qur'an provides that: 'And those who launch a charge against chaste women *and produce not four witnesses* [to support their allegation] flog them with eighty stripes and reject their evidence ever after, for such men are wicked transgressors'.[302] Also the Prophet had stated that: 'The onus of proof lies upon the Claimant, and an oath is required of one who denies the claim'.[303] A possible argument from a Western legal perspective would be that the requirement of an oath to sustain the defendant's denial under Islamic law impugns the

---

[298] *See* Azad (above n.272) at pp.21–23.

[299] This is based on a Prophetic Tradition that: 'Everyone is born inherently pure ...'.

[300] *Istishâb* is a principle of Islamic law which denotes the continuation of an established state of affairs until the contrary is proven. For an analysis of its application *See* e.g. Kamali, M.H., *Principles of Islamic Jurisprudence* (1991) pp.297–309. [301] Q49:6.

[302] Q24:4 (emphasis added). This onus of proof lies upon the accuser of both men and women of any criminal offence.

[303] Reported by al-Bayhâqî. *See* e.g. al-Asqalânî, Ibn Hajar, *Bulugh al-Maram* (With English Translations) (1996) p.499, Hadith 1210.

total presumption of the defendant's innocence. This requirement of an oath to sustain the defendant's denial under Islamic law derives from the need to do substantive justice especially in civil claims, because it is possible that a claimant may sometimes fail to prove his case only for lack of eloquence or simply on technicalities. Thus, in such cases the defendant's oath is only to ensure positive justice. This may be compared with the oath or affirmation undertaken by litigants to speak 'the truth and nothing but the truth' at the commencement of evidence under Western legal systems.

The presumption of the defendant's innocence under Islamic law is further demonstrated by the unanimity of the Islamic jurists that any balance of probabilities or doubt in criminal trials must be resolved in favour of the accused. This is based on the Prophet's instruction that the *hudûd* punishments should be averted with the slightest iota of doubt.[304] Article 19(e) of the OIC Cairo Declaration on Human Rights in Islam thus provides that: 'A defendant is innocent until his guilt is proven in a fair trial in which he shall be given all the guarantees of defence.'

3.15.3 *Accused person's minimum guarantees*

Article 14(3)

In the determination of any criminal charge against him, everyone shall be entitled to the following minimum guarantees, in full equality;

(a) to be informed promptly and in detail in a language which he understands of the nature and cause of the charge against him;

Prompt information of the accused person of the nature and cause of the charges against him aims, *inter alia,* at preventing arbitrary charges and also leaves the accused in no doubt of the charges against him. The HRC has stated in its General Comment 13 that the right of an accused person 'to be informed of the charge "promptly" requires that information is given in the manner described as soon as the charge is first made by a competent authority'.[305] Because the liberty and freedom of an accused person may be restricted to facilitate investigation, prompt information in the language that the accused person understands will ensure certainty of the wrong committed to warrant any such restriction and the subsequent sanction that may be imposed thereafter if found guilty of the alleged wrong. This is in full consonance with Islamic law since the Qur'an provides that blame can only be against those who have certainly committed wrong.[306]

---

[304] *See* Al-Zuhayli (above n.78) at Vol.4, p.3144; and al-'Awwa, M.S., 'The Basis of Islamic Penal Legislation' in Bassiouni, M.C. (ed.), *The Islamic Criminal Justice* (1982) p.127 at pp.143–144.   [305] General Comment 13, para.8.

[306] *See* e.g. Q42:42.

(b) To have adequate time and facilities for the preparation of his defence and to communicate with counsel of his own choosing;

The guarantee in Article 14(3)(b) is related to the accused person's general right to defence, which is examined in detail under paragraph (d) below.

(c) To be tried without undue delay;

The guarantee to be tried without undue delay is consequential to the right to justice, because justice delayed is justice denied. Due to the great emphasis that Islam places on justice, any undue delay in the administration of justice is also prohibited. The Islamic jurists stress that the presentation of evidence for criminal offences must not be delayed. The importance of this is demonstrated in the opinion of some Islamic jurists that delayed evidence in criminal trial amounts to doubtful evidence which cannot sustain punishment for *hudûd* crimes under Islamic law.[307]

(d) To be tried in his presence, and to defend himself in person or through legal assistance of his own choosing; to be informed, if he does not have legal assistance, of this right; and to have legal assistance assigned to him, in any case where the interests of justice so require, and without payment by him in any such case if he does not have sufficient means to pay for it;

The accused person's right of appearance and defence are both very much recognized under Islamic law. The Qur'an establishes the right of defence in its narration that even when Adam violated God's order in the Garden of Eden, he was given the opportunity of defence, even though he apparently had none.[308] Also the Qur'an presents us with scenarios of the fact that even in the hereafter God will give sinners an opportunity to present their defences, if any, before being punished.[309] The Prophet and the Caliphs after him also set examples in that regard. For instance when the Prophet appointed Ali ibn Abî Tâlib as Governor to Yemen he instructed him not to decide any matter brought to him without first hearing the defence of the other party.[310] Caliph Umar ibn Abdul Azîz was also reported to have handed down instructions to judges during his rule as follows: 'If a litigant comes complaining with a blinded eye, do not be quick to decide in his favour until the other party appears, for it is possible that the former has blinded the latter in both eyes'.[311]

Qadri has pointed out that Islamic law 'does not favour the trial of a claim in the absence of the defendant' and that if the court is forced to proceed

---

[307] *See* Salama, M.M., 'General Principles of Criminal Evidence in Islamic Jurisprudence', in Bassiouni, M.C., (ed.), *The Islamic Criminal Justice* (1982) pp.113–115.

[308] *See* Q7: 22–24.   [309] *See* e.g. Q37:22–35; Q67:8–11; Q75:13–15.

[310] Reported by Abû Dâwûd and others. *See* Ibn Rushd al-Qurtubî (above n.121) at p.472. *See also* Nyazee (above n.121) at p.567, para.57.4.

[311] *See* Awad (above n.135) at p.97; and Al-Alwani (above n.274) at p.274.

ex parte by the non-availability of the defendant, a representative must be appointed to protect the defendant's interest.[312] While Imâm Mâlik and Imâm al-Shâfi'î opined that judgment may be rendered against a person who has been absent for a long time, Imâm Abû Hanîfah held that judgment cannot be rendered against an absent person at all.[313] The right to defence has been so much emphasized under Islamic law to the extent that every effort must be made to ensure its adequacy. The right to adequate time and facilities to prepare one's defence under Article 14(3)(b) is very much incidental to the substantive enjoyment of this general right to defence and is thus also protected by the rules stated above. The same applies to the right to counsel of one's choice.[314] It is often erroneously portrayed that representation by counsel is disallowed under Islamic law. Although the early Islamic jurists concentrated largely on the litigant presenting his case personally, they also recognized the right of a litigant to appoint another person to represent him. It is reported for instance that the fourth Caliph, Ali ibn Abî Tâlib disliked litigation, so in any case in which he was a party he usually appointed Ukail ibn Abî Tâlib to represent him.[315] Also in his work, *The History of the Judges of Cordova*, al-Khushânî stated the instance of two men who brought a matter before the judge Ahmad ibn Bâqî. In presenting their cases, the judge observed that one of the men was very eloquent while the other had problems presenting his case eloquently. The judge thus advised the latter saying: 'Would it not be better if you were represented by someone who can match the verbal skills of your opponent?' The man answered saying: 'But I only speak the truth'. The judge in insisting that he engaged an attorney said: 'How many men have perished [due to lack of eloquence even though] telling the truth!'[316] Although representation by counsel is not generally practised in the Islamic judicial system of some Muslim countries, there is nothing in Islamic law that prevents the use of counsel to protect the interest of litigants and to ensure substantive justice. Due to the fact that most individuals are generally ignorant of the law and oblivious of their rights under the *Sharî'ah*, the right to engage counsel and to communicate with counsel of one's own choice has actually become more imperative today under Islamic law. The guarantee of the right to counsel will no doubt ensure equality of arms at law especially in criminal trials between individuals and State Prosecutors who on their part are not oblivious of the law as the accused person often is.

---

[312] Qadri (above n.22) at p.495.

[313] *See* Ibn Rushd al-Qurtubî (above n.121) at p.472. *See also* Nyazee (above n.121) at p.567, para.57.4.   [314] *See* e.g. Al-Alwani (above n.274) at pp.273–276.

[315] *See* al-Bayhâqî, A., *Kitâb al-Sunan al-Kubrâ* (Arabic) (1925) 26 cited in al-Saleh (above n.162) at p.81.

[316] *See* Al-Khushânî, *Târîkh Qudât Qurtubah* (Arabic) cited in Awad (above n.135) at p.99.

Islamic jurists are so particular about the right to defence to the extent that the *Hanafī* School holds that the *hudûd* punishment cannot be inflicted upon a dumb person because perhaps if he were capable of speaking he might have been able to raise some defence that might create some doubt and thus negate the application of the *hudûd* punishment. Many contemporary writers on Islamic law thus argue strongly that the right to engage counsel actually falls within the 'theory of protected interest' of the individual under Islamic law and must be fully ensured by the State.[317] Provision of free legal aid by the State, in accordance with Covenant obligations, to those who cannot afford to pay for such services will be very much advantageous in that regard and will thus not be contrary to Islamic law.

This right to legal representation under Islamic law has recently been acknowledged under the Saudi Arabian criminal justice system. In *Protection of Human Rights in Criminal Procedure and in the Organization of the Judicial System*, issued by the Saudi Arabian Ministry of Foreign Affairs in 2000, it is provided that: 'The accused person has the right to, avail himself of the services of a lawyer or legal representative', and that: 'The suspect has the right to contact his lawyer or legal representative in order to exercise his right of defense and the examiner cannot prevent him from doing so'.[318]

(e) To examine, or have examined, the witnesses against him and to obtain the attend-ance and examination of witnesses on his behalf under the same conditions as witnesses against him;
(f) To have the free assistance of an interpreter if he cannot understand or speak the language used in court;

Both the right to examine witnesses and the right to an interpreter are natural and essential aspects of the substantive right to defence addressed above. Their denial will no doubt lead to injustice. Both guarantees are therefore fully recognized under Islamic law. On the issue of language the Qur'an states that God does not send a messenger 'except in the language of his people, in order to make things clear to them'.[319] This indicates the divine recognition of the right of human beings to be communicated with in the language they understand.

(g) Not to be compelled to testify against himself or to confess guilt.

---

[317] *See* e.g. Al-Alwani (above n.274) at pp.274–276; al-Saleh (above n.162) at pp.81–84; Awad (above n.135) at p.95; Mahmood, T., 'Criminal Procedure at the Shari'ah Law as Seen by Modern Scholars: A Review' (above n.274) at p.300.

[318] *See* KSA Ministry of Foreign Affairs, *Protection of Human Rights in Criminal Procedure and in the Organization of the Judicial System* (2000), Sec. I(2)(a), *The Characteristics of Criminal Examination*, para.6; and Sec. I(2)(b), *Remand in Custody,* para.4. For an official English translation of this document, *see* Saudi Embassy News Website at: http://www.saudiembassy.net/press_release/hr-judicial-1-menu.html [1/3/03].

[319] Q14:4.

Under Islamic law an accused person may be convicted through his voluntary confession *(iqrâr)*, but he is protected against being compelled to confess guilt or incriminate himself. The *Sharî'ah* provides that a person will not be punished for things done involuntarily or under compulsion. Even for the sin of apostasy, compulsion exonerates from God's punishment in the hereafter. The Qur'an provides that:

Anyone who after accepting faith in God, utters disbelief, *except under compulsion,* . . . on them is anger from God and theirs will be a severe punishment.[320]

Prophet Muhammad had also stated that his community is exempted from responsibility for things committed through mistakes, forgetfulness, and under duress.[321] The same rule applies to confession as a means of evidence. Islamic jurists have considered the probability of a forced confession being false as greater than its veracity. In prohibiting the extraction of evidence through coercion, Umar ibn al-Khatâb is reported to have stated that 'A person would not be secure from incriminating himself if you made him hungry, frightened him or confined him'.[322] Also, a man accused of theft was beaten until he confessed and was brought to Abdullah ibn Umar for punishment, but ibn Umar did not punish him because he confessed under coercion.[323] Islamic law thus specifies strict rules for confession and the majority of the Islamic jurists hold that any admission of guilt or confession obtained by coercion or interdiction amounts to inadmissible evidence.[324] The accused person has a right to remain silent and not to respond to questions put to him. Also the accused person has the right to retract his confessions in *hudûd* offences even up to the last minute of executing the punishment.

Where the accused person is however known to be a notorious criminal and there are other contributing circumstances to the effect that he has hidden the stolen property, some scholars hold that he may be coerced to confess. An example has been given of a known thief who denied stealing some goods and was coerced to confess where he had hidden the stolen goods. The jurist, Islam ibn Yusuf, who witnessed the coercion exclaimed saying: 'never have I seen injustice appear so similar to justice than in this case'. That the coercion was described by Ibn Yusuf in this instance as an injustice suffices to indicate its abhorrence. The jurists have therefore contended that conviction in such a situation would not be based on the confession but on the recovery of the stolen goods.[325]

---

[320] Q16:106 (emphasis added).
[321] Reported by Ibn Majâh. *See* e.g. Ibrahim, E., and Johnson-Davies, D., (Trans.) *Forty Hadith, An-Nawawî's* (1985) pp.120–121, Hadith 39.
[322] *See* al-Saleh (above n.162) at p.73.   [323] *ibid.*
[324] *See* e.g. Salama (above n.307) at pp.119–120.
[325] *See* Al-Alwani (above n.274) at p.276ff. *See also* al-Mâwardî, A., *al-Ahkâm as-Sultâniyyah,* trans. Yate, A., (1996) p.310.

3.15.4 Rights of juveniles in criminal proceedings

Article 14(4)

In the case of juvenile persons, the procedure shall be such as will take account of their age and the desirability of promoting their rehabilitation.

Rather than stigmatizing young offenders with criminality and focusing on their punishment, this provision promotes their rehabilitation and reintegration 'back onto the path of socially acceptable conduct'.[326] This is very well supported by the Islamic teachings on the proper upbringing and training of children who are considered as the future generation. In fact the Prophet exonerated immature persons completely from responsibility by stating that 'Three [categories of] people are free from responsibility, the insane until he is sane, the sleeping until he wakes and the child until he reaches maturity'.[327]

3.15.5 Right of appeal to higher tribunal

Article 14(5)

Everyone convicted of a crime shall have the right to his conviction and sentence being reviewed by a higher tribunal according to law.

The right of appeal to a higher forum is recognized under Islamic law. Abû Yûsuf was the first *Qâḍi al-Quḍât* (Chief Justice) in the administration of Islamic justice. He was appointed during the rule of the Abassid Caliph, Hârûn al-Rashîd in Baghdad in the eighth century and could hear appeals and review the decisions of other judges throughout the Islamic Empire.[328] Islamic jurisprudence thus provides for the principles of appeal and revision of judgments. This is under the Islamic legal principle of *murâfa'ah* which exists in the Islamic legal system of many Muslim States.[329]

3.15.6 Right to compensation for wrongful conviction

Article 14(6)

When a person has by a final decision been convicted of a criminal offence and when subsequently his conviction has been reversed or he has been pardoned on the ground that a new or newly discovered fact shows conclusively that there has been a miscarriage

---

[326] *See* Noor Muhammad, N.A., 'Due Process of Law for Person Accused of a Crime' in Henkin (above n.6) at p.155.

[327] Reported by Ahmad. *See* e.g. Al-Zuhayli (above n.78) Vol.4, p.2969.

[328] *See* e.g. Ibn Sa'd Âl Darîb, S., *al-Tandhîm al-Qaḍâ'i fi al-Mamlakah al-Arabiyyah al-Sa'udiyyah fî Daw' al-Sharî'ah al-Islâmiyyah* (Arabic) (1984) Vol.1, p.250.

[329] *See* Qadrî, A.A., *Justice in Historical Islam* (1968) and Qadri (above n.22) at pp.484 and 497–498. Cf. Azad (above n.272) at pp.98–104.

of justice, the person who has suffered punishment as a result of such conviction shall be compensated according to law, unless it is proved that the non-disclosure of the unknown fact in time is wholly or partly attributable to him.

Islamic law also recognizes the right to compensation of a person who suffers injury or is punished through judicial error or miscarriage of justice. The jurists rely on an incident in which Ali ibn Abî Tâlib ruled that the second Caliph Umar ibn al-Khatâb should pay compensation to a woman who suffered miscarriage as a result of the Caliph's orders. There are however differences of opinion among the jurists as to whether the compensation should be paid from public funds or from the private funds of the officer or judge responsible for such error or miscarriage of justice.[330]

3.15.7 *The rule against double jeopardy*

Article 14(7)

No one shall be liable to be tried or punished again for an offence for which he has already been finally convicted or acquitted in accordance with the law and penal procedure of each country.

This provision is to avoid double jeopardy against the offender and is in full conformity with the Islamic principles of justice. Retrying a previously tried and convicted or acquitted person on the same facts is tantamount to injustice and perhaps witch-hunting. This does not however preclude appeals and reviews of lower court decisions by higher tribunals.

It is evident from the above analyses that even though Anglo-American and Civil Law procedure may differ in some respects from Islamic judicial procedure, the principles of fair hearing and rule of law formulated into Article 14 of the ICCPR to ensure proper administration of justice and legal protection of all other human rights are generally compatible with Islamic law. In the Resolution adopted after the First International Conference on the Protection of Human Rights in the Islamic Criminal Justice System held in Siracusa, Italy in 1979, the Conference resolved that 'the letter and spirit of Islamic Law on the subject of the protection of the rights of the criminally accused are in complete harmony with the fundamental principles of human rights under international law'.[331] The Resolution

---

[330] *See* e.g. Al-Alwani (above n.274) at pp.284–286.
[331] The Conference was held at the International Institute of Advanced Criminal Sciences in Siracusa, Italy between 28–31 May 1979 and was attended by 55 penal jurists from 18 different countries including Algeria, Egypt, Jordan, Libya, Mauritania, Syria, Saudi Arabia, Somalia, Sudan, and United Arab Emirates. Also in attendance were jurists from Belgium, France, Italy, Switzerland, United States of America, Yugoslavia, and the United Kingdom. *See* Bassiouni, C.M., (ed.), *The Islamic Criminal Justice* (1982) at p.249.

identified the following minimum guarantees for the criminally accused under Islamic law:

1. the right of freedom from arbitrary arrest, detention, torture, or physical annihilation;
2. the right to be presumed innocent until proven guilty by a fair and impartial tribunal in accordance with the Rule of Law;
3. the application of the Principle of Legality which calls for the right of the accused to be tried for crimes specified in the Qur'an or other crimes whose clear and well-established meaning and content are determined by Shariah Law (Islamic Law) or by a criminal code in conformity therewith;
4. the right to appear before an appropriate tribunal previously established by law;
5. the right to a public trial;
6. the right not to be compelled to testify against oneself;
7. the right to present evidence and to call witnesses in one's defence;
8. the right to counsel of one's own choosing;
9. the right to a decision on the merits based upon legally admissible evidence;
10. the right to have the decision in the case rendered in public;
11. the right to benefit from the spirit of Mercy and the goals of rehabilitation and resocialization in the consideration of the penalty to be imposed; and
12. the right of appeal.[332]

The minimum guarantees identified above are applicable to all individuals under Islamic law without discrimination of any kind.[333] Thus Article 19(b) of the OIC Cairo Declaration on Human Rights in Islam provides that: 'The right to resort to justice is guaranteed to everyone'.

3.16 FREEDOM FROM RETROACTIVE CRIMINAL LAW

Article 15

1. No one shall be held guilty of any criminal offence on account of any act or omission which did not constitute a criminal offence, under national or international law, at the time when it was committed. Nor shall a heavier penalty be imposed than the one that was applicable at the time when the criminal offence was committed. If, subsequent to the commission of the offence, provision is made by law for the imposition of a lighter penalty, the offender shall benefit thereby.

---

[332] *See* a reproduction of the Resolution in Bassiouni (above n.331) at pp.249–250.
[333] *See* text to n.285 above for Qur'anic reference to the fact that the whole of mankind has a right to justice under Islamic law without discrimination.

2. Nothing in this article shall prejudice the trial and punishment of any person for any act or omission which, at the time when it was committed, was criminal according to the general principles of law recognized by the community of nations.

This right which reiterates the principle of legality also falls within the guarantee of the due process of law. The wording of Article 15(1) does not limit this right only to the prohibition of retroactive criminal laws but also prohibits a penalty heavier than the one prescribed by law at the time the offence was committed. This places a duty on the State to ensure that criminal offences and their penalties remain clearly defined by law for legal certainty. The reference to international law in Article 15(1) makes it imperative that international crimes must also be well defined for legal certainty. Article 15(2) excludes from the prohibition of retroactivity, acts or omissions that were, at the time committed, criminal offences under customary international law. Thus States Parties can under this exception possibly punish war crimes, piracy or genocide through retroactive national laws. In that case the punishment is made legal by the prohibition of those offences under international law.

The non-retroactivity principle is also reversed in respect of a lighter punishment enacted after the commitment of an offence. The last sentence of Article 15(1) which allows for the retroactive application of a lighter penalty, was proposed by Egypt during the drafting.[334] It places a duty on the State to apply retroactively a lighter penalty subsequently enacted in place of a heavier one after the commission of the relevant offence. This demonstrates a humanitarian approach to criminal law. Most international law scholars consider this exception to the rule of non-retroactivity as a trend of modern criminal law. It is instructive to note however that, based on the precedent of the Prophet, the classical Islamic jurists had also stated in their writings an exception to the rule of non-retroactivity of criminal law where the new law provides for a lesser penalty than that existing when the offence was committed, in which case the lesser penalty was held to apply retroactively.[335] It is possible therefore that Egypt's proposal in that respect during the drafting of Article 15 of the ICCPR was influenced by Islamic jurisprudence.

The Qur'an had from inception reflected the rule of non-retroactivity in some of its injunctions and so did the Prophet in some of his Traditions. Generally the Qur'an points out that God never punishes a people until He first sends a Messenger with His laws.[336] A specific instance of non-retroactivity of laws in the Qur'an is demonstrated in the laws prohibiting some types of marriage

---

[334] *See* E/CN.4/425; E/CN.4/SR.159 para.94, cited in Nowak (above n.5) at p.279.

[335] *See* e.g. al-Saleh (above n.162) at pp.62–65; *see also* Kamel, T., 'The Principle of Legality and its Application in Islamic Criminal Justice' in Bassiouni (above n.331) at pp.149–169.

[336] *See* e.g. Q4:165; Q17:15–16; Q28:59; Q35:24.

that were formerly legitimate among the Arabs. The Qur'an provided as follows:

And marry not women whom your fathers married, *except what is past*; it was a shameful, odious and abominable custom indeed. Prohibited to you [also] are your mothers, daughters, sisters ... *except what is past*; for God is Most-forgiving, Most Merciful.[337]

Thus, while those who violated the prohibited degrees in marriage after the revelation of these verses were committing a sin, those who did it before the law was revealed (that is to say, *except what was past*) were exempted on grounds of non-retroactivity of the law. Also, during his last sermon the Prophet declared that any blood guilt traced back to the period of ignorance, (namely before the dawn of Islam in Arabia) should be disregarded because the Islamic provision on blood money for homicide and torts was not operative then. That this applies to all other rules of Islamic law is also reflected in the saying of the Prophet that Islam wipes out any prohibited conduct that preceded it.[338] Thus, any person who comes into Islam is not accountable for any prohibited conduct committed before becoming a Muslim. This indicates clearly that there is no liability under Islamic law prior to legislation. Thus Article 19(d) of the OIC Cairo Declaration on Human Rights in Islam provides that 'There shall be no crime or punishment except as provided in the Sharî'ah'.

3.17 THE RIGHT TO RECOGNITION AS A PERSON BEFORE THE LAW

Article 16

Everyone shall have the right to recognition everywhere as a person before the law.

The importance of this right derives from the fact that the violation of any human right may only be remedied through the due process of law. Without recognition as a person before the law an individual will never be able to bring any claims before the law. Conversely, if everyone has a right to be recognized as a person before the law then everyone has capacity to bear rights and duties.[339] This right thus guarantees the legal capacity or legal personality of the individual under international human rights law.

The right to recognition as a person before the law is in full harmony with Islamic law. Under Islamic law, legal capacity or personality is known as

---

[337] Q4:22–23 (emphasis added).
[338] Reported by Muslim. *See* e.g. Karim (above n.248) at Vol. 1, pp.137–138, Hadith No. 63.   [339] *See* Joseph, Schultz and Castan (above n.23) at pp.201–205.

Ahlīyah or *Dhimmah*, and has been defined as 'the capacity or fitness to acquire legal rights and exercise them and to accept duties and perform them'.[340] The acknowledgement of the importance of this right by the classical Islamic jurists is reflected in their very detailed exposition on the topic.[341]

In case of the insane, imbecile or infant, Islamic law provides that their guardian shall represent them in law.[342] Article 8 of the OIC Cairo Declaration on Human Rights in Islam thus provides that:

> Every human being has the right to enjoy his legal capacity in terms of both obligation and commitment, should this capacity be lost or impaired, he shall be represented by his guardian.

3.18 THE RIGHT TO PRIVACY

Article 17

1. No one shall be subjected to arbitrary or unlawful interference with his privacy, family, home or correspondence, nor to unlawful attacks on his honour and reputation.
2. Everyone has the right to the protection of the law against such interference or attacks.

The right to privacy guarantees individual autonomy and is thus an important aspect of freedom, liberty, and respect for human dignity. Article 17(1) however prohibits only arbitrary or unlawful interference with privacy. The HRC has interpreted this to mean that no interference with privacy can take place 'except in cases envisaged by the law . . . which itself must comply with the provisions, aims and objectives of the Covenant' and 'reasonable in the particular circumstances'.[343] Article 17(2) also guarantees the right to protection of the law against such interference or attacks and thus places a positive obligation on the State to enact laws to protect that right both vertically and horizontally. Generally, the right to privacy therefore 'guarantees the respect for the individual existence of the human being'.[344]

The scope of the right to privacy can however be very vague.[345] Volio has notably observed that '[a]lthough it is an old right and some of its manifestations have long been recognized, the right to privacy has acquired a new and special place in the law, as the means for invading the private

---

[340] *See* Nyazee, I.A.K., *Theories of Islamic Law* (n.d.) p.75. *See also* Al-Zuhayli (above n.78) at Vol. 4, p.2960.   [341] *See ibid.*

[342] *See* e.g. Qadri (above n.22) at p.406.   [343] General Comment 16, paras.3 and 4.

[344] Nowak (above n.5) at p.288.

[345] *See* e.g. Dissenting Opinion of Mr. Herndl in *Coeriel and Aurik v. The Netherlands,* Communication No. 453/1991, UN Doc.CCPR/C/52/D/453/1991 (1994).

life of individuals have multiplied and become more sophisticated and intrusive'.[346] Specific aspects of privacy addressed by the HRC include family,[347] home,[348] correspondence,[349] honour and reputation,[350] name,[351] person and body.[352]

The regulation of sexual behaviour that takes place in private has also been considered as interference with privacy under Article 17. The HRC observed in *Toonen v. Australia*[353] that: 'In so far as article 17 is concerned, it is undisputed that adult consensual sexual activity in private is covered by the concept of "privacy" '. The Committee went on to find that a Tasmanian law that criminalized homosexual practices interfered with the claimant's privacy and thus violated Article 17 of the ICCPR even if the provisions had not been enforced for a decade.[354] The Committee had also rejected the State Party's argument that the law was justified on grounds of public morals, which must be left to the domestic law of the State. It held that it 'cannot accept . . . for the purpose of article 17 of the Covenant [that] moral issues are exclusively a matter of domestic concern, as this would open the door to withdrawing from the Committee's scrutiny a potentially large number of statutes interfering with privacy'.[355]

The right to privacy is also generally well stressed under Islamic law. The *Sharî'ah* prohibits any unlawful intrusion into the private life, home and

---

[346] Volio, F., 'Legal Personality, Privacy, and the Family Life' in Henkin (above n.6) at pp.192–3.

[347] *See* General Comment 16, para.5. *See also Shirin Aumeeruddy-Cziffra and 19 Other Mauritian Women v. Mauritius*, Communication No. 35/1978 (9 April 1981), UN Doc. CCPR/C/OP/1 at 67 (1984).

[348] *See* General Comment 16, para.8. 'Searches of a person's home should be restricted to a search for necessary evidence and should not be allowed to amount to harassment'.

[349] *See* General Comment 16, para.8. 'Compliance with article 17 requires that the integrity and confidentiality of correspondence should be guaranteed *de jure* and *de facto* . . . Surveillance, whether electronic or otherwise, interceptions of telephonic, telegraphic and other forms of communications, wire-tapping and recording of conversations should be prohibited'. *See also Miguel Angel Estrella v. Uruguay*, Communication No. 74/1980 (17 July 1980), UN Doc. Supp. No. 40 (A/38/40) at 150 (1983), para.9.2.

[350] *See* General Comment 16, para.11. 'Article 17 affords protection to personal honour and reputation and States are under an obligation to provide adequate legislation to that end'. *See also Tshisekedi v. Zaire*, Communication Nos. 241/1987 and 242/1987.

[351] *Coeriel and Aurik v. The Netherlands* (above n.345) at para.10.2. 'The Committee is of the view that a person's surname constitutes an important component of one's identity and that the protection against arbitrary or unlawful interference with one's privacy includes the protection against arbitrary or unlawful interference with the right to choose and change one's own name'.

[352] *See* General Comment 16, para.8. 'So far as personal and body search is concerned, effective measures should ensure that such searches are carried out in a manner consistent with the dignity of the person who is being searched. Persons being subjected to body search by State officials, or medical personnel acting at the request of the State, should only be examined by persons of the same sex'.

[353] Communication No. 488/1992, Human Rights Committee (04 April 1994), UN Doc. CCPR/C/50/D/488/1992. [354]*ibid.*, paras. 8.1 and 8.2.

[355] *ibid.*, para.8.6.

correspondence of others, or the violation of a person's honour and integrity. There is actually a chapter in the Qur'an titled 'Private Apartments' or 'The Chambers',[356] in which many Islamic rules on privacy and morality are specified. Generally, the *Sharî'ah* prohibits arbitrary suspicion and spying on others by providing that '...Avoid much suspicion;...And spy not on each other...'.[357] More specifically on right to privacy for the family and home, Qur'an 24:27–28 provides that:

> ...Enter not houses other than your own, until you first announce your presence and invoke greetings of peace upon those therein; that is best for you, that you may be heedful. Even if you find no one therein, do not enter until permission is given to you, and if you are asked to go away then go away; that is purer for you; and God knows all that you do.

To drive this point home, the Prophet had stated in one Tradition that a man should not even peep into a house without permission, for if he does so he would have entered it. Islamic law also prohibits interference with the correspondence of others. The Prophet had warned that: 'Anyone who reads the letter of another without permission will read it in hell-fire',[358] and 'He who listens clandestinely to peoples' conversation against their wishes will have molten lead poured into his ears on the Day of Resurrection'.[359] Also in prohibiting the violation of the honour and reputation of others the Qur'an prohibits scoffing, defamation, insults, and offensive nicknames.[360] These rules apply to both State and private intrusions into privacy.

Under Islamic law, only State officials conferred with the necessary jurisdiction may violate the above Islamic injunctions on right to privacy. They may only do so for the purpose of conducting reasonable searches or investigations, and this must be in accordance with the due process of law.[361] It is reported that during the Caliphate of Umar ibn al-Khatâb he used to go round on night patrol of the city of Medina. One night while on patrol he heard some noise of drunkenness coming from a house and he knocked on the door to find out what it was but no one answered him. He then climbed over the wall and saw a drunken party inside, he shouted down and accused the homeowner of breaking the law prohibiting intoxicants. The man replied, 'if I have committed one sin you have committed four sins to find out. You spied on us against God's command that "spy not on each other";[362] You climbed over the wall despite God's command that: "enter houses through the proper doors";[363] You entered without announcing yourself nor greeting in violation of God's command that: "announce your presence and invoke greetings of peace upon those

---

[356] Q49.   [357] Q49:12.

[358] *See* Al-Suyûtî, J., *al-Jâmi' al-Sagîr* (Arabic) (1964) p.165.

[359] Reported by al-Bukhârî and Muslim. *See* e.g. al-Qaradawi (above n.16) at pp.315–6.

[360] Q49:11.   [361] *See* al-Saleh (above n.162) at p.69.   [362]Q49:12.

[363] Q2:189.

therein";[364] You entered without permission in violation of God's command that "do not enter until permission is given you" '.[365] The Caliph Umar was abashed and he said: 'You are right and I must forgive you your sin'. The man then indicted the Caliph saying: 'that is your fifth sin, you claim to be the Caliph and protector of Islamic law, how can you then say you forgive what God has prohibited'.[366] This vividly illustrates the importance of the right to privacy under Islamic law and that the privacy of individuals cannot for any reason be violated contrary to due legal process. Article 18(b) and (c) of the OIC Cairo Declaration on Human Rights in Islam thus provides that:

(b) Everyone shall have the right to privacy in the conduct of his private affairs, in his home, among his family, with regard to his property and his relationships. It is not permitted to spy on him, to place him under surveillance or to besmirch his good name. The State shall protect him from arbitrary interference.
(c) A private residence is inviolable in all cases. It will not be entered without permission from its inhabitants or in any unlawful manner, nor shall it be demolished or confiscated and its dwellers evicted.

Since Islamic law prohibits and criminalizes homosexuality the question may be raised whether the HRC will follow its decision in *Toonen's* case if faced with a Muslim State's domestic law prohibiting homosexuality vis-à-vis the right to privacy under Article 17. The question of reasonableness and public morals are relevant here. *Toonen v. Australia* does not provide a clear answer and may be distinguishable from a Muslim State on grounds, *inter alia,* that: (i) with the exception of Tasmania, all laws criminalizing homosexuality had been repealed throughout Australia; (ii) the Tasmanian law had never been used and there was ongoing debate for its repeal; (iii) the Federal Government of Australia had acknowledged also that a complete prohibition of homosexuality was unnecessary to sustain the moral fabric of Australian society and therefore did not argue that the challenged laws were based on reasonable and objective criteria.[367]

The situation will apparently be different in the case of Muslim States that apply Islamic law. Homosexuality is generally seen to be strongly against the moral fabric and sensibilities of Islamic society and is prohibited morally and legally under Islamic law. The HRC may perhaps distinguish a similar case involving the domestic law of a Muslim State that applies Islamic law from its decision in *Toonen's* case. That will however require a consideration of the public sensibility and morality obtaining within Muslim societies and on that basis concede some margin of appreciation to the Muslim State in that regard. Although the HRC does not presently apply the margin of appreciation

---

[364] Q24:27.   [365] Q24:28.
[366] This incident has been reported in slightly varied versions by different narrators but all depict the same important principle of prohibition of violation of individual privacy under Islamic law. *See* e.g. Tabandeh (above n.259) at pp.31–32, and 'Uthmân (above n.119) at p.82.
[367] *See* above n.353.

doctrine, one of the propositions in this study is that the HRC needs to adopt the margin of appreciation doctrine because of its utility for resolving cases involving public sensibility and moral issues confronted by States Parties to the Covenant.[368] The cultural background and orientation of the HRC Members at the point in time will also play an influential role in such circumstances. It is instructive to observe in relation to this that the US Supreme Court had in *Bowers v. Hardwick* rejected, on grounds, *inter alia*, of public sensibility and morality, the claim that homosexual sodomy was protected by the US constitutional right to privacy.[369]

3.19 THE RIGHT TO FREEDOM OF THOUGHT, CONSCIENCE AND RELIGION

Article 18

1. Everyone shall have the right to freedom of thought, conscience and religion. This right shall include freedom to have or to adopt a religion or belief of his choice, and freedom, either individually or in community with others and in public or private, to manifest his religion or belief in worship, observance, practice and teaching.
2. No one shall be subject to coercion which would impair his freedom to have or to adopt a religion or belief of his choice.
3. Freedom to manifest one's religion or beliefs may be subject only to such limitations as are prescribed by law and are necessary to protect public safety, order, health, or morals or the fundamental rights and freedoms of others.
4. The States Parties to the present Covenant undertake to have respect for the liberty of parents and, when applicable, legal guardians to ensure the religious and moral education of their children in conformity with their own convictions.

Despite the diversity of ideological and religious leanings within the international community there has been an identified need, since the UN was founded, for an acceptance in modern society of the basic notion of the right to freedom of thought, conscience, and religion as contained in the first sentence of Article 18(1).[370] It is one of the foundations of a pluralistic and democratic society. Article 18 of the UDHR also provides for this right. However, the attempt to define the content of Article 18 of the ICCPR in terms of Article 18 of the UDHR to include the clause that 'this right includes freedom to change

---

[368] *See also* Baderin (above n.2) at p.303.

[369] 478 US 186 (1986). *See also* the view of the European Court of Human Rights on public sensibility in *Otto-Preminger-Institut v. Austria* in a case of blasphemy under Article 10 of the European Convention, in text to n.430 below. Cf. Self, J., 'Bowers v Hardwick: A Study of Agression' (1988) 10 *Human Rights Quarterly*, p.395 and Thornton, B., ' The New International Jurisprudence on the Right to Privacy: A Head-on Collision with Bowers v Hardwick' (1995) 58 *Albany Law Review*, p.725.

[370] *See* e.g. Tahzib, B.G., *Freedom of Religion or Belief: Ensuring Effective International Legal Protection* (1996) pp.63–94.

[one's] religion or belief ' met with opposition principally from Muslim countries such as Egypt, Saudi Arabia, Yemen, and Afghanistan, which pressed for its deletion.[371] Similar objections against that clause during the drafting of Article 18 of the UDHR were defeated in 1948. On that occasion the representative of Pakistan did not agree with the objection of other Muslim States by arguing that '[t]he Moslem [sic] religion was a missionary religion: it strove to persuade men to change their faith and alter their way of living, so as to follow the faith and way of living it preached, but it recognized the same right of conversion for other religions as for itself'.[372]

During the drafting of Article 18 of the ICCPR the arguments resurfaced. In opposing the inclusion of the clause 'this right includes freedom to change [one's] religion or belief ', the Saudi Arabian delegate submitted that:

Some religions emphasized the importance of missionary work, and were organized for proselytizing activities, while others were not. Again, a powerful State with a proselytizing State religion, if it had mass media of information at its disposal, might well use them to cast doubt in the minds of members of other faiths . . . [I]f the individual was to enjoy true religious freedom, he had to be protected against pressure, proselytism and also against errors and heresies. Men could in fact be induced to change their religion not only for perfectly legitimate intellectual or moral reasons, but also through weakness or credulity. The second sentence overemphasized the right to change one's religion. Moreover, the unqualified wording adopted did not take into account the State of mind prevailing in some societies, nor did it allow for the situation, in other societies, of individuals who did not conform to established standards and who might for example, have a purely ethical religion.[373]

Instead of a complete deletion of that clause, a compromise was achieved in the change of the language to '[t]his right shall include freedom to have or to adopt a religion or belief of [one's] choice', after which the Article was unanimously adopted without reservations. This formulation was based on the propositions submitted by Brazil, the Philippines, and the United Kingdom.[374] The HRC has however indicated that the freedom 'to have or to adopt' includes the freedom 'to replace one's current religion or belief with another or to adopt atheistic views, as well as the right to retain one's religion or belief '.[375] Tahzib has also observed that the 'Saudi Arabian representative to the Third Committee who had proposed the deletion of the clause concerning freedom to maintain or to change one's religion or belief, mentioned that he did recognize that freedoms

---

[371] *See* Partsch, K.J., 'Freedom of Conscience and Expression, and Political Freedoms', in Henkin (above n.6) at p.211.

[372] *See* UN Doc A/PV.182 at 890 (1948); and Tahzib (above n.370) at p.75.

[373] *See* UN Docs. A/C.3/SR.1021, para.11; A/C.3/SR.1022, para.27 (1960); and Tahzib (above n.370) at p.85.

[374] *See* UN Docs. A/C.3/SR.1026, para.26 (1960); A/C.3/L.877 (1960); and Tahzib (above n.370) at p.86.

[375] General Comment 22, para.5. *See also* the HRC's reiteration of this point after its consideration of Jordan's 3rd Periodic Report to the ICCPR in 1994: UN Doc. A/49/40 (1994).

to change, maintain and even renounce one's religion or belief were implicit in the right to freedom of thought, conscience and religion'.[376]

The interpretation of the right to freedom of thought, conscience, and religion to include freedom to change one's religion or even to adopt atheistic views has not been without controversy among Islamic scholars in relation to the question of apostasy under Islamic law.[377] The different views will be analysed below. However, the trend among contemporary Islamic scholars on the issue of religious freedom under Islamic law has mostly been towards emphasizing the Qur'anic provision which states that:

> There is no compulsion in religion: truth stands out clear from error; whoever rejects evil and believes in God has grasped the most trustworthy handhold that will never break, and God hears and knows all things. [378]

Elaborating on the principle of non-compulsion of religion under Islamic law, Ismail al-Farûqî had emphasized that by the wording of the Qur'an every human is endowed with the capacity to know God if the intellect is exercised with candidness and integrity. He illustrated the human capacity to understand with reference to a story invented by the early Islamic thinkers about a mythical being called *Hayy ibn Yaqzân*[379] 'who grew up on a deserted island devoid of humans and hence tradition, and who gradually led himself by sheer intellectual effort from ignorance, to naïve realism, to scientific truth and finally, to natural reason and the discovery of transcendent God'.[380] There is however also the human capacity to misunderstand, especially when influenced or sometimes misled by the surrounding circumstances of non-isolated existence. Thus the Muslim is obliged by his faith, which he believes to be the only true one, to present its claims to humanity not dogmatically nor by coercion but rationally through intellectual persuasion, wise argument, and fair preaching.[381] The Qur'an points out that whoever accepts it does so for his own good and whoever rejects it does so at his own loss and none may be compelled.[382] To advocate thought or religion by coercion is, in the words of al-Farûqî, '[t]o tamper with the process of intellection [and] constitutes a threat to man's integrity and authenticity' and is null and void from the standpoint of the *Sharî'ah*.[383] 'Uthmân has also observed that although the Islamic State has a duty to promote the religion of Islam, it is not allowed to force anyone to embrace Islam, but rather has a duty to monitor and prevent those who seek to deny people their freedom of belief.[384]

---

[376] *See* Tahzib (above n.370) at p.86; and UN Doc. A/C.3/SR.1026, para.26 (1960).

[377] *See* e.g. Tabandeh (above n.259) at pp.70–73.

[378] Q2:256. *See generally* al-Farûqî, I.R., *Islam and other Faiths*, ed. Siddiqui, A. (1998) especially pp.129–160 and 281–302.   [379] Meaning 'Living' son of 'Awake'.

[380] al-Farûqî (above n.378) at p.45. For an English translation of the story of Hayy ibn Yaqzân see Ockley, S. *The History of Hayy ibn Yaqzan* (1986).   [381] *See* e.g. Q16:125.

[382] *See* e.g. Q10:108.   [383] al-Farûqî (above n.378) at p.291.

[384] 'Uthmân (above n.119) at p.91.

Under Islamic law, a Muslim male who marries a Christian or Jewish wife cannot compel her into Islam. Also, the recognition of the status of non-Muslims within the Islamic State indicates that Islamic law does not advocate forced conversions to Islam. According to the twelfth century *Hanbali* jurist, Ibn Qudâmah:

> It is not permissible to force a non-believer into embracing Islam. For instance if a non-Muslim citizen *(Dhimmî)* or a protected alien *(Musta'min)* is forced to embrace Islam, he will not be considered as a Muslim except his embrace of Islam is of his own choice . . . The authority for this prohibition of coercion is the words of God Most High that says: 'There is no compulsion in religion'. [385]

Some traditional interpreters of the Qur'an such as al-Tabarî however hold that the 'no compulsion' verse applied only to the 'people of the book' (for example, Christians and Jews) and did not extend to the Arab idolaters or polytheists who did not follow any 'heavenly' religion. Al-Tabarî's view was based on the cause of revelation of the verse. He narrated that the two sons of a certain Muslim man of the tribe of Salim ibn 'Awf, both of whom had embraced Christianity before the advent of Islam came to visit their father in Medina. The father was very grieved about them and requested them to convert to Islam but they declined. The father then brought both of them to the Prophet Muhammad and asked him to intervene. It was on this occasion that the 'no compulsion' verse was revealed, and the man had to leave the two sons with their faith. Since the incident of revelation related specifically to Christianity, Al-Tabarî thus opined that the verse applied only to either Christians or other 'peoples of the book' and not to idolaters.[386] Where this view is followed, it will deny polytheists a right to freedom of thought, conscience, and religion as advocated under international human rights law.

Other interpreters such as al-Zamakhsharî however cited additional Qur'anic verses such as Qur'an 10:99 which states that: 'And had your Lord willed, everyone on earth would have believed. Will you then, [O Muhammad] compel mankind until they become believers?', to contend that not only the 'people of the book' but all human beings are free from being compelled into belief since if God had willed, 'everyone on earth would have believed'.[387] Conversely, Ibn Hazm and some other jurists contend that the 'no compulsion'

---

[385] Ibn Qudâmah, *al-Mugnî,* (Arabic) Vol.8, p.144.

[386] *See* al-Tabarî, M., *Tafsîr al-Tabarî,* (Arabic) (1968) Vol.9 p.347.

[387] *See* al-Zamakhsharî, J., *al-Kashâf An Haqâ'iq al-Tanzîl* (Arabic) (n.d.); *See also* Q6:107–108, which says: 'Had God willed, they would not have taken others beside Him in worship and We have not made you a watcher over them nor are you set over them to dispose of their affairs. And insult not those whom they worship besides God, lest they insult God wrong-fully without knowledge. Thus We have made fair-seeming to each people its own doings; then to their Lord is their return and He shall then inform them of all that they used to do'.

verse had been abrogated by the 'verse of the sword' which says: '... and fight the polytheists altogether as they fight you altogether, and know that God is with those who keep their duty [to Him]'[388] and thus, according to him, compulsion is allowed in religion.[389] Some contemporary Muslim scholars and jurists dispel the above view of Ibn Hazm and point out that this was an extreme position that narrows the Qur'anic experience.[390]

Abû Zahrah has stated a precedent of the second Caliph, Umar, which supports no compulsion into Islam. An old Christian woman was reported to have come to the Caliph with some request which the Caliph fulfilled, after which the Caliph invited her to Islam. The woman declined. The Caliph was reported to have then stated his sincerity of purpose in the following words: 'My Lord, I did not intend to compel her, because I am aware that there must be no compulsion in religion ... the right path has certainly become distinct and distinguished from the wrong path'.[391] This incident no doubt indicates an attitude of non-compulsion and freedom of religion.

Today, most Muslim scholars who address the human rights question of freedom of thought, conscience, and religion, follow the moderate view and hold that Islamic law prohibits the compulsion of anyone in matters of faith.[392] The rule of religious dissemination under Islamic law is 'Invite [all] to the Way of thy Lord with wisdom and beautiful preaching and argue with them in ways that are best and most gracious ...'[393] which does not also support or imply any notion of forced conversion. Thus Article 10 of the OIC Cairo Declaration

---

[388] Q9:36.

[389] *See* e.g. Abû Zayd, M., *al-Nâsikh Wa al-Mansûkh: Dirâsah Tashrî'iyyah, Ta'rîkhiyyah Naqdîyyah* (Arabic) (1963) Vol.2, pp.503–583 and Ibn Hazm, A., *al-Muhallâ* (Arabic) (n.d.) Vol. 2, p.195.

[390] *See* e.g. AbnSulaymân, A.A., *Towards An Islamic Theory of International Relations: New Directions for Islamic Methodology and Thought* (1993) pp.44–45.

[391] *See* Abû Zahrah, M., *Tanzîm al-Islâm li al-Mujtama'* (Arabic) (n.d) p.192.

[392] *See* e.g. Chaudhry (above n.86) at pp.26–30; Ahsan, M.M., 'Human Rights in Islam: Personal Dimensions' (1990) 13 *Hamdard Islamicus*, p.3 at pp.7–8; Ishaque, K.M., 'Human Rights in Islamic Law' (1974) 12 *Review of the International Commission of Jurists*, p.30 at p.35; Hussain, S.S., 'Human Rights in Islam: Principles and Precedents' (1983) 1 *Islamic and Contemporary Law Quarterly*, p.103 at pp.113–114 and Mahmood, T., 'The Islamic Law of Human Rights' (1984) 4 *Islamic and Comparative Law Quarterly*, p.32 at pp.34–38; *See also* e.g. Art. 7 of 'Basic Principles of Islamic State' adopted by the Convention of Muslim Scholars and Thinkers representing all schools of Islamic thought in Pakistan in 1951 which stated that: 'The citizens shall be entitled to all the rights conferred upon them by Islamic Law i.e. they shall be assured within the limits of the law, ... freedom of religion and belief, freedom of worship ...' in Maududi, A.A., *The Islamic Law and Constitution* (7th Ed., 1980) p.333. *See also* the Communiqué of the International Conference on Islamic Law held between the leading scholars of Arabia and Europe which stated *inter alia*, that: 'The individual is free in regard to the creed he wishes to embrace, and it is unlawful to compel anyone to embrace a religion' and citing the no-compulsion verse as authority to that effect, in al-Dawalibi, *Nadwah 'Ilmiyyah Hawl al-Sharî'ah al-Islâmiyyah Wa Huqûq al-Insân fî al-Islâm* (Arabic) cited in Kamali, H.M., *Freedom of Expression in Islam* (1997) p.88. *See also* Art. XIII of the Universal Islamic Declaration of Human Rights (1981) which says: 'Every person has the right to freedom of conscience, and worship in accordance with his religious beliefs'.   [393] Q16:125.

on Human Rights in Islam states that: '. . . It is prohibited to exercise any form of compulsion on man or to exploit his poverty or ignorance in order to convert him to another religion or to atheism'. This brings us to the question of apostasy under Islamic law vis-à-vis the right to freedom of thought, conscience, and religion.

3.19.1 The question of apostasy under Islamic law

Apostasy from Islam is a topical issue under the concept of freedom of thought, conscience, and religion because of its classification as a crime punishable with death under traditional Islamic law. This apparently contradicts the basic principle of non-compulsion advanced above. It also conflicts with the international human rights understanding of freedom of thought, conscience, and religion. In paragraph 5 of its General Comment 22, the HRC observed, *inter alia*, that:

Article18.2 bars coercion that would impair the right to have or adopt a religion or belief, including the use of threat of physical force or penal sanctions to compel believers or non-believers to adhere to their religious beliefs and congregations, to recant their religion or belief or to convert.[394]

There had been differences amongst Muslim jurists and scholars about the definition and punishment of apostasy under traditional Islamic law since the early times of Islam. The jurist, Ibn Taimiyyah, had observed that some of the successors to the companions of Prophet Muhammad known as *al-Tâbi'ûn* such as Ibrahim al-Nakha'î (d.95AH/718CE) a leading jurist of his time and Sufyân al-Thawrî (d.161AH/884CE) held the view that a Muslim apostate must never be sentenced to death but should be invited back to Islam.[395] Their views conform to the Qur'anic rule of propagation that says: 'Invite [all] to the way of thy Lord with wisdom and beautiful preaching; and argue with them in ways that are best and most gracious . . .'.[396]

Both El-Awa and Kamali through references to the Qur'an, the *Sunnah,* the practice of the rightly guided Caliphs, and views of some of the classical as well as contemporary Islamic jurists and scholars seek to establish that apostasy *simpliciter* neither constituted a *hadd*-type offence nor attracted the death penalty.[397] They both cited the twelfth century *Mâlikî* jurist, Abu al-Walîd al-Bâjî as stating that apostasy is 'a sin for which there is no *hadd* punishment'.[398] Although Hamidullah included the crime of apostasy in his

[394] General Comment 22, para.5.
[395] *See* Ibn Taymiyyah, T., *al-Sarîm al-Maslûl 'alâ Shâtim al-Rasûl* (Arabic), ed. Abd al-Hamîd, M.M., (1398AH) p.318; al-Sha'rânî, A.W., *Kitâb al-Mîzân* (Arabic) (1329AH) Vol.2, p.134; Ibn Qudâmah, M., *al-Mugnî* (1981) Vol.8, p.126.   [396] Q16:125.
[397] *See* El-Awa, M.S., *Punishment in Islamic Law* (1982) pp.50–56 and Kamali (above n.392) at pp.87–107. *See also* Sachedina, A.A. 'Freedom of Conscience and Religion in the Qur'an' in Little, D., Kelsay, J., and Sachedina, A.A. (eds.), *Human Rights and the Conflict of Cultures: Western and Islamic Perspectives on Religious Liberty* (1988) p.53 at pp.76–83.
[398] El-Awa (above n.397) and Kamali (above n.392).

Muslim Conduct of State, he went on to indicate that: 'The basis of Muslim polity being religious and not ethnological or linguistic, it is not difficult to appreciate the reason for penalizing this act of apostasy. For it constitutes a politico-religious rebellion'.[399] Contemporary Muslim jurists and scholars thus differ as to whether apostasy *simpliciter* in the form of a person denouncing the Islamic faith is a *hadd*-type offence at all, and also as to whether it attracted the death penalty. Many of the scholars and jurists define apostasy in terms of rebellion against the State, where a Muslim-subject of the Islamic State after denouncing Islam joins with those who take arms against the Islamic State and thus commits a political offence against the State.[400]

The contention is that apostasy *simpliciter,* in the sense of an individual denouncing Islam without more, wherever mentioned in the Qur'an does not stipulate any worldly punishment but is only described as attracting severe punishments in the hereafter.[401] The death punishment for apostasy was based on a reported Tradition of the Prophet that said: 'Anyone who changes his religion, kill him'.[402] Some Muslim scholars have however identified this Tradition as a solitary *(âhâd)* Tradition while others allege weakness in its transmission *(isnâd)*. It has been contended also that there is no precedent of the Prophet compelling anyone into Islam or sentencing anyone to death for apostasy *simpliciter*.[403] El-Awa thus concluded that 'the Qur'an prescribes no punishment in this life for apostasy, [and] [t]he Prophet never sentenced a man to death for it, [but] [s]ome of the companions of the Prophet recognized apostasy as a sin for which there was a *ta'zîr* [discretionary] punishment'.[404] Thus this placed the matter within the legislative discretion of the Islamic State.

Under Article 18(3) of the ICCPR, the right to freedom of religion and beliefs is not absolute. There is a restriction by the provision that:

Freedom to manifest one's religion or beliefs may be subject only to such limitations as are prescribed by law and are necessary to protect public safety, order, health, or morals or the fundamental rights and freedoms of others.

[399] Hamidullah (above n.241) at p.174, para.330.

[400] *See* e.g. Abduh, M., *Tafsîr al-Manâr* (1947–48) Vol.5, p.327; El-Awa (above n.397) at pp.49–56; Rahman, S.A., *Punishment of Apostasy in Islam* (1978) Chapter 2; Al-Ganûshî, R., *al-Huriyyât al-Amah fî al-Dawlah al-Islâmiyyah* (Arabic) (1993) pp.47–51; Shaltût, M., *al-Islâm 'Aqîdah Wa Sharî'ah* (Arabic) (n.d.) pp.292–293; al-Samura'î, A.R.N., *Ahkâm al-Murtadd fî al-Sharî'ah al-Islâmiyyah* (Arabic) (1968) p.144; Mahmassânî, S., *Arkân Huqûq al-Insân fî al-Islâm* (Arabic) (1979) pp.123–124.

[401] *See* e.g. Q2:217–'. . . And if any of you turn back from their faith and die in unbelief, their work will bear no fruit in this life and in the hereafter they will be companions of fire and will abide therein'; and also Q3:86–91; Q5:54; Q16:106.

[402] Reported by al-Bukhârî. *See* e.g. al-Asqalânî, Ibn Hajar, *Bulugh al-Maram (with English translations)* (1996) p.428, Hadith 1032.

[403] *See* e.g. Rahman (above n.400) at p.63; al-'Îlî, A.H.H., *al-Huriyyah al-'Âmah* (Arabic) (1983) p.339; and Mahmassânî (above n.400).   [404] El-Awa (above n.397) at p.56.

That would perhaps be in consonance with the argument of contemporary Islamic scholars[405] and that of some Muslim States that it is not the changing of one's religion *simpliciter* that is prohibited under Islamic law but its manifestation in a manner that threatens public safety, morals, and freedom of others, or even the existence of the Islamic State itself. In its second ICCPR periodic report Sudan stated in that regard that 'conversion from Islam is not an offence in Sudan but only the manifestation of such conversion in a manner that adversely affects public safety'.[406] In accordance with the requirements of due process of law the HRC has however further observed that:

Article 18(3) permits restrictions on the freedom to manifest religion or belief *only if limitations are prescribed by law* and are necessary to protect public safety, order, health or morals, or the fundamental rights and freedoms of others. The freedom from coercion to have or to adopt a religion or belief and the liberty of parents and guardians to ensure religious and moral education cannot be restricted. (emphasis added)

3.20 THE RIGHT TO FREEDOM OF OPINION AND EXPRESSION

Article 19

1. Everyone shall have the right to hold opinions without interference.
2. Everyone shall have the right to freedom of expression; this right shall include freedom to seek, receive and impart information and ideas of all kinds, regardless of frontiers, either orally, in writing or in print, in the form of art, or through any other media of his choice.
3. The exercise of the rights provided for in paragraph 2 of this article carries with it special duties and responsibilities. It may therefore be subject to certain restrictions, but these shall only be such as are provided by law and are necessary;
   (a) For respect of the rights or reputation of others;
   (b) For the protection of national security or of public order (*ordre public*), or of public health or morals.

The intellect is the greatest instrument of human life and its full potential can only be achieved through interaction of ideas among individuals. Freedom of opinion and expression is a birthright of every human being which stimulates dialectical intercourse that aids human development and well-being. Expression is the outward manifestation of a person's opinion, thus a person's liberty is completely denied where freedom of expression is denied. Freedom of opinion and expression has therefore been long recognized as 'one of the

---

[405] *See* e.g. above n.403.
[406] *See* e.g. para.127 and 133 of Sudan's 2nd ICCPR Periodic Report of 1997 (UN Doc. CCPR/C/75/Add.2. of 13/03/97).

most precious rights of man'[407] and also of 'great importance for all other rights and freedoms'.[408]

The right to hold opinions, being internal and private, is absolute and is here separated from the right to freedom of expression. 'Opinion' and 'thought' are quite synonymous, but since 'thought' has been associated with religion or beliefs in Article 18 above, 'opinions' here is deemed to point more towards political, secular, and civil matters.[409] Although a person's opinion may be influenced by external factors, it cannot actually be restricted because it is an event of the mind and hardly interferes with the rights of others. In contrast, freedom of expression is a public matter that could easily interfere with the right of others if not controlled. Freedom of expression is thus not absolute. During the drafting of Article 19, it was appreciated that while 'freedom of expression was a precious heritage' it could also be 'a dangerous instrument' against public order and the personality of others.[410] Thus while the right to freedom of expression was made as comprehensive as possible to cover the seeking, receiving, and imparting of information and ideas of all kinds through any media of one's choice, it carried with it 'special duties and responsibilities'[411] and was also subjected to certain restrictions under Article 19(3).

Due to the importance and preciousness of the right to freedom of expression, there were differences of opinion during the drafting as to the scope of the limitations upon the right.[412] In its effort to define that scope, the HRC has pointed out that 'when a State party imposes certain restrictions on the exercise of freedom of expression, these may not put in jeopardy the right itself [and] the restrictions must be "provided by law"; they may only be imposed for one of the purposes set out in subparagraphs (a) and (b) of paragraph 3; and they must be justified as being "necessary" for that State party for one of those purposes'.[413] Moreover, 'the word "necessary" imports "an element of proportionality" into Article 19(3): the law must be appropriate and adapted to achieving one of the enumerated ends'.[414]

The recognition of freedom of expression under Islamic law as a birthright of every human being is confirmed by Qur'an 55:1–4 which states that:

[God] The most Gracious!; [He] Taught the Qur'an; [He] Created Man [and] *Taught him eloquent speech [expression]*. (emphasis added)

---

[407] *See* Art.XI French Declaration of the Rights of Man and of Citizen (1789) Translated in Paine, T., *Rights of Man* (with an Introduction by Eric Foner) (1984) p.110.
[408] Partsch (above n.371) at p.216.   [409] *ibid.*, p.217.
[410] *See* UN Doc. A/2929 (above n.8) at p.148.
[411] These duties and responsibilities were however not defined.
[412] *See* UN Doc. A/2929 (above n.8) at pp.147–152. *See also* Nowak (above n.5) at p.348ff.   [413] General Comment 10, para.4.
[414] *See* Joseph, Schultz and Castan (above n.23) at p.392.

In his pioneering work on freedom of expression in Islam, Kamali has observed that 'it is generally acknowledged that freedom of expression in Islam is in many ways complementary to freedom of religion; that it is an extension and a logical consequence of the freedom of conscience and belief which the *Sharî'ah* has validated and upholds'.[415] There are a whole lot of recorded Traditions and practice during the lifetime of Prophet Muhammad and during the reign of the Rightly Guided Caliphs after him to support that freedom of speech and expression was an acknowledged right from the inception of Islamic law.[416] Under the *Sharî'ah,* the main objective of this right is the 'discovery of truth and upholding human dignity'.[417] Islamic law endeavours a balance between these two principal objectives and does not accommodate the spread of evil or obscenity under its threshold of freedom of expression. While the Qur'an affirms that God gave mankind the power and freedom of expression, it also directs mankind to be always apposite in speech. It states clearly that: 'God loves not the public utterance of evil speech'[418] and that 'Those who love [to see] scandal broadcasted among the believers will have a grievous penalty in this life and in the hereafter'.[419] Thus the freedom of expression under Islamic law is also not absolute but restricted to apposite speech and expressions.

Under Islamic law, examples of expressions and speech that amount to abuse of this right are specifically stated by the Qur'an and some Traditions of the Prophet. Kamali classified these *Sharî'ah* limitations on freedom of expression into 'moral restraints' and 'legal restraints'. The moral restraints are essentially 'addressed to the conscience of the believer' and include, *inter alia*, defamation, backbiting, lying, derision, exposing the weaknesses of others, and acrimonious disputation. The legal restraints, some of which are backed by specific sanctions include, *inter alia*, public utterance of evil or hurtful speech, slanderous accusation, libel, insult, cursing, seditious speech, and blasphemy.[420] Of all these *Sharî'ah* restraints, blasphemy is perhaps portrayed as the most controversial limitation on freedom of expression under international human rights law as was demonstrated through the reactions attracted by the Salman Rushdie affair from both international human rights advocates and Islamic jurists and scholars worldwide.[421]

---

[415] Kamali (above n.392) at p.6. [416] *See* e.g. Chaudhry (above n.86) at pp.31–33.

[417] *See* Kamali (above n.392) at p.8. [418] Q4:148. [419] Q24:19.

[420] *See* Kamali (above n.392) at pp.117–258. It is interesting to note that the section on the restraints makes up the largest portion of Professor Kamali's work *Freedom of Expression in Islam.* This perhaps portrays the non-absolute nature of the right to freedom of expression and the difficulty of balancing between the right itself and the restraints upon it.

[421] *See* e.g. *generally* Appignanesi, L., and Maitland, S., *The Rushdie File* (1990); also Kidwai, A.R., and Ahsan, M.M. (eds.), *Sacrilege versus Civility: Muslim Perspectives on the Satanic Verses Affair* (1991).

Blasphemy is broadly referred to under Islamic law as *'Sabb Allah aw Sabb al-Rasûl'*, meaning 'Reviling God or Reviling the Messenger'. Blasphemy overlaps with apostasy in the sense that an act of blasphemy by a Muslim also amounts to apostasy. Thus classical Islamic jurists often paired the two together in their legal treatises and prescribed the death penalty for both under traditional Islamic law.[422] Blasphemy is however separable from apostasy especially when committed by a non-Muslim against Islam.[423]

The *Encyclopaedia of Religion and Ethics* defines blasphemy in Islam broadly as 'All utterances expressive of contempt for Allah [God] Himself, for His Names, attributes, laws, commands or prohibitions [and] All scoffing at Muhammad or any other prophets or apostles of Allah [God]'.[424] Being a religious law, Kamali points out that the prohibition of blasphemy under Islamic law is mainly 'to defend the dogma and belief-structure of Islam'.[425] It is noteworthy that despite Islam's claim to being 'the [only] religion acceptable to God',[426] it however recognizes the reciprocal rule with respect to other faiths under its prohibition of blasphemy. The Qur'an enjoins Muslims also 'not to revile those whom they [non-Muslims] worship beside God, lest they [non-Muslims] revile God wrongfully without knowledge. Thus We [God] have made fair-seeming to each people its own doings; to their Lord is their final return and He shall inform them of all that they did'.[427]

The *Sharî'ah* prohibition of blasphemy as a limitation to freedom of expression thus aims at protecting the sensibilities and beliefs of the Muslim community in particular and that of other faiths in general. Seen in that perspective, that limitation is explicable within the proviso of Article 19(3)(b) of the ICCPR on the protection of public order or morals. The ability of blasphemous expressions to incite Muslims to public disorder is evidenced, for example, by the upheavals in many parts of the world that followed the publication of Salman Rushdie's *Satanic Verses*, which was considered as being offensive to the religious sensibilities of Muslims not only by Muslims, but even by non-Muslim religious leaders.[428] There is need however in this realm

---

[422] *See* section on apostasy at para.3.19.1 above.

[423] *See* Kamali (above n.392) at p.217. Professor Kamali concluded (at p.244) after a detailed analysis of blasphemy under Islamic law that 'The Qur'an has made no reference to the death penalty for blasphemy, and the text does not warrant the conclusion that it is a Qur'anic obligation, or a prescribed punishment or a mandate. On the contrary, we would submit that the general language of the Qur'an can only sustain the broad conclusion that the perpetrator of blasphemy disgraces himself and invokes the curse of God upon himself, and that it is a criminal offence which carries no prescribed mandatory punishment, and, as such, automatically falls under the category of *ta'zîr* offences, whose punishment may be determined by the head of State or competent judicial authorities.'

[424] Hastings, J., (Ed.), *Encyclopaedia of Religion and Ethics* (1909) Vol. 2, p.672.

[425] *See* Kamali (above n.392) at p.8.   [426] Q3:19.   [427] Q6:108.

[428] *See* e.g. Appignanesi and Maitland (above n.421) at pp.235–236.

always carefully and objectively to distinguish constructive reasonable intellectual critiques of religious interpretations from expressions that insult or revile the sensibilities of reasonable adherents of particular religions under the guise of freedom of expression. Maududi has pointed out in that regard that Islam does not prohibit decent intellectual debate and religious discussions: what it prohibits is evil speech that encroaches upon the religious beliefs of others.[429] Article 22 of the Cairo Declaration on Human Rights in Islam provides that:

(a) Everyone shall have the right to express his opinion freely in such manner as would not be contrary to the principles of the Sharî'ah.
(b) Everyone shall have the right to advocate what is right, and propagate what is good and warn against what is wrong and evil according to the norms of Islamic Sharî'ah.
(c) Information is a vital necessity to society. It may not be exploited or misused in such a way as may violate sanctities and the dignity of Prophets, under moral and ethical values or disintegrate, corrupt or harm society or weaken its faith.

Applying the margin of appreciation doctrine to a case of blasphemy under Article 10 of the European Convention, the European Court of Human Rights held in the case of *Otto-Preminger-Institut v. Austria* [430] that the seizure and forfeiture of a blasphemous film in which God, Jesus Christ, and the Virgin Mary were ridiculed did not violate the author's right to freedom of expression guaranteed under Article 10 of the European Convention. The Court observed, *inter alia,* that:

The Court cannot disregard the fact that the Roman Catholic religion is the religion of the overwhelming majority of Tyroleans. In seizing the film, the Austrian authorities acted to ensure religious peace in that region and to prevent that some people should feel the object of attacks on their religious beliefs in an unwarranted and offensive manner. It is in the first place for the national authorities, who are better placed than the international judge, to assess the need for such a measure in the light of the situation obtaining locally at a given time. In all the circumstances of the present case, the Court does not consider that the Austrian authorities can be regarded as having overstepped their margin of appreciation in this respect.[431]

It is submitted that the HRC should follow a similar approach in considering issues of moral and religious sensibilities, especially in its interpretation of Article 19 of the ICCPR. This will facilitate an appropriate balance between respect for religious beliefs and the right to freedom of expression under international human rights law.

---

[429] *See* Maududi (above n.229) at p.30.
[431] *ibid.*, para.56.
[430] [1994] ECHRR, Series A, Vol.295-A.

3.21 THE PROHIBITION OF PROPAGANDA FOR
WAR AND INCITEMENT TO HATRED

Article 20

1. Any propaganda for war shall be prohibited by law.
2. Any advocacy of national, racial or religious hatred that constitutes incitement to discrimination, hostility or violence shall be prohibited by law.

Differences of race, nationality, and religion are part of the realities of human society that do not by themselves create any problems. It is the advocacy of or incitement to hatred on grounds of those differences that creates problems which lead to serious violations of human rights. Article 20 thus aims at the important objective of promoting tolerance, mutuality, and peaceful co-existence despite human differences.

This provision constitutes a further limitation on the freedom of expression guaranteed under Article 19 above. The HRC has opined that 'these required prohibitions are fully compatible with the right of freedom of expression as contained in article 19 the exercise of which carries with it special duties and responsibilities'. The Committee has also stated that the propaganda prohibited under Article 20(1) 'extends to all forms of propaganda threatening or resulting in an act of aggression or breach of the peace contrary to the Charter of the United Nations'.[432] The object of Article 20(2) is also to combat the reoccurrence of the horrors of Nazism that resulted mainly from incitement of racial hatred. There is a positive obligation on States to enact laws prohibiting such propaganda of war and advocacy of hatred.

The *Sharî'ah* also prohibits aggression and mischief on earth, prohibits racial or religious hatred and incitement to discrimination, violence or hostility. The Qur'an condemns, in many verses, those who spread mischief on earth and incite to hatred. Prophet Muhammad had also stated in one of his Traditions that 'Whoever incites to [racial] partisanship is not of us'.[433] Article 22(d) of the OIC Cairo Declaration on Human Rights in Islam also provides that: 'It is not permitted to arouse nationalistic or doctrinal hatred or to do anything that may be an incitement to any form of racial discrimination'.

Islamic law however approves the call to war in case of self-defence and to counter aggression or persecution. The Qur'an states that 'Permission to fight is given to those against whom war is made because they are wronged, and certainly God is most capable to aid them'.[434] In that case, the authority to call to war lies with the Head of State and not with individuals. In similar vein the HRC has also stated that Article 20(1) of the ICCPR does 'not prohibit

---

[432] General Comment 11, para.2.
[433] Reported by Abû Dâwûd. *See* e.g. Karim (above n.248) at Vol.1, p. 488, Hadith No. 244.
[434] Q22:39.

advocacy of the sovereign right of self-defence or the right of peoples to self-determination and independence in accordance with the Charter of the United Nations'.[435]

3.22 THE RIGHT OF PEACEFUL ASSEMBLY

Article 21

The right of peaceful assembly shall be recognized. No restrictions may be placed on the exercise of this right other than those imposed in conformity with the law and which are necessary in a democratic society in the interests of national security or public safety, public order (*ordre public*), the protection of public health or morals or the protection of the rights and freedoms of others.

Article 21 guarantees the right of peaceful assembly and prohibits any restriction of the right except as is necessary in a democratic society in the interests of national security or public safety, public order, protection of public health or morals or protection of the rights and freedoms of others. Such restriction where necessary must also be in conformity with the law. This aims at protecting the right of people to come together and peacefully pursue a common purpose. The right is usually related to political liberty. Nowak has however observed that the limiting proviso 'is so broad that more than enough possibilities are available to suppress assemblies critical of the regime or threatening to the State'.[436]

The right of peaceful assembly is recognized under Islamic law by virtue of the Qur'anic provision enjoining co-operation in the pursuit of righteousness and goodness and not in nurturing transgression and hostility.[437] There is nothing in the *Shari'ah* that prohibits the right to participate in peaceful assembly for a rightful cause of one's choice as long as it is not an incitement to aggression or public disorder as stressed in the proviso of Article 21. This same Islamic principle applies to the right to freedom of association addressed in Article 22 below.

3.23 THE RIGHT TO FREEDOM OF ASSOCIATION

Article 22

1. Everyone shall have the right to freedom of association with others, including the right to form and join trade unions for the protection of his interests.

---

[435] General Comment 11, para.2.

[436] *See* Nowak (above n.5) at p.371 and p.380–383 for an analysis of the permissible purposes for interference on freedom of assembly. *See also* Joseph, Schultz and Castan (above n.23) pp.425–432. [437] Q5:2.

2. No restrictions may be placed on the exercise of this right other than those which are prescribed by law and which are necessary in a democratic society in the interests of national security or public safety, public order (*ordre public*), the protection of public health or morals or the protection of the rights and freedoms of others. This article shall not prevent the imposition of lawful restrictions on members of the armed forces and of the police in their exercise of this right.
3. Nothing in this article shall authorize States Parties to the International Labour Organisation Convention of 1948 concerning Freedom of Association and Protection of the Right to Organize to take legislative measures which would prejudice, or to apply the law in such a manner as to prejudice, the guarantees provided for in that Convention.

Freedom of association is linked to freedom of assembly in Article 21 above. Freedom of association is here associated with the right to form and join trade unions, which is an economic right.[438] Although the right is subjected to similar restrictions imposed upon freedom of assembly, the State is granted the possibility of further restricting members of the armed forces and the police in the exercise of this right due to its link with trade unions.[439]

While the freedom of peaceful assembly and freedom of association are not treated separately in the legal treatises of classical Islamic jurists, Kamali has pointed out that the *Sharî'ah* certainly 'takes an affirmative stand on rights and encourages association in pursuit of lawful objectives'. He further elaborated that 'the Qur'ânic principle of *hisbah*, that is commanding good and forbidding evil, the principle of *nasîhah*, sincere advice, and *shûrâ*, consultation, can equally be quoted *mutatis mutandis* as the basic authority in the *Sharî'ah* for freedom of association'.[440]

Article 22 also mentions the right to form and join trade unions for the protection of the interest of workers. This is very legitimate under Islamic law, considering the tendency of exploitation that often exists in employer-employee relationships all over the world today. The Prophet had enjoined in one of his Traditions that the adequate wage of the employee should be paid by the employer before the labour-sweat of the employee dries out. There is no doubt that the individual employee is always the weaker party in every employer-employee relationship. It is through the formation of trade unions that the above injunction of the Prophet can be realized and the interest of employees adequately protected within modern economies. Within the modern economic practices that operate in modern Muslim States today, it will be inconsistent with the Islamic injunction of fair-dealing not to allow the formation of trade unions to protect the interests of employees as provided under Article 22.

---

[438] *See* Art. 8 of the ICESCR in Chapter 4, para.4.8.
[439] *See* Joseph, Schultz and Castan (above n.23) at pp.432–441.
[440] Kamali (above n.392) at p.73ff.

3.24 THE RIGHT TO MARRY AND FOUND A FAMILY

Article 23

1. The family is the natural and fundamental group unit of society and is entitled to protection by society and the State.
2. The right of men and women of marriageable age to marry and to found a family shall be recognized.
3. No marriage shall be entered into without the free and full consent of the intending spouses.
4. States Parties to the present Covenant shall take appropriate steps to ensure equality of rights and responsibilities of spouses as to marriage, during marriage and at its dissolution. In the case of dissolution, provision shall be made for the necessary protection of any children.

Article 23 of the ICCPR is unique in the sense that it provides for an institutional guarantee. It recognizes the family institution as 'the natural and fundamental group unit of society' that is 'entitled to protection by society and the State'. It also recognizes the 'right of men and women of marriageable age to marry and to found a family', and makes mandatory 'the free and full consent of the intending spouses' in every marriage. Neither the ICCPR nor the ICESCR gives a definition of family. The HRC has however stated that:

In giving effect to recognition of the family in the context of article 23, it is important to accept the concept of the various forms of family, including unmarried couples and their children and single parents and their children and to ensure the equal treatment of women in these contexts . . .[441]

The recognition and importance of the family institution under Islamic law cannot be overemphasized. However, marriage is the legitimate means of founding a family under Islamic law. In that regard paragraphs (1), (2), and (3) of Article 23 are in full consonance with Islamic law, they in fact re-echo important principles of Islamic family law.

There are however some apparent differences between the thresholds of Islamic law and international human rights law regarding equality of rights and responsibilities of spouses during marriage and at its dissolution under Article 23(4). Similar provision is found in Article 16 of the Convention on the Elimination of all forms of Discrimination Against Women.[442] During the discussions of the draft Women's Convention in the Third Committee of the General Assembly, Muslim countries raised some objections with respect to Article 16 and its conformity with principles of Islamic law on rights and responsibilities of spouses during marriage and at its dissolution. They

---

[441] General Comment 28, para.27. The matters addressed here are further considered under family rights in Article 10 of ICESCR in Chapter 4, para.4.10.   [442] Above, n.61.

succeeded in achieving only a few amendments to the original draft.[443] In consequence, most Muslim countries that ratified the Women's Convention entered a reservation to Article 16.[444] The Committee on the Elimination of Discrimination Against Women, believing that it would be useful for it to have material on the subject, requested the UN in its reports of 1987 and 1988 to 'promote or undertake studies on the status of women under Islamic laws and customs'.[445] The request was however turned down at the meetings of both the Economic and Social Council (ECOSOC) and the UN General Assembly due to objections by some Muslim States.[446] According to Lijnzaad this has so far made it difficult to 'reconcile the cause of women's rights with Islamic law'.[447] We will therefore examine in detail here those specific areas of differences with regard to equality of rights and responsibilities of spouses under Islamic law.

The first important issue in this regard is the presumed concept of superiority of the male over the female in Islamic law. 'Abd al 'Atî has observed that almost all writers, Oriental and Occidental, classical and modern, have variously interpreted the following Qur'anic verses to mean the superiority of men (husbands) over women (wives) in Islamic law:

... And women shall have rights similar to the rights against them, according to what is equitable; but *men have a degree above them* ...[448]

Men are the protectors and maintainers of women because God has given the one more strength than the other, and because they support them from their means ...[449] (emphasis added)

In addressing this question, Ibn Qudâmah in his highly esteemed legal treatise, *al-Mugnî*, began by indicating the complementary role of the two genders, but went on to state that the husband's rights were greater than the wife's because

---

[443] *See* UN Doc. A/C.3/34.SR, pp.70–73. *See also* Khaliq, U., 'Beyond the Veil?: An Analysis of the Provisions of the Women's Convention and the Law as Stipulated in Sharî'ah' (1995) 2 *The Buffalo Journal of International Law*, p.1 at p.29.

[444] For texts of reservations *see* e.g. Lijnzaad, L., *Reservations to UN-Human Rights Treaties: Ratify and Ruin?* (1995) pp.320–322. *See also* Cook, R.J., 'Reservations to the Convention on the Elimination of All forms of Discrimination Against Women' (1990) 30 *Yale Journal of International Law*, p.644 at pp.687–706. *See also* UN Treaty Website http://www.unhchr.ch/html/menu3/b/e1cedaw.htm [1/3/03].

[445] *See* (1987) Report of the Committee on the Elimination of Discrimination Against Women Sixth Session, UN Doc. A/42/38 (1987), para.580, (Decision 4); and (1988) Report of the Committee on the Elimination of Discrimination Against Women, Seventh Session, UN Doc. A/43/38 (1988), para.61.

[446] *See* UN Doc. E/1987/SR.10-SR.14 (1987); UN Doc. A/C.3/42/SR.22 (1987); UN Doc. A/C.3/42/SR.26-SR.28 (1987) and UN Doc. A/C.3/42/SR.30 (1987). *See also* Byrnes, A.C., 'The "Other" Human Rights Treaty Body: The Work of the Committee on the Elimination of Discrimination of Discrimination Against Women' (1989) 14 *Yale Journal of International Law*, p.1 at pp.53–55.

[447] *See* Lijnzaad (above n.444) at p.320. *See however*, Ali, S.S., *Gender and Human Rights in Islam and International Law: Equal before Allah, Unequal before Man?* (2000).

[448] Q2:228.   [449] Q4:34.

God says that '*men have a degree above them*'. He also referred to a Tradition in which the Prophet Muhammad is reported to have said that if it were lawful for a human being to prostrate before another, wives would have been ordered to prostrate to husbands due to the rights of husbands over wives.[450] This has often been taken to mean a confirmation of the superiority of the husband over the wife under Islamic law. Thus, for example, the French writer Gaudefroy-Demombynes asserted that Islamic law and customs 'give the husband absolute authority over his wife and children . . . The husband is superior to his wife: "men having a degree above them", says the Qur'an'.[451]

The idea of superiority of men over women is inferred from the 'degree' that men are stated to have above women in Qur'an 2:228. But what is meant by this degree, 'a degree' of what? One observes that both classical and contemporary interpreters of the Qur'an differ on the meaning of this 'degree'. An example of the contrast in interpretations of the 'degree' is found for instance, in the English interpretations of Yusuf Ali which says '. . . men have a degree *(Of advantage)* over them'[452] and that of Muhsin Khan which says '. . . men have a degree *(of responsibility)* over them'.[453] The parenthesizing of the phrases '*Of Advantage*' and '*of responsibility*' by the respective interpreters indicate that those are not express statements of the Qur'an but the understanding of the content by the interpreters. 'Abd al 'Atî has therefore pointed out that such interpretations are 'probably better understood as a reflection of certain psychological dispositions or of the *actual* status of women, which has been low on the whole, at least on the surface', and that the 'idea that men are superior to women and have power over them without reciprocity or qualifications stemmed from sources apparently alien to the spirit as well as the letter of the Qur'anic verses.[454]

It is noteworthy that both Qur'an 2:228 and Qur'an 4:34 revolve around the family institution. Rather than advocating the superiority of one gender above the other, the verses must be understood in the context of the Islamic appreciation of role differentiation within the family. From sociological perspectives, authority and power are necessary elements of any group structure.

---

[450] *See* Ibn Qudâmah, M.A., *al-Mugnî* (Arabic) (1981) Vol.7, p.223.

[451] Gaudefroy-Demombynes, M., *Muslim Institutions*, trans. MacGregor, J.P., (1968) p.132. *See also* Honarver, N., 'Behind The Veil: Women's Rights in Islamic Societies' (1988) 6 *Journal of Law and Religion*, p.355 at pp.384–385.

[452] *See* Ali, A.Y., *The Meaning of The Holy Qur'ân (New Edition with Revised Translation and Commentary)* (1992) p.92 (emphasis added). In footnote 255 to the translation Yusuf Ali states that 'The difference in economic position between the sexes makes the man's rights and liabilities a little greater than the woman's. Q.4:34 refers to the duty of the man to maintain the woman, and to a certain difference in nature between sexes. Subject to this, the sexes are on terms of equality in law, and in certain matters the weaker sex is entitled to special protection'.

[453] *See* Muhsin Khan, M., and Taqi-ud-Din Al-Hilali, M., *Interpretations of the Meanings of the Noble Qur'an in English Language: A Summarized Version of At-Tabari, Al-Qurtubi and Ibn Kathir with Comments from Sahih Al-Bukhari* (1996) p.57 (emphasis added).

[454] 'Abd al 'Atî, (above n.65) at pp.178–182.

The family structure is not an exception. Bernard, quoting Allport, pointed out that the concepts of status, authority, power, etc, 'run through all human and animal relationships', and that 'the social psychologist sees ascendance-submission or dominance-compliance wherever two persons are in contact with each other'.[455] This explains why Islam required leadership in every group activity to ensure cohesion in human relationships. For instance in acts of worship involving two or more people, one of them who is more qualified will lead the others. Also when two or more people travel together, the Prophet instructed that one of them must be selected as leader of the group. In all these situations the leader is not considered as being superior to the others, it is only to ensure cohesion in the group. To enhance the success of family life therefore, there arises the need to differentiate and identify roles within the family structure. The husband would necessarily be more influential in certain roles while the wife would be in others. Zeldich has pointed out that in most societies the instrumental and protective roles are played by the husband-father, while the wife-mother plays the expressive roles.[456] It is in exceptional cases that the wife-mother assumes the protective role within the family structure. That perhaps explains the degree of responsibility that men have above women and which is consistent with the second verse that says:

> Men are the protectors and maintainers of women because God has given the one more strength than the other, and because they support them from their means . . .[457]

The word interpreted here as protectors and maintainers *(qawâmûn)* is also sometimes translated as 'guardians' which in that case involves some element of authority on the part of the husband. However the role of a guardian, protector or maintainer is substantially rather that of responsibility than of authority. It would be more consistent therefore to understand the 'degree' that men are stated to have above women in Qur'an 2: 228 as a degree of responsibility. It is clear that neither the two verses under examination nor any other verse of the Qur'an mentions specifically that men are superior to women. It is also not mentioned directly that men have absolute authority over women.

Where the husband/father adequately discharges the degree of responsibility placed upon him, some reflective rights will reciprocally ensue to him from the wife/mother in the family relationship. Thus the authority of the male is at best inferred only as a consequence of the structural role of the husband/father in the family. Authority and leadership is thus not really generalized or attached per se to the idea of the male being superior to the female. It relates to specific roles in the family structure and is delegated to the gender better suited for that

---

[455] *See* Bernard, J., *American Family Behaviour* (1942) p.420.
[456] Zeldich, M., *Family*, 'Marriage and Kinship' in Faris, R.E.L., *Handbook of Modern Sociology* (1964) p.680 at pp.699 and 703.   [457] Q4:34.

role within Islamic teachings. Whether men are better suited for that role than women is an open question subject to diverse cultural arguments.

Marriage and the family institution are very strong traditions of Islam that cannot be neglected except for valid necessities. Islamic law does not promote celibacy and also generally prohibits sexual relations outside wedlock. The Prophet Muhammad is reported to have said that marriage was part of his Traditions (*Sunnah*) which should not be neglected.[458] Esposito has thus pointed out that:

Islam considers marriage, which is an important safeguard for chastity, to be incumbent on every Muslim man and woman unless they are physically or financially unable to lead conjugal life.[459]

Muslim jurists therefore tend to protect the family institution resolutely and are cautious in accommodating any norms that would tend to disrupt that tradition of Islam. Khan, as quoted by Badawi, expressed the fear of Muslim societies about disintegration of the family institution in the following words:

Of all the family problems in advanced countries, divorce tops the list. The fact that the majority of marriages in these countries end up in divorce has ruined family life completely, for children do not enjoy the love and care of parents who are still alive, whereas it was formerly only death which separated children from their parents.[460]

The urge to protect the family institution while guaranteeing equality of the spouses is not peculiar to Islamic law. It was such considerations, *inter alia*, that defeated the ratification of the Equal Rights Amendment to the US Constitution by the American States in 1982.[461] Also as of March 2003 the United States of America had not ratified the Women's Convention on the ground, *inter alia*, that the Convention has the potential of prohibiting even 'non-invidious gender distinctions'.[462]

Meron has alluded to the wide scope of the Women's Convention with regard to the prohibition of religious inspired norms within the family and suggested that 'religious practices within the family which have relatively less significance for women's ability to function as full human beings in society might be permitted even though those practices perpetuate stereotype roles while

---

[458] Reported by al-Bukhâri. *See* e.g. al-Asqalânî, Ibn Hajar, *Bulugh al-Maram (with English translations)* (1996) p.342, Hadith 825.

[459] Esposito, J.L., *Women in Muslim Family Law* (1982) p.15.

[460] *See* e.g. Badawi, J.A., *The Muslim Woman's Dress According to the Qur'an and Sunnah* (n.d.) pp.13–14.

[461] *See* Feinberg, R., *The Equal Rights Amendment. An Annotated Bibliography of the Issues 1976–1985* (1986) p.3.

[462] *See* Zearfoss, S., 'The Convention for the Elimination of All Forms of Discrimination against Women: Radical, Reasonable, or Reactionary?' (1991) 12 *Michigan Journal of International Law*, p.905. The USA signed the Women's Convention on 17 July 1980 but has yet to ratify it.

practices which impair women's ability to exercise their rights and foreclose opportunities to function outside stereotyped roles (for instance a prohibition on women working outside the home) must not be allowed'.[463] He submitted that to require the elimination of sex-roles in the family structure as required by religious teachings could constitute coercion to alter religious practice or belief, contrary to Article 1(2) of the Declaration on the Elimination of All Forms of Intolerance and of Discrimination Based on Religion or Belief.[464]

Of relevance here is also the issue of abortion. The Women's Convention does not specifically sanction abortion, but a wide interpretation of Article 16(1)(e) of the Women's Convention which provides for the same rights to decide *freely* on the number and spacing of the couple's children can accommodate the right to abortion under the Convention where the wife decides that she has had enough children and then finds that she is pregnant.[465]

With regard to equality of rights 'as to marriage, within marriage and at its dissolution' under Article 23(4) the apparent areas of conflict with Islamic law are: the right of conditional polygamy for men with no right of polyandry for women; the right of Muslim men to marry women of the 'people of the book' (i.e. Christian and Jewish women), but no similar right for Muslim women to marry men of the 'people of the book', i.e. female religious endogamy; the female's share in inheritance; and the right to divorce. We shall now examine these issues together with the juristic views and justifications advanced for them under Islamic law and their implications for international human rights law.

3.24.1 Polygamy in Islamic law and equality of rights in marriage

The HRC observed in its General Comment 28 that polygamy is incompatible with equality of rights in marriage under the Covenant and that 'it should be definitely abolished wherever it continues to exist'.[466] Muslim scholars and jurists have advanced reasons such as demographic needs, economic factors, barrenness of the wife, chronic illness of the wife, higher sexual needs of men, etc, in their attempt to justify the conditional permissibility of polygamy in Islamic law.[467] Most of these justifications may be stiffly contested

---

[463] *See* Meron, T., *Human Rights Law-making in the United Nations: a Critique of Instruments and Process* (1986) p.159, *see* pp.62–66 and pp.153–160.   [464] *ibid.*, pp.159–160.

[465] *See* e.g. Meron (above n.463) at p.72. *See also* the issue of 'unwanted pregnancy' and the presumption that the decision is that of the woman addressed in text to n.151 above.

[466] General Comment 28, para.24. *See also* the Committee's Concluding Observations on Nigeria (1996), UN Doc. CCPR/C/79/Add.65; para.291; Concluding Observations on Libya (1998), UN Doc. CCPR/C/79/Add.101; para.17; Concluding Observations on Cameroon (1999), UN Doc. CCPR/C/79/Add.116; para.10. *See also* CEDAW's General Recommendation 21, UN Doc. HRI\GEN\1\Rev.1 at 90 (1994), para.14.

[467] *See* e.g. Ibn Qayyim al-Jawziyyah, *Kitâb Akhbâr al-Nisâ'* (Arabic) (1900) Vol.2, pp.85–87; Doi (above n.86) at p.146, and al-Qaradawi (above n.16) at pp.192–193.

in the light of present day circumstances. Problems like the barrenness of the wife are however quite tenacious in the arguments for the justification of conditional polygamy in Islamic law. Similar arguments exist also in other cultures. In traditional African society for instance, procreation is usually the main purpose of marriage. Thus where the wife is found barren, the husband is usually inclined towards taking another wife, even though he does not divorce his barren wife.[468] The obvious question here is, what of when the man is the one barren? It is often assumed, albeit wrongly, amongst the local populace in many developing countries that the fault for lack of conception in marriage is always with the wife. Islamic law however recognizes defects of the husband such as impotence, lack of semen or ejaculation during intercourse, lack of testicles and amputated sexual organ, all of which constitute grounds on which the wife may seek dissolution of the marriage. Al-Zaylâ'î, the twelfth century *Hanafi* jurist stated that since these defects defeat the very purpose of marriage, that is to say, satisfaction of sexual urge and procreation of children, the wife has a right to demand for dissolution.[469] Thus, the woman may seek dissolution where the man is found barren. The question then would be, why a right to dissolution for the woman and not a right to polyandry like her male counterpart? The medieval Islamic jurist, Ibn Qayyim al-Jawziyyah, has responded with a list of socio-legal arguments to this question, the most compelling perhaps of which is that polyandry can more easily lead to family and societal disintegration because both the concepts of legitimacy of offspring and family lineage would be impaired. There would always be a contest for legitimacy between the male spouses each time a child is born in a polyandrous union, which is not the case in a polygamous marriage.[470]

In case of a barren woman it is often argued that to take a second wife is better than either divorcing the barren wife or having offspring outside the marriage through adulterous relationships with other women. For such exceptional reasons, some Muslim scholars have argued that 'Islam permitted polygamy—as a remedy for some social diseases—under certain conditions without which plurality of wives shall be prohibited . . . [because] Islam, since the very beginning, favours monogamy'.[471] According to 'Abd al 'Atî, polygamy should not be viewed entirely as a blessing for one sex and a curse for the other, but 'as a legitimate alternative applicable to some difficult, "crisis" situations'.[472]

---

[468] *See* Doi (above n.86) at pp.153–154 and footnote 15 thereof.

[469] *See* al-Zaylâ'î, *Tabyîn al-Haqâ'iq: Sharh Kanz al-Daqâ'iq* (Arabic) (1313AH) Vol.3, p.25.

[470] Ibn Qayyim al-Jawziyyah (above n.467). *See also* 'Abd al'Atî (above n.65) at pp.125–126.

[471] *See* e.g. El-Bahnassawi (above n.59) at p.157; and Al-Zuhayli (above n.78) at Vol.9, p.6670.   [472] 'Abd al'Atî (above n.65) at p.126.

The permissibility of polygamy in Islamic law is based on Qur'an 4:3 which provides that:

> ... marry women of your choice, two, three, or four; but if you fear that you shall not be able to deal justly [with them] then only one, or [a captive] that your right hands possess. That is nearer to prevent you from doing injustice.

Men are thus allowed to have a maximum of four wives at a time. Both classical and contemporary Muslim jurists generally agree that the ability to treat co-wives justly, as stated in the Qur'anic verse above, is a prerequisite to this permissibility of polygamy.[473] Some of the classical jurists such as Imâm al-Shâfi'î, the eponym of the *Shâfi'î* school of Islamic jurisprudence, did not consider the requirement for doing justice between co-wives as an essential legal requirement but only as a 'moral exhortation binding on the husband's conscience'.[474] Many contemporary Islamic scholars and jurists however hold that the mere apprehension of not being able to deal justly between co-wives removes the permissibility of polygamy and advocates monogamy. They refer to the concluding sentence of the Qur'an 4:3 above, which says: '... That [monogamy] is nearer to prevent you from doing injustice', and conclude that monogamy is the rule while polygamy is only an exception.

The view that the ability to deal justly between co-wives is a legal prerequisite to polygamy had been further argued by other scholars and taken together with Qur'an 4:129, which says 'You will never be able to do perfect justice between wives even if it is your ardent desire . . .', to reach a conclusion that polygamy is actually prohibited under Islamic law. Advocates of that view argue that the Qur'an itself confirms the inability of men to fulfil the prerequisite of dealing justly with co-wives. The pioneer advocate of that interpretation was the nineteenth century Egyptian jurist, Muhammad Abduh, who, at the close of that century, argued that the abuse of polygamy created injustice to women and he advocated its proscription through a combined interpretation of those two Qur'anic verses. However, that view was and is still strongly opposed by Muslim scholars who support the traditional interpretation that permits polygamy provided that justice is ensured between co-wives.[475]

Despite the trend in the Muslim world today generally favouring, at least, a restricted polygamy if not outright monogamy, most Muslim scholars and jurists would hesitate to declare its outright prohibition for the fear of violating the sanctity of its Qur'anic permissibility. The combined interpretation of Qur'an 4:3 and Qur'an 4:129 as advocated by Muhammad Abduh was subsequently relied upon by some Muslim States either to restrict or abrogate polygamy.

---

[473] *See* e.g. Tanzil-ur-Rahman, *A Code of Muslim Personal Law* (1978), Vol.1, pp.92–101; and Al-Zuhayli (above n.78) at Vol.9, pp.6669–6670.

[474] *See* Coulson, N.J. *History of Islamic Law* (1964) p.208.

[475] *See* e.g. Doi (above n.86) at pp.149–154; and Al-Zuhayli (above n.78) at Vol. 9, p.6670.

In 1956 Tunisia enacted the Tunisian Code of Personal Status,[476] which provided that:

Polygamy is forbidden. Any person who, having entered into a bond of marriage, contracts another marriage before the dissolution of the preceding one, is liable to one year's imprisonment or to a fine . . .[477]

That prohibitory approach has been controversial under Islamic law and it has been criticized as contravening the Qur'an.[478] This has been particularly so because, for example, the Tunisian code criminalized polygamy with a sentence of one year's imprisonment, despite the fact that some schools of Islamic jurisprudence consider it permissible in exceptional circumstances. Iraq had also followed the prohibitory approach in 1959 and specified imprisonment and a fine for any violator. Due to strong opposition and non-compliance by Muslims who considered it as contrary to Qur'anic provisions, the law was revised in 1963 and the article prohibiting polygamy was removed. The Tunisian Code was however retained despite similar opposition.[479]

Syria had also in 1953 enacted the Syrian Code of Personal Status restricting the right to polygamy. Article 17 of the Syrian Code, which remains operative, provided that:

The judge is empowered to refuse permission to a married man to marry another woman if it is established that he is not in a position to support two wives.[480]

Although this is substantively a restrictive approach, it could almost serve as a procedural means of closing the door to polygamy since the discretion of determining the ability to do justice is taken away from the husband and placed with the judiciary.[481]

In many Muslim societies where polygamy is practised, the prerequisite of being able to do justice between co-wives is seldom given any consideration by men. The permissibility of polygamy is often abused in a way that actually works against the family institution itself. Quoting Ibn Qayyim, 'Abd al-'Atî, has observed that 'polygamy in Islam is no more and no less than that of a permissible act, [which] like any other act lawful in principle, it becomes forbidden if it involves unlawful things or leads to unlawful consequences such

---

[476] Law of 13 August 1956 (as amended).

[477] *ibid.*, Art. 18.

[478] *See* Qadri (above n.22) at p.368; and Doi (above n.86) at pp.149–154.

[479] *See* Khadduri, M., 'Marriage in Islamic Law: The Modernist Viewpoints' (1978) 26 *American Journal of Comparative Law*, p.213 at p.216.

[480] *See also* the Moroccan Code of Personal Status of 1958 and the Pakistan Family Law Ordinance of 1961. *See also* Mahmood, T., *Statutes of Personal Law in Islamic Countries, History, Texts and Analysis* (2nd Ed., 1995) pp.246–248.

[481] *See* e.g. Al-Zuhayli (above n.78) at Vol.9, p.6674 for a critique of this approach.

as injustice'.[482] It is arguable on the above grounds that the permissibility could be controlled under Islamic law for reasons of welfare *(maslahah)*.[483]

It is noteworthy that most discussants of women's rights proceed from the premise that there is only one way of redressing the inequality and abuse of polygamy, that is, by 'equalizing down' through a direct prohibition to strip men of that right. In relation to Islamic law this will continue to be controversial in view of its Qur'anic permissibility. Are there other means through which Muslim countries may therefore address the problem of polygamy within acceptable limits of Islamic law to remove any disadvantage against women and also satisfy their obligations under international human rights law? One approach that has not been fully utilized and which could prove realistic is the 'equalizing up' approach of redressing inequality.

There are normally two alternative routes to redress situations of inequality or disadvantage: either by raising the rights of victims of the inequality, namely 'equalizing up' or by lowering the rights of those advantaged, namely 'equalizing down'.[484] Will situations where women have a right to polyandry similar to that of men to polygamy not satisfy the requirements of equality of rights to marriage? Although that could satisfy the requirements because nothing prohibits polyandry in international law, practical considerations indicate that most societies would not endorse such an alternative as a solution to polygamy.[485] Islamic law actually prohibits polyandry by *ijmâ'* (legal consensus), so 'equalizing up' in that manner is not legally possible under Islamic law, and that is not what is suggested here either. Rather, there are provisions within Islamic law that allow for a sort of 'equalizing up' by legally activating the rights of women to 'suspended repudiation' *(ta'lîq al-talâq)* and/or 'delegated repudiation' *(tafwîd al-talâq)* of marriage. The legal activation of such rights will not only redress any disadvantage or abuse of polygamy against women but also lead to a smooth harmonization of the conflict in this area between Islamic law and international human rights law. How can that be achieved?

There is consensus in Islamic law that polygamy can neither be imposed upon a woman or a man, it is only a permissible act. Also, most of the schools of Islamic jurisprudence, except the *Shî'ah*, endorse the doctrines of 'suspended repudiation' *(ta'lîq al-talâq)* and 'delegated repudiation' *(tafwîd al-talâq)*.[486]

---

[482] 'Abd al'Atî (above n.65) at p.119. He made reference to Ibn Qayyim's, *Kitâb Akhbâr al-Nisâ* (above n.467), and observed that Ibn Qayyim al-Jawziyyah 'cites ninety-nine cases in confirmation of this principle and makes extensive reference to the Qur'an and Sunnah, and the rulings of leading jurists'. *See* endnote 44 thereof.

[483] However, for the doctrine of welfare *(maslahah)* to apply the abuse that makes such control necessary needs to be sufficiently established.

[484] *See* e.g. Harris, D.J., and Joseph, S. (eds.), *The International Covenant on Civil and Political Rights and United Kingdom Law* (1995) p.594.

[485] *See* e.g. *Dietmar Pauger v. Austria*, Communication 415/1990; *see also* Joseph, Schultz and Castan (above n.23) at p.570.

[486] *See* e.g. Al-Zuhayli (above n.78) at Vol.9, pp.6935–6941; and 'Abd al'Atî (above n.65) at p.119. The *Shî'ah* (Twelvers) recognize the right of the husband to delegate his right of divorce

By the first doctrine of 'suspended repudiation', the husband stipulates at the time of marriage that the marriage becomes repudiated if he does certain things unfavourable to the wife, which may include taking another wife. By the second doctrine of 'delegated repudiation' the wife is vested, by the husband, during the marriage contract with the right to divorce herself should there arise circumstances unfavourable to her, which may include taking another wife by the husband.[487] It is possible therefore for Muslim countries, for reasons of public welfare, to enact that women shall be specifically informed of these rights during the marriage contract, and thus have the discretion either to utilize it or not.[488] The State would have in that way legally activated the relevant rights of women within Islamic law and 'equalized up' their formerly available but suppressed rights against the rights of men to polygamy, and thus given them a choice in the matter. Supplementary to this, women should also be adequately educated of the existence of such rights to them in law. The importance of educating Muslim women about their rights in Islamic law, is manifested in the observation of Coulson that:

There has perhaps been a natural tendency in recent years to exaggerate the picture of Muslim wives labouring under the shackles of the traditional law. Miserable though the lot of Muslim wives may have been in practice, this was often not so much the direct result of the terms of the law itself as the responsibility of society. The customary seclusion of women, and especially the lack of educational facilities, left them ignorant of their rights and unable to insist upon the proper use of machinery which the law had provided for their protection.[489]

Any disadvantage of polygamy could thus be redressed by women utilizing an alternative legal right available to them within Islamic law, while at the same time the liberty of women who may still like to be co-wives, when exceptional circumstances so demand, would still be guaranteed without the law interfering in their way by the prohibitory approach. Neither monogamy nor polygamy would then be an imposition upon men and women respectively, but would actually be put in its correct perspective under Islamic law as a matter of choice. This would not contravene the *Sharî'ah* and would also indirectly satisfy the obligations of the Muslim States to ensure equality of rights in

to his wife, by appointing her as an agent to do so. This is called *Tawkîl*. Although the rules differ technically, this can also achieve similar results with *Tafwîd* and *Ta'lîq*. See e.g. Mir-Hosseini, Z., 'The Delegated Right To Divorce: Law and Practice in Morocco and Iran', in Carroll, L., and Kapoor, H., (eds.), *Talaq-i-Tafwid: The Muslim Woman's Contractual Access to Divorce* (1996) pp.121–133.

[487] *See* Ibn Qudâmah, M.A., *al-Mugnî* (Arabic) (1981) Vol.7, p.13; 'Abd al'Atî (above n.65) pp.119–120 and Coulson (above n.474) at p.207.

[488] Similar rules can be found in the Jordan, Morocco and Egypt Personal Status Laws respectively, allowing the wife to stipulate that the husband shall not take another wife and entitling her to sue for divorce if he does. *See generally* Carroll and Kapoor (above n.486); Mahmood (above n.480) at pp.246–248; and Nasir, J.J., *The Islamic Law of Personal Status* (3rd Ed., 2002) pp.66–68.   [489] Coulson (above n.474) at p.207.

marriage. This way the focus of international human rights law would be seen to be specifically on human rights and not on questioning the basis of religious teachings per se, and thus promote a complementary approach to solving human rights problems.[490]

3.24.2 Female endogamy in Islamic law and equality of rights as to marriage

Based on Qur'an 2:221 and Qur'an 60:10 there is consensus among both *Sunni* and *Shî'ah* jurists that a Muslim woman is prohibited under Islamic law from marrying any non-Muslim man.[491] Conversely, Qur'an 5:5 permits Muslim men to marry 'women of the people of the Book' (that is, Christian and Jewish women). In international human rights law this will be considered discriminatory against women. The HRC has observed in that regard that:

> . . . the right to choose one's spouse may be restricted by laws or practices that prevent the marriage of a woman of a particular religion with a man who professes no religion or a different religion. States should provide information on these laws and practices and on the measures taken to abolish the laws and practices . . .[492]

Muslim jurists have advanced some justifications for this provision under Islamic law.[493] The foremost being that, under Islamic law a Muslim man who marries a Christian or Jewish woman has a religious obligation to honour and respect both Christianity and Judaism. Thus the woman's religious beliefs and rights are not in jeopardy through the marriage, because she would be free to maintain and practise her religion as a Christian or Jew. Conversely, a Christian or Jewish man who marries a Muslim woman is not under such obligation within his own faith, so allowing a Muslim woman to marry a Christian or a Jewish man may expose her religious beliefs and rights to jeopardy. This justification is therefore hinged mainly on wanting to protect the religious beliefs and rights of Muslim women. Al-Qaradawi has thus argued that:

> . . . while Islam guarantees freedom of belief and practice to the Christian or Jewish wife of a Muslim, safeguarding her rights according to her own faith, other religions, such as Judaism and Christianity, do not guarantee the wife of a different faith freedom of belief and practice, nor do they safeguard her rights. Since this is the case, how can Islam take chances on the future of its daughters by giving them into the hands of people who neither honor their religion nor are concerned to protect their rights?[494]

On grounds of the guarantee of freedom of thought, conscience, and religion under international human rights law, it could be argued that other religions,

---

[490] *See* Levitt, M.A., 'The Taliban, Islam and Women's Rights in the Muslim World' (1998) 22 *The Fletcher Forum*, p.113 at p.115.   [491] *See* e.g. Nasir (above n.488) at pp.69–70.

[492] General Comment 28, para.24.

[493] *See* e.g. 'Abd al 'Atî (above n.65) at pp.140–145.

[494] *See* e.g. al-Qaradawi (above n.16) at p.184–186.

such as Judaism and Christianity, would now also be under an international obligation to guarantee the freedom of belief and religion to a Muslim wife and thus safeguarding her rights according to her own faith. If so, will this remove the prohibition of Muslim women from marrying men of the 'people of the book' (that is, Christians and Jews)? 'Abd al 'Atî, has observed that the honour and reverence that the Muslim must give to the faith of his Christian or Jewish counterpart is an integral part of the Islamic faith while the same 'reciprocity' is not an integral part of either the Christian or Jewish faith. The required unreserved honour and reverence is a matter of faith that cannot be imposed by law. For the same reason the Muslim male is prohibited in Islamic law from marrying an idolatress because of the psychological factors involved. Faith, concluded 'Abd al 'Atî, 'is the most private relationship between man and God; it cannot be imposed or conferred. Nor is it the question of discrimination between men and women in Islam'.[495] Can this then be categorized as 'differentiation' for the purpose of protecting the religious rights of Muslim women instead of discrimination? We will then also have to consider whether the prohibition causes any disadvantages to women. Love does transcend religious boundaries.

The prohibition under Islamic law may therefore, on some occasions, prevent a Muslim woman from marrying a man she loves, where he happens to be a non-Muslim. According to 'Abd al 'Atî, 'Of course, love may be invoked . . . as omnipotent, capable of solving all problems, emotional, ideological, or social. But love is perhaps one of the most abused words; and if it were so omnipotent as is sometimes claimed, social interaction would be much simpler and human life much less problematic'.[496] The socio-legal arguments are quite broad and can no doubt be continued, for and against, ad infinitum.

Naturally, every religion, ideology or sect treasures its adherents and will have rules that close the door to, or at least minimize, defections. Such rules may often be contrary to the right to freedom of thought, conscience, and religion under international human rights law. The prohibition of Muslim women from marrying non-Muslim men thus seems to be one of the areas where achieving complete equality is difficult between Islamic law and international human rights law for the reason stated by al-Qaradawi above. No non-secular Muslim State has enacted any law to abrogate that prohibition of Islamic law. Nasir has thus observed that:

Under the Sharia and all modern Islamic laws, both for the Sunni and Shia schools, a marriage of a Muslim woman to a non-Muslim man is null and void, even if it is validly solemnized according to the laws of any given non-Muslim state. For such a marriage to be valid the man must have converted to Islam at the time of the contract.[497]

---

[495] *See* 'Abd al 'Atî (above n.65) at p.143.   [496] *ibid.*, p.142.
[497] Nasir (above n.488) at p.82, also pp.69–70.

However, the juristic view of some contemporary Muslim jurists is that since Muslim women are prohibited completely from marrying non-Muslim men, the Muslim men would also be temporarily prohibited from marrying women of the 'people of the book' in a situation where there is apprehension of a high number of Muslim women remaining unmarried, until the situation is remedied.[498] This is based on the doctrine of public welfare *(maslahah)* under Islamic law.

3.24.3 Female's share in Islamic inheritance and equality of rights in marriage

While advocates of Islamic law assert that the 'Islamic inheritance scheme contains one of the most comprehensive and detailed systems of succession known to the world',[499] the females' share in the Islamic law of inheritance is viewed under international human rights law as being inconsistent with the principle of equality for women. According to the HRC, 'Women should have equal inheritance rights to those of men when the dissolution of marriage is caused by the death of one of the spouses'.[500] Basically, under Islamic law the male heir receives double the share of the female heir. This is based on the Qur'anic provision which states that:

> God directs you as regards your children's [inheritance]: to the male, a portion equal to that of two females . . .[501]

This rule of double share for the male does not however apply in all cases under Islamic law.[502] There are some instances where the female gets the same share of inheritance as the male. For example a father and mother get equal share (a sixth each) when they survive and inherit from their deceased son in the same capacity as parents;[503] the uterine sister gets equal share (in the same capacity) with her uterine brother;[504] and where the sole inheritors are a husband and a full sister of the deceased, the husband gets one-half and the full sister of the deceased equally gets one-half. There are also instances where the female could receive double the share of the male.[505] The female will also receive the entire estate if she inherits alone.[506] This contradicts any emphatic allegation of unqualified discrimination on grounds of sex in the scheme of Islamic inheritance.

---

[498] *See* e.g. al-Qaradawi (above n.16) at p.184.
[499] *See* Chaudry (above n.59) at p.527.
[500] General Comment 28, para.26.   [501] Q4:11.
[502] *See generally* Chaudry (above n.59).   [503] Q4:11.   [504] Q4:12.
[505] An instance is where the inheritors are a husband, one daughter and one full brother. In that case, the husband gets one quarter of the estate, the daughter as an only child gets one-half and the full brother gets the remaining one-quarter. *See* Chaudry (above n.59) at pp.535–536.
[506] *See* e.g. Nasir (above n.488) at p.223.

Historically, Islamic law was the first legal system to grant women a fixed portion in inheritance either as a mother, wife, daughter, or sister at a time when such a right was not available to them in any civilization or under any legal system. This was on the basis of the Qur'anic verse which provided that:

From what is left by parents and those nearest related, there is a share for men and a share for women, whether the property be small or large—a determinate share.[507]

Muslim scholars thus argue that Islamic law must actually be seen as having removed the pre-Islamic discrimination which the female was subjected to in every society which had denied her any inheritance alongside her male counterpart.

The fact that there are instances when the female obtains equal share in the same capacity with the male, and can also obtain a higher share than the male in some instances, shows that the basic rule of double share for the male is not an indication of superiority of the male above the female nor discrimination on grounds of sex. Badawi summarizes the justifications for the double-share rule as follows:

The variation in inheritance rights is only consistent with the variations in financial responsibilities of man and woman according to the Islamic Law. Man in Islam is fully responsible for the maintenance of his wife, his children, and in some cases of his needy relatives, especially the females. This responsibility is neither waived nor reduced because of his wife's wealth or because of her access to any personal income gained from work, rent, profit, or any other legal means. Woman, on the other hand, is far more secure financially and is far less burdened with any claims on her possessions. Her possessions before marriage do not transfer to her husband. She has no obligation to spend on her family out of such properties or out of her income after marriage. She is entitled to 'Mahr' [Dowry] which she takes from her husband at the time of marriage. If she is divorced she may get an alimony from her ex-husband. An examination of the inheritance law within the overall framework of the Islamic Law reveals not only justice but also an abundance of compassion for woman.[508]

Thus, while the share of the male and the female, where the double share applies, appears arithmetically unequal, Muslim scholars argue that the shares are morally equitable in the final analysis, considering the varied financial responsibilities of each gender.[509] This argument indicates that the variation in the Islamic inheritance scheme takes the overall family structure under Islamic law into consideration. From that perspective, will counter arguments that the family structure has already changed, that the nuclear family is now dominant even in many Muslim countries, that many women for one reason or the other are breadwinners of the family, coupled with feminist calls for the empowerment of women and the promotion of their non-dependence on

[507] Q4:7.
[508] Badawi, J., *The Status of Woman in Islam* (1971) 8 *Al-Ittihad*, No.2, September, 33.
[509] *See* e.g. 'Abd al 'Atî (above n.65) at p.268.

men, make any difference? This relates to the economic, social, and cultural rights of women. It is important to note here that the financial responsibilities of men within the family structure of Islamic law are without prejudice to the financial independence of the women.[510] While it is reasonable and appreciative that a financially buoyant wife can assist with the financial responsibilities of the family, Islamic law does not impose this responsibility on her. Such responsibility is legally placed on the husband and where he fails to discharge it without necessity, the man becomes an irresponsible husband under Islamic law, against whom the wife has a right of dissolution on grounds of lack of maintenance.[511]

In addressing any problem of inheritance, succession rules can hardly be imposed upon any person who does not intend to follow such rules. There is always a way of circumventing any such imposition, the most legally approved of which is gifting away the estate to whomever one pleases during one's lifetime. It is the belief in the divine basis of the *Sharî'ah* rules on Islamic inheritance that keeps Muslims attached to it. If the Islamic law of succession is considered generally, it would be observed that the fixed-shares actually make it impossible for some certain heirs to be completely disinherited for any reason. A displacement of Islamic law will therefore actually expose those secured heirs, which include women, to the possibility of being completely disinherited through testamentary dispositions and put them at a greater disadvantage.[512] It may actually be more difficult to compel any individual through secular law to dispose of his estate equally and non-discriminatorily among his male and female heirs. People usually prefer to distribute their estate as it pleases them. What Islamic law has successfully established through the fixed-shares is to ensure that certain close relations are not disinherited by the testator. That does not however prevent testators from exercising their discretion to make a gift of any part of their estate during their lifetime to any of their heirs (male or female) through the doctrine of *hibah* (gift) which is an in-built mechanism in Islamic law for legally tilting the balance of the fixed-shares as one pleases during one's lifetime.[513]

In 1959 Iraq enacted the Personal Status Act giving equal shares to males and females in all cases. Due to its unpopularity the provision was abrogated

[510] *See* 'Abd al 'Atî (above n.65) at pp.269–270. *See also* Chaudry (above n.59) at pp.544–545.

[511] *See* e.g. Tanzil-ur-Rahman (above n.473) at Vol.1, pp.641–652. Note the observation of the HRC that: 'Equality during marriage implies that husband and wife should participate equally in responsibility and authority within the family'. General Comment 28, para.25.

[512] *See* e.g. the Nigerian case of *Adesubokan v. Yinusa* [1971] Northern Nigerian Law Reports, p.77.

[513] *See* e.g. Powers, D.S., 'The Islamic Inheritance System: A Socio-Historical Approach' in Mallat, C., and Connors, J., *Islamic Family Law* (1990) p.11 at pp.19–21; Chaudry (above n.59) at p.546; and Nasir (above n.488) at pp.249–255.

in 1963 and the *Sharî'ah* provisions restored.[514] Islamic inheritance rules continue to apply to Muslims within the personal law codes of many Muslim States.[515] During the consideration of its initial report before the Committee on the Rights of the Child, the Saudi Arabian representative, Mr Al-Nasser, stated that 'because Saudi inheritance law was taken directly from the Koran, it was considered to be the word of God, hence there was no room for interpretation or the adoption of another system' and that 'in some cases, a woman's entitlement could be much greater than that of a man'.[516]

3.24.4 Dissolution of marriage in Islamic law and equality rights of women

In its General Comment 28, the HRC observed that in the dissolution of marriages States must ensure that 'grounds for divorce and annulment should be the same for men and women'.[517]

Under Islamic law, marriage may be dissolved either through Unilateral Repudiation by the husband *(talâq)*, Discharge at wife's request *(khul')*, Dissolution by Mutual Agreement *(mubâra'ah)*, or Dissolution through Judicial Order *(faskh)*. Unilateral Repudiation *(talâq)* is a right of the husband while the other three forms *(khul', mubâra'ah,* and *faskh)* are invocable by the wife. Unilateral Repudiation *(talâq)* is however the simplest method of marriage dissolution and can be legally exercised exclusively by the husband at his discretion for any or no reason at all. Thus, although it may be morally wrong or even sinful in some circumstances, a husband could legally divorce his wife by a simple statement such as 'I divorce you'. Conversely, the wife can dissolve the marriage through either a Discharge *(khul')*, Mutual Agreement *(mubâra'ah)* with the husband's consent or through a Judicial Order *(faskh)* on certain limited legal grounds only. According to Jeffery therefore, 'The Qur'an grants man complete liberty of divorce and demands of him no justification for divorcing his wife. Thus he can divorce her at his own caprice, but no such facility exists for her'.[518] While it may be a misconception to state that men have an exclusive right of marriage dissolution under Islamic law, it will also be misleading to suggest that men and women have 'equal' or the 'same' rights of divorce under Islamic law. Men certainly have an advantage over women in the procedure of marriage dissolution under traditional Islamic law. This is most probably connected to the fact that it is men who ordinarily

---

[514] *See* Anderson, J.N.D., 'Modern Trends in Islam: Legal Reform and Modernisation in the Middle East' (1971) 20 *International and Comparative Law Quarterly*, p.1 at p.11.

[515] *See* e.g. Arts.139–179 of the Algerian Family Code (1988). *See also* Mahmood (above n.480) and Nasir (above n.488) at pp.200–201.

[516] *See* Summary Record of the 688th Meeting of CRC: Saudi Arabia, UN Doc. CRC/C/SR.688 of 24/01/2001, para.59.   [517] General Comment 28, para.26.

[518] Jeffery, A., 'The Family in Islam' in Anshen, R.N. (ed.), *The Family: Its Future and Destiny* (1949) p.39 at p.60.

propose marriages and pay the dowry and are also expected to be able to act more resolutely when difficulties arise in the marriage relationship.

Although the Qur'anic verses permitting marriage dissolution begin and end with strong moral admonitions for husbands to safeguard their wives' welfare in the matter of divorce,[519] yet there is evidence of this right of Unilateral Repudiation *(talâq)* being abused by men from quite an early period of Islam.[220] Furthermore, even though divorced women are free to remarry under Islamic law, men in many Muslim countries consider it as a taboo to marry divorced women. They are thus often subjected to misery and destitution. On the other hand, even in the exercise of the right to Discharge *(khul')* by a wife, the husband may, in bad faith, also withhold consent and thus continue to punish the woman and keep her under retention.[521] Thus the woman will be left only with the alternative of seeking a Judicial Order of dissolution *(faskh)* which she may also not be able to obtain if her grounds of dissolution fall outside the traditional legal limits for granting such order. As observed by Coulson above,[522] this was certainly not the spirit by which Islamic law was ordained to be applied, rather it is the men who have often failed to meet the moral expectation of Islam with respect to piety and prudence in the exercise of their procedural advantage in marriage dissolution. It is evidenced that the abuse of this procedural advantage by men in marriage dissolution had in fact been a matter of concern as early as the seventh century during the rule of Umar ibn al-Khatâb, the Second Caliph, who legislated against its abuse by men. Ibn Taimiyyah also addressed it in the fourteenth century,[523] and the problem persists in many Muslim societies today. There is reasonable ground therefore to argue for the need to combine the moral content with the procedural aspect of marriage dissolution in Islamic law.

Some Muslim States already have sections in their Personal Status Laws that modify, in a variety of ways, the traditional rules of marriage dissolution under Islamic law.[524] The most radical modifications prohibit the husband's right to divorce his wife extra-judicially through Unilateral Repudiation *(talâq)*. For example, Article 30 of the Tunisian Code of Personal Status (1956) provides that 'Divorce outside a court of law is without legal effect'.[525] This was achieved by reference to the Qur'anic verse which provides that: 'If you fear a breach between the two of them [husband and wife], appoint two arbiters . . .'.[526] The Court is placed in the position of 'two arbiters' to ensure

---

[519] Q2:229–232.   [520] *See* 'Abd al 'Atî (above n.65) at pp.220–221.
[521] It is however morally wrong and very sinful to do so in Islam.
[522] *See* above n.489 and text thereto.
[523] *See* e.g. 'Abd al 'Atî (above n.65) at p.221 and Coulson (above n.474) at pp.194–195.
[524] *See* Mahmood (above n.480) and Nasir (above n.488) at pp.106–136.
[525] *See also* Art. 49 of the Algerian Family Code (1988).
[526] Q4:35. This verse however mentions specifically that the arbiters shall be: 'one from his (husband's) family and one from her (wife's) family'. Here the State considered itself best to take over that role through its judiciary on grounds of public interest.

a combination of the moral content and procedural aspect of the divorce and thus placing the couple on the same procedural footing in the dissolution of marriage. In other countries such as Morocco, Syria, Algeria, and Iran, the court is empowered to order the husband to pay compensation to the wife where the Unilateral Repudiation *(talâq)* is for no just cause.[527] In Pakistan, Unilateral Repudiation *(talâq)* by the husband will only be effective 90 days after it has been reported to an Arbitration Council, which tries to reunite the couple during the period.[528]

Considering the consensus of Muslim jurists that divorce is recommended only as a last resort when it has become clearly impossible for the couple to remain together, coupled with evidence that the procedural advantage enjoyed by men over women in the matter of divorce has often been misused, the judicial control of marriage dissolution by the State can as well be justified under the doctrine of public welfare *(maslahah)*.[529] The doctrine of *hisbah* could also be relied upon here, so that the State would be seen as encouraging good and preventing evil by such judicial control whereby marriage dissolution is restricted to dissolution by Judicial Order to facilitate the amalgamation of both the moral and legal content of the rules of divorce. Since dissolution by Judicial Order *(faskh)* is a method sanctioned already by Islamic law, this will not amount to making any new law but the removal of a procedural advantage which has been generally subjected to abuse. However, Khallâf considered such abrogation of men's right of Unilateral Repudiation and vesting dissolution of marriages entirely in the courts as dubious and non-genuine welfare (that is, *maslahah wahmiyyah)*.[530] One could disagree with this view of Khallâf, on the grounds that the approach does not violate or come in conflict with any direct Qur'anic verse on Unilateral Repudiation *(talâq)*. The approach is consistent with the Prophet's Tradition which states that: 'There should be no harming nor should any harm be remedied with another harm'.[531] That approach will remove genuine hardship from women without placing any consequential hardship on men, since it does not totally block every avenue to divorce for men, but only ensures that they divorce for justifiable reasons.

An alternative approach is through the exercise of the right of stipulation by women during the marriage contract. This is known in Islamic law as

---

[527] Perhaps as a deterrent for unjustifiable use of the right of Unilateral Repudiation *(talâq)* by the man. *See* e.g. Art. 49 of Algerian Family Code (1988) and Art. 117 Syrian Code of Personal Status (1953) (as amended). *See also* Al-Zuhayli (above n.78) at Vol.9, pp.7065–7066.

[528] This is more like a supervisory role over the traditional waiting period under Islamic law after the *talâq* has been pronounced.

[529] *See* e.g. the reported view of Sheikh al-Qaradawî by Heba Raouf Ezzat on the possibility of the control of the abuse of the power of divorce by men through the doctrine of *maslahah*, in Lawyers Committee on Human Rights, *Islam and Justice* (1997) pp.122–123.

[530] Khallâf, A.W., *'Ilm Usûl al-Fiqh* (1398AH) p.86.

[531] Reported by Ibn Mâjah. *See* e.g. Ibrahim, E., and Johnson-Davies, D. (trans.), *Forty Hadith, An-Nawawî's* (1985) pp.106–107, Hadith 32.

khiyâr al-talâq meaning the option (of the wife) to divorce. Under traditional Islamic law, the wife has a right to stipulate during the marriage contract that the husband delegates to her, absolutely or conditionally, the right of Unilateral Repudiation whereby she will have a right to invoke it when absolutely necessary. This does not divest the husband of his own original right to divorce. Both he and the wife can then exercise the right unilaterally.[532] Fyzee has observed that: 'This form of delegated divorce is perhaps the most potent weapon in the hands of a Muslim wife to obtain her freedom without the intervention of any court and is now beginning to be fairly common in India'.[533] As stated in the case of polygamy above, the same approach could be adopted in the case of divorce whereby the State will make it mandatory under law that the wife shall be informed during the marriage contract, of this right to stipulate. Supplementary to that is the need to create awareness and educate women of this legal right under Islamic law.[534] There is nothing under the *Sharî'ah* that prohibits the State from ensuring that women are adequately informed about their rights under the law, especially if it is for removing difficulties from them within society. In fact they have a right to be informed if they are so ignorant.

The above analysis reveals that the questions raised by gender equality and rights are not as simplistic as sometimes portrayed. In relation to Islamic law, the issues are of great socio-legal importance and a great demonstration of good faith is required in addressing them from both the Islamic law and international human rights perspectives. Only a superficial view of Islamic law or a very restrictive interpretation of its sources gives an impression of total deadlock between Islamic law and international human rights law on the issues of gender equality. But the differences are not trivial either. There are certainly issues to be resolved but which may not be possible if addressed monologically from either the single perspective of secular international human rights jurisprudence or the single perspective of restrictive hardline interpretations of the *Sharî'ah*. There is need for complementary understanding of the issues. Feminist human rights advocates need to appreciate the importance of the family institution to Islamic society and the importance of the female gender to its subsistence. The obvious question here may be, why must it be women that have to bear the brunt for the subsistence of the family institution? In redressing the disadvantages and inequalities that have existed against women, it is important not to swing from one extreme to another in a manner that may create a conflict of cultures or portray the arguments as an attack against Islamic institutions rather than against non-justifiable discriminations. The socio-legal justifications of Islamic jurists in the instances where differences exist must

---

[532] *See* e.g. Ibn Âbidîn, M.A., *Radd al-Muhtâr* (Arabic) (1994) Vol.2, p.497.

[533] Fyzee, A.A.A., *Outlines of Muhammadan Law* (4th Ed., 1974) p.159. This is still true today. *See generally* Carroll and Kapoor (above n.486).

[534] *See generally* Carroll and Kapoor (above n.486). *See also* Tanzil-ur-Rahman (above n. 473) at Vol.1, pp.339–352.

be examined in good faith. Some of the arguments are certainly rebuttable, without consensus, and not really absolute. A study of them from a combined pragmatic and transcendental perspective will certainly help to argue the unsustainable ones out. While it is true that the male gender enjoys some role-advantage under Islamic law in accordance with the structural roles within the Islamic family institution, such role-advantage is meant for the cohesion and success of the family. Conversely, there are in-built rights within Islamic law that may be activated for the benefit of the female gender whenever there is apprehension of abuse of the role-advantage enjoyed by the male. The debilitating factor is that women are generally ignorant of their rights under Islamic law and men often callously abuse that ignorance.

The *Sharî'ah* promotes the normative equality of both sexes, and women have rights within Islamic law, some of which have been suppressed over the centuries due to ignorance on their part and callousness on the part of some men in many Muslim countries.[535] However, in recent times due to the challenges of the international human rights movement, women in many parts of the Muslim world are becoming more aware of their rights within the legal sources of Islamic law through education and enlightenment. It is important therefore to take both the Islamic law and international human rights law discourses seriously if the inequalities against women in Muslim States are to be realistically redressed. It is believed that as more women become aware of Islamic legal sources that support their equal status they will not fail to utilize that knowledge to their advantage in order to activate their inherent rights within Islamic law. Where they do, the barriers of gender discrimination and inequality will definitely be broken, or at least further minimized.

Article 23(4) of the ICCPR also provides that in case of dissolution of marriage, 'provision shall be made for the necessary protection of any children'. Islamic law does fully recognize the need for the necessary protection of any children in case of marriage dissolution. Under the rules of *hidânah* (child custody) in Islamic family law, there are elaborate rules for the protection of children in case of divorce, which essentially reflect consideration for the best interest of the child.[536]

3.25 THE RIGHTS OF THE CHILD

Article 24

1. Every child shall have, without any discrimination as to race, colour, sex, language, religion, national or social origin, property or birth, the right to such measures of

---

[535] *See generally* Bouthaina, S., 'The Muted Voices of Women Interpreters' in Afkhami, M. (ed.), *Women's Human Rights in the Muslim World* (1995) pp.61–77.
[536] *See* e.g. Qadri (above n.22) at pp.406–409; and Doi (above n.86) at p.214.

protection as are required by his status as a minor, on the part of his family, society and the State.

2. Every child shall be registered immediately after birth and shall have a name.

3. Every child has the right to acquire a nationality.

Despite the fact that all the other provisions of the Covenant apply *mutatis mutandis* to children, Article 24 provides further for the special protection of children due to their vulnerability as minors.[537] Article 24(1) places the responsibility of protecting the child on family, society, and State. As to how this obligation is to be fulfilled between family, society, and State, the HRC Committee has observed that:

> Responsibility for guaranteeing children the necessary protection lies with the family, society and the State. Although the Covenant does not indicate how such responsibility is to be apportioned, it is primarily incumbent on the family, which is interpreted broadly to include all persons composing it in the society of the State party concerned, and particularly on the parents, to create conditions to promote the harmonious development of the child's personality and his enjoyment of the rights recognized in the Covenant. However, since it is quite common for the father and mother to be gainfully employed outside the home, reports by States parties should indicate how society, social institutions and the State are discharging their responsibility to assist the family in ensuring the protection of the child. Moreover, in cases where the parents and the family seriously fail in their duties, ill-treat or neglect the child, the State should intervene to restrict parental authority and the child may be separated from his family when circumstances so require. If the marriage is dissolved, steps should be taken, keeping in view the paramount interest of the children, to give them necessary protection and, so far as is possible, to guarantee personal relations with both parents. The Committee considers it useful that reports by States parties should provide information on the special measures of protection adopted to protect children who are abandoned or deprived of their family environment in order to enable them to develop in conditions that most closely resemble those characterizing the family environment.[538]

Article 24 together with other provisions on children's rights, guarantees a secure foundation for the proper development of the child and, in that regard, the best interest of the child is always paramount.[539]

Islamic law obviously also recognizes the need for special protection of children due to their vulnerable nature. The Qur'an describes children as the 'comfort of our eyes'[540] and there are many verses of the Qur'an and Traditions of the Prophet that remind parents and society about their responsibility to children. Islam emphasizes that children are born innocent and should therefore not be made part of the conflicts and viciousness of adult society. The right of the child to have a good name is specifically stated by Prophet Muhammad in one of his Traditions[541] and this accommodates the right to be registered after

---

[537] *See* General Comment 17, para.1.   [538] General Comment 17, para.6.

[539] *See* the Convention on the Rights of the Child (1989), 1577 UNTS, p.3; *and generally* Van Bueren, G., *The International Law on the Rights of the Child* (1995). *See also* Joseph, Schultz and Castan (above n.23) at pp.467–494.   [540] Q25:74.

[541] *See* Karim (above n.248) at Vol.2, p.620, Hadith No. 379w.

birth. From the context of the Qur'an and the Prophet's Traditions, Omran has identified that children have at least 'ten cardinal rights' under Islamic law, which he listed as:

1. The right [of the child] to genetic purity.
2. The right [of the child] to life.
3. The right [of the child] to legitimacy and good name.
4. The right [of the child] to breast-feeding, shelter, maintenance and support, including health care and nutrition.
5. The right [of the child] to separate sleeping arrangements for children.
6. The right [of the child] to future security.
7. The right [of the child] to religious training and good upbringing.
8. The right [of the child] to education, and training in sports and self-defence.
9. The right [of the child] to equitable treatment regardless of gender or other factors.
10. The right [of the child] that all funds used in their support come only from legitimate sources.[542]

Although all Muslim States have ratified the UN Convention on the Rights of the Child (CRC)[543] many of them have however entered reservations on grounds of Islamic law or *Sharî'ah*.[544] Many of the reservations are in respect of the issue of adoption.[545] Instead of adoption, Islamic law provides for a guardianship system *(kafâlah)* to provide alternative family-care for children deprived of natural parental care.[546] Another area of possible conflict is the position of Islamic law on the status of children conceived out of wedlock, which has been raised by the HRC in its concluding observations on many Muslim States.[547]

Nevertheless, Muslim States generally believe that 'the provisions set forth in [the Children's] Convention are in conformity with the teachings of Islamic law concerning the need to fully respect the human rights of the child'.[548] Thus

---

[542] Omran (above n.149) at p.32.

[543] The only two exceptions being Somalia and Palestine. Somalia has not had a stable government since 1991, while Palestine is not yet recognized as a State under international law.

[544] *See* UN Treaty Website at: http://www.unhchr.ch/html/menu3/b/treaty15_asp.htm [1/3/03]. *See also* Baderin (above n.2) at pp.297–301.

[545] *See also* Leblanc, L.J., 'Reservations to the Convention on the Rights of the Child: A Macroscopic View of State Practice' (1996) 4 *International Journal of Children's Rights*, pp.357–381.

[546] *See* e.g. The Initial Report of the Kingdom of Saudi Arabia on the CRC, UN Doc CRC/C/Add.2, (29/3/2000) para.60. *Kafâlah* is recognized under Art. 20(3) and Art. 21 of the CRC (above n.539).

[547] *See* Baderin (above n.2) at pp.297–301 for more detailed analyses of these issues. *See also* Ch. 4 under Article 10(3) of the ICESCR, text to notes 115–125 inclusive below.

[548] *See* Initial Report of Saudi Arabia to the CRC (above n.546) at para.27. *See also* the General Statement of the United Arab Emirates during the drafting of the CRC that: 'The provisions of the draft Convention contradict neither the principles of Islamic law nor the provisions of the Provisional Constitution of the United Arab Emirates': Detrick, S. (ed.), *The United Nations Convention on the Rights of the Child: A Guide to the 'Travaux Préparatoires'* (1992), p.50.

Article 7 of the OIC Cairo Declaration on Human Rights in Islam provides that:

(a) As of the moment of birth, every child has rights due from the parents, society and the state to be accorded proper nursing, education and material, hygienic and moral care. Both the fetus and the mother must be protected and accorded special care.

(b) Parents and those in such like capacity have the right to choose the type of education they desire for their children provided they take into consideration the interest and future of the children in accordance with ethical values of the principles of Shari'ah.

3.26 POLITICAL RIGHTS

Article 25

Every citizen shall have the right and the opportunity, without any of the restrictions mentioned in article 2 and without unreasonable restrictions;

(a) To take part in the conduct of public affairs, directly or through freely chosen representatives;

(b) To vote and to be elected at genuine periodic elections which shall be by universal and equal suffrage and shall be held by secret ballot, guaranteeing the free expression of the will of the electors;

(c) To have access, on general terms of equality, to public service in his country.

The only provisions of the ICCPR on political rights in the strict sense of the word are those contained in Article 25. The provisions reflect a democratic process that calls for the right and opportunity of every citizen to participate directly or indirectly in the conduct of public affairs of State. Thus autocratic regimes 'which offer no opportunities for political participation by citizens' are incompatible with Article 25.[549] The HRC has indicated that: 'The conduct of public affairs, referred to in paragraph (a), is a broad concept which relates to the exercise of political power, in particular the exercise of legislative, executive and administrative powers. It covers all aspects of public administration, and the formulation and implementation of policy at international, national, regional and local levels. The allocation of powers and the means by which individual citizens exercise the right to participate in the conduct of public affairs protected by article 25 should be established by the constitution and other laws.'[550] It is important to note that the political rights, unlike the civil rights, do not apply to every individual but only to citizens of particular States. The Covenant does not prescribe the criteria for citizenship of States Parties

---

[549] Joseph, Schultz and Castan (above n.23) at p.498. *See also* Steiner, H., 'Political Power as a Human Right' (1988) 1 *Harvard Human Rights Yearbook*, p.77.

[550] General Comment 25, para.5.

but the HRC has indicated that 'State reports should outline the legal provisions which define citizenship in the context of the rights protected by Article 25', and that '[n]o distinctions are permitted between citizens in the enjoyment of these rights on the grounds of race, colour, sex, language, religion, political or other opinion, national or social origin, property, birth, or other status'.[551]

The discussion of political principles is often very topical from an Islamic perspective. This is due to the fact that the Qur'an and *Sunnah* have not laid down any specific political system for the Islamic State. The *Sharî'ah* only emphasizes good governance based on justice, equity and responsibility but leaves its actual administration in the hands of the community. There is evidence within the *Sharî'ah* however that the community has the right to elect its leaders either directly or indirectly.[552] The Qur'an states in many verses that sovereignty of the heavens and earth belongs to God[553] but also mentions in other verses that God has made human beings agents and representatives on Earth.[554] Islamic scholars and jurists agree that this representative capacity of human beings is conferred upon all human beings alike. Based on these Qur'anic provisions and with reference to the practices of election of Caliphs after the demise of Prophet Muhammad, almost all contemporary Islamic legalists concur that every Muslim has the right and the opportunity to participate, either directly or indirectly in the public affairs and electoral processes of the State. For example Maududi, writing on the right of Muslims to participate in the public affairs of the Islamic State, stated as follows:

According to Islam, governments are representatives (*khalifa*) of the Creator of the universe: this responsibility is not entrusted to any individual or family or to any particular class or group of people, but to the entire Muslim community. The Holy Qur'an says: 'God has promised to appoint those of you who believe and do good deeds as (His) representatives on earth' (24:55). This clearly indicates that *khilâfa* (representation) is a collective gift of God in which the right of every individual Muslim is neither more nor less than the right of any other person.

The method recommended by the Holy Qur'an for running the affairs of the state is as follows: 'And their business is (conducted) through consultation among themselves' (Q43:38). According to this principle it is the right of every Muslim either to have a direct say in the affairs of the state or to have a representative chosen by him and other Muslims to participate in the running of the state.

Under no circumstances does Islam permit an individual or a group or party of individuals to deprive the common Muslims of their rights or usurp powers of the state. Nor does Islam regard it as right and proper for an individual to put on a false show of setting up a legislative assembly and by means of such tactics as fraud, persecution, bribery and so on, get himself and men of his choice elected to the assembly. This is not only treachery against the people whose rights are illegally usurped, but also against the Creator who has entrusted Muslims to rule on earth on His behalf, and has prescribed the procedure of an assembly for exercising these powers. The *shûrâ* or

---

[551] General Comment 25, para.3.
[552] *See* e.g. Zaidan, A.K., *Individual and the State in Islamic Law* (1982) pp.16–26.
[553] *See* e.g. Q3:189.   [554] *See* e.g. Q24:55.

legislative assembly should embrace the following principles:

1. The executive head of the government and the members of the assembly should be elected by free and independent choice of the people.
2. The people and their representatives should have the right to criticize and freely express their opinions.
3. The real conditions of the country should be brought before the people without suppression of fact so that they are in a position to judge whether the government is working properly or not.
4. There should be adequate guarantee that only those people who have the support of the masses should rule over the country and those who fail to win this support should be removed from their position of authority.[555]

The Qur'anic principle of consultation (*shûrâ*) to which Maududi referred above, has been interpreted by most contemporary Islamic legalists to accommodate the process of democratic free and fair elections for the selection of leaders. In fact some Islamic scholars consider free and fair elections as the best way to reflect the principle of *shûrâ*, because this involves the participation of all citizens in selecting their ruler and giving him the contract to govern them known as *bay'ah* (allegiance) under Islamic law.[556] This clearly indicates that the democratic process of societal participation in governance and state affairs envisaged under Article 25 is compatible with Islamic principles of justice, equity and good governance. Thus Article 23(b) of the OIC Cairo Declaration on Human Rights in Islam provides that:

Everyone shall have the right to participate directly or indirectly in the administration of his country's public affairs. He shall also have the right to assume public office in accordance with the provisions of Shari'ah.

Two issues remain to be examined here. It is often assumed that the political rights of non-Muslims and women are totally constrained under Islamic law and thus inconsistent with the opening clause of Article 25 which provides that every citizen shall have the right and the opportunity to exercise the political rights 'without any of the restrictions mentioned in article 2 and without unreasonable restrictions'. With respect to voting and taking part in the conduct of public affairs of the State, there is nothing under Islamic law that prohibits women or non-Muslim citizens of the Islamic State from voting and participating in the public affairs of the State. The contemporary problem with the status of non-Muslims under Islamic law is principally due to the traditional interpretation of Islam as both a religion and a nationality. Thus a Muslim subject was traditionally considered as possessing full religious and political nationality in the Islamic State while the non-Muslim subject was considered

---

[555] Maududi (above n.229) at pp.33–34.
[556] *See* e.g. Hussein, G.M., 'The *Shura* and Human Rights in Islamic Law', (paper delivered at the Cairo Conference on Democracy and the Rule of Law, December 1997) pp.5–6; and also, Chaudhry (above n.86) at pp.56–60.

as possessing only the political nationality but not the religious nationality.[557] Doi has therefore pointed out that the distinction between Muslims and non-Muslims was and remains merely that of political administration and not of human rights, and concluded that: 'It is wrong presumption that since an Islamic State is based on a definite ideology, the State will annihilate the non-Islamic elements within its fold'.[558] The lack of religious nationality by non-Muslims in the Islamic State only exempted them from both duties and rights that involved the religious aspects of the State and 'not due to a tendency of imposing on them an inferior social position nor minimising the humane treatment they are entitled to'.[559] The situation is comparable to the issue of citizenship and the prohibition of all forms of racial discrimination in international human rights law. Although the International Convention on the Elimination of all Forms of Racial Discrimination[560] prohibits 'any distinction, exclusion, restriction or preference based on race, colour, descent, or national or ethnic origin which has the purpose or effect of nullifying or impairing the recognition, enjoyment or exercise, on an equal footing, of human rights and fundamental freedoms in the political, economic, social, cultural or any other field of public life', it exempted 'distinctions, exclusions, restrictions or preferences made . . . between citizens and non-citizens'.[561] The distinction that traditional Islamic law made between Muslims and non-Muslims in aspiring to leadership of the Islamic State was therefore in the nature of the distinction made between citizens and non-citizens in a secular State. Al-Ghunaimi thus contended that:

> The conditions of acquiring the nationality of a particular state is a matter of its own discretion. It is not to be construed as an indication of contempt of those who could not acquire the necessary qualifications . . . Consequently, in a modern state, we often come across restrictions imposed on non-nationals, in one way or another, for a better organization of the society. This is likewise with the rights of the *dhimmis* in the Islamic state.[562]

Under traditional Islamic law, the theory was that of totality of religious citizenship whereby 'as soon as a Muslim migrates from his non-Muslim home and comes to Islamic territory with the intention of residing there, he at once becomes a full-fledged Muslim citizen of the Muslim state; he has the same rights as the other Muslim citizens and the same obligations as they'.[563] However, all modern Muslim States of today seem to have departed from that traditional theory of totality of religious citizenship to the extent that a foreign Muslim does not today acquire citizenship of any modern Muslim State for merely being a Muslim. Citizenship is generally based on national and

---

[557] *See generally* al-Qardâwî, Y., *Non Muslims in the Islamic Society*, Hamad, K.M., and Shah, M.A. (trans.) (1985).   [558] Doi (above n.86) at p.427.
[559] *See* Al-Ghunaimi, M.T., *The Muslim Conception of International Law and the Western Approach* (1968) p.189.   [560] 660 UNTS, p.195.
[561] *ibid.*, Art.1(1),(2).   [562] Al-Ghunaimi (above n.559) at p.189.
[563] Hamidullah (above n.241) at pp.110–111, para.199.

geographical grounds in the Muslim countries of today. Conversely, neither the religious nationality nor the political nationality is enough on its own for the enjoyment of certain political rights within many Muslim States today. Only through the combination of both religious and political nationality in an individual may he, for instance, have a right to the highest political office in many Muslim States of today. It is noteworthy that all the Qur'anic verses on leadership and authority do not merely emphasize religiosity but equally emphasize righteousness to all and upholding justice for all. Thus, while for ideological reasons the ideal is to have a Muslim as the Head of State in an Islamic State, there are, otherwise, many instances right from the time of Prophet Muhammad of non-Muslims being appointed to very important public offices in the Islamic State.[564]

Next is the question of the political rights of women under Islamic law. The question whether Islamic law prohibits women from voting, having a say or participating in the public affairs of the State is often misrepresented by the practice in some Muslim States. At its ratification of CEDAW, Kuwait for instance entered a reservation 'regarding article 7(a), inasmuch as the provision contained in that paragraph conflicts with the Kuwaiti Electoral Act, under which the right to be eligible for election and to vote is restricted to males'.[565] That reservation, as it clearly stated, is on grounds of the Kuwaiti Electoral Act and not on Islamic law per se.

On the rights of women under the *Sharî'ah* to vote and to participate in the *shûrâ* and generally in the public affairs of the State, Hussein has summarized the position as follows:

> Nowhere in the *Qur'an* or *Sunna* does exist any verse or rule which prevents or can be construed to prevent women from participating in the *Shura* process. Women did participate in the *Shura* and participated and continue to participate in the running of the affairs of various Islamic states through the holding of various governmental top positions and through the *Shura* process.
>
> Those who do not support women's participation in the *Shura* process and in running the affairs of the state base their views not on the principles and rules of the Islamic religion and the Islamic *Sharî'a* but on mere social concerns and fears which do not rest on any Islamic principle or rule. Of course, social concerns and fears do change from state to state, and from time to time within the same state. It should be stressed that most recent writers on the topic support the right of women to participate in the *Shura* process and in running the affairs of their own countries. It is therefore, an Islamic principle that women do indeed have the right to participate in the *Shura* process and in running the public and governmental affairs of their states.[566]

However, with respect to the right of being elected to the highest public office, Islamic jurists differ on whether a woman can be elected to head an Islamic

---

[564] *See* e.g. Ramadan, S., *Islamic Law, Its Scope and Equity* (1970) pp.144–145. *See also* al-Qardâwî (above n.557) at pp.12–14.

[565] *See* UN Treaty Website at: http://www.unhchr.ch/html/menu3/b/treaty9_asp.htm [1/3/03].   [566]Hussein (above n.556) at p.5.

State. The differences of opinion arise from the interpretation of a Tradition in which it is reported that when the Prophet heard that the Persians had enthroned a daughter of the Chosroe as their Queen he said: 'Any nation that leaves its affairs in the hands of a woman would not prosper'.[567] Although the wording of the Tradition does not specifically contain a prohibition on a woman being elected as a head or leader of an Islamic State, one school of thought construes from it such a prohibition on the argument that consideration of the nation's prosperity is an important determinant of who is elected to its leadership. Some scholars however considered it to be an isolated Tradition (*âhâd*) and some others have expressed doubts about its authenticity on the grounds, *inter alia*, that the Tradition was reported by Abû Bakratah during the 'Battle of the Camel' in which A'ishah, the widow of Prophet Muhammad led and commanded an army against Ali ibn Abî Tâlib, the fourth Caliph. Usmani argues that despite its report on the said occasion many of the illustrious companions of the Prophet still participated in the battle under the leadership of A'ishah without anyone disclaiming her leadership. He thus concluded that the Tradition did not connote a prohibition of the appointment of a woman as Head of State but it is generally an advice indicating that it may not be advisable to appoint a woman as Head of State.[568]

On the basis of that Tradition, a petition was brought before the Federal Shariat Court of Pakistan in 1982 challenging the appointment of women judges as being violative of Islamic law. In his judgment, the Chief Judge of the Court, Aftab Hussain, CJ, extensively examined the different opinions of Islamic jurists on the Tradition. The learned judge cited a list of classical and contemporary Islamic legal works[569] to establish that Imam Ibn Jarîr al-Tabarî, for instance, supported the appointment of a woman both as a judge and as a Head of State and that a similar view was attributed to Imam Mâlik, which was favoured by the *Mâlikî* jurists as well. In dismissing the petition the learned judge observed, *inter alia*, that:

It is on account of this Hadis [Tradition] that in the 22 points of the Ulema [learned scholars] of Pakistan which were presented to the Government as necessary preliminaries to the framing of a Constitution, point No. 12 specifically said that the Head of the State will be a Muslim male. This point was re-examined during the course of campaigne [sic] for the Presidential Elections of 1964 in which Miss Fatima Jinnah was nominated by the opposition parties to fight the election to the office of the President of Pakistan against Field Martial [sic] Muhammad Ayub Khan. After a research the view as about a woman being qualified for the office of the Head of the State was changed on the basis of opinions of two of the most renowned Ulema of the

---

[567] Reported by al-Bukhâri. *See* e.g. Karim (above n.248) at Vol.2, p.570, Hadith No. 7.

[568] Usmani, U.A., *Fiqh al-Qur'an*, Vol.III, pp.286–287 and Usmani, U.A., *I'lâ al-Sunan*, Vol.15, p.28 cited in the judgment of Aftab Hussain CJ, in *Ansar Burney v. Federation of Pakistan*, PLD 1983 Federal Shariat Court, p.73 at p.86.

[569] For example, *Durr al-Muhtâr*, *Sharh al-Waqâyâ*, *Fath al-Bârî*, *Hedaya*, *al-Muhallâ* and *al-Ahkâm al-Sultâniyyah*.

20th Century in Indo Pakistan, namely Maulana Ashraf Ali Thanvi and Allama Syed Sulaiman Nadvi. The Jamait-e-Islamia Pakistan endorsed this view after retracting its earlier stand on the matter which was reflected in the above-mentioned point No. 12. Maulana Maudoodi was severely criticised for this by Kalim Bahadur in his book 'Jamait-i-Islami of Pakistan'. But this criticism was not justified since it is duty of a Muslim to accept the truth and to change and retract his earlier view. In technical parlance this is known as the doctrine of [Raju' or retreat].[570]

There is no verse of the Qur'an that specifically prohibits a woman from being elected to any public office under Islamic law. The wording of the Tradition itself leaves room for the different opinions that have been expressed by Islamic jurists concerning its interpretation. This provides flexibility on the matter as was demonstrated by the change of the initial view of the Pakistani religious scholars in 1964 as expressed in Justice Hussain's judgment above.

The controversy surrounding the election of women to the highest political office of the State is not unique to Islam. The problem exists in almost all societies of today in different forms, albeit informally. The provisions of Article 25 however only demand that women's right and opportunity to be elected be not denied, which the Tradition of the Prophet quoted above does not specifically deny as rightly opined by some of the Islamic jurists.

3.27 THE RIGHT TO EQUALITY BEFORE THE LAW

Article 26

All persons are equal before the law and are entitled without any discrimination to the equal protection of the law. In this respect, the law shall prohibit any discrimination and guarantee to all persons equal and effective protection against discrimination on any ground such as race, colour, sex, language, religion, political or other opinion, national or social origin, property, birth or other status.

Reference has earlier been made to Article 26 together with Articles 2(1) and 3 on right to equality and non-discrimination.[571] Article 26 is more general and extends further than Articles 2(1) and 3. The HRC has observed that Article 26 is not limited to the rights provided under the Covenant but 'prohibits discrimination in law or in fact in any field regulated and protected by public authorities'.[572] It prohibits discrimination in both the legislation and application of laws by States Parties. Article 26 fortifies the right to recognition as a person before the law guaranteed under Article 16. While Article 16

---

[570] *Ansar Burney v. Federation of Pakistan*, PLD 1983 Federal Shariat Court, p.73 at p.85.
[571] *See* para.3.6 above.
[572] General Comment 18, para.12. *See also Zwaan-de Vries v. The Netherlands*, and *Broeks v. The Netherlands*, Communication No. 172/1984, 42 UN GAOR Supp. (No. 40) at p.139, UN Doc. A/42/40 (1987), para.12.3.

guarantees a standing in law for every individual, Article 26 goes further to guarantee an *equal standing* before the law for every individual. Judges and public administrators must thus apply the law without discrimination.

The HRC has however observed also that 'not every differentiation of treatment will constitute discrimination, if the criteria for such differentiation are reasonable and objective and if the aim is to achieve a purpose which is legitimate under the Covenant'.[573] The HRC has addressed the question of reasonable and objective differentiation on a case-by-case basis.[574] The onus however lies on a State Party to prove the reasonableness and objectivity of any differentiation under the Covenant.

A State Party may also need to take affirmative action to redress existing discrimination against some members of society. The HRC has observed in that regard that:

> ... the principle of equality sometimes requires States parties to take affirmative action in order to diminish or eliminate conditions which cause or help to perpetuate discrimination prohibited by the Covenant. For example, in a State where the general conditions of a certain part of the population prevent or impair their enjoyment of human rights, the State should take specific action to correct those conditions. Such action may involve granting for a time to the part of the population concerned certain preferential treatment in specific matters as compared with the rest of the population. However, as long as such action is needed to correct discrimination in fact, it is a case of legitimate differentiation under the Covenant.[575]

The general notion of equality and non-discrimination is also quite fundamental in Islamic law. The *Sharî'ah* recognizes that all human beings are created equal. The Prophet Muhammad had declared in his farewell sermon as follows:

> O People! be aware: your God is One ..., No Arab has any superiority over a non-Arab and no non-Arab any superiority over an Arab, and no white one has any superiority over a black one nor any black one over a white one, except on the basis of piety. The most honourable among you in the Sight of God is the most pious and righteous.

The *Sharî'ah* does accord additional honour (in the sight of God) to the most pious and righteous. This is a special right conferred by God on those who worship Him. This additional honour is 'in the sight of God' because the determination of the 'most pious and righteous' lies exclusively with Him. Article 19(a) of the OIC Cairo Declaration on Human Rights in Islam provides that 'All individuals are equal before the law, without distinction between the ruler and the ruled'.

---

[573] General Comment 18, para.13. *See also* the Dissenting Opinion of Judge Tanaka in the ICJ *South West Africa Cases* (1966) ICJ Report of Judgments p.305 and McKean, W., *Equality and Discrimination Under International Law* (1983) p.260.

[574] *See* Joseph, Schultz and Castan (above n.23) at pp.540–556.

[575] General Comment 18, para.10. *See also* Art. 2(2) of the International Convention on the Elimination of all Forms of Racial Discrimination (1966) 660 UNTS, p.195.

The right to equality before the law for every individual under Islamic law has been discussed extensively under the right to fair hearing and due process in Article 14 above. We have also examined the differences between Islamic law and international human rights law regarding equality and non-discrimination on grounds of sex and religion under other relevant articles in this chapter and thus this needs no further examination here.

3.28 THE RIGHTS OF ETHNIC, RELIGIOUS OR LINGUISTIC MINORITIES

Article 27

In those States in which ethnic, religious or linguistic minorities exist, persons belonging to such minorities shall not be denied the right, in community with the other members of their group, to enjoy their own culture, to profess and practise their own religion, or to use their own language.

There is today in every part of the world some minority group that is, unfortunately, being denied some right for the mere fact of being in minority. While the general prohibition of discrimination on grounds of race, religion, language, and other status aims also at guaranteeing that individuals belonging to minority groups enjoy all the rights under the Covenant in the same manner as every other human being, Article 27 additionally guarantees the right of individuals belonging to ethnic, religious, or linguistic minorities to enjoy their own culture, profession and practice of their own religion and/or the use of their own language.[576] Notwithstanding the vagueness and non-definition of the term 'minority' in the Covenant, the provision in Article 27 reflects an appreciation of the diversity in human nature and culture, which must be respected.

The HRC has observed that 'this article establishes and recognizes a right which is conferred on individuals belonging to minority groups and which is distinct from, and additional to, all the other rights which, as individuals in common with everyone else, they are already entitled to enjoy under the Covenant', and that 'the persons designed to be protected are those who belong to a group and who share in common a culture, religion and/or a language'. The Committee also pointed out that 'the individuals designed to be protected need not be citizens of the State party'.[577]

From an Islamic perspective, the Qur'an specifically recognizes this diversity in human nature and culture and also prohibits the employment of

[576] For a full discussion on Art. 27 *see* e.g. Sohn, L.B., *The Rights of Minorities*, in Henkin (above n.6) at p.270ff.

[577] General Comment 23, para.1 and 5.1. *See further* Joseph, Schultz and Castan (above n.23) at pp.572–595.

this diversity as a basis for discrimination amongst human beings. Rather, human diversity is indicated as a basis for identification and appreciation of the powers and divine wisdom of God, the Creator of humanity. In respect of ethnic differences the Qur'an states that:

O Mankind! We created you from a single [pair] of a male and female, and made you into nations and tribes that you may know each other [not that you may despise (or discriminate against) each other]. The most honoured of you in the sight of God is he who is most righteous amongst you. And God has full knowledge and is well-acquainted with all things.[578]

And in respect of linguistic differences the Qur'an states that:

And among His [God's] signs is the creation of the heavens and earth, *and the difference of your language and colours.* Verily in that are indeed signs for men of sound knowledge.[579]

Thus, ethnic or racial discrimination is prohibited under Islamic law, and consequently the rights of ethnic minorities to enjoy their own culture and use their own language must be protected without discrimination.

Regarding the question of religious minorities in Muslim States, this needs some elaboration more than that of ethnic or linguistic minorities. Generally, on the question of religious differences, the Qur'an states, *inter alia*, that:

Say: [O Muhammad to the non-believers]: 'O you that reject faith! I worship not that which you worship. Nor will you worship that which I worship. And I shall not worship that which you are worshipping. Nor will you worship that which I worship. *To you be your religion, and to me my religion.*[580]

Although the above Qur'anic verses point towards the reality of possible religious differences among humans, the point has been raised that '[n]on-Muslim minorities within an Islamic state do not enjoy rights equal to those of the Muslim majority'.[581] Two oft-cited examples of such denial of rights of religious minorities in modern Muslim States are the *Bahai* in Iran and *Ahmadi* in Pakistan.[582] Both countries however tend to consider the two groups respectively as Islamic heretics rather than religious minorities.[583] That approach has

---

[578] Q49:13.   [579] Q30:22 (emphasis added).   [580] Q109:1–6 (emphasis added).

[581] *See* An-Na'im, A.A., 'Religious Minorities under Islamic law and the Limits of Cultural Relativism (1987) 9 *Human Rights Quarterly*, p.1.

[582] *See* e.g. Monshipouri, M., *Islamism, Secularism, and Human Rights in the Middle East* (1998) pp.192–193; and Mahmud, T., 'Freedom of Religion and Religious Minorities in Pakistan: A Study of Judicial Practice' (1995) 19 *Fordham International Law Journal*, p.40.

[583] *See* e.g. the judgment of the Pakistani Supreme Court in *Zaheer-ud-din and Others v. The State and Others* [1993] SCMR (S.Ct) p.1718 where the court saw the matter as an issue of 'religious misrepresentation' by the Ahmadis rather than that of freedom of religion *simpliciter*.

attracted a lot of criticism from international human rights circles.[584] Reference
has been made in that regard to the fact that traditionally, Islamic law treated
non-Muslims as inferior beings within the Islamic State and thus encouraged
the violation of the rights of religious minorities in Muslim States.[585]

Inhabitants of the early Islamic State were either Muslim subjects, non-
Muslim subjects or non-Muslim aliens. The Muslim subjects had a sort of full
citizenship within the State, the non-Muslim subjects had the status of *Dhimmîs* (protected citizens) and the non-Muslim aliens had the status of *Musta'min*
(safe aliens).[586] The *Dhimmîs* were mostly 'people of the book' (for example
Christians and Jews) while the *Musta'min* were mostly polytheists. While
Hamidullah perceived the *Dhimmîs* as being even better off with regards to
their duties and rights under Islamic law,[587] Khadduri saw them as second-
class citizens[588] and al-Ghunaimi considered them as not being 'citizens
stricto sensu of the Muslim State' but 'rather subjects who enjoy a particular
status'.[589] Piscatori referred to Qur'an 9:5 to argue that 'the law is clear' on
how Muslims must treat polytheists—slay them wherever they were found.[590]
This is contradictable.

The Qur'anic verse (Q9:5) quoted by Piscatori was specific to those polytheists who violated their covenant of peace with the Muslims and attacked the
Muslim allies and is thus not the general position of the law on how polytheists
should be treated within the Islamic State. On the contrary al-Ghunaimi has
given a detailed contextual analysis of that and other similar Qur'anic verses
that are often quoted out of context as general injunctions on the slaying of
the polytheists.[591] Hamidullah has also elaborated extensively in his classical
work on *Muslim Conduct of State* that all non-Muslims—'people of the book'
as well as polytheists—are entitled to enjoy and did enjoy protection under

---

[584] *See* e.g. UN Doc. E/CN.4/1999/32, para.40–45; and Human Rights Watch, *Iran: Religious and Ethnic Minorities, Discrimination in Law and Practice* (1997); Baha'i International
Community, *Iran's Secret Blueprint for the Destruction of a Religious Community* (1999). *See
also* the Pakistani case of *Zaheer-ud-din and Others v. The State and Others* (above n.583); *and*
Mayer, A.E., 'Judicial Dismantling of Constitutional Protections for Religious Freedom: The
Grim Legacy of *Zaheeruddin v State*', (Conference Paper at the Cairo Conference on Democracy
and the Rule of Law, December 1997).   [585] *See* e.g. An-Nai'm (above n.581) at p.10ff.
[586] *See* e.g. Doi, A.R., *Sharî'ah: the Islamic law* (1984) pp.426–435, Hamidullah (above
n.241) at pp.110–130.   [587] Hamidullah (above n.241) at p.112.
[588] Khadduri, M., *War and Peace in the Law of Islam* (1955) p.177 and pp.195–198.
[589] Al-Ghunaimi, M.T., *The Muslim Conception of International Law and the Western
Approach* (1968) p.151.
[590] Piscatori, J.P., 'Human Rights in Islamic Political Culture' in Thompson, K. (Ed.), *The
Moral Imperatives of Human Rights: A World Survey* (1980) p.139 at p.146; and An-Na'im
(above n.581) at p.12. *See also* Nanda, V.P., 'Islam and International Human Rights Law: Selected
Aspects' (1993) *American Society of International Law Proceedings*, p.327 at p.329 for a similar
view.
[591] Al-Ghunaimi (above n.589) at pp.165–183. See also Moinuddin, H., *The Charter of the
Islamic Conference and Legal Framework of Economic Co-operation Among its Member States*
(1987) pp.24–26.

Islamic law both in times of peace and war.[592] Evidence abounds in Islamic legal sources and the precedents of the early Islamic State which shows that it was those polytheists who tormented the Muslim State that should be fought and subdued. It is thus difficult to justify any blanket opinion under Islamic law for the violation of the fundamental rights of religious minorities within Muslim States.[593]

3.29 CONCLUDING REMARKS

We have endeavoured in this chapter to examine elaborately the substantive guarantees of the ICCPR in the light of Islamic law, and have shown that the Covenant is for the most part not inconsistent with Islamic law. The myth that the *Sharî'ah* is an antithesis to civil and political rights has been sustained for so long mainly due to the generalized and confrontational approach often adopted in comparisons between Islamic law and international human rights law. The right by right investigative approach adopted here opens the door for a better understanding of the socio-legal problems and how to handle them in a manner that promotes the noble objective of enhancing human dignity and fostering an ideal human community, which are common objectives of both the *Sharî'ah* and international human rights law.

The analyses reveal that the *Sharî'ah* does not oppose or prohibit the guarantee of civil and political rights, liberal and democratic principles or the liberty and freedom of individuals in relation to the State. The areas of conflict identified, particularly concerning the scope of equality of rights between men and women, prohibition of inhuman and degrading punishments, freedom of religion, and some death penalty cases are also shown to be not insurmountable where addressed open-mindedly and in a well-informed manner. With a better understanding of the socio-legal problems as expounded herein, Islamic law, being the domestic law of many Muslim States, can serve as a vehicle for the full realization of the civil and political rights guaranteed under the ICCPR with the result that Muslim States would not only consider themselves under an international legal duty but also under a religious obligation to respect and ensure the civil and political rights guaranteed under the Covenant.

A most practical approach, *inter alia*, as is fully argued in Chapter 5, is that the HRC should, in appreciation of the varied social values and ideological varieties of the UN Member States, adopt the margin of appreciation doctrine in its interpretation of the Covenant. The doctrine has been vindicated in practice

---

[592] *See generally* Hamidullah (above n.241) at pp.104–131 and pp.201–224 for Islamic law rules governing persons within the Islamic State.

[593] *See* e.g. Ramadan (above n.564) at pp.146–148. *See also* Article 25 above for the discussion of the recognition of the political rights of non-Muslim minorities. The right to the enjoyment of cultural life under Islamic law is further addressed under Art. 15 of the ICESCR in Ch. 4 para.4.14 below.

within the European Human Rights regime. It will enable the Committee to maintain a reasonable universal standard of the rights guaranteed under the Covenant and at the same time respect reasonable and justifiable social and moral values of all its States Parties. Correlatively, Muslim States that apply Islamic law also have a duty to demonstrate the highest humanitarian and political will in respect of their obligations under the Covenant through a constructive interpretation and implementation of the *Sharî'ah* in a manner that enhances the protection of our human rights.

4

The International Covenant on Economic, Social, and Cultural Rights (ICESCR) in the Light of Islamic Law

4.1 INTRODUCTION

As the ICCPR does for civil and political rights, so does the International Covenant on Economic, Social, and Cultural Rights (ICESCR) represent the positive law on economic, social, and cultural rights under the international human rights objective of the UN. It entered into force on 3 January 1976 and has, as of December 2002, been ratified by 146 States, including 41 of the 57 Member States of the Organization of Islamic Conference (OIC).[1]

Following the approach of Chapter 3, this chapter similarly examines the ICESCR in the light of Islamic law. We will endeavour to determine whether or not the *Sharî'ah* contradicts the provisions of the ICESCR in any way and whether or not the *Sharî'ah* can serve as a vehicle for the full realization of the rights recognized under the Covenant in Muslim States that apply Islamic law fully or as part of domestic law. Reference is made to the General Comments and practice of the Committee on Economic, Social, and Cultural Rights (ESCR Committee) and to other scholarly expositions on the Covenant. The reporting guideline formulated by the ESCR Committee is also used as an interpretational guide for relevant Articles of the Covenant.[2] We analyse each of the substantive rights from an international law perspective followed by an Islamic law perspective as was done in Chapter 3. Reference is also made to the OIC Cairo Declaration on Human Rights in Islam and reports of Muslim States parties to the Covenant where relevant.

---

[1] *See* the Status of Ratification of the ICESCR at the UN Human Rights Treaty Website at: http://www.unhchr.ch/html/menu3/b/a_cescr.htm [1/3/03].

[2] *See* Revised General Guidelines Regarding The Form And Contents Of Reports To Be Submitted By States Parties Under Articles 16 And 17 Of The International Covenant On Economic, Social, And Cultural Rights (Basic Reference Document) UN Doc E/C.12/1991/1 of 17 June 1991 (hereinafter referred to as *Revised Guidelines*).

4.2 IMPORTANCE OF ECONOMIC, SOCIAL, AND CULTURAL RIGHTS

The UN Charter had provided the basic foundation for economic, social, and cultural rights in its Article 55 which provided, *inter alia*, that the UN shall promote:

(a) higher standards of living, full employment, and conditions of economic and social progress and development; and
(b) solutions of international economic, social, health, and related problems; and international cultural and educational co-operation.

Articles 22–27 of the UDHR also followed with some general provisions on economic, social, and cultural rights.

The adoption of the ICESCR as part of the UN International Bill of Rights legally put to rest, at least for the States parties thereto, the old opposing argument that economic, social, and cultural rights were not human rights per se.[3] Although economic, social, and cultural rights are still often termed 'second generation' rights this does not suggest that they are in any way 'second class' rights to the civil and political rights. Many human rights scholars argue strongly that economic, social, and cultural rights are very essential for the full realization and enjoyment of civil and political rights. In his State of the Union address in 1944 the US President Roosevelt had observed that:

... true individual freedom cannot exist without economic security and independence. 'Necessitous men are not free men.' People who are out of a job are the stuff of which dictatorships are made.[4]

Given the choice, most individuals, especially in developing nations, would practically choose a genuine guarantee of economic, social, and cultural rights before thinking of civil and political rights. Shue thus considered economic, social, and cultural rights as basic rights and argued that '[n]o one can fully, if at all, enjoy any right that is supposedly protected by society if he or she lacks the essentials for a reasonably healthy life'.[5] Craven has submitted similarly that 'freedom of expression, for example, has little importance to the starving or homeless'.[6] Realistically, no human right or dignity can still be said to

---

[3] *See* Arambulo, K., *Strengthening the Supervision of the International Covenant on Economic, Social, and Cultural Rights, Theoretical and Procedural Aspects* (1999) especially Chapters III and IV, for an analysis of the arguments against and in support of the human rights character of economic, social, and cultural rights.

[4] *See* Eleventh Annual Message of Congress (11 January 1944) in Israel. J. (ed.), *The State of the Union Messages of the Presidents* (1966), Vol. 3, pp.2875 and 2881.

[5] Shue, H., *Basic Rights, Subsistence, Affluence, and U.S. Foreign Policy* (1979) pp.24–25.

[6] Craven, M.C.R., *The International Covenant on Economic, Social, and Cultural Rights: A Perspective on its Development* (1995) p.13.

be inherent in a hungry, sick, homeless, jobless, illiterate, and impoverished human being, except perhaps only the right to the life that still flows in him or her, which under those circumstances can hardly be a life of dignity. The relevance and importance of the ICESCR in developing nations cannot therefore be overemphasized.

Most of the countries of the Muslim world today fall within the category of developing nations. The promotion of the ICESCR in the Muslim world is thus very important if the dignity of the individual is to be enhanced and even if the civil and political rights are to be ensured.

4.3 THE RIGHTS 'RECOGNIZED' UNDER THE ICESCR

Apart from the right of self-determination in Article 1 and the equality of rights between men and women in Article 3, the ICESCR 'recognizes' nine substantive economic, social, and cultural rights. They are:

Article 6	The right to work.
Article 7	The right to enjoy just and favourable conditions of work.
Article 8	Trade union rights.
Article 9	The right to social security and social insurance.
Article 10	Family rights.
Article 11	The right to an adequate standard of living.
Article 12	The right to the highest attainable standard of physical and mental health.
Articles 13–14	The right to education.
Article 15	The right to cultural life and benefits of scientific progress.[7]

The provisions in Article 1 on the right of self-determination and Article 3 on equality of rights between men and women are identical with those of the ICCPR already examined in Chapter 3. Those two Articles will thus not be readdressed in this chapter, rather their analysis in Chapter 3 will be applicable here *mutatis mutandis*.[8] Again we will first identify the fundamental purpose of the ICESCR and also analyse the obligation of States Parties under Article 2 before proceeding to examine the substantive rights.

4.4 THE OBJECT AND PURPOSE OF THE ICESCR

The object and purpose of the ICESCR is similar to that of the ICCPR in the sense that it guarantees the recognized economic, social, and cultural rights of

[7] All these rights are contained in Part III of the ICESCR.
[8] *See* Ch. 3, paras.3.5 and 3.6 above.

the individual from the States Parties to it. The preamble of the ICESCR refers to the fact that the rights recognized in it derive from the inherent dignity of the human person and that enjoyment of economic, social, and cultural rights will lead to the realization of 'the ideal of free human beings enjoying freedom from fear and want'.[9] Economic, social, and cultural rights deal essentially with subsistence and basic needs of human beings, thus the principal purpose of this group of rights is the realization of an adequate and dignified standard of living for every human being. The purpose and ethical basis of the ICESCR are thus very laudable and commensurate with the overall objectives of the *Shari'ah* and the purpose of Islamic law. They are ideals which any Muslim State that purports to pursue the noble objectives of the *Shari'ah* has both a moral and legal obligation to uphold under its application of Islamic law. The Qur'an states that all the good things and rich resources of the universe are created for the basic needs of humanity[10] and it specifically alluded to the significance of freedom from hunger and fear to human existence as follows:

He [God] provided them with food against hunger, and with security against fear.[11]

4.5 OBLIGATIONS OF STATES PARTIES UNDER THE ICESCR

Article 2

1. Each State Party to the present Covenant undertakes to take steps, individually and through international assistance and co-operation, especially economic and technical, to the maximum of its available resources, with a view to achieving progressively the full realization of the rights recognized in the present Covenant by all appropriate means, including particularly the adoption of legislative measures.
2. The States Parties to the present Covenant undertake to guarantee that the rights enunciated in the present Covenant will be exercised without discrimination of any kind as to race, colour, sex, language, religion, political or other opinion, national or social origin, property, birth or other status.
3. Developing countries, with due regard to human rights and their national economy, may determine to what extent they would guarantee the economic rights recognized in the present Covenant to non-nationals.

The description of the obligations of States under the ICESCR differs significantly from that of the ICCPR. The obligations of States Parties are recognized under the ICESCR as being subject to the availability of resources and require only the 'progressive realization' of the recognized rights.[12] This tends to remove the steam from the speedy realization of the economic, social, and

---

[9] *See generally* the Preamble of the ICESCR. [10] *See* e.g. Q2:29 and Q31:20.
[11] Q106:4.
[12] *See* Steiner, H.J., and Alston, P., *International Human Rights in Context: Law Politics Morals* (2nd Ed., 2000) p.246.

cultural rights, especially in developing nations. The ESCR Committee has endeavoured through its General Comment 3 to impress the point that these differences must not be seen as watering down the obligations of States under the Covenant.[13] It noted that 'while the Covenant provides for progressive realization and acknowledges the constraints due to the limits of available resources, it also imposes various obligations which are of immediate effect'.[14] For example, the obligation to ensure the right of everyone to form and join a trade union (Article 8) is of immediate effect.

The obligations of States under the Covenant are thus a combination of 'obligations of conduct' and 'obligations of result'.[15] While the undertaking of States Parties 'to take steps' under Article 2(1) to realize the rights protected in the Covenant is an 'obligation of conduct' and has immediate application, the realization of the relevant rights, in most cases, is an 'obligation of result' that may be achieved progressively.[16] The ESCR Committee has interpreted the obligations of States Parties under Article 2(1) by first stressing the 'obligations of conduct' as follows:

... while the full realization of the relevant rights may be achieved progressively, steps towards the goal must be taken within a reasonably short time after the Covenant's entry into force for the States concerned. Such steps should be deliberate, concrete and targeted as clearly as possible towards meeting the obligations recognized in the Covenant. The means which should be used in order to satisfy the obligation to take steps are stated in article 2(1) to be 'all appropriate means, including particularly the adoption of legislative measures'.[17]

The Committee then went on to explain the 'obligations of result' and the progressive realization of the rights as follows:

... the fact that realization over time, or in other words progressively, is foreseen under the Covenant should not be misinterpreted as depriving the obligation of all meaningful content. It is on the one hand a necessary flexibility device, reflecting the realities of the real world and the difficulties involved for any country in ensuring full realization of economic, social, and cultural rights. On the other hand, the phrase must be read in the light of the overall objective, indeed the raison d'être, of the Covenant which is to establish clear obligations for States parties in respect of the full realization of the rights in question. It thus imposes an obligation to move as expeditiously and effectively as possible towards that goal. Moreover, any deliberately retrogressive measures in that regard would require the most careful consideration and would need

---

[13] General Comment 3. All the Committee's General Comments are available on the UN Website at: http://www.unhchr.ch/tbs/doc.nsf [1/3/03].   [14] General Comment 3, para.1.
[15] *See* e.g. Report of the International Law Commission (1977) 2 *Yearbook of the International Law Commission* 20, para. 8. *See also* Alston, P., and Quinn, G., 'The Nature and Scope of States Parties' Obligations under the International Covenant on Economic, Social, and Cultural Rights' (1987) 9 *Human Rights Quarterly*, p.156 at pp.165–166; and Craven (above n.6) at pp.107–109.
[16] *See* Alston and Quinn (above n.15).   [17] *See* General Comment 3, paras.2 and 3.

to be fully justified by reference to the totality of the rights provided for in the Covenant and in the context of the full use of the maximum available resources.[18]

Although the Committee confers upon itself 'the ultimate determination as to whether all appropriate measures have been taken' in respect of the above obligations,[19] there is no doubt that in respect of both 'obligations of conduct' and 'obligations of result' much will still depend on the humane volition and good faith of the States Parties to take the appropriate steps towards the realization of the economic, social, and cultural rights. In appreciation of the onerous and resource-demanding nature of economic, social, and cultural rights, Article 2(1) states the obligation of contracting parties to 'take steps *individually and through international assistance and co-operation, especially economic and technical'* to realize the rights guaranteed. Developing nations would certainly favour the argument that this places some level of obligation on the international community, especially on the developed and wealthy nations to assist and co-operate with the poor and developing nations in the realization of the economic, social, and cultural rights.[20] The ESCR Committee also seemed to have suggested this when it emphasized in its General Comment 3 that:

... in accordance with Articles 55 and 56 of the Charter of the United Nations, with well-established principles of international law, and with the provisions of the Covenant itself, international co-operation for development and thus for the realization of economic, social, and cultural rights is an obligation of all States. *It is particularly incumbent upon those States which are in a position to assist others in this regard.* The Committee notes in particular the importance of the Declaration on the Right to Development adopted by the General Assembly in its resolution 41/128 of 4 December 1986 and the need for States parties to take full account of all of the principles recognized therein. *It emphasizes that, in the absence of an active programme of international assistance and co-operation on the part of all those States that are in a position to undertake one, the full realization of economic, social, and cultural rights will remain an unfulfilled aspiration in many countries.*[21] (emphasis added)

Developed nations do not however seem to accept that they are under a legal obligation under the ICESCR to provide international assistance to developing nations or co-operate with them for the realization of economic, social, and cultural rights. In their view, while developing nations may seek the assistance or co-operation of developed nations, they cannot claim it as a legal right in the strict sense of the word. They make reference, for example, to the wording

---

[18] *See* General Comment 3, para.9.   [19] *ibid.*, para.4.
[20] *See* e.g. Chile's argument during the drafting of the Covenant that 'international assistance to under-developed countries had in a sense become mandatory as a result of commitments assumed by States in the United Nations'. E/CN.4/SR.1203, at p.342, para.10 (1962) cited in Craven (above n.6) at p.148.
[21] General Comment 3, para.14. *See also* the Committee's GC2 on International Technical Assistance Measures; UN Doc. HRI\GEN\1\Rev.1 at 45 in E/1990/23.

of Article 11 of the ICESCR which, in recognizing the right of everyone to an adequate standard of living, also recognizes that international co-operation in that regard is 'based on free consent' of States.[22] The full realization of economic, social, and cultural rights in developing States tends therefore to depend on an ethical duty and the humane volition of developed States rather than any international legal obligation on their part. Ethical and religious values can therefore give the legal obligations under the Covenant a human face that will contribute to the effective realization of those rights, especially in developing nations.

From an Islamic legal perspective, the *Sharî'ah* places both a moral and legal obligation on the State to ensure the economic, social, and cultural welfare of individuals. Limitation of resources should not be an excuse for the neglect of the welfare of the people by the State. Under Islamic law, the State must always sincerely strive to ensure the people's welfare within its available resources. The general Qur'anic principle here is for the wealthy State to provide according to its means and the poor State according to its means,[23] performed expeditiously, with prudence and the intention to do what is best. This is consistent with the principle of 'minimum core obligation' established by the ESCR Committee, which is to the effect that:

> ...a minimum core obligation to ensure the satisfaction of, at the very least, minimum essential levels of each of the rights is incumbent upon every State party. Thus, for example, a State party in which any significant number of individuals is deprived of essential foodstuffs, or essential primary health care, of basic shelter and housing, or of the most basic forms of education is, prima facie, failing to discharge its obligations under the Covenant.[24]

There is nothing under the *Sharî'ah* that contradicts the above eagerness to oblige States Parties to ensure the minimum possible enjoyment of economic, social, and cultural rights even in the face of resource constraints. As will become evident below, sensitivity to the injunctions of the *Sharî'ah* had spurred the early Caliphs to fulfil the economic, social, and cultural rights of individuals in the early Islamic State even in very difficult periods of its history. Also, the notion of international assistance and co-operation under Article 2(1) of the ICESCR is equally tenable under the Qur'anic principle of co-operation for the realization of human well-being.[25] Islamic law thus generally accommodates the obligations undertaken by States Parties under Article 2 for the realization of the rights recognized under the ICESCR. More so when the rights, as will become evident from their analyses below, are well sustainable within the provisions of the *Sharî'ah*. The legislative obligation of States Parties reflected in Article 2(1) and the obligation of non-discrimination in Article 2(2) have already been addressed in Chapter 3.

---

[22] *See* Craven (above n.6) at pp.148–150.   [23] *See* e.g. Q2:236.
[24] General Comment 3, para.10.   [25] *See* Q5:2.

4.6 THE RIGHT TO WORK

Article 6

1. The States Parties to the present Covenant recognize the right to work, which includes the right of everyone to the opportunity to gain his living by work which he freely chooses or accepts, and will take appropriate steps to safeguard this right.
2. The steps to be taken by a State Party to the present Covenant to achieve the full realization of this right shall include technical and vocational guidance and training programmes, policies and techniques to achieve steady economic, social, and cultural development and full and productive employment under conditions safeguarding fundamental political and economic freedoms to the individual.

Work is traditionally recognized as the legitimate means of earning a livelihood in every human society. Sieghart has thus rightly pointed out that work is 'an essential part of the human condition'.[26] It is through work that a dignified source of income is often guaranteed and the material well-being of an individual and a harmonious development of his personality may be realized. The popular saying that 'there is dignity in labour' substantiates the fact that the right to work is fundamental to the maintenance of the dignity of the individual. Article 6 therefore recognizes the value of work as 'an element integral to the maintenance of the dignity and self-respect of the individual'.[27]

While the intendment of Article 6 may not be to guarantee full employment and total elimination of unemployment (as States may argue), it places an obligation on the States Parties to provide at least the opportunity of work for everyone who wants to work and narrow the channels of unemployment.[28] Also, while the right to work under Article 6(1) may be subject to progressive realization, as is the case with most of the rights recognized under the ICESCR, Article 6(2), as read with Article 2(1), provides that certain steps must be taken by the States Parties to achieve the full realization of the right. Such steps, which include 'technical and vocational guidance and training programmes, policies and techniques to achieve steady economic, social, and cultural development and full and productive employment under conditions safeguarding fundamental political and economic freedoms to the individual', are very demanding for many developing nations and may still take some time to be achieved, depending on available resources.

The wording of Article 6(1) indicates that the recognition of the right to work includes freedom of choice of employment by everyone. This excludes forced labour or forced employment upon any individual.[29] Article 6 would

---

[26] Sieghart, P., *The Lawful Rights of Mankind: An Introduction to the International Legal Code of Human Rights* (1986) p.123.   [27] Craven (above n.6) at p.194.

[28] *See* Art. 23(1) of the UDHR which provides that 'Everyone has the right to work . . . and protection against unemployment'.

[29] Art. 8(3)(a) of the ICCPR provides that 'No one shall be required to perform forced or compulsory labour'. *See also* Art. 1 of the ILO Abolition of Forced Labour Convention No. 105

however not accommodate a choice by an individual of 'work' or 'trade' legally prohibited by the State. Drzewicki has also pointed out that the freedom of choice in the right to work may be limited by 'provisions designed to prevent vulnerable persons, such as women, children and young persons, from working in certain conditions'.[30] Conversely, Article 2(2) and Article 3 of the ICESCR would prohibit any discriminatory legislation or practice that inhibits certain groups such as women, the elderly, or the disabled from employment.[31] Other aspects of this right include the right not to be arbitrarily dismissed from work.[32]

The right to work and dignity of labour is fully recognized under Islamic law. This is evidenced by many verses of the Qur'an and by the *Sunnah* of the Prophet Muhammad that extol the value of labour and work.[33] For example the Qur'an states categorically that God has ordained the daytime for seeking sustenance (through work) by humans,[34] and has also made trade lawful.[35] The Prophet himself set many examples on the dignity of labour both in deeds and words. In one Tradition he is reported to have said: 'There is no better way of sustenance than through the labour of one's own hands, because even the Prophet David used to feed from the labour of his own hands'.[36] And in answer to a question put to him as to which was the best means of sustenance the Prophet gave a similar answer that: '... the best means of sustenance is through the labour of your own hands or through lawful trade'.[37] He also stated in another Tradition that it is better and dignifying for an individual to earn a living by cutting and selling firewood than through begging.[38] The Prophet himself is recorded to have worked for his livelihood.

---

of 1957. *See* ILO Treaty Website at: http://ilolex.ilo.ch:1567/public/english/docs/convdisp.htm [1/3/03].

[30] For example, ILO Convention No. 45 prohibiting underground work for women and ILO Conventions Nos. 5, 10, 33, 59, 60, and 123 concerning minimum age for admission to employment. *See* Drzewicki, K., 'The Right to Work and Rights in Work', in Eide, A., Krause, C., and Rosas, A. (eds.), *Economic, Social, and Cultural Rights: A Textbook* (1995) p.169 at p.179.

[31] For example, agitation about the discriminatory effects of the ILO Convention No. 89 of 1948, which excluded women from night work, led the ILO to adopt a Protocol in 1990 amending the earlier provisions of Convention No. 89. *See* Drzewicki (above n.30).

[32] *See generally* Craven (above n.6) pp.194–225 for a detailed discussion of the right to work in the context of the ICESCR.

[33] *See* e.g. al-Ghazâlî, M., *Huqûq al-Insân Bayn T'âlîm al-Islâm Wa I'lân al-Umam al-Mutahidah* (Arabic) (1993) pp.177–203; Al-Zuhayli, W., *Al-Fiqh Al-Islami wa-Adillatuh* (Arabic) (1997) Vol. 7, pp.4986–4989 and 'Uthmân, M.F., *Huqûq al-Insân Bayn al-Sharî'ah al-Islâmiyyah Wa al-Fikr al-Qânûniy al-Garbiyy* (Arabic) (1982) pp.151–155; where the authors discuss many Qur'anic verses and Prophetic Traditions on dignity of labour and work in Islamic law. [34] *See* Q78:11.

[35] *See* Q2:275.

[36] Reported by al-Bukhâri, *see* e.g. Karim, F., *Al-Hadis, An English Translation and Commentary of Mishkat-ul-Masabih With Arabic Text* (3rd Ed., 1994) Vol.1, p.403, Hadith No. 109.

[37] Reported by Ahmad, *see* Karim (above n.36) at p.406, Hadith No. 131w.

[38] Reported by al-Bukhâri, *see* e.g. Karim (above n.36) at Hadith No. 108.

It is clear from the above Traditions that Islam discourages begging and dependence upon others but rather encourages labour and working for one's sustenance. The State therefore has a duty under Islamic law to respect the right of every individual to work, and in fact to encourage them to do so. The duty of the State to recognize the right to work and to take steps to ensure the provision of opportunity for work and the protection of individuals from unemployment is often inferred by Muslim scholars from a precedent laid down by Prophet Muhammad when a man came to him begging for alms. The Prophet asked the man to bring two items from his house, which he sold for two silver coins. He then gave the coins to the man instructing him to feed his family with one of the coins and to buy an axe with the other coin. The Prophet fixed a handle to the axe and gave it to the man saying: 'Go, cut wood and sell it, and do not come back to me for fifteen days'. The man did as he was told and returned thereafter to the Prophet having earned up to ten silver coins from a few days' work, and was able to fulfil his needs conveniently from his own labour. The Prophet then advised him that this was better and more dignifying for him than begging. Based on this precedent of the Prophet of Islam, as an embodiment of the State during his time, Chaudhry concluded that the 'Islamic State is, thus, responsible to provide employment to its citizens if they have no employment or occupation to earn their livelihood'.[39] Al-Zuhayli reached the same conclusion by reference both to this Tradition[40] and also through another Tradition in which the Prophet stated that the ruler (that is, the State) is like a shepherd over the people and is thus responsible for the affairs of the people.[41]

Scholars also argue from the facts of the above precedent of the Prophet that there is a corresponding duty to work on every individual who has the capacity to do so under Islamic law.[42] As is the case under Article 6 of the ICESCR this corresponding duty to work would not accommodate forced labour, the prohibition of which is evidenced by the verse of the Qur'an that says: 'God does not burden a person beyond his scope . . .'.[43] Tabandeh has also cited a precedent of the fourth Caliph, Ali ibn Abî Tâlib to show that forced labour has no place under Islamic law. One of the governors under the Caliph was reported to have requested the Caliph's permission to force people to work for the repair of a canal to improve the flow of water in the province for agricultural purposes. The Caliph was reported to have replied: 'I would never compel a single person to do any work he has not a mind to do. If the stream

---

[39] Chaudhry, M.S., *Islam's Charter of Fundamental Rights and Civil Liberties* (1995) p.41. *See also* 'Uthmân (above n.33) at p.153. and Karim (above n.36) at p.401, Hadith No. 107.

[40] *See* Al-Zuhayli (above n.33) at Vol.7, p.5010.

[41] *ibid.*, p.4989. The Tradition in reference here is further discussed more elaborately below under the right to social security in text to n.87 and n.88 below.

[42] See e.g. Art. 36(1) of the Syrian Constitution of 1973 which provides that: (1) Work is a right and duty of every citizen. The state undertakes to provide work for all citizens.

[43] Q2:286.

and its canal are in the condition you describe, invite the people to do the work needed voluntarily, and give them every encouragement, promising that the water of the stream shall afterwards be the property of anyone who worked on it, but that such people as did not work shall have neither lot nor portion in its water'.[44]

Under Islamic law, the rights of the individual to do any work which he freely chooses and accepts will not include the right to choose any 'work' prohibited by the *Sharî'ah* such as prostitution, gambling, usury, and alcohol business. These are all prohibited 'work' under Islamic law and are considered as detrimental to both the ultimate well-being of the individual and that of society at large. It is on that basis for example, that Article 14 of the OIC Cairo Declaration on Human Rights in Islam while providing that 'Everyone shall have the right to legitimate gains without monopolization, deceit or harm to oneself or to others', added also that 'Usury (riba) is absolutely prohibited'.[45] As earlier argued above, Article 6 of the ICESCR does not seem to restrain a State from prohibiting certain types of work considered to be against public interest as long as such prohibition is not discriminatory and does not inhibit certain groups from legitimate work.

4.6.1 Women and the right to work under Islamic law

Regarding non-discrimination in the right to work, the right of women under Islamic law freely to choose or accept work of their own choice becomes relevant. For instance, the ESCR Committee expressed concern in its concluding observations on the initial report of the Islamic Republic of Iran in 1993 on the prohibition of women from magisterial appointments in Iran.[46] The 2000 report of the Special Representative on the situation of human rights in the Islamic Republic of Iran also questioned the requirement in the Iranian Civil Code for 'women to obtain the permission of their husbands to take jobs'.[47] The report however acknowledged that 'the provision is widely disregarded and can ... be circumscribed by a suitable provision in a marriage contract'. The Representative of the Islamic Republic of Iran had in his answer to questions on the issue at the eighth Session of the ESCR Committee stated that the situation

---

[44] Tabandeh, S., *A Muslim Commentary on the Universal Declaration of Human Rights* (1970) p.77. *See also* Chapter 3, para.3.9 above on the prohibition of slavery under Islamic law.

[45] This is based on Q2:275. While there is consensus among Muslim jurists about the prohibition of usury there are differences of opinion on its contemporary definition. *See* e.g. Moinuddin, H., *The Charter of the Islamic Conference and Legal Framework of Economic Co-operation among its Member States* (1987).

[46] *See* Concluding Observations on Islamic Republic of Iran, (1993), UN Doc. E/C.12/1993/7, para.6.   [47] UN Doc. E/CN.4/2000/35 of 18 January 2000, para.22.

was being corrected and 'a text had been submitted to the Government' in that regard.[48]

Under traditional Islamic jurisprudence, jurists hold different opinions on the question of appointing women as judges. While a majority of the traditional jurists excluded women from the bench, Imâm Abû Hanîfah held the view that a woman can be appointed as a judge in civil matters. Other jurists like Ibn Jarîr al-Tabarî and Ibn Hazm however held the view that a woman can be appointed as a judge in all cases as her male counterpart. Al-Tabarî's argument was that since a woman could be appointed as a jurisconsult (*muftî*) then she can equally be appointed as a judge. We have pointed out in Chapter 3 that there is neither a verse of the Qur'an nor a Tradition of the Prophet that specifically prohibits the appointment of women as judges.[49] On that basis, the Federal Shariat Court of Pakistan when faced with this question in the case of *Ansar Burney v. Federation of Pakistan*[50] in 1982, held that women could be appointed as judges under Islamic law. The court preferred the views of al-Tabarî and Ibn Hazm to that of other jurists who excluded women from working as judges.

Generally, one finds nothing within the Qur'an and *Sunnah* that specifically excludes women from doing any legitimate work of their choice provided they possess the required skills and expertise and are not exposed to any hazards therefrom. As observed in Chapter 3, the *Sharî'ah* recognizes the independence of women within basic moral and ethical rules that equally apply to men. Most contemporary Muslim scholars support the view that women may not be legally discriminated against in the right to work and choice of profession. For instance, Hamidullah has observed that:

> In every epoch of Islamic history, including the time of the Prophet, one sees Muslim women engaged in every profession that suited them. They worked as nurses, teachers, and even as combatants by the side of men when necessary, in addition to being singers, hair-dressers, cooks, etc. Caliph 'Umar employed a lady, Shifa' bint 'Abdullah as inspector in the market at the capital [Madinah] as Ibn Hajar [*Isabah*] records. The same lady had taught Hafsah, wife of the Prophet, how to write and read. The jurists admit the possibility of women being appointed as judges of tribunals, and there are several examples of the kind. In brief, far from becoming a parasite, a woman could collaborate with men, in Muslim society, to earn her livelihood and to develop her talents.[51]

Similarly Abdulati has also stated that:

> Historical records show that women participated in public life with the early Muslims, especially in times of emergencies. Women used to accompany the Muslim armies engaged in battles to nurse the wounded, prepare supplies, serve the warrior, and so on. They were not shut behind iron bars or considered worthless creatures and

---

[48] *See* Summary Record of 8th Meeting: Iran (Islamic Republic of) E/C.12/1993/SR.8 of 20/12/93 paras.36 and 40.   [49] *See* Ch.3 text to n.570ff above.
[50] (1983) 65 PLD (FSC) 73.   [51] Hamidullah, M., *Introduction to Islam* (1982) p.139.

deprived of souls. Islam grants woman equal rights to contract, to enterprise, to earn and possess independently.[52]

Badawi, while also subscribing to the legal view that there is no decree in Islam which forbids women from seeking employment, added that:

with regard to the woman's right to seek employment it should be stated first that Islam regards her role in society as a mother and a wife as the most sacred and essential one. Neither maids nor baby-sitters can possibly take the mother's place as the educator of an upright, complex free, and carefully-reared children [sic]. Such a noble and vital role, which largely shapes the future of nations, cannot be regarded as 'idleness'.[53]

Badawi's observation above expresses a moral consideration upon which Muslim scholars discourage women from choosing any work capable of preventing them from fulfilling their important role as mothers and wives. Reciprocally, the man is also prevented from choosing any work capable of preventing him from fulfilling his role as a father or husband. It is upon the same basis that both spouses may confer not only on choice of work but on all aspects of the family relationship. Ideally it is not a question of consent or permission but mutual agreement between the couple in the best interest of the family. In a strict Islamic legal sense, the right to work and freely to choose or accept work of one's choice is very much sustainable within the provisions of the *Sharî'ah* and general principles of Islamic law, and is applicable both to the male and female gender without discrimination. Article 12 of the OIC Cairo Declaration on Human Rights in Islam thus provides that:

Work is a right guaranteed by the State and society for each person able to work. Everyone shall be free to choose the work that suits him best and which serves his interests and those of society. The employee shall have the right to safety and security as well as to all other social guarantees. He may neither be assigned work beyond his capacity nor be subjected to compulsion or exploited or harmed in any way.[54]

In that regard most Muslim States need to redress the misconception about the right of women to work and also ensure their safety and security in that respect both in the private and public sectors of society.

---

[52] Abdulati, H., *Islam in Focus* (1997) pp.364–5; *see also generally* Badawi, J., 'The Status of Woman In Islam' (1971) 8 *Al-Ittihad,* No. 2, September, p.33.   [53] Badawi (above n.52).

[54] Note that the pronouns 'he', 'his' and 'him' are generically used for both male and female in the Declaration.

4.7 THE RIGHT TO JUST AND FAVOURABLE CONDITIONS OF WORK

Article 7

The States Parties to the present Covenant recognize the right of everyone to the enjoyment of just and favourable conditions of work which ensure, in particular:

(a) Remuneration which provides all workers, as a minimum, with:
    (i) Fair wages and equal remuneration for work of equal value without distinction of any kind, in particular women being guaranteed conditions of work not inferior to those enjoyed by men, with equal pay for equal work;
    (ii) A decent living for themselves and their families in accordance with the provisions of the present Covenant;
(b) Safe and healthy working conditions;
(c) Equal opportunity for everyone to be promoted in his employment to an appropriate higher level, subject to no considerations other than those of seniority and competence;
(d) Rest, leisure and reasonable limitation of working hours and periodic holidays with pay, as well as remuneration for public holidays.

If the individual is not to be exploited in the enjoyment of his right to work, and if work is to fulfil its role as a crucial source of income upon which the material well-being and the harmonious development of the individual's personality depends, then the right to work must be enjoyable under some minimum favourable and just conditions. As stated earlier, labour is not to be considered merely as a commodity but must be linked with human dignity. Thus while Article 6 provides for the *right to* work, Articles 7 and 8 provide for *rights in* work.[55]

The reporting guidelines formulated by the ESCR Committee in respect of Article 7 make reference to some Conventions of the International Labour Organization (ILO).[56] That is because the precedent of recognizing the right to just and favourable conditions of work had been laid earlier by the ILO through the adoption of many Conventions and Recommendations such as: Hours of Work (Industry) Convention (No. 1) of 1919; Weekly Rest (Industry) Convention (No. 14) of 1921; Minimum Wage-Fixing Machinery Convention (No. 26) of 1928 and (No. 131) of 1970; Weekly Rest (Commerce and Offices) Convention (No. 106) of 1957; Equal Remuneration Convention (No. 100) of 1951; Safety Provisions (Building) Convention (No. 62) of 1937; Holidays With Pay Convention (No. 52) of 1936 and (No. 132) of 1970.[57] This early formal recognition of rights in work by the ILO arose from revolutionary

---

[55] *See* e.g. Craven (above n.6) at pp.226–247 for elaborate analysis of these provisions.
[56] *See Revised Guidelines* (above n.2) at Art. 7(1).
[57] Many of the modern Muslim States have ratified these and other ILO Conventions. *See* the ILO Treaty Website for these and similar Conventions and their status of ratification at: http://ilolex.ilo.ch:1567/public/english/docs/convdisp.htm [1/3/03].

unrest that swept across Europe after the First World War and the appreciation of the 'interdependence between labour conditions, social justice and universal peace'.[58] By the establishment of these rights in work as fully fledged human rights, the individual worker is depicted as a subject and not an object of labour under the Covenant. As clearly stated under the provision of Article 7, the rights in work mainly aim at ensuring fair wages, decent living, safety at work, equal treatment and adequate rest and leisure for every worker, which all contribute to enhance the dignity of the working human being.

Although the right to just and favourable conditions of work has not been specifically codified and itemized as such under traditional Islamic law, it is very much sustainable and recognized within the provisions of the *Sharî'ah*. The *Sharî'ah* injunctions on non-exploitation, equity, humane treatment of peers and underlings etc, provide the basis in Islamic law for, in the words of Qadri, 'social controls and administrative techniques for the general welfare, social security, wages of labour and hours of work together with the rules on the relations of the employees and the employers'.[59] For example the Qur'an provides that:

Woe to those who give less in measure and weight. Those who, when they receive from Men demand full measure; But when they have to give by measure or weight, give less than due.[60]
... Give just measure and weight, and do not withhold from people things that are their due and do not do mischief on earth after its perfection, that is best for you if you had faith.[61]

The above verses serve as a basis for fair trade, fair and equitable wages for workers as well as equal remuneration for work of equal value under Islamic law. The injunctions here are for equity and fairness in labour transactions generally. There are also many Prophetic Traditions that specifically encourage equity and fairness in wages of workers. In one Tradition the Prophet is reported to have enjoined that: 'When anyone of you hires a worker he should inform him of his wages',[62] and in another he enjoined that the employee should be paid his or her wages before his or her labour sweat dries out.[63] The Prophet also warned that in the hereafter God would be displeased with an employer who engaged an employee and enjoyed his full labour but failed

[58] Drzewicki (above n.30) at p.169. For example the 2nd preambular paragraph of the ILO Constitution recognized the capability of 'conditions of labour involving such injustice, hardship and privation to large numbers of people as to produce unrest so great that the peace and harmony of the world are imperilled'. *See* ILO Treaty Website: http://www.ilo.org/public/english/about/iloconst.htm [8 July 2002] for the ILO Constitution.
[59] Qadri, A.A., *Islamic Jurisprudence in the Modern World* (1986) p.306.   [60] Q83:1–3.
[61] Q7:85.
[62] Reported by al-Bayhâqî, *see* al-Shawkânî, M., *Nayl al-Awtâr* (Arabic) (n.d.) Vol.5–6, pp.292–293.
[63] Reported by Ibn Majah, *see* e.g. Karim (above n.36) at Vol.2, p.301, Hadith No. 6.

to pay him his fair wages.[64] Another Tradition which says: 'Good treatment of persons under one's control brings fortunes while their bad treatment brings misfortune'[65] reflects the wisdom that ensuring just and favourable conditions of work increases the well-being of workers which in return improves productivity and brings fortunes to the employer and society at large. The Prophet thus generally enjoined the good and humane treatment of servants, employees and workers.

Correlative to the right of the worker to a fair wage and favourable working conditions is also his duty to discharge his contract properly and justly. The Qur'anic rule in employer/employee and human relationships generally is that 'Deal not unjustly and you shall not be dealt with unjustly'.[66] The Prophet is also reported to have stated that: 'God loves to see that when someone does some work he does it perfectly'.[67] From the above provisions and principles, Weeramantry has correctly identified that under Islamic law 'work [is] looked upon more as a partnership between employer and employee than as a relationship of superiority and subordination' and that the 'right to a fair wage and of the employer's obligation to implement the contract justly are deeply ingrained in Islamic doctrine'.[68]

The recognition of rest and leisure in relation to work under Islamic law is evidenced in the Qur'anic verses which state that 'We have made your sleep for rest... And made the day as a means of [seeking] subsistence'.[69] Overworking without rest and lack of leisure certainly results in stress and weakness, which is detrimental to workers. This is prohibited within the provision of the Qur'anic verse which says: '... let there be transactions [between you] by mutual good will, and do not kill [or destroy] yourselves...'[70] The Prophet had also admonished that the human body has a right of rest and leisure that must be respected.[71] Tabandeh has, in that regard, referred to an Islamic Tradition which recommends the division of the 24 hours of a day into three periods 'viz: 8 hours for work; 8 hours for worship, food and recreation; 8 hours for sleep and repose' as a demonstration of Islam's recognition of the right to rest, leisure, and reasonable limitation of working hours.[72]

Islamic law thus fully recognizes and strongly encourages the right of everyone to enjoy just and favourable conditions of work as provided under

[64] Reported by al-Bukhâri, *see* e.g Karim (above n.36) at p.299, Hadith No. 3.
[65] Reported by Abû Dâwûd, *see* e.g. Karim (above n.36) at Vol. 1, p.228, Hadith No. 96.
[66] Q2:279.
[67] Reported by al-Bayhâqî *see* e.g. Al-Zuhayli (above n.33) at Vol. 7, p.5011.
[68] Weeramantry, C.G., *Islamic Jurisprudence: An International Perspective* (1988) pp.63 and 64.   [69] Q78:9–11.
[70] Q4:29.
[71] Reported by al-Bukhâri and Muslim, *see* Karim (above n.36) at Vol.1, pp.431–432, Hadith No. 146.
[72] *See* Tabandeh, S., *A Muslim Commentary on the Universal Declaration of Human Rights* (1970) p.78.

Article 7 without discrimination of any kind. This is acknowledged in Article 13 of the OIC Cairo Declaration on Human Rights in Islam:

> ... The employee shall have the right to safety and security as well as to all other social guarantees. He may neither be assigned work beyond his capacity nor be subjected to compulsion or exploited or harmed in any way. He shall be entitled—without any discrimination between males and females—to fair wages for his work without delay, as well as to the holidays allowances and promotions which he deserves. For his part, he shall be required to be dedicated and meticulous in his work.

The provisions on the rights and duties of the employee apply to both the private and public sectors of labour. Based on the Tradition in which the Prophet described the ruler (that is, the State) as being the 'shepherd' that is responsible for the affairs of the 'flock' (that is, the people), the State has the duty under Islamic law to ensure that the right of everyone to enjoy just and favourable conditions of work is ensured both in the private and public sectors of labour. The State may enact legislation and create institutions through which the rights of workers can be ensured. For example, the public institution called *al-hisbah* is an important organ in Islamic law under which the *muhtasib* (officer for public order) is conferred with a broad jurisdiction, *inter alia*, to monitor and control trade and labour standards, investigate trade and labour disputes and generally ensure fair practices in trade, the welfare and rights of consumers and labourers under Islamic law.[73] This strongly complements the obligation of Muslim States under the Covenant to ensure that the rights of employees are fully guaranteed both in the private and public sectors.

4.8 TRADE UNION RIGHTS

Article 8

1. The States Parties to the present Covenant undertake to ensure:
   (a) The right of everyone to form trade unions and join the trade union of his choice, subject only to the rules of the organization concerned, for the promotion and protection of his economic and social interests. No restrictions may be placed on the exercise of this right other than those prescribed by law and which are necessary in a democratic society in the interests of national security or public order or for the protection of the rights and freedoms of others;
   (b) The right of trade unions to establish national federations or confederations and the right of the latter to form or join international trade-union organizations;
   (c) The right of trade unions to function freely subject to no limitations other than those prescribed by law and which are necessary in a democratic society in the interests of national security or public order or for the protection of the rights and freedoms of others;

---

[73] *See* e.g. al-Mâwardî, A., *al-Ahkam as-Sultaniyyah, The Laws of Islamic Governance* (trans. Yate, A.) (1996) p.337ff.

(d) The right to strike, provided that it is exercised in conformity with the laws of the particular country.

2. This article shall not prevent the imposition of lawful restrictions on the exercise of these rights by members of the armed forces or of the police or of the administration of the State.

3. Nothing in this article shall authorize States Parties to the International Labour Organization Convention of 1948 concerning Freedom of Association and Protection of the Right to Organize to take legislative measures which would prejudice, or apply the law in such a manner as would prejudice, the guarantees provided for in that Convention.

The recognition of the right of all workers to just and favourable conditions of work under Article 7 does not often come easily and must sometimes be negotiated and pressed for collectively. Sieghart has observed that although 'work continues to be an essential part of the human condition' it also 'continues to be one of the most persistent occasions for the exploitation of human beings by their own kind'.[74] Trade unions are thus essentially meant for the promotion and protection of the economic and social interests of workers. During the drafting of the Covenant, the Lebanese and Pakistani representatives emphasized that trade union rights were a 'necessary instrument for implementing economic, social, and cultural rights' and 'satisfactory working conditions in particular'.[75] It is important to note that the States Parties do not merely recognize the right to form and join trade unions but undertake in Article 8 to *ensure* this right. The obligation here is therefore seen to require positive action, is immediate and not progressive.[76] The ESCR Committee has observed that this Article was capable of immediate application and that any suggestion to the contrary would be difficult to sustain.[77]

While, like the general right to freedom of association guaranteed under Article 22 of the ICCPR, everyone is free under Article 8 of the ICESCR 'to form trade unions and join the trade union of his choice, subject only to the rules of the organization concerned', the inclusion that trade unions are 'for the promotion and protection of [workers'] economic and social interests' tends to restrict trade unions from being used as political instruments.[78] Article 8(2) also allows the State to impose lawful restrictions on the trade union rights of members of the armed forces, the police, and members of the administration of State.

There are no direct provisions on trade unionism within the *Sharî'ah*. The Qur'an however enjoins co-operation (*ta'âwun*)-and thus organization–for good purposes (*al-birr*) and common causes.[79] There is also no provision

---

[74] Sieghart (above n.26).
[75] *See* Malik (Lebanon) E/CN.4/SR.298, at p.8 (1952); and Chaudhury (Pakistan) A/C.3/SR.719 at p.199, para.19 (1956) cited in Craven (above n.6) at p.250.
[76] *See* e.g. Craven (above n.6) at p.251.   [77] *See* General Comment 3 para. 5.
[78] *See* Craven (above n.6) at p.254.
[79] *See also* under Art. 22 of the ICCPR in Ch. 3 para. 3.23 above.

for the right to form or join trade unions or the right to freedom of association in the OIC Cairo Declaration on Human Rights in Islam. That leaves a big gap to be filled in respect of those rights. Article 13 of the OIC Declaration only provides that:

> ... Should workers and employers disagree on any matter, the State shall intervene to settle the dispute and have the grievances redressed, the rights confirmed and justice enforced without bias.

While the above provision appreciates the possibility of disagreement between workers and employers, it fails to provide a legal basis for the formation of trade unions that can formally represent workers to promote and protect their economic and social interests. If the argument is that the State has a duty under Islamic law to intervene and protect the confirmed rights of workers in such instances, the problem with that is, this can hardly be guaranteed where the employer is the State itself. Where there is no opportunity of unionism, workers would then have to pursue their rights in work on an individual basis, which then denies them the benefit and strength in collectivity.

Nevertheless, nothing in the *Sharî'ah* prohibits trade unionism for the promotion and protection of the economic and social interests of workers as specifically indicated in Article 8(1)(a) of the ICESCR. Kamali has argued that both the Qur'an and *Sunnah* 'enjoin co-operation (*ta'âwun*) in good and beneficial work', and stressed that 'co-operation in good work (*al-birr*) . . . is a broad concept which can apply to all forms of beneficial co-operation, whether in the form of a political party, a professional association, or a workers' union which aims at ensuring fair practices in trade and the equitable treatment of workers'.[80] Considering the tendency of exploitation that often exists in employer-employee relationships all over the world today, the right of trade unionism for the purpose of promoting and protecting the economic and social interests of workers is very legitimate under Islamic law. As earlier indicated above, the Prophet of Islam has in many ways enjoined the welfare of workers. It is a fact that the individual worker is always the weaker party in every employer-employee relationship. It is only through trade unionism that the welfare of workers may truly be realized and the interest of employees adequately protected, especially within the capitalist oriented economy that exists in most parts of the modern world. Since modern Muslim States participate in the capitalist oriented economy, it would be inconsistent with the Islamic injunction of fair-dealing not to allow the formation of trade unions to protect the interest of workers against any exploitative tendencies of employers. Apart from the confrontational trait often associated with trade unions, they also are necessary vehicles for the social, cultural, and professional

---

[80] Kamali, M.H., *Freedom of Expression in Islam* (1997) p.79.

interaction of workers both nationally and internationally, which goes a long way to improving their productivity.

Many Muslim States have ratified the ILO Convention No. 87 on Freedom of Association and Protection of the Right to Organize (1948)[81] and Convention No. 98 Right to Organize and Collective Bargaining Convention (1949),[82] which are the two key ILO trade union Conventions. It is important to note in this regard that Muslim States have an important obligation to ensure that the rights of workers to form trade unions and join trade unions of their choice are ensured within both the public and private sectors of the State.

4.9 THE RIGHT TO SOCIAL SECURITY AND SOCIAL INSURANCE

Article 9

The States Parties to the present Covenant recognize the right of everyone to social security, including social insurance.

Apart from the general statement that social security includes social insurance, the scope and nature of social security is not defined under the Covenant. Article 22 of the UDHR also provides that: 'Everyone, as a member of society, has the right to social security and is entitled to realization, through national effort and international co-operation and in accordance with the organization and resources of each State, of the economic, social, and cultural rights indispensable for his dignity and the free development of his personality', but fails to define the scope of social, and economic rights indispensable for the dignity and free development of the individual. The reporting guidelines for Article 9 of the ICESCR however refer to the ILO Social Security (Minimum Standards) Convention (No.102) of 1952[83] and also request each State Party to indicate which of the following branches of social security exist in their country, viz: medical care; cash sickness benefits; maternity benefits; old-age benefits; invalidity benefits; survivors' benefits; employment injury benefits; unemployment benefits; and family benefits.[84] This list clearly indicates that the social security system is meant to be an alleviative arrangement for ensuring a guaranteed income and basic sustenance from the State to 'labour inactive'

---

[81] 34 of the 56 Member States of the OIC have ratified this ILO Convention. *See* ILO Treaty Website at: http://www.ilo.org/ilolex/english/convdisp1.htm.

[82] 41 of the 56 Member States of the OIC have ratified this ILO Convention. *See* ILO Treaty Website (above n.81).

[83] *See* ILO Website at: http://ilolex.ilo.ch:1567/scripts/convde.pl?query=C102&query0=102 &submit=Display [1/3/03].

[84] These are exactly the nine specific branches of social security covered by the ILO Social Security (Minimum Standard) Convention (No. 102) of 1952. *See Revised Guidelines* (above n.2).

members of society who may for obvious reasons not be able to earn income or sustenance through work. This in essence is aimed at protecting the dignity of the individual in such situations and preventing him from having to engage in the undignified act of begging or resorting to other degrading and unacceptable means of sustenance.

Scheinin has noted that '[i]n developing countries, the economic protection of other, "inactive", persons may be seen more as a moral duty of the family than as a legal right of the individual in relation to public authorities'. He however further argued that '[t]he place of the right to life in the international code of human rights certainly puts limits on leaving the responsibility of the basic well-being of the members of society to families'.[85] While Scheinin's observation in respect of the concept of social security in developing countries describes what one finds today in Muslim States, there are precedents in early Islamic State practice where responsibility for the basic well-being of everyone and especially the economic protection of labour inactive persons was taken as an obligation of the State.

The *Sharî'ah,* in fact, enjoins the concept of social security as a State policy rather than purely a family responsibility. The *Zakât* tax is, for example, an obligatory State institution basically for ensuring the social security of indigent individuals within the State. The State has the legal responsibility of collecting the *Zakât* which must only be expended for the specific category of indigent persons to ensure their social security within the State. Apart from that, the State itself has a primary responsibility under the *Sharî'ah*, to provide members of the society with the economic and material welfare 'necessary for the maintenance of human happiness and dignity'.[86] This is evidenced by the oft-quoted Tradition of Prophet Muhammad in which he says:

> Behold, every one of you is a shepherd; and everyone of you is responsible for his flock. The ruler [the State] that governs over a people is a shepherd, and is responsible for his flock [the people]; The man is a shepherd over his family and is responsible for his flock; The woman is a shepherdess over her husband's household and children, and is responsible for them; The servant is a shepherd over his master's property, and is responsible for it. Behold, everyone of you is a shepherd, and everyone of you is responsible for his flock.[87]

Analysing the above Tradition, Muhammad Asad has pointed out the need to note that the ruler's (that is, the State's) responsibility to the people 'has been put at par with a father's or a mother's responsibility toward their children'. Just as the father and mother are 'shepherds' and are morally and legally responsible for the well-being of their family, the State is also morally and

---

[85] Scheinin, M., 'The Right to Social Security', in Eide *et al.* (above n.30) at p.161.

[86] *See* Asad, M., *The Principles of State and Government in Islam* (1980) p.87.

[87] Reported by al-Bukhâri and Muslim, *see* e.g. Karim (above n.36) at Vol. 2, p.567, Hadith No. 1.

legally responsible for the economic and social well-being of its people. 'It follows, therefore', Asad concluded, 'that a state, in order to be truly Islamic, must arrange the affairs of the community in such a way that every individual, man and woman shall enjoy that minimum of material well-being without which there can be no human dignity, no freedom and, in the last resort, no spiritual progress'.[88]

There are numerous recorded precedents of social security arrangements for the welfare of the labour inactive members in the history of the early Islamic State. For example, Hamidullah (quoting the great eighth century jurist, Imam Abû Yûsuf), has documented the position in his well-known work, *The Muslim Conduct of State,* first published in 1941, as follows:

> Social security in favour of non-Muslim subjects, at the expense of the Central Exchequer, was introduced as early as the time of Abû Bakr. In a State document, the commander, Khâlid ibn al-Walîd informs the Caliph of the conquest of the city of al-Hîrah, and says: 'I counted the male population. They were seven thousand. On further examination, I found that one thousand of them were permanently sick and invalid. So I excluded them from the imposition of the *jizyah* [tax]; and those susceptible of the tax thus remained six thousand... I have accorded them that any old man who could no more earn his livelihood for his weakness, or who should otherwise be afflicted by a calamity, or one who was rich but became poor to the extent that he requires the charity of his co-religionists, I shall exonerate him from the *jizyah* [tax] *and he and his family will be supported by the Muslim treasury so long as he lives in the Islamic territory* ...[89] [emphasis supplied]

The second Caliph, 'Umar ibn al-Khatâb, also laid down a formal precedent in that respect by demonstrating clearly during his rule that the State has an obligation under the *Sharî'ah* to ensure the social security and welfare of every member of the society, especially that of the 'labour inactive' along the lines envisaged under Article 9 of the ICESCR. 'Umar is recorded to have issued formal instructions during his Caliphate that grants must be provided from the State Treasury (*bayt al-mâl*) to the elderly and to the sick in the State without discrimination. Abû Yûsuf has documented in his *Kitâb al-Kharâj* that the Caliph 'Umar once 'passed along a street where somebody was asking for charity. He was old and blind. 'Umar tapped his shoulder from behind and said: From which community art thou? He replied: A Jew. He said: And what hath constrained thee to what I see thee in? He replied: I have to pay the capitation tax: I am poor; and I am old. At this 'Umar took him by the hand and led him to his own house and gave him something from his private coffers. Then he sent word to the cashier of the *bayt al-mâl* [State Treasury]: Look at him and his like. By God! We should never be doing justice if we eat out of his youth and leave him deserted in the old age. "The government taxes are meant

---

[88]   Asad (above n.86) at p.88.
[89]   Hamidullah, M., *The Muslim Conduct of State* (7th Revised Ed., 1977) p.117, para.211. *See also* Abû Yûsuf's *Kitâb al-Kharaj* (trans. Ali, A.A.) (1979) pp.289–290.

for the poor and the indigent." '[90] Al-Balâdhurî is also quoted to have recorded that when 'Umar came to a city called al-Jâbiyah 'he passed en route by some Christians suffering from leprosy, so he gave order that they should be aided out of *sadaqât*, i.e. *zakât*, and that they should be given a life pension'.[91]

Describing the precedent of Caliph 'Umar in respect of the formal inauguration of the concept of social security in the early Islamic State, Muhammad Asad observed exhaustively as follows:

> If some readers suppose that the idea of ... a social insurance scheme is an invention of the twentieth century, I would remind them of the fact that it was in full swing many centuries before its present name was coined, and even before the need for it became apparent under the impact of modern industrial civilization: namely, in the Islamic Commonwealth, at the time of the Right-Guided Caliphs. It was 'Umar the Great who, in the year 20A.H.(643CE) inaugurated a special government department, called *dîwân*, for the purpose of holding a census of the population at regular intervals. On the basis of this census, annual state pensions were fixed for (a) widows and orphans, (b) all persons who had been in the forefront of the struggle for Islam during the lifetime of the Prophet, beginning with his widows, the survivors of the Battle of Badr, the early *muhâjirs*, and so forth, and (c) all disabled, sick and old persons. The minimum pension payable under this scheme amounted to two hundred and fifty *dirhams* annually. In time, a regular allowance, payable to their parents or guardians, was settled even on children (on the principle that they were unable to fend for themselves) from the moment of their birth to the time when they would reach maturity; and during the last year of his life, 'Umar said more than once: 'If God grants me life, I shall see to it that even the lonely shepherd in the mountains of San'â' shall have his share in the wealth of the community.' With his characteristic grasp of the practical issues, 'Umar even went so far as to make experiments with a group of thirty people with a view to finding out the minimum amount of food an average person needed to maintain full health and vigor; and on the conclusion of these experiments he ordained that every man and woman in the country should receive from the government storehouses (in addition to the monetary pension of which he or she might be a recipient) a monthly allowance of wheat sufficient for two square meals a day.[92]

Most Muslim States today hardly operate a full social security scheme in the manner contemplated under Article 9 of the ICESCR. Asad has thus posed a question to Muslim States, based on the precedent of 'Umar narrated above, that: 'Is it not our duty [that is, the Muslim States], with thirteen centuries [now fourteen] of historical experience at our disposal, to rectify that shameful negligence and to bring 'Umar's work to completion?'.[93] This clearly indicates that the social security scheme is very much accommodated under Islamic law and is in fact a strong obligation upon Muslim States within available economic resources. The obligatory *zakât* fund is specifically meant for that purpose as specifically enjoined by the Qur'an. Thus, if Muslim States can properly

[90] See Hamidullah (above n.89) at pp.113–114.
[91] al-Balâdhurî, *Futûh al-Buldân*, (Arabic) p.129, cited in Hamidullah (above n.89) at p.114.　　　　　[92] Asad (above n.86) at p.92.
[93] *ibid.*

organize and utilize this important public institution, the social security system in the Muslim world would be greatly reformed and enhanced. Notably, the challenges of international human rights seem to spur some Muslim States into action in that respect. For instance, Libya in its initial report on the ICESCR, reiterated the importance of social security in promoting human welfare especially of labour inactive persons and further stated that an important distinguishing feature of the country's social security scheme was that:

> It is an Islamic scheme founded on the modern scientific and organizational experience of the developed countries. The underlying principles of the scheme were inspired by the magnanimous Islamic Shari'a, which ensures social solidarity and communal concern and promotes reform of the individual and the community based on justice, mercy and fellowship.[94]

In a similar vein Morocco also stated in its second periodic report on the ICESCR that it intends a thorough reform of its social strategy to benefit the most deprived members of society and that the country's 'social strategy will be reinforced by a social development fund and the establishment of a transparent mechanism for mobilizing the *zakat*'.[95]

As stated during examination of the right to work above, the able-bodied individual has a correlative duty to work under Islamic law. The individual is urged to work to earn a living whenever he can, rather than depend totally on benefits from the State. Islam discourages any form of parasitical or indolent way of life for the fit and able. The upper hand (that is, the giving hand) according to the Prophet, is always better than the lower hand (that is, the receiving hand). The OIC Cairo Declaration on Human Rights in Islam contains no specific provision on a right to social security and social insurance.

4.10 FAMILY RIGHTS

Article 10

The States Parties to the present Covenant recognize that:

1. The widest possible protection and assistance should be accorded to the family, which is the natural and fundamental group unit of society, particularly for its establishment and while it is responsible for the care and education of dependent children. Marriage must be entered into with the free consent of the intending spouses.

---

[94] *See* Initial Report: Libyan Arab Jamahiriya (1996), UN Doc. E/1990/5/Add.26, para.55(a).

[95] *See* para.210 of Second Periodic Report: Morocco, UN Doc. E/1990/6/Add.20 of 9 January 1999.

2. Special protection should be accorded to mothers during a reasonable period before and after childbirth. During such period working mothers should be accorded paid leave or leave with adequate social security benefits.
3. Special measures of protection and assistance should be taken on behalf of all children and young persons without any discrimination for reasons of parentage or other conditions. Children and young persons should be protected from economic and social exploitation. Their employment in work harmful to their morals or health or dangerous to life or likely to hamper their normal development should be punishable by law. States should also set age limits below which the paid employment of child labour should be prohibited and punishable by law.

The recognition of the family as an important natural unit of society and its role in the positive development of the individual can be found in most human rights instruments. For example, the African Charter identifies the family as 'the custodian of morals and traditional values recognized by the community'[96] and the European Social Charter identifies the family as 'a fundamental unit of society'.[97] Also Article 17(1) of the American Convention on Human Rights, Article 16(3) of the UDHR and Article 23(1) of the ICCPR all recognize that '[t]he family is the natural and fundamental group unit of society and is entitled to protection by society and the State'. It is in the same vein that Article 10(1) of the ICESCR not only recognizes the family as 'the natural and fundamental group unit of society', but also recognizes it as 'responsible for the care and education of dependent children'.

There is however no treaty definition for the term 'family' in international human rights law. This raises the problem of identifying which model or family structure would be entitled to the above protections by society and the State. Lagoutte and Arnason have argued that reference to the family in almost all human rights instruments as a 'natural' unit also refers to natural law, which, they further argued, 'is a direct translation of the anthropological theorization of kinship'.[98] Apart from the traditional classification of family into the nuclear and extended types, new notions of 'family' have today emerged in many societies other than those based on natural and traditional heterosexual biological relations. There are today new reproductive means like artificial insemination, surrogacy and, more controversially, same-sex relationships through which 'families' are formed. The ESCR Committee has not adopted any specific definition of family under the ICESCR, but seems to appreciate the possibility of differences in the concept of family under its reporting guidelines for Article 10. It requires States Parties to indicate in their report 'what meaning

---

[96] Art. 18(2) African Charter of Human and Peoples' Rights (1981).
[97] Art. 16 European Social Charter (1961).
[98] Lagoutte, A., and Arnason, A.T., 'Article 16' in Alfredsson, G., and Eide, A. (eds.), *The Universal Declaration of Human Rights: A Common Standard of Achievement* (1999) p.324 at p.338.

is given in your society to the term "family" '.[99] The HRC had also noted in its General Comment 19 issued in 1990 on Article 23 of the ICCPR that:

the concept of the family may differ in some respects from State to State, and even from region to region within a State, and that it is therefore not possible to give the concept a standard definition. However, the Committee emphasizes that, when a group of persons is regarded as a family under the legislation and practice of a State, it must be given the protection referred to in article 23. Consequently, States parties should report on how the concept and scope of the family is construed or defined in their own society and legal system.[100]

Also in the case of *Shirin Aumeeruddy-Cziffra and 19 Other Mauritian Women v. Mauritius*[101] the HRC had earlier observed *inter alia* that the 'legal protection or measures that a society can afford to the family may vary from country to country and depend on different social, economic or cultural conditions and traditions'.[102] That view placed the scope of definition of family under both the ICCPR and ICESCR upon each State and legal system concerned. The HRC has however moved further from that view by observing in its General Comment 28 issued in 2000 on Article 3 of the ICCPR that:

. . . in giving effect to the recognition of the family in the context of article 23 [of the ICCPR], it is important to accept the concept of the various forms of family, including unmarried couples and their children and single parents and their children and to ensure the equal treatment of women in these contexts . . .[103]

Although this current broad interpretation of 'family' by the HRC is said to be 'in the context of article 23' of the ICCPR, it can be equally relative to Article 10 of the ICESCR due to the similarity in wording of both Articles on family rights. This broad interpretation is however contrary to the concept of family under Islamic law as will emerge below.

Generally, the importance of the family and its protection is very well established under Islamic law. It is an important institution within Islamic society that is closely guarded, and family rights and duties are specifically defined under Islamic family law and jurisprudence for its establishment and protection.[104] Every Muslim individual is encouraged to be family-oriented and to assist in the realization of a socially stable society through the establishment of a stable family. The *Sharî'ah* also places responsibility on both the society and State in respect of protecting the family institution. There should therefore be no problem in reconciling the general protection and assistance of the family recognized under the ICESCR with Islamic law principles. The

[99] *See Revised Guidelines*, (above n.2) at para.2.   [100] General Comment 19, para.2.
[101] Communication No.35/1978 (9 April 1981), UN Doc. CCPR/C/OP/1 at 67 (1984).
[102] *ibid.*, para.9.2(b)2(ii)1.   [103] HRC General Comment 28, para.27.
[104] *See generally* e.g. Pearl, D., and Menski, W., *Muslim Family Law* (1998) and generally 'Abd al 'Atî, H., *The Family Structure in Islam* (1977).

Prophet is reported to have stated in one Tradition that: 'The best of you are those who are best to their families and I am best to my family'.[105] The Tradition earlier cited under Article 9 above in which the Prophet described the ruler, the father, and mother as shepherds in respect of the people and family respectively, also illustrates the recognition of the duty to protect and assist the family under Islamic law. There are also precedents of practical demonstration by the Prophet and the early Caliphs after him of the State's duty to protect and support the family, especially its vulnerable members such as children, the elderly, the handicapped, the widowed, and divorced.[106]

Article 10(1) of the ICESCR recognizes the institution of marriage and provides that marriage 'must be entered into with the free consent of the intending spouses'. The requirement of free consent of intending spouses is also an important condition of marriage under Islamic law. It is reported that a lady called Khansâ'a bint Khidhâm was given in marriage by her father, she disliked it and so complained to the Prophet Muhammad. The Prophet annulled the marriage.[107] Also in another Tradition it was reported that a girl came to the Prophet to complain that her father had given her in marriage against her will. The Prophet gave her the option of annulment.[108] On the basis of this Tradition, a girl forced into marriage before maturity has the option to revoke such marriage on reaching maturity under Islamic law. This is what is termed 'option of puberty' (*khiyâr al-bulûg*) under Islamic family law.[109]

In Muslim societies the definition of family is based on principles prescribed by the religion, reinforced by law, and observed by individuals as a religious obligation. For example the Egyptian Constitution provides that 'The family is the basis of the society founded on religion, morality and patriotism.'[110] Article 5 of the OIC Cairo Declaration on Human Rights in Islam also provides that:

(a) The family is the foundation of society, and marriage is the basis of its formation. Men and women have the right to marriage, and no restrictions stemming from race, colour or nationality shall prevent them from enjoying this right.
(b) Society and the State shall remove all obstacles to marriage and shall facilitate marital procedure. They shall ensure family protection and welfare.

This clearly states the Islamic law position that 'marriage is the basis of its (family) formation'. The concept of family is thus strictly limited within the confines of legitimate marriage under Islamic law. There are defined rules for legitimate marriage through which a legitimate family may be formed.[111]

---

[105] Reported by Tirmidhî and Ibn Mâjah, *see* Karim (above n.36) at Vol.1, p.200, Hadith No. 35.   [106] *See* e.g. 'Uthmân (above n.33) at pp.137–140.
[107] Reported by al-Bukhâri *see* e.g. Karim (above n.36) at Vol. 2, p.635, Hadith No. 37.
[108] Reported by Abâ Dâwûd, *see* Karim (above n.36) at Hadith No.36.
[109] *See* Karim (above n.36) at p.635.
[110] *See* Art. 9 The Constitution of the Arab Republic Of Egypt (1971).
[111] *See* e.g. 'Abd al 'Atî (above n.104) at pp.50–145.

The husband/father and wife/mother constitute the primary actors, and only the consequential natural blood-ties of such relationships can create a legitimate family under Islamic law.[112] Same-sex relationships and sexual relationships outside marriage are prohibited and not tolerated as a basis for family under Islamic law.[113] Interpreted within an appreciation of the different concepts of family from State to State, as acknowledged in the earlier General Comment 19 of 1990 by the HRC,[114] this Islamic conception of family would generally raise no problem under the provisions of Article 10 of the ICESCR.

The current broader view of the HRC in its General Comment 28 would however raise questions about recognizing unmarried couples and their children as a family. Article 10(3) of the ICESCR also provides that all children and young persons should enjoy special protection and assistance 'without any discrimination for reasons of parentage or other conditions'. This also raises the issue of the right of children conceived out of wedlock to enjoy such protection and assistance under Islamic law. For example, the Committee on the Rights of the Child observed in its concluding observation on Kuwait's initial report on the Convention on the Right of the Child that:

> The Committee is concerned at the potential for stigmatization of a woman or couple who decide to keep a child born out of wedlock, and at the impact of this stigmatization on the enjoyment by such children of their rights.[115]

In response, the Kuwait representative indicated that:

> extramarital sex was proscribed by Islamic law, and sex with a minor under 18 years of age was considered a crime, even with the girl's consent. In cases where it did occur and a child was born as a result, the tendency was for the parents to rid themselves of the child, since they were forbidden under Islamic law to keep a child conceived out of wedlock. In that event, the child was initially provided for by the Ministry of Public Health, and subsequently by the Ministry of Social Affairs and Labour.[116]

Islamic law emphasizes a child's right to legitimacy and that a child shall be linked naturally to only one mother and one father. But while maternity is naturally conspicuous, paternity can be subjected to doubt. Apparently, Islamic law considers maternal legitimacy as an inalienable right of legitimacy because a child can naturally have only one mother, conspicuous by the fact of birth.[117]

---

[112] *See* e.g. 3rd Periodic Report on Implementation of the ICESCR by Syrian Arab Republic. UN Doc. E/1994/104/Add.23 of 17/11/99, para.111.

[113] *See* e.g. 'Abd al 'Atî (above n.104) at pp.50–145.   [114] *See* above n.100.

[115] *See* Concluding Observations of the Committee on the Rights of the Child: Kuwait (1998) UN Doc. CRC/C/15/Add.96, para.23; *see also* Concluding Observations of the ESCR Committee: Morocco (2000) UN Doc. E/C.12/1/Add.55, para.23.

[116] *See* para.2 of Summary Record of 489th Meeting: Kuwait. CRC/C/SR.489 of 2 October 1998.

[117] Thus, although Islamic law prohibits conception outside wedlock, it does not legally forbid the mother from keeping a child conceived outside wedlock as stated in the Kuwait Report

Islamic law also emphasizes that every child shall have one natural father only, and in order to shut out any iota of doubt about paternity, the father's legitimacy is restricted within the confines of marriage, excluding any other man. Thus any conception that begins within marriage is presumed paternally legitimate until the contrary is proved. Once the father's legitimacy is established within marriage, an inalienable right of paternal legitimacy is created also in respect of father and child. Consequently, fornication/adultery is correlatively prohibited, *inter alia*, to promote and ensure an active sense of moral and familial responsibility within Islamic society. To protect the institution of marriage and the concept of legitimacy within marriage, a child conceived outside wedlock is considered under Islamic jurisprudence as a 'child of fornication/adultery' and its 'descent will derive from the mother only, while the adulterer, the father, will be denied paternity as a punitive measure for his misconduct'.[118] The main consequence of this under Islamic jurisprudence is that, while the child sustains its maternal legal inheritance rights to the mother, it is deprived of legal paternity and barred from paternal inheritance rights to the adulterous father.[119]

While the Qur'an specifically prohibits fornication/adultery and prescribes punishment for the direct offenders, it does not contain any direct provision on the status of a child conceived outside wedlock. However, the Prophet is reported to have stated in one Tradition that: 'Any man who commits fornication/adultery with either a free woman or a slave-girl, the child [of such relationship] is a child of fornication/adultery who has no right of inheritance'.[120] 'Abd al 'Atî has thus raised the tangible question of 'why should the child be deprived of a legal father or denied a father's name? The child has committed no offence, and it is unjust to "penalize" an innocent party'.[121]

It is apparent from the juristic views on this question that the denial of legal paternity in this case is intended only as a punitive measure against the adulterous father and not against the child, and to deter against fornication/adultery in the Muslim society. In finding answers to this question, 'Abd al 'Atî has

above. In one Tradition the Prophet Muhammad was reported to have instructed a woman who conceived and delivered a baby outside wedlock to keep and look after the child and postponed her punishment for *zinâ* till after the child had fully weaned. It is the societal stigmatization, as observed by the Committee, that often prevents a mother from wanting to keep a child conceived out of wedlock. *See* arguments by 'Abd al 'Atî against such stigmatization against the child further below.

[118] *See* 'Abd al 'Atî (above n.104) at p.191.

[119] According to *Shî'ah* (Twelvers) jurisprudence, the child loses both maternal and paternal rights of inheritance. *See* e.g. Al-Zuhayli (above n.33) at Vol. 10, pp.7905–7906. *See also* Art. 43 of the Egyptian Inheritance Act, which provides that: 'A child born out of wedlock inherits from his or her mother and maternal kin, who likewise inherit from the child', *see* Replies to List of Issues: Egypt, UN Doc. HR/CESCR/NONE/2000/6 of 28/03/2000. Article 18(2) of the Constitution of Kuwait also provides that: 'Inheritance is a right governed by the Islamic Sharî'ah'.

[120] Reported by al-Tirmidhî, *see* e.g. Karim (above n.36) at Vol. 2, p.333, Hadith No. 50.

[121] 'Abd al 'Atî (above n.104) at p.192.

argued *inter alia* that since children were highly valued and eagerly sought after, the need to minimize disputes and confusion about their paternity justifies the Islamic rule that children 'were to be conceived in wedlock, placed with, and entrusted to, devoted parents of unsuspected characters'. Bearing in mind that fornication/adultery is a crime under Islamic law and naturally abhorrent in most societies, he contended that those were conditions which 'adulterers could hardly qualify for'.[122] While he thus concluded on one hand that it may be in the child's interest to deny it to a father of such questionable integrity and character, he argued on the other hand that:

> This denial, however, does not affect the child's basic rights to security and full community membership. In fact, such a position may be a testimony to the child's own credit, to the society's openness, to the social response of the community, and to the degree of social integration. It would seem to reaffirm the basic principle that every Muslim individual has equal access to whatever is of value for Muslim society, hindered neither by a family name nor by the lack thereof. The chief criterion of excellence in the value system of Islam is personal piety and religio-moral achievement. No one may claim the credit of another nor is any one responsible for or penalized by the actions of anyone else. Whenever an offence is committed against God, e.g. adultery or fornication, it is only God Who exempts or forgives the offender. Thus, if there is any stigma of illegitimacy, it would cling not so much to the innocent child as to the guilty parents, and its effects shall not be allowed to hurt the innocent. ... The stigma need not arise in the first place for an innocent party; but if it does, reparations obtain by way of giving the child complete access to equal life chances and the right to grow up free from prejudice or stigmas of any kind.[123]

While the prohibition of fornication/adultery falls within the State's duty of protecting the family institution and public morality under Islamic law, the recognition and protection of the best interest of the child is also very well recognized. Coupled with the Qur'anic principle that 'No bearer of burdens shall bear the burden of another',[124] the argument that the innocent child should not be vicariously imperilled as a consequence of the illegitimate act of its de facto parents is therefore a valid and strong argument that compels States to guarantee the special protection and assistance of every child without any discrimination for reasons of parentage or other conditions. Answering questions on the status of children conceived out of wedlock in Saudi Arabia, the country's representative, Dr Bayari, informed the Committee on the Rights of the Child that:

> Pregnancies outside wedlock were carried to term and a decision was taken on whether the family would keep the child or place it in an institution. Most families accepted to keep the child, who had the same right to name and nationality as children born in wedlock.[125]

---

[122] 'Abd al 'Atî (above n.104) at p.195.   [123] *ibid.*, p.193.
[124] *See* Q6:164; Q17:15; Q35:18; Q39:7; Q53:38.
[125] *See* Summary Record of the 688th Meeting of CRC: Saudi Arabia, UN Doc. CRC/C/SR.688, para.52.

Marriage is thus an important institution on the basis of which family rights are determined under Islamic law. While unmarried persons or children conceived out of wedlock may, as individuals, be entitled to other guaranteed individual rights they will not qualify for family rights under Islamic law because family rights can only be claimed through the link of an Islamically legitimate marriage. This is a religio-moral principle that is evidently incompatible with the broad interpretation adopted by the HRC on the concept of family in its General Comment 28, and is reflective of the need for the adoption of the margin of appreciation doctrine by the UN human rights treaty bodies in resolving such differences with relevant States Parties to international human rights treaties.

4.11 THE RIGHT TO AN ADEQUATE STANDARD OF LIVING

Article 11

1. The States Parties to the present Covenant recognize the right of everyone to an adequate standard of living for himself and his family, including adequate food, clothing and housing, and to the continuous improvement of living conditions. The States Parties will take appropriate steps to ensure the realization of this right, recognizing to this effect the essential importance of international co-operation based on free consent.
2. The States Parties to the present Covenant, recognizing the fundamental right of everyone to be free from hunger, shall take, individually and through international co-operation, the measures, including specific programmes, which are needed:
   (a) To improve methods of production, conservation and distribution of food by making full use of technical and scientific knowledge, by disseminating knowledge of the principles of nutrition and by developing or reforming agrarian systems in such a way as to achieve the most efficient development and utilization of natural resources;
   (b) Taking into account the problems of both food-importing and food-exporting countries, to ensure an equitable distribution of world food supplies in relation to need.

The importance of Article 11 cannot be overemphasized because it restates in general terms the overall purpose of economic, social, and cultural rights, which is the realization of an adequate standard of living for every human being. A specific definition is not given of what constitutes an 'adequate standard of living' but it is stated to include 'adequate food, clothing and housing and . . . continuous improvement of living conditions'.[126] This will essentially be interpreted to mean a standard of living that ensures the dignity of the human person. That is, the ability, *inter alia*, for every person to enjoy the basic

---

[126] *See also* Art. 25 of the UDHR which provides that adequate standard of living includes 'food, clothing, housing and medical care and necessary social services, and the right to security in the event of unemployment, sickness, disability, widowhood, old age or lack of livelihood in circumstances beyond his control'.

necessities of life without resort to any degrading or dehumanizing means in that regard.[127]

Food, clothing, and housing are, without doubt, important basic necessities of life. The physical well-being of an individual essentially depends, *inter alia*, on whether he has (i) adequate food not only to free him from hunger but also nourish and provide him with energy required for a healthy life; (ii) adequate clothing to cover and protect his body and (iii) adequate shelter that provides him with security, peace of mind, and dignity. Without the guarantee of these three rights the inherent dignity of the human person will be greatly imperilled and hardly can any other human right make sense to anyone denied of those three. They are basic subsistence rights that are absolutely necessary for human survival.[128]

In furtherance of the right to food, the States Parties recognize also in Article 11(2) the '*fundamental* right of everyone to be free from hunger' and they undertake, individually and through international co-operation, to pursue measures and specific programmes to 'improve methods of production, conservation and distribution of food by making full use of technical and scientific knowledge, by disseminating knowledge of the principles of nutrition and by developing or reforming agrarian systems in such a way as to achieve the most efficient development and utilization of natural resources'. States shall also take into account 'the problems of both food-importing and food-producing countries, to ensure an equitable distribution of world food supplies in relation to need'. It is noteworthy that the right of everyone to be free from hunger is recognized here as a *fundamental* right, which places an obligation on the State to recognize this right under all circumstances.[129] In its General Comment 12 the ESCR Committee affirmed that:

> . . . the right to adequate food is indivisibly linked to the inherent dignity of the human person and is indispensable for the fulfilment of other human rights enshrined in the International Bill of Human Rights. It is also inseparable from social justice, requiring the adoption of appropriate economic, environmental and social policies, at both the national and international levels, oriented to the eradication of poverty and the fulfilment of all human rights for all.[130]

The States Parties undertake 'to take appropriate steps to ensure the realization' of the rights under Article 11. Eide has notably observed that '[t]he individual is also expected to use his/her own property or working capacity, to the best of his/her judgement', to realize his/her right to an adequate standard of living.[131] Thus, adopting Shue's typology of duties correlating to subsistence rights, the duties of the State in this regard are namely: (i) the duty to avoid deprivation,

---

[127] *See* e.g. Eide, A., 'The Right to an Adequate Standard of Living Including the Right to Food' in Eide *et al.* (above n.30) at p.90.

[128] *See generally* Shue (above n.5).   [129] *See* Craven (above n.6) at p.307ff.

[130] General Comment 12, para.4.   [131] Eide (above n.127) at p.100.

which places a duty on the State not to eliminate any individual's legitimate means of subsistence; (ii) the duty to protect from deprivation, which places a duty on the State to protect individuals against deprivation of their available legitimate means of subsistence; and (iii) the duty to aid the deprived, which places a duty on the State to provide for the subsistence of those unable to provide for themselves.[132] Starting with General Comment 12 on right to food the ESCR Committee has adopted this tripartite view of States Parties obligations under the Covenant consisting of the obligations to *respect, protect* and *fulfil*, thus observing that:

The right to adequate food, like any other human right, imposes three types or levels of obligations on States parties: the obligations to *respect*, to *protect* and to *fulfil*. In turn, the obligation to *fulfil* incorporates both an obligation to *facilitate* and an obligation to *provide*. The obligation to *respect* existing access to adequate food requires States parties not to take any measures that result in preventing such access. The obligation to protect requires measures by the State to ensure that enterprises or individuals do not deprive individuals of their access to adequate food. The obligation to *fulfil (facilitate)* means the State must pro-actively engage in activities intended to strengthen people's access to and utilization of resources and means to ensure their livelihood, including food security. Finally, whenever an individual or group is unable, for reasons beyond their control, to enjoy the right to adequate food by the means at their disposal, States have the obligation to *fulfil (provide)* that right directly. This obligation also applies for persons who are victims of natural or other disasters.[133]

Regarding international co-operation in respect of right to food, the ESCR Committee has also emphasized the duty of States not only individually and collectively to take positive steps to ensure the realization of adequate rights to food for every individual but also to 'refrain at all times from food embargoes or similar measures which endanger conditions for food production and access to food in other countries. Food should never be used as an instrument of political and economic pressure'.[134]

The duty in respect of right to housing seems much more onerous on the State than the right to food and clothing. This is due to the resource-demanding nature of that right and the obvious fact that, unlike food and clothing, most individuals in developing States would not be able to afford to build or buy houses on their own. The ESCR has issued two General Comments (GC4 and GC7) on the right to adequate housing.[135] In its General Comment 4 the Committee noted that '[t]he human right to adequate housing, which is ... derived from the right to an adequate standard of living, is of central importance for the enjoyment of all economic, social and cultural rights'.[136]

---

[132] Shue (above n.5) at pp.52–53. *See also* UN Centre for Human Rights, *Right to Adequate Food as a Human Right* (1989) pp.21–50.

[133] General Comment 12, para.15.   [134] *ibid.*, paras.36–41.

[135] General Comment 4 issued in 1991 covers the right to adequate housing generally, and General Comment 7, issued in 1997 addresses the problem of forced evictions.

[136] General Comment 4, para.1.

The Committee then indicated that 'the right to housing should not be interpreted in a narrow or restrictive sense which equates it with, for example, the shelter provided by merely having a roof over one's head or views shelter exclusively as a commodity' but 'should be seen as the right to live somewhere in security, peace and dignity'.[137] The UN 'Global Shelter Strategy to the Year 2000' adopted by the UN General Assembly in 1988 defined adequate shelter to mean 'adequate privacy, adequate space, adequate security, adequate lighting and ventilation, adequate basic infrastructure and adequate location with regard to work and basic facilities—all at a reasonable cost'.[138] In guaranteeing the right to adequate housing, the ESCR Committee has therefore identified that the following seven aspects must be taken into consideration by States, namely: (i) legal security of tenure; (ii) availability of tenure; (iii) affordability; (iv) habitability; (v) accessibility; (vi) location; and (vii) cultural adequacy.[139] Another important observation of the Committee is that 'the right to housing should be ensured to all persons irrespective of income or access to economic resources'. This obviously places a duty on the State to formulate national housing policies and strategies to alleviate homelessness. Where any step being taken by a State to realize this right is considered to be beyond the maximum resources available to the State, the Committee has reiterated that 'it is appropriate that a request be made as soon as possible for international co-operation in accordance with articles 11(1), 22 and 23 of the Covenant, and that the Committee be informed thereof'.[140]

In its General Comment 7 the Committee addressed extensively the problem of forced evictions, emphasizing its incompatibility with the provisions of the Covenant. It identified this to include forced eviction of communities that occur during developmental projects such as construction of dams or other large-scale energy projects.[141] The Committee then pointed out the duty of the State to ensure, where eviction is considered justified, that such evictions 'are carried out in a manner warranted by a law which is compatible with the Covenant and that all the legal recourses and remedies are available to those affected'.[142] The Committee has also listed a set of procedural protections that must be guaranteed to the individual in case of any forced eviction.[143]

Apart from the specific mention of rights to food, clothing, and housing, Article 11(1) also recognizes the right of everyone to 'the continuous improvement of living conditions'. This notably indicates that the right to an adequate standard of living under the Covenant is generally not static but places a

---

[137]   General Comment 4, para.7.

[138]   Global Strategy for Shelter to the Year 2000, UN Doc A/43/8/Add.1. *See also* G.A. Res. 42/191 of 9 March 1988 and UN Doc. A/RES/43/181 of 20 December 1988.

[139]   *See* General Comment 4, para.8, for the explanation of these elements by the Committee. *See also* Craven (above n.6) at p.335ff.

[140]   General Comment 4, para.10.   [141]   General Comment 7, para.8.

[142]   *ibid.*, para.12.   [143]   *ibid.*, para.16.

continuous dynamic obligation upon the State in line with economic and social developments.

From the perspective of Islamic law, both the substantive provisions of Article 11 and the Committee's interpretations of the right to an adequate standard of living are commensurate with *Sharî'ah* provisions and with the principles of Islamic law. The Qur'an confirms that the good things of life are created for the benefit and good living of human beings,[144] and it expresses disapproval of any attempt to deprive humanity of the good things of life that ensure an adequate standard of living for them.[145] Under Islamic law, the State must endeavour to prevent hardship and has a specific duty to ensure that everyone, especially the poor, enjoys an adequate standard of living. This is evident from the Qur'anic verse which states that: 'And in their wealth there is a right for the indigent who ask and for him who does not ask'.[146] The Prophet is also reported to have prayed as follows: 'Oh God, give hardship to anyone who rules over my people and gives them hardship, and show mercy to anyone who rules over my people and shows them mercy'.[147] The enjoyment of an adequate standard of living was ensured in the early Islamic State through a proper implementation and application of the *zakât* (Compulsory Tax) and *bayt al-mâl* (State Treasury) institutions.

There are ample provisions in both the Qur'an and *Sunnah* indicating that everyone has a right to adequate food, clothing, and housing within an Islamic State. For instance the Qur'anic verse which provides that: 'And they feed, for the love of God, the indigent, the orphan and the captive. [Saying] We feed you for the sake of God alone; no reward do we desire from you nor thanks'[148] indicates clearly that no one is expected to go hungry in the Islamic State. The principle of freedom from hunger, from fear, and from want stands established under Islamic law through the Qur'anic verse which stipulates that God has provided mankind 'with food against hunger and with security against fear'.[149] Thus under Islamic law, feeding the poor and indigent is not considered as a favour to them, rather the Qur'an stipulates it as a right which the poor and indigent have in the wealth of the affluent and in the resources of the State.[150] The Prophet corroborated this with his saying that no true Muslim goes to bed with a full stomach while his neighbour goes hungry. From an Islamic perspective, it is obnoxious that millions of people do starve and die of starvation in a world where there is naturally no food shortage. There is already an in-built

---

[144] *See* e.g. Q2:29 which says 'It is He Who created for you all things that are on earth' and Q28:77 which says: '... And forget not your portion of lawful enjoyment in this world'.

[145] Q7:32 which says: 'Who has forbidden the beautiful gifts of God which He has produced for His servants and the things clean and pure which He has produced for sustenance?'.

[146] Q51:19.

[147] Reported by Muslim, *see* e.g. Karim (above n.36) Vol. 2, p.569, Hadith No. 5.

[148] Q76:8–9.   [149] Q106:4.   [150] *See* Q51:19.

institution under Islamic law for ensuring freedom from hunger for everyone, if well implemented. It is the obligatory agricultural tax whereby a fixed percentage of all agricultural produce and that of cattle is deductible every year for the maintenance of the poor and indigent as of right. This could be emulated both as a national and international humanitarian policy for promoting freedom from hunger and ensuring the right to food for even the most indigent persons of the world. Not only is the right to food substantiated within Islamic law, one finds that the Qur'an also often emphasizes wholesomeness whenever it makes reference to food or drink. For instance the Qur'an 2:168 says: 'Oh Mankind, eat of what is on earth, lawful and good . . . ' and Qur'an 5:88 says: 'Eat of the things which God has provided for you, lawful and good . . . '. Lawful and good food, in the context of rights to food, would include adequate, nutritious, and wholesome food that ensures a healthy and dignified life for everyone.

The second Caliph 'Umar is recorded as having demonstrated during his rule in the early Islamic State that the State has a duty to ensure the right of everyone to food. He went to great lengths to ensure that the populace was free from hunger. He would go round disguised on night patrol listening to comments and to find out about the welfare of the populace. On one of such patrols the Caliph was reported to have come to a house from wherein he heard the crying of children. He knocked at the door to find out what was the cause and found a woman cooking something on fire with her children milling hungrily around her and crying in anticipation of the 'meal' being cooked. Upon enquiry, the woman informed 'Umar that, having nothing to feed her children that night, she had only placed some stones in the pot on the fire to hoodwink the children that something was being cooked for them, hoping that they would eventually fall asleep while waiting for the 'meal' to cook. The Caliph felt highly aggrieved and rushed to his palace and brought back a sack of wheat and some local butter from the State storage for the woman and her children. The Caliph was reported to have insisted on carrying the food personally to the indigent family, lamenting that he feared being questioned in the hereafter concerning anyone who was left to wallow in hunger during his rule as Caliph.[151] The Caliph was alluding to the Tradition of the Prophet earlier quoted which stated, *inter alia*, that the ruler (namely the State) is like a shepherd that would be held responsible for the welfare of his flock. He did not consider his action as a favour to that family but rather as a duty that correlatively ensured the right of the woman and her children to food in the Islamic State as provided by the *Sharî'ah*.

The Prophet Muhammad also demonstrated restraint from using food embargoes as a weapon of political or economic pressure even against enemies.

---

[151] This is a very well-known incident during the Caliphate of 'Umar, which has been narrated in slightly different versions by most Islamic historians and traditionists.

The Chief of Yamamah, Thumamah ibn Uthal had embraced Islam during the early period when Mecca was still very hostile to the Muslims. Yamamah was then the main source of grain supplies to Mecca. The Chief, after his embrace of Islam, decreed an embargo on grains from Yamamah to Mecca. The Prophet Muhammad however intervened and ordered the lifting of the embargo.[152]

In respect of rights to clothing, evidence is found, for example, in the Qur'anic verse which says: 'Oh Children of Adam, We have bestowed garments upon you to cover yourselves [screen your private parts] and also to serve as adornment . . .'[153] and also in another verse which says: '. . . He [God] has provided you with garments to protect you from heat [and cold] . . .'.[154] The stated purposes of clothing here, namely cover, adornment, and protection, certainly also depict the enhancement of human dignity. The Prophet also greatly encouraged the provision of clothing to those in need as a most rewarding religious obligation. Evidence for a right to housing is equally found, for example, in the verse of the Qur'an which states that: 'And God has made for you your homes as habitations of rest and quiet; and made for you out of the hides of cattle [tents] for dwelling, which you find so light [and handy] when you travel and when you stop in [your travels] . . .'.[155] It is clear from the last verse that the right to habitation is not limited to the domiciled but extended even to those constantly on the move, like Nomads and Gypsies.

In line with the above provisions, Article 17(c) of the OIC Cairo Declaration on Human Rights in Islam thus also recognizes the right of everyone to an adequate standard of living by providing that:

> The State shall ensure the right of the individual to a decent living which will enable him to meet all his requirements and those of his dependants, including food, clothing, housing, education, medical care and all other basic needs.

The Declaration also provides in Article 18(c) that neither shall a private residence be demolished, confiscated, nor its dwellers evicted.

4.12 THE RIGHT TO HIGHEST ATTAINABLE STANDARD OF PHYSICAL AND MENTAL HEALTH

Article 12

1. The States Parties to the present Covenant recognize the right of everyone to the enjoyment of the highest attainable standard of physical and mental health.
2. The steps to be taken by the States Parties to the present Covenant to achieve the full realization of this right shall include those necessary for:
   (a) the provision for the reduction of the stillbirth-rate and of infant mortality and for the healthy development of the child;

---

[152] *See* Hamidullah, M., *The Muslim Conduct of State* (Rev. 7th Ed., 1977) p.196, para.392.
[153] Q7:26.   [154] Q16:81.   [155] Q16:80.

(b) the improvement of all aspects of environmental and industrial hygiene;
(c) the prevention, treatment and control of epidemic, endemic, occupational and other diseases;
(d) the creation of conditions which would assure to all medical service and medical attention in the event of sickness.

The adage that 'health is wealth' explains the importance of health to the well-being of the human person. Apart from the right to food, clothing, and housing, the right to health and medical care are also specifically mentioned in the UDHR as elements of an adequate standard of living for the individual and his family.[156] The ESCR Committee has also observed that health is a 'fundamental human right indispensable for the exercise of other human rights' and that every human being 'is entitled to the enjoyment of the highest attainable standard of health conducive to living a life in dignity'.[157] Article 12(1) thus recognizes 'the right of everyone to the enjoyment of the highest attainable standard of physical and mental health' and the States Parties undertake to take necessary steps for the full realization of this right.

Article 12 creates two broad sets of norms in respect of health rights. The first is the guarantee of the rights of the individual to the enjoyment of the highest attainable standard of health, while the second is the protection of public health as a necessary step for the realization of the first. Sometimes, the protection of public health may however tend to restrict the liberty and freedom of movement of individuals.[158] This could occur during the control of epidemic or endemic diseases by the State under Article 12(2)(c). Such restrictions would then have to be, strictly, for the protection of public health and in accordance with law.

The maintenance of both individual and public health depends on a lot of other factors, such as waste disposal, environmental sanitation, nutrition and even housing provisions, which thus makes the right to the enjoyment of the highest attainable standard of physical and mental health quite complex. Apart from its demand for a great level of economic and human resources, it also depends a lot on the developmental level of each State. In defining the normative content of this right the ESCR Committee has observed that the right to health in all its forms and at all levels will include elements of availability, accessibility, acceptability, and quality,[159] and using its tripartite interpretation of States Parties obligations, the Committee has observed that:

> The right to health, like all human rights, imposes three types or levels of obligations on States parties: the obligations to *respect, protect* and *fulfil*. In turn, the obligation to fulfil contains obligations to facilitate, provide and promote. The obligation to *respect*

---

[156] *See* Art. 25(1) UDHR (1948).   [157] General Comment 14, paras.1 and 3.
[158] *See* e.g. Art. 12(3) of the ICCPR (1966).   [159] General Comment 14, para.12.

requires States to refrain from interfering directly or indirectly with the enjoyment of the right to health. The obligation to *protect* requires States to take measures that prevent third parties from interfering with article 12 guarantees. Finally, the obligation to *fulfil* requires States to adopt appropriate legislative, administrative, budgetary, judicial, promotional and other measures towards the full realization of the right to health.[160]

It is manifest that the realization of the right to health in the above terms remains one of the greatest problems confronting developing nations. Although international co-operation is not specifically mentioned under Article 12, as in Article 11, such co-operation is very pertinent to the realization of a reasonable standard of health care in developing nations. The international obligation in the realization of the right to health is also emphasized by the ESCR Committee as follows:

> To comply with their international obligations in relation to article 12, States parties have to respect the enjoyment of the right to health in other countries, and to prevent third parties from violating the right in other countries, if they are able to influence these third parties by way of legal or political means, in accordance with the Charter of the United Nations and applicable international law. Depending on the availability of resources, States should facilitate access to essential health facilities, goods and services in other countries, wherever possible and provide the necessary aid when required. States parties should ensure that the right to health is given due attention in international agreements and, to that end, should consider the development of further legal instruments. In relation to the conclusion of other international agreements, States parties should take steps to ensure that these instruments do not adversely impact upon the right to health. Similarly, States parties have an obligation to ensure that their actions as members of international organizations take due account of the right to health. Accordingly, States parties which are members of international financial institutions, notably the International Monetary Fund, the World Bank, and regional development banks, should pay greater attention to the protection of the right to health in influencing the lending policies, credit agreements and international measures of these institutions.[161]

The Committee's comprehensive General Comment 14 broadens the perspective of the right to health in a manner that greatly envisages the enhancement of the quality of human life in relation to the enjoyment of good health.

Islam also emphasizes the importance of both mental and physical health. Great importance is attached to medical and health sciences as it is to religious sciences because without good health neither religious nor secular activities can be performed by anyone. The training of medical personnel and establishment of hospitals was considered as an important duty of the State and was greatly encouraged very early in Islamic history. Isaacs has pointed out that:

---

[160] General Comment 14, para.33.　　[161] *ibid.*, para.39.

Islam not only put medicine on a high level but also conferred the title of *hakîm* [wise] on medical practitioners, a term used by Muslims up to the present day in many areas. The association of medicine with religious learning is noteworthy, and is a pleasing feature of Muslim life: for according to a Tradition of the Prophet: 'science is twofold, theological science for religion and medical science for the body'.[162]

Saud has also recorded that:

From the time of the Banû Umayyah rule the Muslims developed the institution of hospitals. During the reign of the 'Abbâsî Caliph Hârûn al-Rashîd, a hospital was built in Baghdad, which was the first in the history of this city. Many new hospitals were established shortly afterwards. Some of them had their own gardens in which the medicinal plants were cultivated. The large hospitals had medical schools attached to them. Beside such hospitals there were a large number of travelling hospitals in the Muslim world.[163]

These were all in recognition of the importance of health and medical assistance within human society. The duty of ensuring the highest attainable standard of health in society through the adequate training of medical personnel and provision of necessary medical and health facilities remains binding upon modern Muslim States under Islamic law.

Islamic law advocates both the preventive and curative approaches to health and encourages cleanliness as the best preventive approach to both mental and physical health. Both individuals and the State are thus encouraged to maintain personal and societal cleanliness as the natural and first step towards ensuring the highest attainable standard of both physical and mental health in society. The Prophet emphasized this by declaring that: 'Cleanliness is half of faith'.[164] This will include all aspects of personal, environmental, and industrial hygiene. There are Islamic instructions on the removal of dirt and prohibition of urination and defecation in open places or in stagnant waters. The prevention and control of epidemic and endemic diseases under Islamic law is also evidenced by a Tradition in which the Prophet is reported to have instructed that: '... When there is plague in any city don't enter it and when it breaks out in any city while you are there don't go out fleeing from it'.[165] The State thus has a duty to control and protect public health to ensure the ultimate enjoyment of the right to health by individuals.

The curative aspect of health is also stressed under Islamic law through the belief that there is a cure for every disease. The Prophet is reported to have stated that 'God sent no disease for which He sent no cure'[166] and that

---

[162] *See* Young M.J.L., *et al.* (eds.), *Religion, Learning and Science in the 'Abbasid Period* (1990) p.342.   [163] Saud, M., *Islam and Evolution of Science* (1994) p.95.
[164] Reported by Muslim, *see* e.g. Karim (above n.36) at Vol. 1, p.663, Hadith No. 1.
[165] Reported by al-Bukhâri and Muslim, *see* e.g. Karim (above n.36) at Vol. 1, p.284 Hadith No.44.   [166] Reported by al-Bukhâri, *see* e.g. Karim (above n.36) at Vol. II, p. 71, Hadith 1.

'For every disease there is a cure'.[167] This encourages belief in the possibility and seeking of a cure for every disease, which consequently promotes the right to health. The nursing, caring, and treatment of both the physically and mentally ill is also considered as a very rewarding duty under Islamic law. It is thus an important duty of the State to ensure the availability of medical services and medical attention in the event of illness. In recognition of the above ideals, Article 17 of the OIC Cairo Declaration on Human Rights in Islam provides that:

Everyone shall have the right to live in a clean environment, away from vice and moral corruption, an environment that would foster his self-development, and it is incumbent upon the State and society in general to afford that right.

Everyone shall have the right to medical and social care, and to all public amenities provided by society and the State within the limits of their available resources.

4.13 THE RIGHT TO EDUCATION

Article 13

1. The States Parties to the present Covenant recognize the right of everyone to education. They agree that education shall be directed to the full development of the human personality and the sense of its dignity, and shall strengthen the respect for human rights and fundamental freedoms. They further agree that education shall enable all persons to participate effectively in a free society, promote understanding, tolerance and friendship among all nations and all racial, ethnic or religious groups, and further the activities of the United Nations for the maintenance of peace.
2. The States Parties to the present Covenant recognize that, with a view to achieving the full realization of this right:
   (a) Primary education shall be compulsory and available free to all;
   (b) Secondary education in its different forms, including technical and vocational secondary education, shall be made generally available and accessible to all by every appropriate means, and in particular by the progressive introduction of free education;
   (c) Higher education shall be made equally accessible to all, on the basis of capacity, by every appropriate means, and in particular by the progressive introduction of free education;
   (d) Fundamental education shall be encouraged or intensified as far as possible for those persons who have not received or completed the whole period of their primary education;
   (e) The development of a system of schools at all levels shall be actively pursued, an adequate fellowship system shall be established, and the material conditions of teaching staff shall be continuously improved.
3. The States Parties to the present Covenant undertake to have respect for the liberty of parents and, when applicable, legal guardians to choose for their children schools, other than those established by the public authorities, which conform to such minimum educational standards as may be laid down or approved by the State and to

---

[167] Reported by Muslim, *see* e.g. Karim (above n.36) at Vol. II, p.72, Hadith 2.

ensure the religious and moral education of their children in conformity with their own convictions.

4. No part of this article shall be construed so as to interfere with the liberty of individuals and bodies to establish and direct educational institutions, subject always to the observance of the principles set forth in paragraph 1 of this article and to the requirement that the education given in such institutions shall conform to such minimum standards as may be laid down by the State.

Article 14

Each State Party to the present Covenant which, at the time of becoming a Party, has not been able to secure in its metropolitan territory or other territories under its jurisdiction compulsory primary education, free of charge, undertakes, within two years, to work out and adopt a detailed plan of action for the progressive implementation, within a reasonable number of years, to be fixed in the plan, of the principle of compulsory education free of charge for all.

Education is the key to mental liberation which helps the individual not only to develop his own personality but also to be useful to his society. The right to education is thus comprehensively covered under Articles 13 and 14 of the ICESCR. Apart from recognizing the right of everyone to education, the States Parties also *agree* under Article 13(1) that 'education shall be directed to the full development of the human personality and the sense of dignity, and shall strengthen the respect for human rights and fundamental freedoms' and 'that education shall enable all persons to participate effectively in a free society, promote understanding, tolerance and friendship among all nations and all racial, ethnic or religious groups and further the activities of the United Nations for the maintenance of peace'.[168] There is therefore a form of consensus among States Parties to the ICESCR on the fact that education is an important tool of individual and societal development.

Apart from being a right in itself, education is also an essential tool for the exercise and full enjoyment of human rights. It has been described as an empowerment right.[169] Without some minimum level of education and literacy, an individual's awareness about his human rights would be greatly impaired. Article 13(1) states that education 'shall strengthen the respect for human rights and fundamental freedoms'. This is achieved through both general education and provision of specific human rights education in the educational curriculum. The Vienna Declaration and Programme of Action after the 1993 World Conference on Human Rights called on all States and institutions 'to include human rights, humanitarian law, democracy and rule of law as subjects in the curricula of all learning institutions in formal and non-formal settings'.[170]

The ESCR Committee has observed that the right to education in all its forms and at all levels shall exhibit the essential features of availability, accessibility,

---

[168] *See also* Art. 26(2) of the UDHR (1948).   [169] *See* General Comment 13, para.1.
[170] UN Doc A/CONF.157/23. Part II para.79.

acceptability, and adaptability.[171] Based on its tripartite interpretation of States Parties' obligations, the Committee also observed that:

The right to education, like all human rights, imposes three types or levels of obligations on States parties: the obligations to *respect, protect* and *fulfil*. In turn, the obligation to fulfil incorporates both an obligation to facilitate and an obligation to provide. The obligation to respect requires States parties to avoid measures that hinder or prevent the enjoyment of the right to education. The obligation to protect requires States parties to take measures that prevent third parties from interfering with the enjoyment of the right to education. The obligation to fulfil (facilitate) requires States to take positive measures that enable and assist individuals and communities to enjoy the right to education. Finally, States parties have an obligation to fulfil (provide) the right to education. As a general rule, States parties are obliged to fulfil (provide) a specific right in the Covenant when an individual or group is unable, for reasons beyond their control, to realize the right themselves by the means at their disposal. However, the extent of this obligation is always subject to the text of the Covenant.[172]

Under Article 13, every State shall provide at least free compulsory primary education for all, and under Article 14 each State Party that has not yet attained the provision of free compulsory primary education for all, undertakes to work out and adopt a detailed plan of action for the progressive implementation of the principle of compulsory free primary education for all within a reasonable number of years.[173] Secondary and higher education shall also be made available and accessible to all with the progressive introduction of free education at those levels as well. Article 13 covers both formal and informal education as well as fundamental education for those who for one reason or another miss out on primary education. It also recognizes the need to improve the conditions of teaching staff to ensure the full achievement of the right to education.

Although the State has an obligation to provide free and compulsory primary education, it undertakes to respect the liberty of parents and legal guardians to enrol their children, in conformity with their religious or moral convictions, in private institutions other than those established by the State, provided those private institutions conform with minimum educational standards approved by the State. The parents and guardians would be under an obligation here to act in the best interest of the child.[174] The State shall also not interfere with the establishment of private institutions subject to their observance of required minimum standards and their pursuance of the principles of individual and societal development set out in Article 13(1).[175]

The Covenant does not contain a provision on academic freedom but the Committee has observed that academic freedom and institutional autonomy constitute an important aspect of the right to education and stated in that regard that:

---

[171] General Comment 13, para.6.

[172] *ibid.*, paras. 46–47.   [173] *See also* General Comment 11.

[174] *See* Art. 3(1) of the Convention on the Rights of the Child (1989) which provides that: 'In all actions concerning children...the best interest of the child shall be a primary consideration'.   [175]*See* Art. 13(3–4).

Members of the academic community, individually or collectively, are free to pursue, develop and transmit knowledge and ideas, through research, teaching, study, discussion, documentation, production, creation or writing. Academic freedom includes the liberty of individuals to express freely opinions about the institution or system in which they work, to fulfil their functions without discrimination or fear of repression by the State or any other actor, to participate in professional or representative academic bodies, and to enjoy all the internationally recognized human rights applicable to other individuals in the same jurisdiction. The enjoyment of academic freedom carries with it obligations, such as the duty to respect the academic freedom of others, to ensure the fair discussion of contrary views, and to treat all without discrimination on any of the prohibited grounds.[176]

These ideals and aspirations concerning the right to education under the ICESCR are very much in consonance with the Islamic ideals on education as well. There is consensus among all Islamic schools of thought that education is absolutely important and compulsory under Islamic law. Right from its inception, Islam had laid great emphasis on the importance of education and its role in the development of the human person. The very first five revealed verses of the Qur'an were related to education and learning. The verses were as follows:

Read! In the name of your Lord Who created [everything]. He created Man from a clot of congealed blood. Read! And your Lord is Most Generous. He has taught [writing] by the Pen. He has taught Man that which he knew not.[177]

These five verses continue to be the basic reference point for advocating the right to education under Islamic law. There are also many other references in both the Qur'an and *Sunnah* on the importance of education, the obligation of seeking knowledge, and the superiority of scholarship. The Qur'an summarizes the importance of education and scholarship with an affirmatory interrogative statement that: '. . . Can those who are learned be compared with those who are unlearned? It is those who are endowed with understanding that receive admonition'.[178] The Prophet had also stressed the paramount value of education in many Traditions, a few of which are quoted below:

Whoever goes out seeking knowledge is on the path of God till he returns.[179]
Whoever follows a path seeking knowledge, God will thereby make it an easy way for him to Paradise.[180]
The superiority of the scholar over the [mere] worshipper is like the superiority of the full moon over the stars.[181]

The Prophet had emphatically stated in one Tradition that seeking of knowledge (education) is compulsory on every Muslim.[182] Asad thus concluded that

---

[176] General Comment 13, para.39.   [177] Q96:1–5.   [178] Q39:9.
[179] Reported by Tirmidhî, *see* e.g. Karim (above n.36) at Vol. 1, p.351, Hadith No. 38.
[180] Reported by Tirmidhî, Abû Dâwûd, *see* Karim (above n.36) at pp.348–349, Hadith No. 32.   [181] *ibid.*
[182] Reported by Ibn Mâjah, *see* Karim (above n.36) at Vol. 1, p.351, Hadith No. 37.

from an Islamic perspective 'it is the citizens' right and the government's duty to have a system of education which would make knowledge freely accessible (and compulsory) to every man and woman in the state'.[183] This recognition and emphasis on the importance of education under Islamic law thus fully accommodates the duty of the State under the Covenant to provide at least free and compulsory primary school education to everyone. In appreciation of the importance of the right to education, Article 9 of the OIC Cairo Declaration on Human Rights in Islam provides that:

(a) The quest for knowledge is an obligation and the provision of education is a duty for society and the State. The State shall ensure the availability of ways and means to acquire education and shall guarantee educational diversity in the interest of society so as to enable man to be acquainted with the religion of Islam and the facts of the Universe for the benefit of mankind.
(b) Every human being has the right to receive both religious and worldly education from the various institutions of education and guidance, including the family, the school, the university, the media, etc., and in such an integrated and balanced manner as to develop his personality, strengthen his faith in God and promote his respect for the defence of both rights and obligations.

The need for human rights education under Islamic law is also buttressed by the common saying that: 'A person will often oppose concepts that he knows nothing about'. Lack of human rights education can (and does) create misconceptions about the international human rights objective and actually deny individuals the right to know their rights as human beings under both domestic and international law. Human rights education would certainly increase the awareness and the understanding necessary for the realization of the rights that everyone is entitled to as human beings. This thus makes human rights education as important as the enjoyment of human rights itself.

4.14 THE RIGHT TO CULTURAL LIFE AND BENEFITS OF SCIENTIFIC PROGRESS

Article 15

1. The States Parties to the present Covenant recognize the right of everyone:
   (a) To take part in cultural life;
   (b) To enjoy the benefits of scientific progress and its applications;
   (c) To benefit from the protection of the moral and material interests resulting from any scientific, literary or artistic production of which he is the author.
2. The steps to be taken by the States Parties to the present Covenant to achieve the full realization of this right shall include those necessary for the conservation, the development and the diffusion of science and culture.

---

[183] Asad (above n.86) at p.86.

3. The States Parties to the present Covenant undertake to respect the freedom indispensable for scientific research and creative activity.
4. The States Parties to the present Covenant recognize the benefits to be derived from the encouragement and development of international contacts and co-operation in the scientific and cultural fields.

Cultural life has been described as 'everything which makes life worth living' and 'that which separates human society from its animal counterpart' and thus 'closely related to human dignity'.[184] Its enabling factors would thus include a host of other rights such as freedom of association, freedom of thought, conscience and religion, freedom of expression, right of self-determination, right to be different, and right to education. Culture is however one of the distinguishing factors of human society, the scope of which is sometimes very difficult to determine. It may be perceived from different dimensions. It is often used to describe the way of life of a particular community referring to their customs, civilization, spiritual, and material heritage. For instance, Article 27 of the ICCPR provides for the right of members of minorities 'to enjoy their own culture' 'in community with the other members of their group'. Also Article 27 of the UDHR provides for 'the right to freely participate in cultural life of the community'. If this is understood to mean the cultural life of the community to which the individual belongs, then the group or community is the cultural creator, and the right to cultural life would mean the right of individuals to lead their own way of life as members of that community in distinction from others. It, in that sense, signifies the right to be different. That is often the basis for cultural identity and cultural relativism, and is sometimes criticized as capable of jeopardizing the universal concept of human rights.[185] As a matter of reality, it is impossible to deny the natural diversity of cultures among the human population of the world. Stavenhagen has pointed out that: 'In some instances, all or most of a country's population share a common culture; in others, a State is made up of a variety of different cultures'.[186] The recognition of cultural identity or cultural relativism should however not jeopardize the universality of human rights but rather enhance it. Article 1 of the UNESCO Declaration of the Principles of International Cultural Co-operation of 1966,[187] had identified that:

1. Each culture has a dignity and value which must be respected and preserved.
2. Every people has the right and the duty to develop its culture.

---

[184] *See* Adalsteinsson, R., and Thorhallson, P., 'Article 27', in Alfredsson and Eide (above n.98) at p.575.

[185] *See* e.g. Donnelly, J., *Universal Human Rights in Theory and Practice* (1989) pp.109–124; and UN Dept. of Public Information, *Is Human Rights in Jeopardy?* (1987).

[186] *See* Stavenhagen, R., 'Cultural Rights and Universal Human Rights', in Eide *et al.* (above n.30) at p.66.

[187] Adopted on 4 November 1966. *See* UNESCO's Standard-Setting Instruments, Incorporating Supplement 1, (1982) IV.C. 1.

3. In their rich variety and diversity, and in the reciprocal influences they exert on one another, all cultures form part of the common heritage belonging to all mankind.

The universality of human rights is actually better projected through the recognition of the right to cultural life, because it signifies that individuals can still maintain their diverse cultural inclinations within the universal atmosphere of human rights. This is subject only to the proviso that discriminatory or other invidious elements of any traditional culture may have to be rejected in order to fit into the universal atmosphere of international human rights. The challenge that the right to cultural life poses, in the context of cultural identity or cultural relativism, is the need to understand adequately the different cultures and interpret them as instruments of universalism in human rights. In that respect and from an Islamic legal perspective, the Qur'anic verse which states that mankind has been created from a single pair of male and female and 'made into nations and tribes that [they] may know each other' is very instructive.[188]

It is important to note that the wording of Article 15(1)(a) of the ICESCR is however not qualified with 'community', it provides simply for the right of everyone to 'take part in cultural life'. This tends to amplify the recognition of the right to cultural life as an individual right. The right to take part in cultural life can certainly also be perceived as 'the process of artistic and scientific creation', in which case the individual is the cultural creator (as an artist, writer, or performer) and has the right 'to freely create [his own] cultural "*oeuvres*", with no restrictions, and the right of all persons to enjoy free access to these creations'.[189] This is further expressed in Article 15(1)(c) through the recognition of the right of everyone 'to benefit from the protection of the moral and material interests resulting from any scientific, literary or artistic production of which he is the author'.[190] It is also very much related to freedom of expression of the individual.

The non-association, in Article 15, of the right to take part in cultural life with 'the community' does not however de-emphasize the fact that cultural life will often be defined in relation to a particular social group or community. Stavenhagen has thus observed that cultural rights 'can only be enjoyed in community with others and that community must have the possibility to preserve, protect and develop what it has in common'. He further stated that while the beneficiaries of cultural rights may be individuals, 'their content evaporates without the preservation and the collective rights of groups'.[191] The enjoyment of the right to take part in cultural life may thus be fully realized in relation to the identification of a particular community (even if in minority), which preserves

---

[188] Q49:13; *See also* generally Anyaoku, E., *Managing Diversity in Our Contemporary World* (1997); Mandela, N., *Renewal and Renaissance: Towards a New World Order* (1997); Annan, K., *Dialogue of Civilizations And The Need For A World Ethic* (1999).

[189] *See* Stavenhagen (above n.186) at pp.65–66.   [190] Art. 15(1)(c) ICESCR.

[191] *See* Stavenhagen (above n.186) at p.68.

such culture and with which the individual associates.[192] The general nature of Article 15(1)(a) also has the potential of allowing a cross-border participation in cultural life. This would however raise the question of whether an individual in a particular State may have the right to practise within it a cultural life considered 'alien' to that community. Due to their presumed vulnerability in the area of right to cultural life, attention is often focused on the protection of cultural rights of minorities and indigenous peoples.

The right to cultural life can also be perceived in the universal sense of the accumulated material heritage and the universal civilization of humanity as a whole, and the right of every individual to that heritage and civilization. An extension of this perception would be the right of everyone to enjoy the benefits of scientific progress and its application as recognized under Article 15(1)(b). This is an interpretation of cultural life in developmental terms. UNESCO adopted a 'Recommendation on Participation by the People at Large in Cultural Life and Their Contribution to It' in 1976, in which it defined participation in cultural life as 'the concrete opportunities guaranteed for all—groups or individuals—to express themselves freely, to communicate, act and engage in creative activities with a view to the full development of their personalities, a harmonious life and cultural progress of society'.[193] It has been observed that '[t]his aspect of cultural rights has enormous potential for further development in law and society'[194] because it would afford the opportunity for everyone to have access to and benefit from international scientific progress and thereby contribute to the overall enrichment of each individual culture and consequently narrow down the gap of diversity between the different cultures of the world. The guidelines for reports under the ICESCR suggest a comprehensive perspective by the ESCR Committee, which accommodates all the aspects of culture stated above. States Parties are required to provide information, *inter alia*, on: 'Promotion of cultural identity as a factor of mutual appreciation among individuals, groups, nations and regions'; 'Promotion of awareness and enjoyment of the cultural heritage of national ethnic groups and minorities and of indigenous peoples'; and 'Preservation and presentation of mankind's cultural heritage'.[195]

There is scope within Islamic law for the recognition of the right to cultural life in all the contexts analysed above. Defined in terms of community, Islam identifies itself as a religio-cultural community *(ummah)* for every individual that professes to belong or attach to that community. It is a universal community that accommodates different tribes and peoples and thus transcends

---

[192] Cf Eide, A., 'Cultural Rights as Individual Rights' in Eide *et al.* (above n.30) at pp.229–240.
[193] 26 November 1976. *See* UNESCO Standard-Setting Instruments, Incorporating Supplement 1 (1982), IV.B.7, Sec.1(2)(b).
[194] Adalsteinsson and Thorhallson (above n.184) at p.593.
[195] *See* Art.15(1)(c), (d), (f) *Revised Guidelines* (above n.2).

geographical and jurisdictional boundaries of the modern nation-state. The right to take part in cultural life with other members of the Islamic community could therefore often mean with a community beyond the jurisdiction of a State. Although there are general religio-cultural norms prescribed by the *Sharî'ah* for the Islamic community, Islamic law also recognizes the possibility of differences in some cultural practices of the community due to the diversity of its members. That was the basis for the recognition of *'urf* (known practices) and *âdât* (customs) of the different tribes and nations that make up the community as a subsidiary source of law by all Islamic schools of jurisprudence, and especially by the *Mâlikî* school, provided that such practices and customs are not contradictory to the norms of the Qur'an or the *Sunnah*.[196] Muslims are thus still able to maintain their local customs within the scope of the universal Islamic culture.[197] Islamic law also recognizes the presence of other cultures apart from the Islamic culture. Thus non-Muslims are free and entitled to follow their own culture and way of life within the Islamic State, subject only to the protection of public order and morality, and in accordance with due process of law. Hamidullah has even argued that the traditional rule which prohibited non-Muslims from imitating Muslims in dress or other similar social manifestations within the Islamic State, was a rule that bolstered the communal culture of non-Muslims within the Islamic State, because it enabled them to maintain their own cultural and social manifestations within the Islamic State.[198]

The right of the individual to enjoy the benefit resulting from any scientific, literary or artistic production of which he is the author is also recognized under Islamic law. So also is the right of everyone individually or as part of a group to participate and benefit from the accumulated material heritage and the universal civilization of humanity as a whole. In respect of cultural rights, the OIC Cairo Declaration on Human Rights in Islam only provides for the right of the individual to 'enjoy the fruits of his scientific, literary, artistic or technical production and the right to protect the moral and material interests stemming therefrom, provided that such production is not contrary to the principles of Shari'ah'.[199] This does not however necessarily exclude the right to the other aspects of cultural life analysed above under Islamic law. What Islamic law would obviously prohibit in respect of cultural rights is any cultural practice that promotes obscenity and nudity in violation of the moral code of the *Sharî'ah*, because the Qur'an has specifically prohibited the spread of lewdness within the Islamic society.

---

[196] *See* e.g. Doi, A.R., *Sharî'ah: The Islamic Law* (1984) p.84.
[197] *See* e.g. Second Periodic Report of Jordan (1998), UN Doc. E/1990/6/Add.17, para.126, where it is stated, *inter alia*, that: 'Cultured Jordanians feel that their cultural identity . . . is open to Arab and Islamic culture . . .'. [198] Hamidullah (above n.89) at pp.117–118.
[199] *See* Art. 16 of the OIC Cairo Declaration on Human Rights in Islam (1990).

4.15 CONCLUDING REMARKS

It can be deduced from the above expositions that the economic, social, and cultural rights recognized under the ICESCR are generally compatible with the *Sharî'ah* and realizable within the principles of Islamic law. Thus, Islamic law can actually serve as a vehicle for the promotion and realization of economic, social, and cultural rights in Muslim States. The problem areas concern mainly the issues of women in employment and the concepts of the family and of children out of wedlock. While the issue of women in employment in most Muslim States has been circumscribed by custom rather than Islamic law per se, the issue of the family and children out of wedlock is strictly dictated by the Islamic religion and regulated by Islamic law. As has been shown, there is ample room within Islamic law for Muslim States to remedy the problem of women in employment and enhance their societal roles. However, the question of the family and children out of wedlock involves an Islamic religio-moral principle and requires the recognition of some margin of appreciation for Muslim States as is further elaborated in Chapter 5.

For those Muslim States that have ratified the ICESCR, this chapter shows that they have an obligation under Islamic law as they do have under international law to respect and ensure the economic, social, and cultural rights recognized under the Covenant. For those Muslim States that have not yet ratified the ICESCR, the foregoing exposition shows that their non-ratification does not absolve them from ensuring those rights under Islamic law. The analysis can also be of motivational value towards their ratification of the Covenant to participate in the international co-operation to ensure the universal guarantee of economic, social, and cultural rights.

5

Conclusion

5.1 A COMPLEMENTARY APPROACH

It emerges from the preceding chapters that there is certainly a human rights discourse in Islamic law. The analyses impugn the incompatibility theory and reveal the existence of a wide positive common ground between international human rights law and Islamic law. This does not however obscure some areas of differences in scope and application, but rather advocates a positive basis for managing such differences through the development of complementary methodologies between the two legal regimes. The detailed examination of both the ICCPR and the ICESCR in the light of Islamic law demonstrates the possibility of constructive harmonization of international human rights norms with Islamic law. This however requires good faith and the abandonment of prejudice between Islamic law and international human rights scholars and advocates.

The eliminative and 'end of history' approaches to the interpretation of international human rights law and Islamic law respectively have herein been challenged and need to be discarded. Only an inclusive, evolutionary, and constructive method of interpretation can bring the best out of the two regimes for the enrichment of human rights universally and especially in the Muslim world. Through mutuality and accommodation, the legitimizing force of Islamic law in many Muslim States can be positively utilized for the enforcement of international human rights law in the Muslim world.

The scope of international human rights can be positively enhanced in the Muslim world through moderate, dynamic, and constructive interpretations of the *Sharî'ah* rather than through hardline and static interpretations of it. This is particularly so in respect of women's rights, minority rights, and the application of Islamic criminal punishments. We have shown by reference to the different schools of Islamic jurisprudence and classical juristic views that even the early Islamic jurists and scholars emphasized the importance of moderation and had adopted constructive views that can be relied upon today greatly to enhance the realization of international human rights norms within the dispensation of Islamic law. The Qur'an described the Muslim *Ummah* as 'justly balanced', a description signifying moderation.[1] This Islamic legal

---

[1] Q2:143. 'Thus have We made of you an *Ummah* justly balanced ...'. Yusuf Ali comments, *inter alia*, on this verse as follows: '*Justly balanced*: The essence of Islam is to avoid all extravagances on either side. It is a sober, practical religion'. A Tradition of the Prophet also instructs Muslims thus: 'Beware of extremism in religion. People before you have perished as

analysis of the two international human rights Covenants establishes the need for review of some traditional interpretations of the *Sharî'ah*, in the light of equally valid moderate opinions that had existed even from the time of the earliest Islamic jurists, for the full realization of the rights contained in them within the application of Islamic law. The rules of Islamic jurisprudence do actually encourage interpretations of the *Sharî'ah* that promote the benevolent nature of Islam, especially where the reasoning for such interpretations is commensurate with prevalent needs of social justice and human well-being.

The representative of Iran, Mr Nasseri, stated, *inter alia*, before the ESCR Committee in 1993 that 'it was not always easy to apply traditional Islamic law without falling short of the commitments undertaken in acceding to the Covenant', but also added that '[t]he Islamic Republic of Iran…was sincerely endeavouring to reconcile Islamic law and the provisions of the Covenant'.[2] Also, when Egypt ratified both the ICCPR and ICESCR in 1982 it entered a general declaration 'taking into consideration the provisions of the Islamic Shari'a', but in paragraph 3 of its initial report on the ICESCR submitted in 1998, it stated in respect of the said declaration as follows:

Egypt expressed a general reservation to the effect that account should be taken of the need to ensure that the Covenant was not incompatible with the provisions of the Islamic Shari'a. *However, the practical implementation in Egypt of the provisions of the Covenant, as one of the country's laws, from 14 April 1982 to date has not revealed any incompatibility between the provisions of the Islamic Shari'a and the principles and rights set forth in the Covenant and relating to its field of application.*[3] (emphasis added)

The Egyptian representative before the ESCR Committee, Mr Salama, had pointed out that: 'Enlightened interpretations of Islamic law were permitted … [in Egypt] and had actually contributed to the positive developments mentioned by the delegation in many fields, such as women's and family issues'.[4] This demonstrates the possibility of rapprochement and reflects the importance of good faith and humanitarian will on the part of State authorities in endeavouring to realize international human rights within the ample limits of the *Sharî'ah* and their application of Islamic law.

Conversely, there is a similar need to depart from the exclusionist approach in the interpretations of the provisions of international human rights treaties. To encourage the promotion and realization of international human rights in the Muslim world, the UN international human rights treaty bodies must develop

a result of such extremism'. *See also generally*, al-Qaradawi, Y., *Islamic Awakening between Rejection and Extremism* (1990).

[2] *See* paras 36 and 37 of Summary Record of the 8th Meeting: Iran; E/C.12/1993/SR.8 of 20 December 1993.

[3] Initial State Party Report: Egypt; E/1990/5/Add.38 of 30 June 1998.

[4] Summary Record of the 13th Meeting: Egypt; E/C.12/2000/SR.13 of 9 May 2000 and para. 64 of Summary Record of the 11th Meeting: Egypt; E/C.12/2000/SR.11 of 8 May 2000.

consideration for Islamic values when dealing with States that apply Islamic law. This is possible through the adoption of the margin of appreciation doctrine on moral issues relating especially to Islamic religio-ethical and family norms.

Due to the obvious relevance of Islamic law in the quest for universalism in international human rights in the Muslim world, there is a positive need for the inclusion of highly qualified experts in Islamic international law and jurisprudence on the membership of international human rights treaty bodies to reflect the 'representation of the different forms of civilization and of the principal legal systems' of the world on the Committees.[5] This would boost the confidence of Muslim States and Islamic legalists in the international human rights treaty bodies and lead to a more positive inclination towards interpretations and general comments of the relevant Committees of international human rights treaties. It might also encourage the ratification by Muslim States not only of substantive human rights treaties but also Optional Protocols that provide for individual complaints systems within the international human rights regime. With reference to the HRC for instance, McGoldrick has observed that:

> The presence of experts from different legal systems can assist the HRC in its consideration of reports under article 40. For example, during consideration of the report of Morocco it was useful to have members of the HRC who were conversant with Islamic laws. The provision in article 31(2) can give States parties the confidence that their approach will at least be understood even if disagreed with ...[6]

Joseph, Schultz, and Castan have however observed that 'a Western representative bias can be detected in recent years, with over half of the (HRC) members serving from 1998 to 2000 coming from the United States, Canada, Australia, the United Kingdom, France, Italy, Israel, Finland, Germany and Poland'.[7] Thus the need for the reflection of a more 'equitable distribution of membership' not only of the HRC but of all the UN human rights treaty bodies cannot be overemphasized.[8]

Both international human rights and Islamic law jurists and scholars need to adopt an accommodative and complementary approach to achieve the noble objective of enhancing human dignity. The objective must be towards combining the best in both systems for all humanity. This strikes at the unilateral approach, which demands that the harmonization between international human rights and Islamic law depends only on reforming the *Sharî'ah* to conform

---

[5] *See* e.g. Art. 31(2) of the ICCPR and Art. 8 of the International Convention on the Elimination of All Forms of Racial Discrimination (ICERD) (1965).

[6] McGoldrick, D., *The Human Rights Committee: Its Role in the Development of the International Covenant on Civil and Political Rights* (1994) p.55 n.5.

[7] Joseph, S., Schultz, J., and Castan, M., *The International Covenant on Civil and Political Rights, Cases, Materials, and Commentary* (2000) p.10.

[8] For example the balance of State Party membership of the European Court of Human Rights does make easier its search for a 'European Consensus' in cases brought before it. Art. 20 of the European Convention provides that: '*The Court shall consist of a number of judges equal to that of the High Contracting Parties*'.

totally with current international human rights interpretations, some of which are considered by Muslims as insensitive to Islamic religious and moral viewpoints. For example, one advocate of the unilateral approach, while answering the question 'How should international law respond to the incompatibility of claims based on *Shari'a* with international human rights norms?', submitted that: 'international law norms must not be compromised, and that it may be desirable for Muslim scholars to explore alternative interpretations of Islamic sources under which *Shari'a* can be reconciled with developments in international human rights law'.[9] The difficulty of such a unilateral demand upon Islamic law is quite obvious and tantamount to an attempt to clap with only one hand.

By the complementary approach, the necessary means for harmonization, in respect of Islamic law are: (i) adopting an 'enlightened interpretations' approach, as observed by the Egyptian representative above, and (ii) a 'sincere endeavour to reconcile' as observed by the Iranian representative. We have observed earlier that the *maqâsid al-Sharî'ah* approach and the Islamic law doctrine of *maslahah* are very relevant for this purpose.[10] And in respect of international human rights law the necessary means are: (i) accommodation of a necessary margin of appreciation in respect of Islamic ethical and moral values, and (ii) appreciation that human rights are not inherently non-achievable within the scope of Islamic law. Following are some salient practical means of achieving the above, domestically, regionally, and universally.

5.2 DOMESTIC MEANS OF ENHANCING HUMAN RIGHTS

5.2.1 Human rights education

Similar to most other countries, ignorance about contemporary human rights principles and lack of human rights education constitute a major debilitating factor against the enhancement of human rights in most Muslim States. While, as shown in our comparative analysis, Islamic law substantially recognizes the duty of the State to promote and protect the human rights of individuals, most of the populace in Muslim States are ignorant about these rights. They do not often understand what human rights is all about. Some individuals even believe that it is a conspiracy against their religious values. They do not see international human rights law as a means of protecting the individual against the abuse of State power. There is, therefore, an important need to encourage extensive formal and informal human rights education for the populace in Muslim States.

---

[9] Nanda, V.P., 'Islam and International Human Rights Law: Selected Aspects' (1993) *American Society of International Law Proceedings*, p.327 at p.331.

[10] *See* Ch. 2 para.2.4.5 above.

Under Islamic law, the populace have a right to know and to be informed of everything of benefit to them, not only for the hereafter but for their well-being in this world as well. There are many Qur'anic verses and Traditions of the Prophet, as earlier referred to,[11] that enjoin the promotion of education and condemn the concealment of knowledge, which in this case includes human rights education due to its value for the ultimate benefit of the individual in every society of today's world. An Islamic and international human rights curriculum for primary, secondary, and tertiary institutions would be of great benefit in that regard.

Due to the importance and role of religion and religious institutions in the Muslim world, human rights education should not be limited to secular institutions but also extended to the religious institutions. The provisions of the Qur'an and *Sunnah* that promote the ideals of human rights must be stressed. The provisions of international human rights instruments need also to be explained and illustrated through the Islamic legal tradition as demonstrated in our comparative analyses in Chapters 3 and 4 above. To put into practice their assertion in the OIC Declaration on Human Rights in Islam that human rights are a divine part of the Islamic legal tradition, which no authority can withhold,[12] Muslim States must disseminate what those rights are through a massive human rights education amongst their populace.

The importance of human rights education in Muslim States has been acknowledged by the adoption of the Cairo Declaration on Human Rights Education and Dissemination at the Second International Conference of Human Rights Movements in the Arab World held in Cairo, Egypt in October 2000. The Declaration recognized human rights education as a fundamental human right and that governments in particular have a responsibility to 'expatiate, propagate and disseminate human rights principles and their protection mechanisms'.[13]

This duty of promoting human rights education is not restricted to the State alone, Non-Governmental Organizations (NGOs) and religious bodies also have an important role to play in that regard and should be encouraged and not be hindered by the State to do so. It is suggested that a decade of human rights education and dissemination be declared by the OIC and Muslim States be encouraged to adopt national plans for human rights education in that regard, reviewable periodically. Such an approach would be a big and bold step towards the realization of the ideal Islamic society, wherein human beings will enjoy the inherent *Karâmah* (dignity) which their Creator had endowed upon them from their inception.

---

[11] *See* Ch. 4 text to notes 177–183 inclusive above.

[12] *See* 4th Preambular Paragraph of OIC Cairo Declaration on Human Rights in Islam (1990).

[13] *See* a copy of this Declaration at: http://www.euromedrights.net/english/barcelona-process/civil_society/HR_activities/Decl_cairoHRE.htm [1/3/03].

5.2.2 *Judicial training in human rights*

The primacy of domestic enforcement of human rights is acknowledged in both universal and regional human rights instruments.[14] In respect of the exhaustion of all available domestic remedies by victims of human rights violations, the HRC has stressed that this 'clearly refers in the first place to judicial remedies'.[15] This confirms the importance of the judiciary in the domestic enforcement of human rights guarantees.

Going by the rule of law, the judiciary is the ultimate resort to claiming one's right in case of its denial by the State. However, justice is, to a degree, relative to a judge's understanding and values. Thus, for the reflection of a human rights approach to justice in the Muslim world, the courts and the judges must be human rights conscious. Judges are expected to demonstrate a clear rational perspective of issues based on evidence placed before them and not to be biased by emotions or zealousness. Judges in Muslim States and courts must, in their dispensation of justice, be disposed to adopt a human rights approach based on the humane objective of the *Sharî'ah (maqâsid al-sharî'ah)*, which is the protection and promotion of human welfare. Islamic law judges may, in that regard, be introduced to international human rights jurisprudence to afford a reflective comparison in their legal thinking.

Another important relative factor in this regard is the need to ensure access to justice and adequate remedies for individuals within the application of Islamic law in Muslim States. The need for legal aid, which includes proper legal representation for those who cannot afford it, is paramount and will go a long way to ensure that judges are not oblivious of human rights perspectives in the cases before them.

5.2.3 *National Human Rights Commissions*

The UN has encouraged its Member States to establish independent National Human Rights Commissions (NHRCs) for promoting the observation of human rights in individual States. The establishment of such NHRCs by Muslim States would certainly enhance their human rights practice. There is nothing under Islamic law that prohibits the establishment of such institutions. They would be independent bodies conferred with adequate autonomy for the general promotion of human rights ideals in the States. The Commissions would also play complementary roles in realizing human rights education and judicial training in human rights as suggested above. The presence of such

---

[14] *See* e.g. Art. 8 UDHR, Art. 2(3) ICCPR, Art. 6 ICERD, Art. 14(1) CAT, Art 25 ACHR, Art. 13 ECHR, and Art. 7 ACHPR.

[15] *R.T. v. France*, Communication No. 262/1987 (30 March 1989), UN Doc. Supp. No. 40 (A/44/40) at 277 (1989), para.7.4. For provisions on the exhaustion of domestic remedies *see* e.g. Art. 5(2)(b) OP1 to the ICCPR, Art. 35 ECHR, Art. 46(1)(a) ACHR, and Art. 50 ACHPR.

commissions has contributed to the awareness about human rights in some Muslim countries already.[16]

While the above domestic means, coupled with the goodwill of State authorities can go a long way in enhancing the ideals of human rights in individual States, it must be appreciated that individual State mechanisms cannot, for obvious reasons, be solely adequate for the full realization of international human rights guarantees. To promote and encourage the universalization of human rights, there is the need for inter-State co-operation as an important means for further enhancement of international human rights. Regionalism has proved to be a very effective means to achieve that, but one which the Muslim States have not adequately utilized.

5.3 REGIONAL MEANS OF ENHANCING HUMAN RIGHTS

While the State, as the main duty-bearer, is a very important institution for the realization of human rights, the traditional concept of the modern nation-state is itself absolutist and to a large extent inhibits the realization of a common universal human rights practice. Community is thus an important vehicle of ensuring the effective universalization of international human rights. This has been demonstrated through the establishment of the European, Inter-American and African regional human rights regimes. These regional arrangements do not constitute a deviation from the universal aspiration of international human rights pursued by the UN as it may appear. Rather, they narrow down the diverse cultural differences and difficulties that may confront the universal enforcement of international human rights in practice. The UN has itself welcomed the regional human rights regimes and has also appealed for the establishment of regional human rights institutions where none exists.[17]

The Islamic culture and civilization transcends geographical boundaries and creates a strong heritage between modern Muslim States. According to Hurewitz, 'all the countries of North Africa and most of those of the Middle East are Arab and view themselves as belonging to a regional community of states ... The Arab states, moreover, form part of a bigger yet more deeply

---

[16] For example the Indonesian National Commission on Human Rights. For information on its functions and role in promoting human rights ideals in Indonesia *see* its 1999 Annual Report. Available online at: http://www.komnas.go.id/english/report/index.html [1/3/03]; and the Nigerian National Human Rights Commission established under the National Human Rights Commission Decree No.22 of 1995. *See* a commendation of the work of the Nigerian National Human Rights Commission in the Report on the Situation of Human Rights in Nigeria by the Special Rapporteur of the UN Commission on Human Rights, UN Doc. E/CN.4/1999/36 of 14/1/99, paras.69–72.

[17] *See* UN Doc. GA Res. 32/127 (1977), which has been reiterated yearly since then. The Vienna Declaration and Programme of Actions (1993) also reiterated this call. *See* (1993) 32 *International Legal Materials* p.1661 at p.1672, para.37.

fractured Islamic world'.[18] Despite their geographical spread, the historical bond of Islam provides modern Muslim States with a strong sense of commonality. This can be utilized for the achievement of an effective collective supervision and enforcement of human rights in the Muslim world that will greatly enhance the universal practice of international human rights law. The Organization of Islamic Conference (OIC) is a body founded, *inter alia*, to 'consolidate co-operation in the economic, social, cultural, scientific and other vital fields of activities' among Muslim States,[19] which can provide a community framework among modern Muslim States within the international order as a regional mechanism for the practical realization of international human rights law in the Muslim world.

5.3.1 The Organization of Islamic Conference (OIC) as a regional mechanism for human rights protection in the Muslim world

The OIC was founded by Muslim Heads of State and Governments in 1969 with the main objective of promoting 'Islamic solidarity among member States'.[20] The Charter[21] establishing the OIC entered into force on 28 February 1973. As of March 2003 the OIC had a total membership of 57 Muslim States, all of whom are also Member States of the UN.[22] This constitutes almost one-third of the present membership of the UN, an indication of the viability of the OIC serving as a regional institution for a community approach to international human rights within the dispensation of Islamic law in the Muslim world. In the preamble of the OIC Charter, the Member States both '[r]esolved to preserve Islamic spiritual, ethical, social and economic values' and '[reaffirmed] their commitment to the UN Charter and Fundamental Human Rights, the purposes and principles of which provide the basis for fruitful co-operation amongst all people'. The OIC Charter was registered as an international treaty with the UN on 1 February 1974 in conformity with Article 102 of the UN Charter, making the charter evocable before the organs of the UN.[23]

After a conference on *'Liberties and Human Rights in Islam'* in the Republic of Niger in 1979, the Tenth Conference of Foreign Ministers of the OIC agreed, in line with its Charter commitment on fundamental human rights,

---

[18] Hurewitz, J.C., (ed.), *The Middle East and North Africa in World Politics: A Documentary Record* (1975) Vol. 1, p.xvii.   [19] *See* Art. II(A)(2) of the OIC Charter.

[20] Article II(A)(1) of the OIC Charter.   [21] 914 UNTS p.111.

[22] This is with the exception of Palestine, which is not a full member of the UN but has only an observer status.

[23] Art. 102 of the UN Charter provides that: '(1) Every Treaty and every international agreement entered into by any Member of the United Nations after the present Charter comes into force shall as soon as possible be registered with the Secretariat and published by it. (2) No party to any such treaty or international agreement which has not been registered in accordance with the provisions of paragraph 1 of this Article may invoke that treaty or agreement before any organ of the United Nations.'

to set up a consultative commission of Muslim experts to draft an Islamic human rights document for the Organization.[24] Through that and subsequent efforts the OIC Cairo Declaration on Human Rights in Islam emerged and was endorsed by the OIC Foreign Ministers in 1990. In further pursuance of its commitment to the promotion of human rights, the OIC in co-operation with the UN organized a seminar in 1998 on *'Enriching the Universality of Human Rights: Islamic Perspectives on the Universal Declaration of Human Rights'* as part of the activities marking the Fiftieth Anniversary of the UDHR at the UN Secretariat in Geneva. The then OIC Secretary-General, Azzedine Laraki, described the initiative as 'a positive step forward among nations and a building block in the edifice of inter-civilizational dialogue [and to which] the Organization of the Islamic Conference possesses all the potential and desire to contribute actively in furthering and enriching'.[25] Also in his address at the Fifty-Sixth Session of the Commission on Human Rights in March 2000, the then Secretary-General of the OIC stated, *inter alia*, that:

At the threshold of the 21st Century it is imperative to put an end to all [the] blatant violations of human rights so that all people of the world may enjoy the same rights to education, health, development and welfare in a decent moral environment by eradicating poverty, misery, hunger, illiteracy etc. We can achieve these objectives, especially through a decisive and voluntary international cooperation deriving from an understanding and mutual respect of the cultural idiosyncracies of each people ... I am pleased to announce to you that the Organization of the Islamic Conference is actively working in this regard.[26]

The UN has itself demonstrated the desire to co-operate with the OIC in the search for solutions to global problems. Such co-operation can be traced back to 1975 when the General Assembly adopted a resolution to invite the OIC to participate in the sessions and work of the General Assembly and of its subsidiary organs in the capacity of observer.[27] From 1982 the General Assembly has also adopted resolutions on co-operation with the OIC and continues to include on its agenda the item entitled 'Cooperation between the United Nations and the Organization of the Islamic Conference'.[28]

The above endeavours of co-operation and mutuality are fully accommodated within the founding objectives of the OIC without discarding the Islamic

---

[24] *See* al-Ahsan, A., *OIC, The Organization of the Islamic Conference: An Introduction to an Islamic Political Institution* (1988) p.113.

[25] For the OIC Secretary-General's Opening Address *see* UN Human Rights Website at: http://www.unhchr.ch/huricane/huricane.nsf/(Symbol)/OHCHR.981129.B.En?OpenDocument [1/3/03].

[26] *See* Address of Secretary-General of OIC Before the 56th Session of the UN Commission on Human Rights, Geneva, on 24 March 2000, at: http://www.oic-un.org/Statements/SG56.html [8 July 2002].   [27] Res. 3369 (XXX) of 10 October 1975.

[28] *See* e.g. A/RES/53/16 of 11 November 1998. *See also* the Report of the UN Secretary General A/53/430 of 24 September 1998 on Cooperation between the United Nations and the Organization of the Islamic Conference.

religious ideology of its Member States. Such co-operation and mutuality are also encouraged by the *Sharî'ah* on the basis of equity and good faith. Ensuring the realization of international human rights in the Muslim world demands priority in these endeavours. The OIC needs to encourage among Muslim States the practical interpretation of the general 'Islamic spiritual, ethical, social and economic values', which they hold as 'one of the important factors of achieving progress for mankind'[29] in a manner that enhances the realization of international human rights. It is suggested that human rights should be placed permanently on the Organization's agenda for at least twenty years, with the review of human rights situations in Member States discussed every two years.

It is important to note, however, that while Islam is a strong value-unifier in the Muslim world, there presently exists no interpretative or enforcement organ with the competence of a 'universal' interpretation of the *Sharî'ah* in relation to international human rights, or with the jurisdiction of determining the scope of the *Sharî'ah* on any violation that might arise even under the Cairo Declaration on Human Rights in Islam adopted by the OIC in 1990. This situation gives room to each Member State to individually determine its own scope of the *Sharî'ah*, which is sometimes vaguely pleaded by some States to restrict even the most basic human rights. The lack of an interpretative or enforcement organ has rendered the OIC Cairo Declaration on Human Rights in Islam a dormant document which neither the Muslim States individually nor the OIC as a body formally refers to in the face of the sometimes obvious violations of basic and fundamental human rights in some Muslim States. There is thus a real need for a supervisory and enforcement organ for the rights guaranteed by the Declaration. In the absence of such an enforcement organ, the political authorities will, for example, not be restricted in any way from clawing back whatever rights may be apparently guaranteed even by the OIC Cairo Declaration on Human Rights in Islam.

The nearest to having a judicial organ by the OIC was in 1981 when the Organization decided at its Third Islamic Summit Conference in Saudi Arabia to create an Islamic Court of Justice in Kuwait with the competence to hear, *inter alia*, cases 'which the concerned Member States of the Organization of the Islamic Conference agree to refer to it' and cases 'whose referral to the Court is provided for in any treaties or conventions in force'.[30] The court has so far not been established.

The existing regional and the UN human rights enforcement organs have contributed greatly to the protection of international human rights by serving as independent determiners of the scope of human rights within the regional

---

[29] *See* para.4 of the Preamble of the OIC Charter.
[30] *See* Art. 25 Organization of the Islamic Conference, Statute of the Islamic Court of Justice, ICJ/2–86/D.1(FINAL). Available at the OIC Permanent Mission to the UN in Geneva.

and UN systems respectively. The OIC as a unifying organization of the modern Muslim States can emulate the regional institutions in that regard for the Muslim world. In his exposition on Human Rights in Islam, Maududi had stated that:

The charter and the proclamations and the resolutions of the United Nations cannot be compared with the rights sanctioned by God; the former are not obligatory on anybody, while the latter are an integral part of the Islamic faith. All Muslims and all administrators who claim to be Muslim have to accept, recognize and enforce them.[31]

The reverse seems to be the case today in respect of actual enforcement of human rights. Due to lack of any enforcement or monitoring mechanism, the administrators of modern Muslim States often violate those 'rights sanctioned by God' and even on some occasions vaguely cite the *Sharî'ah* as an excuse to violate basic human rights. And when this happens, other Muslim States stand by and watch hopelessly. Perhaps the Muslim States have resigned the redress of such violations to God in the judgment of the hereafter. Yet one finds in the Qur'an such provisions as follows:

And what is wrong with you that you fight not in the cause of God and for those weak, ill-treated and oppressed among men, women, and children, whose cry is: Our Lord! Rescue us from this town whose people are oppressors; and raise for us from You one who will protect, and raise for us from You one who will help.[32]

5.3.2 A binding covenant and a regional Islamic Court of 'Mazâlim' for Muslim States

To realize the OIC's commitment to the enforcement of human rights among its Member States, there is, first, the need for a fully binding Islamic Human Rights Covenant, to be ratified by all its Member States. This is necessary because, apart from the present OIC Cairo Declaration on Human Rights in Islam not being legally binding, it also leaves out many essential rights as depicted in our analysis of the ICCPR and ICESCR above. Secondly, there is the need for a regional supervisory and enforcement organ that will bind all the Member States. The establishment of such a regional enforcement organ is not unknown under Islamic law. Classical books on Islamic jurisprudence document the existence of an institution called *Wilâyah al-Mazâlim* from the very early periods of the Islamic State. This was a sort of complaints or grievances tribunal with inter-provincial jurisdiction throughout the Islamic Empire to redress any alleged violation of individual rights by State officials.[33]

---

[31] Maududi, A.A., *Human Rights in Islam* (1993) p.16.   [32] Q4:75.

[33] For further expatiation on the institution of *Mazâlim, see* Baderin, M.A., 'Establishing Areas of Common Ground between Islamic Law and International Human Rights Law' (2001) 5

The proposed regional enforcement organ can thus be in the form of a regional Islamic Court of *Mazâlim* with jurisdiction to adjudicate on allegations of human rights violations against any of the OIC Member States, and also to interpret the scope of the rights guaranteed under the present OIC Cairo Declaration on Human Rights in Islam, any subsequent binding Covenant, and also rights guaranteed under the *Sharî'ah* in general. The Court would be composed of highly qualified Islamic law jurists not only learned in Islamic jurisprudence, but also conversant with international human rights law and jurisprudence. That would provide a definite and unified Islamic parameter for determining the scope of human rights within the application of Islamic law by Muslim States.

The proposed regional Islamic Court of *Mazâlim* would need to adopt an evolutionary approach in its interpretation of the law whereby it would accommodate the jurisprudence of all the established Islamic schools and juristic views. It would take advantage of the utility of the doctrine of *maslahah* enabling it to adopt the juristic opinions that ultimately enhance human well-being and benefit and avert human difficulty and hardship.[34] The Islamic legal principle of *takhayyur* (eclectic choice) permits movement within the different schools of Islamic jurisprudence and is supported by the Tradition that whenever the Prophet had a choice between equally lawful situations, he always chose the easiest and most beneficial option.[35] The regional Islamic Court of *Mazâlim* would then consciously develop a definite human rights jurisprudence that would serve as a specific departure point for international human rights practice in the Muslim world.

Thirdly, the proposed regional Islamic Court of *Mazâlim* should have compulsory jurisdiction for individual complaints against human rights violations in the OIC Member States. This would afford a more collective approach to guaranteeing human rights practice amongst Muslim States based on a common interpretation of Islamic law, and a more unified and determinable approach towards international human rights practice in the Muslim world.

The regional Islamic Court of *Mazâlim*, the UN human rights bodies and the other regional human rights bodies would be expected to co-operate with the aim of combining the best in all cultures and legal traditions for the realization of a 'universal universalism' in international human rights law for all human beings universally.

The International Journal of Human Rights, No. 2, p.72 at pp.97–98. *See also* Qadri, A.A., *Islamic Jurisprudence in the Modern World* (1986) p.488; Kamali, M.H., 'Appellate Review and Judicial Independence in Islamic Law' in Mallat, C., *Islam and Public Law: Classical and Contemporary Studies* (1993) p.49.

[34] *See* Ch. 2 para.2.4.6 above.

[35] *See* e.g. Kamali, M.H., 'Have We Neglected the Sharî'ah Law Doctrine of Maslahah?' (1988) 27 *Islamic Studies*, p.287 at p.290.

5.4 THE 'MARGIN OF APPRECIATION' DOCTRINE AS A UNIVERSAL MEANS OF ENHANCING HUMAN RIGHTS

Complementary to the Islamic regional human rights regime proposed above, we also earlier mentioned the need for the adoption of the margin of appreciation doctrine by the UN human rights treaty bodies in interpreting international human rights treaties.[36] The margin of appreciation doctrine exists within the European human rights regime and it has been defined as 'the line at which international supervision should give way to a State Party's discretion in enacting or enforcing its laws'.[37] While the doctrine has its critics, it no doubt allows for the sustenance of justifiable moral values of different societies through 'striking a balance between a right guaranteed . . . and a permitted derogation [or limitation]'.[38] In practice, the UN Human Rights Committee has not formally adopted the margin of appreciation doctrine[39] but has alluded to it only on one occasion in *Hertzberg and Others v. Finland*[40] where the authors had brought a complaint alleging violation of their freedom of expression under Article 19 of the ICCPR. The State Party had in that case censured TV programmes dealing with homosexuality. The State Party argued that the restrictions were for the protection of public morals. In finding that there had been no violation of Article 19, the HRC stated that:

> It has to be noted, first, that public morals differ widely. There is no universally applicable common standard. Consequently, in this respect, a certain *margin of discretion* ought to be accorded to the responsible national authorities.[41]

The Committee however rejected the doctrine later in *Ilmari Lansman et al v. Finland*[42] where the authors had brought a complaint alleging violation of their right to enjoy their own culture under Article 27 of the ICCPR. The State Party had argued that the acts complained of were in pursuance of national development and that 'a margin of discretion must be left to national authorities

---

[36] On the 'margin of appreciation' doctrine *see* e.g. Steiner, H.J., and Alston, P., *International Human Rights in Context, Law, Politics, Morals* (2nd Ed., 2000) pp.854–857; Harris, D.J., O'Boyle, M., and Warbrick, C., *Law of the European Convention on Human Rights* (1995) pp.12–15; Clayton, R., and Tomlinson, H., *The Law of Human Rights* (2000) Vol.1, pp.273–278; and Ghandhi, P.R., *The Human Rights Committee and the Right of Individual Communication: Law and Practice* (1998) pp.311–314 and n.96 at p.326.

[37] *See* Yourow, H.C., *The Margin of Appreciation Doctrine in the Dynamics of European Human Rights Jurisprudence* (1996) p.13, citing Wong, W.M., 'The Sunday Times Case: Freedom of Expression Versus English Contempt-of-Court Law in the European Court of Human Rights' (1984) 17 *New York University Journal of International Law and Politics*, p.35 at p.58.

[38] *ibid.* [39] *See* Ghandhi (above n.36) at p.314.

[40] Communication No. 61/1979 Finland: 2/4/82. UN Doc. Supp. No.40 (A/37/40) at 161 (1982). [41] *ibid.*, para.10.3 (emphasis added).

[42] Communication No. 511/1992: Finland 08/11/94. CCPR/C/52/D/511/1992.

in the application of article 27' in that regard.[43] Although the HRC did not find a breach of Article 27, it however pointed out that the scope of a State Party's freedom to encourage development 'is not to be assessed by reference to a margin of appreciation, but by reference to the obligations it has undertaken in article 27'.[44] It is however probable that the rejection of the margin of appreciation by the HRC in the latter case was due to its non-relatedness to the issue of public morals.

The HRC has obviously refrained from adopting the margin of appreciation doctrine due to the fear of its potential abuse by States Parties to limit important rights like freedom of expression or as justification for imposing states of emergency on grounds of threat to the existence of the State. The issues of public morals and religious values do not however give rise to such fears because the application of a margin of appreciation on these grounds is based on public sensibility and morality rather than for the protection of the State per se. Its application on grounds of public sensibility and morality will thus be justifiable on the obvious accepted practice in the State or region concerned.

The European Court of Human Rights has effectively applied the doctrine in a variety of cases under the European Convention on Human Rights. Macdonald has observed that '[t]he margin of appreciation is now the primary tool of the Court in ensuring the efficacy of the application of Articles 8 to 11, 14 and 15 and Article 1 of Protocol No.1'.[45] This has consisted of cases brought under the European Convention involving issues such as protection of morals, protection of reputation of others, commercial speech, respect for private and family life, matrimonial status, family life and home, sexual morality, respect for private life, peaceful enjoyment of possessions, expropriation and nationalism, control of rental property, licensing and regulations, non-discrimination, liberty and security of the person.[46] The relevance and rationality of the proposal for the adoption of the margin of appreciation doctrine within the UN international human rights regime cannot be better buttressed than in the following conclusion of Macdonald after his detailed exposition of the doctrine. He justified the doctrine as follows:

> The margin of appreciation which is more a principle of justification than interpretation, aims to help the Court show the proper degree of respect for the objectives that a Contracting Party may wish to pursue, and the trade-offs that it wants to make, while

---

[43] Communication No. 511/1992: Finland 08/11/94. CCPR/C/52/D/511/1992, para.7.13.

[44] *ibid.*, para.9.4. *See also* the debate on cultural practices during consideration of Nigeria's initial report to the ICESCR, where in response to the cultural arguments of the Nigerian delegation the ESCR Committee Members stated, *inter alia*, that 'it was not the Committee's mandate to evaluate cultural practices and pass judgement on them, but rather to determine whether a State party to the Covenant was conforming with the obligations it had entered into'. UN Doc. E/C.12/1998/SR.7 of 09/09/98.

[45] Macdonald, St. J.R., 'The Margin of Appreciation' in Macdonald, J., *et al.* (eds.), *The European System for the Protection of Human Rights* (1993) p.83.

[46] *See generally ibid.*, pp.83–124; *see also* Yourow (above n. 37).

at the same time preventing unnecessary restrictions on the fullness of the protection which the Convention can provide.[47] This flexibility has enabled the Court to avoid any damaging dispute with Contracting States over the respective areas of authority of the Court and the Convention and the Contracting States and their respective legislatures. The margin of appreciation has also helped the Court strike a proper balance between the application of the Convention by national organs and the central institutions of the Court and Commission. Practices within States vary. In one State a law viewed in the abstract outside other national circumstances might be seen as violating the Convention, but viewed in the light of some other national matter or practice it may not. The intention of the drafters of the Convention was not that each Contracting State would have uniform laws but that there would be a European standard which, if violated, would give redress to the Members of the Contracting State. The margin of appreciation has very much assisted in this task. The justification of the margin of appreciation is usually a pragmatic one. The argument is that the margin of appreciation is a useful tool in the eventual realization of a European-wide system of human-rights protection, in which a uniform standard of protection is secured. Progress towards that goal must be gradual, since the entire legal framework rests on the fragile foundations of the consent of the Contracting Parties. The margin of appreciation gives the flexibility needed to avoid damaging confrontations between the Court and Contracting States over their respective spheres of authority and enables the Court to balance the sovereignty of Contracting Parties with their obligation under the Convention.[48]

It will be observed that the margin of appreciation doctrine is likened to the principle of justification, which we had also referred to as an important principle in our analysis of the two Covenants in the light of Islamic law. Expressing the fears of the HRC on the adoption of the doctrine, Schmidt has argued that the adoption of the margin of appreciation doctrine by the Committee 'might prompt some states parties to rely on arguments of "cultural relativism", however ill-defined or inappropriate in the circumstances of a given case, or to seek to justify serious human-rights abuses'.[49] The proposal here is not for an arbitrary or unjustifiable application of the doctrine. The margin of appreciation will be exercised proportionately and supervised by the Treaty Bodies to prevent its abuse. A State Party that pleads the doctrine would be saddled with the onus of establishing a legal justification for exercising its margin of discretion in any alleged violation of right. The scope of the doctrine would thus be determined by the circumstances of each case as has been demonstrated in the practice of the European Court. The approach of the European Court in that regard is to search for a 'European consensus' in interpreting the provisions of the Convention. Whenever the practice among Member States achieves a certain measure of uniformity the Court raises 'the

---

[47] *See also* Mahoney, P., 'Judicial Activism and Judicial Self-Restraint in the European Court of Human Rights: Two Sides of the Same Coin' (1990) 11 *Human Rights Law Journal* p.57.

[48] Macdonald (above n.45) at p.123.

[49] Schmidt, M.G., 'The Complementarity of the Covenant and the European Convention on Human Rights—Recent Developments' in Harris, D.J., and Joseph, S., *The International Covenant on Civil and Political Rights and United Kingdom Law* (1995) p.628 at p.657.

standard of rights-protection to which all states must adhere'.[50] According to Helfer, the Court, broadly speaking, relies 'on three distinct factors as evidence of [a European] consensus: legal consensus, as demonstrated by European domestic statutes, international treaties, and regional legislation; expert consensus; and European public consensus'.[51] In the absence of any such consensus, the Court gives a wide margin of appreciation to the State concerned.[52]

The European human rights regime is regarded as the most developed human rights regime. If, as observed by Macdonald above, the margin of appreciation has provided the system with the 'flexibility needed to avoid confrontations' and is considered as a 'useful tool in the eventual realization of a European-wide system of human-rights protection, in which a uniform standard of protection is secured', then the adoption of the doctrine, complemented with the Islamic regional approach proposed above, would ultimately lead to a similar stability within the international human rights regime in relation to Muslim States, which constitute a significant proportion of the parties to the Covenants and whose practice is relevant to any consensus as to the meaning of Covenant rights.

In respect of the International Bill of Rights as examined in this book, the margin of appreciation doctrine will be a useful tool in addressing issues such as definition of family, homosexuality, blasphemy, abortion, and other moral questions in relation to Muslim States Parties that apply Islamic law. The consensus approach will also require an equitable balance of membership of both the HRC and the ESCR Committee to reflect at least the civilizations and legal systems of all the States Parties if not of the world as a whole. This will facilitate a universal interpretation that accommodates the norms of all the States Parties to the Covenants as observed by McGoldrick earlier above.[53]

To assist the international human rights committees on questions of Islamic law the proposed regional Islamic Court of *Mazâlim* will be a harmonizing institution on Islamic law for matters brought before it among Muslim States, and its jurisprudence and opinions would thus serve as the reference point on Islamic values and norms in the determination of any necessary margin of appreciation for Islamic values by the UN international human rights treaty bodies. This will eliminate any problems of differences of opinion in respect of Islamic legal norms under consideration before the international treaty bodies.

---

[50] *See* Helfer, L., 'Consensus, Coherence and The European Convention on Human Rights' (1993) 26 *Cornell International Law Journal*, No.1, p.133 at p.139.   [51] *ibid.*, at p.134.
[52] *See* e.g. *Rees v. United Kingdom* (1986) 106 ECHR (Series A) at 15; *Cossey v. United Kingdom* (1990) 184 ECHR (Series A) at 16; and *B v. France* (1992) 232-C ECHR (Series A) 1.   [53] *See* text to n.6 above.

The above propositions, implemented in good faith and backed with political and humanitarian will, are capable of providing the flexibility needed to avoid confrontation between Islamic law and international human rights law and create 'breathing space' or 'elbow room' for a closer rapport that will gradually and ultimately lead to the realization of a common standard of universalism in human rights between international human rights law and Islamic law in the Muslim world.

Annexe

The Cairo Declaration on Human Rights in Islam adopted by the Organization of Islamic Conference in Cairo on 5 August 1990

The Member States of the Organization of the Islamic Conference,

Reaffirming the civilizing and historical role of the Islamic *Ummah* which God made the best nation that has given mankind a universal and well-balanced civilization in which harmony is established between this life and the hereafter and knowledge is combined with spiritual faith; and the role that this *Ummah* should play to guide a humanity confused by competing trends and ideologies and to provide solutions to the chronic problems of this materialistic civilization.

Wishing to contribute to the efforts of mankind to assert human rights, to protect man from exploitation and persecution, and to affirm his freedom and right to a dignified life in accordance with the Islamic *Shari'ah*.

Convinced that mankind which has reached an advanced stage in materialistic science is still, and shall remain, in dire need of faith to support its civilization and of a self motivating force to guard its rights.

Believing that fundamental rights and universal freedoms in Islam are an integral part of the Islamic religion and that no one as a matter of principle has the right to suspend them in whole or in part or violate or ignore them in as much as they are binding divine commandments, which are contained in the Revealed Books of God and were sent through the last of His Prophets to complete the preceding divine messages thereby making their observance an act of worship and their neglect or violation an abominable sin, and accordingly every person is individually responsible and the *Ummah* collectively responsible for their safeguard.

Proceeding from the above-mentioned principles, Declare the following:

Article 1
a) All human beings form one family whose members are united by submission to God and descent from Adam. All men are equal in terms of basic human dignity and basic obligations and responsibilities, without any discrimination on the grounds of race, colour, language, sex, religious belief, political affiliation, social status or other considerations. True faith is the guarantee for enhancing such dignity along the path to human perfection.

b) All human beings are God's subjects, and the most loved by Him are those who are most useful to the rest of His subjects, and no one has superiority over another except on the basis of piety and good deeds.

Article 2

a) Life is a God-given gift and the right to life is guaranteed to every human being. It is the duty of individuals, societies and states to protect this right from any violation, and it is prohibited to take away life except for a *Shari'ah* prescribed reason.

b) It is forbidden to resort to such means as may result in the genocidal annihilation of mankind.

c) The preservation of human life throughout the term of time willed by God is a duty prescribed by *Shari'ah*.

d) Safety from bodily harm is a guaranteed right. It is the duty of the State to safeguard it, and it is prohibited to breach it without a *Shari'ah* prescribed reason.

Article 3

a) In the event of the use of force and in case of armed conflict, it is not permissible to kill non-belligerents such as old men, women and children. The wounded and the sick shall have the right to medical treatment; and prisoners of war shall have the right to be fed, sheltered and clothed. It is prohibited to mutilate dead bodies. It is a duty to exchange prisoners of war and to arrange visits or reunions of the families separated by the circumstances of war.

b) It is prohibited to fell trees, to damage crops or livestock, and to destroy the enemy's civilian buildings and installations by shelling, blasting or any other means.

Article 4

Every human being is entitled to the inviolability and the protection of his good name and honour during his life and after his death. The State and Society shall protect his remains and burial place.

Article 5

a) The family is the foundation of society, and marriage is the basis of its formation. Men and women have the right to marriage, and no restrictions stemming from race, colour or nationality shall prevent them from enjoying this right.

b) Society and the State shall remove all obstacles to marriage and shall facilitate marital procedure. They shall ensure family protection and welfare.

Article 6
a) Woman is equal to man in human dignity, and has rights to enjoy as well as duties to perform; she has her own civil entity and financial independence, and the right to retain her name and lineage.
b) The husband is responsible for the support and welfare of the family.

Article 7
a) As of the moment of birth, every child has rights due from the parents, Society and the State to be accorded proper nursing, education and material, hygienic and moral care. Both the fetus and the mother must be protected and accorded special care.
b) Parents and those in such like capacity have the right to choose the type of education they desire for their children, provided they take into consideration the interest and future of the children in accordance with ethical values and the principles of the *Shari'ah*.
c) Both parents are entitled to certain rights from their children, and relatives are entitled to rights from their kin, in accordance with the tenets of the *Shari'ah*.

Article 8
Every human being has the right to enjoy his legal capacity in terms of both obligation and commitment, should this capacity be lost or impaired, he shall be represented by his guardian.

Article 9
a) The quest for knowledge is an obligation and the provision of education is a duty for Society and the State. The State shall ensure the availability of ways and means to acquire education and shall guarantee educational diversity in the interest of Society so as to enable man to be acquainted with the religion of Islam and the facts of the Universe for the benefit of mankind.
b) Every human being has the right to receive both religious and worldly education from the various institutions of education and guidance, including the family, the school, the university, the media, etc., and in such an integrated and balanced manner as to develop his personality, strengthen his faith in God and promote his respect for and defence of both rights and obligations.

Article 10
Islam is the religion of unspoiled nature. It is prohibited to exercise any form of compulsion on man or to exploit his poverty or ignorance in order to convert him to another religion or to atheism.

Article 11

a) Human beings are born free, and no one has the right to enslave, humiliate, oppress or exploit them, and there can be no subjugation but to God the Most-High.

b) Colonialism of all types being one of the most evil forms of enslavement is totally prohibited. Peoples suffering from colonialism have the full right to freedom and self-determination. It is the duty of all states and peoples to support the struggle of colonized peoples from the liquidation of all forms of colonialism and occupation, and all states and peoples have the right to preserve their independent identity and exercise control over their wealth and natural resources.

Article 12

Every man shall have the right, within the framework of *Shari'ah*, to free movement and to select his place of residence whether inside or outside his country and if persecuted, is entitled to seek asylum in another country. The country of refuge shall ensure his protection until he reaches safety, unless asylum is motivated by an act which *Shari'ah* regards as a crime.

Article 13

Work is a right guaranteed by the State and Society for each person able to work. Everyone shall be free to choose the work that suits him best and which serves his interests and those of Society. The employee shall have the right to safety and security as well as to all other social guarantees. He may neither be assigned work beyond his capacity nor be subjected to compulsion or exploited or harmed in any way. He shall be entitled without any discrimination between males and females to fair wages for his work without delay, as well as to the holidays allowances and promotions which he deserves. For his part, he shall be required to be dedicated and meticulous in his work. Should workers and employers disagree on any matter, the State shall intervene to settle the dispute and have the grievances redressed, the rights confirmed and justice enforced without bias.

Article 14

Everyone shall have the right to legitimate gains without monopolization, deceit or harm to oneself or to others. Usury (*riba*) is absolutely prohibited.

Article 15

a) Everyone shall have the right to own property acquired in a legitimate way, and shall be entitled to the rights of ownership, without prejudice to oneself, others or to society in general. Expropriation is not permissible except for the requirements of public interest and upon payment of immediate and fair compensation.

b) Confiscation and seizure of property is prohibited except for a necessity dictated by law.

Article 16

Everyone shall have the right to enjoy the fruits of his scientific, literary, artistic or technical production and the right to protect the moral and material interest stemming therefrom, provided that such production is not contrary to the principles of *Shari'ah*.

Article 17

a) Everyone shall have the right to live in a clean environment, away from vice and moral corruption, an environment that would foster his self-development and it is incumbent upon the State and Society in general to afford that right.
b) Everyone shall have the right to medical and social care, and to all public amenities provided by Society and the State within the limits of their available resources.
c) The State shall ensure the right of the individual to a decent living which will enable him to meet all his requirements and those of his dependants, including food, clothing, housing, education, medical care and all other basic needs.

Article 18

a) Everyone shall have the right to live in security for himself, his religion, his dependants, his honour and his property.
b) Everyone shall have the right to privacy in the conduct of his private affairs, in his home, among his family, with regard to his property and his relationships. It is not permitted to spy on him, to place him under surveillance or to besmirch his good name. The State shall protect him from arbitrary interference.
c) A private residence is inviolable in all cases. It will not be entered without permission from its inhabitants or in any unlawful manner, nor shall it be demolished or confiscated and its dwellers evicted.

Article 19

a) All individuals are equal before the law, without distinction between ruler and ruled.
b) The right to resort to justice is guaranteed to everyone.
c) Liability is in essence personal.
d) There shall be no crime or punishment except as provided for in the *Shari'ah*.
e) A defendant is innocent until his guilt is proven in a fair trial in which he shall be given all the guarantees of defence.

Article 20

It is not permitted without legitimate reason to arrest an individual, restrict his freedom, to exile or to punish him. It is not permitted to subject him to physical or psychological torture or to any form of humiliation, cruelty or indignity. Nor is it permitted to subject an individual to medical or scientific experimentation without his consent or at the risk of his health or of his life. Nor is it permitted to promulgate emergency laws that would provide executive authority for such actions.

Article 21
Taking hostages under any form or for any purpose is expressly forbidden.

Article 22
a) Everyone shall have the right to express his opinion freely in such manner as would not be contrary to the principles of the *Shari'ah*.
b) Everyone shall have the right to advocate what is right, and propagate what is good, and warn against what is wrong and evil according to the norms of Islamic *Shari'ah*.
c) Information is a vital necessity to Society. It may not be exploited or mis-used in such a way as may violate sanctities and the dignity of Prophets, undermine moral and ethical values or disintegrate, corrupt or harm Society or weaken its faith.
d) It is not permitted to arouse nationalistic or doctrinal hatred or to do anything that may be an incitement to any form of racial discrimination.

Article 23
a) Authority is a trust; and abuse or malicious exploitation thereof is absolutely prohibited, so that fundamental human rights may be guaranteed.
b) Everyone shall have the right to participate directly or indirectly in the administration of his country's public affairs. He shall also have the right to assume public office in accordance with the provisions of *Shari'ah*.

Article 24
All the rights and freedoms stipulated in this Declaration are subject to the Islamic *Shari'ah*.

Article 25
The Islamic *Shari'ah* is the only source of reference for the explanation or clarification of any of the articles of this Declaration.

Glossary

Adâlah:	Justice; probity; uprightness.
Âdât:	Customs.
Âhâd:	Solitary *Hadîth* transmitted through a single chain of narration.
Amr bi al-ma'rûf wa nahy an al-munkar:	The Islamic public-order principle of commanding what is good and prohibiting what is wrong.
Asîr:	Prisoner.
Bay'ah:	Pledge of allegiance.
Bayt al-mâl:	State treasury.
al-Birr:	Goodness, righteousness.
Darûrah:	Necessity.
Darûriyyât:	Indispensable benefits or rights—comprising: (right to) life, intellect, religion, family and property.
Dhimmî:	Non-Muslim citizen of the Islamic State.
Diyah:	Blood money—compensation for murder or injuries under Islamic Law.
Faskh:	Judicial annulment of marriage.
Fatwâ:	Legal or religious opinion by a qualified Islamic jurisconsult.
Fiqh:	Islamic jurisprudence.
Habs:	Imprisonment.
Habs Ihtiyâtî:	Preventive detention pending investigation of a crime.
Hadîth:	Saying; Traditions of the Prophet Muhammad.
Hâjiyyât:	Necessary benefits or rights—comes next in line to *Darûriyyât*.
Hâkim:	Law giver.
Haqq:	Right.
Haqq al-'afw 'an al-'uqûbah:	Right of clemency from punishment; amnesty.
Haqq Allah al-khâlis:	Special right of God.
Hibah:	Gift.
Hidânah:	Child custody and care.
Hirâbah:	Highway robbery; brigandage.

Hisbah:	Public order; commanding what is good and prohibiting what is wrong.
Hudûd:	Limits; the fixed punishments for certain crimes under Islamic law.
Hukm:	Legal ruling; injunction; decision.
Huqûq:	Rights.
Huqûq Adamiyyîn:	Rights of humans; individual rights; human rights.
Huqûq Allah:	Rights of God; public rights.
al-Huqûq al-Fitriyyah:	Natural rights; fundamental rights.
Huqûq al-Ibâd:	Rights of (God's) servants, i.e. rights of humans; individual rights; human rights.
Huqûq al-Insân:	Rights of human beings; human rights.
Hurriyyah:	Freedom; liberty.
Ibâd:	Servants (of God).
Ibâdât:	Acts of worship.
Ihsân:	Benevolence; goodness.
Ijmâ':	Islamic legal consensus.
Ijtihâd:	Juridical reasoning of a qualified Islamic legist.
Insâniyyah:	Humanity; humaneness; civility.
Isnâd:	Chain of narrators of *Hadîth*.
Istihsân:	Juristic preference.
Istishâb:	Legal presumption of continuity of a state until contrary is proved.
Istislâh:	Welfare; benefit.
Jâhiliyyah:	Ignorance.
Kafâlah:	Legal guardianship.
Karâmah:	Honour; human dignity.
Khilâfah:	Representation; rule by representation.
Khiyâr al-Bulûg:	Option of puberty.
Khiyâr al-Talâq:	Option of divorce.
Khul':	Divestiture; dissolution of marriage initiated by the wife.
Madhhab:	School of Islamic jurisprudence.
Mahkûm alayh:	Subject of the law.
Mahkûm fîh:	Object of the law.
Mahr:	Dowry; marriage endowment (in cash or service) paid by the husband to the wife.
Mahram:	Unmarriageable male relation of a Muslim woman.

Maqâsid al-Sharî'ah:	Overall objective of the *Sharî'ah*; object and purpose of the *Sharî'ah*.
Ma'rûf:	Convention; fairness; goodness; common good of humanity.
Maslahah:	Welfare; benefit.
Maslahah Mursalah:	Released benefit; communal welfare.
Maslahah Shakhsiyyah	Individual benefit or individual welfare.
Maslahah al-'Ummah	Benefit or welfare of the Muslim community as a whole.
Maslahah Wahmiyyah:	Dubious welfare; non-genuine benefit.
Mas'ûlîyyah:	Responsibility.
Mazâlim:	Complaints tribunal; court of grievances.
Mu'âmalât:	Social intercourse; inter-human relations; civil and temporal human affairs.
Mubâra'ah:	Dissolution of marriage by mutual/bilateral agreement of the couple.
Muftî:	Islamic jurisconsult.
Muhtasib:	Officer for public order.
Mujtahidûn (singular: *Mujtahid):*	Islamic legists competent enough to formulate independent legal or theological opinion based on the sources and methods of Islamic law.
Murâfa'ah:	Defence; appeal; legal proceedings.
Musâwâh:	Equality.
Musta'man:	Safe alien; non-national of the Islamic State who enjoys safe conduct in it.
Mutaw'ah:	Religious law enforcers or volunteers.
Naqd al-Hâkim:	Governmental criticism: Governmental censorship.
Nasîhah:	Admonition; advice.
Naskh:	Abrogation.
Qadâ':	Judgment.
Qadhf:	Slanderous accusation (of adultery or fornication).
Qâdî:	Judge.
Qâdî al-Qudât:	Chief Justice.
Qawâmûn:	Guardians; protectors; defenders.
Qisâs:	Law of retaliation; *lex talionis* (life for life, injury for injury).
Qiyâs:	Legal analogy.

Rajm:	Punishment by stoning.
Riddah:	Apostasy.
Sabb Allah aw Sabb al-Rasûl:	Reviling God or reviling the Prophet; blasphemy.
Sadaqât:	Charity; voluntary alms.
Sâhib al-Mazâlim:	Complaints officer; Ombudsman.
Sariqah:	Theft as defined under Islamic law.
Sharb al-Khamr:	Wine-drinking.
Sharî'ah:	The Right Path; Qur'an and *Sunnah*; The divine source of Islamic law.
Shûrâ:	Consultation.
Siyâsah Shar'iyyah:	Legitimate governmental policy based on the *Sharî'ah*.
Sunnah:	Practice; the practices of the Prophet Muhammad.
Ta'âwun:	Co-operation.
al-Tâbi'ûn:	The early Muslims who witnessed the era of the Prophet's Companions but not that of the Prophet himself.
Tadrîj:	Islamic legal principle of gradualism.
Tafwîḍ al-Talâq:	Delegated repudiation of marriage.
Tahsînîyyât:	Improvement benefits or rights—comes next in line to *Hâjîyyât*.
Takhayyur (also *Takhyîr):*	Eclectic choice (moving between opinions of the schools of Islamic jurisprudence to arrive at a decision).
Ta'lîq al-Talâq:	Suspended repudiation of marriage.
Taqlîd:	Legal conformism; following of a juristic view by a layperson.
Taqnîn:	Codification.
Tashrî':	Legislation.
Ta'zîr:	Discretionary punishment under Islamic law.
'Ulamâ':	Traditional Islamic scholars.
Ummah:	Community (nation).
'Urf:	Custom; usage; practice.
Zakât:	Annual obligatory alms (tax) payable by Muslims in favour of the indigent.
Zinâ:	Adultery; fornication.

Bibliography

ENGLISH LANGUAGE SOURCES

ABA-NAMAY, R., 'The Recent Constitutional Reforms in Saudi Arabia' (1993) 42 *International and Comparative Law Quarterly*, 295.

'ABD AL 'ATI, H., *The Family Structure in Islam* (Indianapolis: American Trust Publications, 1977).

ABDULATI, H., *Islam in Focus* (Cairo: El-Falah Foundation, 1997).

ABU RABI', I. M., 'Review of A. S. Monsalli, Radical Islamic Fundamentalism: The Ideological and Political Discourse of Sayyid Qutb' (1994) 1 *Al-Mizan*, Issue 1, 133.

ABU-SAHLIEH, S. A., 'Muslims and Human Rights: Challenges and Perspectives', in Schmale, W., (ed.) *Human Rights and Cultural Diversity* (Goldbach: Keip, 1993) 239.

ABUSULAYMAN, A. A., *Towards an Islamic Theory of International Relations: New Directions for Islamic Methodology and Thought* (Herndon: International Institute of Islamic Thought, 1993).

ADALSTEINSSON, R., and THORHALLSON, P., 'Article 27', in Alfredsson, G., and Eide, A., (eds.) *The Universal Declaration of Human Rights: A Common Standard of Achievement* (The Hague: M. Nijhoff Publishers, 1999) 575.

AFSHAR, H., 'Women, State and Ideology in Iran', in Women Living Under Muslim Laws, (ed.) *Dossier No.3* (Grabels: Women Living Under Muslim Laws, 1988) 42.

AFSHARI, R., 'An Essay on Islamic Cultural Relativism in the Discourse of Human Rights' (1994) 16 *Human Rights Quarterly*, 235.

AHMAD, F., 'Turkey', in Esposito, J. L., (ed.) *The Oxford Encyclopaedia of the Modern Islamic World*. (Oxford: Oxford University Press, 1995) Vol.4, 241.

AHMAD, K., 'The Nature of the Islamic Resurgence', in Esposito, J.L., (ed.) *Voices of Resurgent Islam* (New York: Oxford University Press, 1983) 225.

AHMED, A. S., *Living Islam* (London: Penguin, 1995).

AHMED, B. D., and UMRI, J., 'Suicide and Euthanasia: Islamic Viewpoint', in Mahmood, T., *et al.*, (eds.) *Criminal Law in Islam and the Muslim World* (Delhi: Institute of Objective Studies, 1996) 164.

AL-AHSAN, A., *OIC, The Organization of the Islamic Conference: An Introduction to an Islamic Political Institution* (Herndon: International Institute of Islamic Thought, 1988).

AHSAN, M. M., 'Human Rights in Islam: Personal Dimensions' (1990) 13 *Hamdard Islamicus*, 3.

AL-ALFI, A. A., 'Punishment in Islamic Criminal Law', in Bassiouni, M. C., (ed.) *The Islamic Criminal Justice System* (New York: Oceana Publications, 1982) 227.

ALGAR, H., (trans.) *Islam and Revolution: Writings and Declarations of Imam Khomeini* (Berkeley: Mizan Press, 1981).

ALI, A. A., (trans.) *Kitab-ul-Kharaj* (Lahore: Islamic Book Centre, 1979).

ALI, A. Y., *The Meaning of the Holy Qur'an* (Maryland: Amana Corporation, 1992).

ALI, S. S., 'Women's Rights in Islam: Towards a Theoretical Framework' (1997–98) 4 *Yearbook of Islamic and Middle Eastern Law*, 117.

—— *Gender and Human Rights in Islam and International Law: Equal before Allah, Unequal before Man?* (The Hague: Kluwer, 2000).

ALLOT, A. N., *New Essays in African Law* (London: Butterworth, 1970).

ALSTON, P., and QUINN, G., 'The Nature and Scope of States Parties' Obligations under the International Covenant on Economic, Social and Cultural Rights' (1987) 9 *Human Rights Quarterly*, 156.

AL-ALWANI, T. J., *Ijtihad* (Herndon: International Institute of Islamic Thought, 1993).

—— 'Judiciary and Rights of the Accused in Islamic Criminal Law', in Mahmood, T., *et al.*, (eds.) *Criminal Law in Islam and the Muslim World* (Delhi: Institute of Objective Studies, 1996) 256.

American Anthropological Association, 'Statement on Human Rights' (1947) 49 *American Anthropologist*, 539.

—— 'Declaration on Anthropology and Human Rights' (1999) http://www.aaanet.org/stmts/humanrts.htm [1/3/2003].

AMIN, T., *Nationalism and Internationalism in Liberalism, Marxism and Islam* (Islamabad: International Institute of Islamic Thought, 1991).

Amnesty International, *Iran Briefing* (London: Amnesty International [MDE 13/08/87], 1987).

—— *Iran: Violations of Human Rights, Documents Sent by Amnesty International to the Government of the Islamic Republic of Iran* (London: Amnesty International Publications [MDE 13/09/87], 1987).

—— *Tunisia: Rhetoric Versus Reality: The Failure of a Human Rights Bureaucracy* (London: Amnesty International [MDE 30/01/94], 1994).

—— *Iran, Violations Against Shi'a Religious Leaders and their Followers* (London: Amnesty International [MDE/13/08/1997], 1997).

—— *Saudi Arabia, Behind Closed Doors: Unfair Trials in Saudi Arabia* (London: Amnesty International [MDE 23/08/97], 1997).

ANDERSON, J. N. D., 'Modern Trend in Islam: Legal Reform and Modernisation in the Middle East' (1971) 20 *International and Comparative Law Quarterly*, 1.

AN-NA'IM, A. A., 'Religious Minorities Under Islamic Law and the Limits of Cultural Relativisim (1987) 9 *Human Rights Quarterly*, 1–18.

—— 'Human Rights in the Muslim World: Socio-Political Conditions and Scriptural Imperatives' (1990) 3 *Harvard Human Rights Journal*, 13.

—— *Towards an Islamic Reformation: Civil Liberties, Human Rights and International Law* (New York: Syracuse University Press, 1990).

—— 'Problems of Universal Cultural Legitimacy for Human Rights', in An-Na'im, A. A., and Deng, F. M., (eds.) *Human Rights in Africa: Cross-Cultural Perspectives* (Washington DC: The Brookings Institution, 1990) 331.

—— 'Towards a Cross-Cultural Approach to Defining International Standards of Human Rights: The Meaning of Cruel, Inhuman or Degrading Treatment or Punishment', in An-Na'im, A. A. (ed.) *Human Rights in Cross-Cultural Perspectives: A Quest for Consensus* (Philadelphia: University of Pennsylvania Press, 1992) 19.

—— 'What Do We Mean By Universal?' (1994) *Index On Censorship,* September/October, 120.

—— 'Toward an Islamic Hermeneutics for Human Rights', in An-Nai'm, A. A. *et al.,* (eds.) *Human Rights and Religious Values: An Uneasy Relationship?* (Michigan: W. B. Eerdman's Pub. Co., 1995) 229.

—— 'Islamic Law and Human Rights Today' (1996) 10 *Interights Bulletin,* No.1, 3.

—— 'The Position of Islamic States Regarding the Universal Declaration of Human Rights', in Baehr, P., *et al.,* (eds.) *Innovation and Inspiration: Fifty Years of the Universal Declaration of Human Rights* (Amsterdam: Royal Netherlands Academy of Arts and Sciences, 1999) 177.

—— 'Universality of Human Rights: An Islamic Perspective', in Ando, N., (ed.) *Japan and International Law: Past, Present and Future* (The Hague: Kluwer Academic Publishers, 1999) 311.

ANNAN, K., *Dialogue of Civilizations and the Need for a World Ethic* (Oxford: Oxford Centre for Islamic Studies, 1999).

ANSAY, T., and WALLACE, D., (eds.) *Introduction to Turkish Law* (The Hague: Kluwer Law International, 1996).

ANYAOKU, E., *Managing Diversity in Our Contemporary World* (Oxford: Oxford Centre for Islamic Studies, 1997).

APPIGNANESI, L., and MAITLAND, S., (eds.) *The Rushdie File* (Syracuse: Syracuse University Press, 1990).

ARAMBULO, K., *Strengthening the Supervision of the International Covenant on Economic, Social and Cultural Rights* (Antwerp: Intersentia, 1999).

ARZT, D.E., 'The Application of International Human Rights Law in Islamic States' (1990) 12 *Human Rights Quarterly,* 202.

ASAD, M., *The Principles of State and Government in Islam* (Gibraltar: Dar Al-Andalus, 1980).

EL-AWA, M. S., *Punishment in Islamic Law* (Indianapolis: American Trust Publications, 1982).

AWAD, A. M., 'The Rights of the Accused under Islamic Criminal Procedure', in Bassiouni, M. C., (ed.) *The Islamic Criminal Justice System* (New York: Oceana Publications, 1982) 91.

AL-AWWA, M.S., 'The Basis of Islamic Penal Legislation' in Bassiouni, M.C., (ed.) *The Islamic Criminal Justice System* (New York: Oceana Publications, 1982) 127.

AZAD, G. M., *Judicial System of Islam* (Islamabad: Islamic Research Institute, 1987).

BADAWI, J., 'The Status of Woman in Islam' (1971) 8 *Al-Ittihad,* No. 2, September, 33.

BADAWI, J. A., *The Muslim Woman's Dress According to the Qur'an and Sunnah* (London: Ta Ha Publishers, n.d.).

BADERIN, M. A., 'The Evolution of Islamic Law of Nations and the Modern International Order: Universal Peace through Mutuality and Cooperation' (2000) 17 *The American Journal of Islamic Social Sciences,* No. 2, 57.

—— 'Establishing Areas of Common Ground between Islamic Law and International Human Rights' (2001) 5 *The International Journal of Human Rights,* No.2, 72–113.

BADERIN, M. A., 'A Macroscopic Analysis of the Practice of Muslim States Parties to International Human Rights Treaties: Conflict or Congruence?' (2001) 1 *Human Rights Law Review*, No.2, 265–303.

—— 'Dialogue Among Civilisations as a Paradigm for Achieving Universalism in International Human Rights: A Case Study with Islamic Law' (2001) 2 *Asia-Pacific Journal of Human Rights and the Law*, No.2, 1–41.

Baha'i International Community, *Iran's Secret Blueprint for the Destruction of a Religious Community* (New York: Baha'i International Community, 1999).

BAHAR, S., 'Khomeinism, The Islamic Republic of Iran, and International Law: The Relevance of Islamic Political Ideology' (1992) 33 *Harvard International Law Journal*, No.1, 145.

EL-BAHNASSAWI, S., *Women between Islam and World Legislations* (Safat: Dar-ul-Qalam, 1985).

BANNERMAN, S., *Islam in Perspective: A Guide to Islamic Society, Politics and Law* (London: Routledge, 1988).

BARI, M. E., 'Human Rights in Islam with Special Reference to Women's Rights' (1994) 5 *Dhaka University Series*, No.1, Part F, 1.

BARR, J., *Fundamentalism* (London: SCM Press Ltd, 1981).

BASRI, G., *Nigeria and Shari'ah: Aspirations and Apprehensions* (Markfield: The Islamic Foundation, 1994).

BASSIOUNI, M. C., 'Sources of Islamic Law, and the Protection of Human Rights in the Islamic Criminal Justice System', in Bassiouni, M. C., (ed.) *The Islamic Criminal Justice System* (New York: Oceana Publications, 1982) 3.

BAUER, J. R., and BELL, D. A., (ed.) *The East Asian Challenge for Human Rights* (Cambridge: Cambridge University Press, 1999).

BAYEFSKY, A. F., 'The Principle of Equality or Non-Discrimination in International Law' (1990) 11 *Human Rights Law Journal*, 1.

BELLIOTTI, R., 'Do Dead Human Beings Have Rights?' (1979) 60 *Personalist*, 201.

BENN, S. I., *A Theory of Freedom* (Cambridge: Cambridge University Press, 1988).

BERKES, N., *The Development of Secularism in Turkey* (London: Hurst and Co, 1998).

BERLIN, I., *Four Essays on Liberty* (Oxford: Oxford University Press, 1979).

BERNARD, J., *American Family Behaviour* (New York: Harper and Brothers, 1942).

BIELEFELDT, H., 'Muslim Voices in the Human Rights Debate' (1995) 17 *Human Rights Quarterly*, 587.

BINDER, L., *Islamic Liberalism: A Critique of Development Ideologies* (Chicago: The University of Chicago Press, 1988).

BOBBIO, N., *The Age of Rights* (Cambridge: Polity Press, 1996).

BOKHARI, A. H., *The Protection of Human Rights in Islamic Republic of Pakistan with Special Reference to Islamic Shari'ah under 1973 Constitution* (University of Nottingham, PhD thesis, 1998).

BOROUJERDI, M., *Iranian Intellectuals and the West* (Syracuse: Syracuse University Press, 1996).

BOUTHAINA, S., 'The Muted Voices of Women Intepreters', in Afkhami, M., (ed.) *Faith and Freedom, Women's Human Rights in the Muslim World* (New York: I. B. Tauris Publishers, 1995) 61.

BREINER, B., 'A Christian View of Human Rights in Islam', in Breiner, B., (ed.) *Two Papers on Shari'ah* (Birmingham: Centre of Islam & Christian Relations, 1992) 1.

BROHI, A. K., 'Islam and Human Rights', in Gauher, A., (ed.) *The Challenge of Islam* (London: The Islamic Council of Europe, 1980) 179.

BUERGENTHAL, T., 'To Respect and to Ensure: State Obligations and Permissible Derogations', in Henkin, L., (ed.) *The International Bill of Rights: The Covenant on Civil and Political Rights* (New York: Columbia University Press, 1981) 72.

BULLOCH, J., *Reforms of the Saudi Arabian Constitution* (London: Gulf Centre for Strategic Studies, 1992).

BURGERS, H. J., 'The Function of Human Rights as Individual and Collective Rights', in Berting, J., *et al.*, (eds.) *Human Rights in a Pluralistic World: Individuals and Collectivities* (Westport: Meckler, 1990) 63.

BYRNES, A. C., 'The "Other" Human Rights Treaty Body: The Work of the Committee on the Elimination of Discrimination Against Women' (1989) 14 *Yale Journal of International Law*, No. 1, 53.

CARROLL, L., 'Rejoinder to the Proceedings of the Seminar on Adultery and Fornication in Islamic Jurisprudence: Dimensions and Perspectives' (1983) 3 *Islamic and Comparative Law Quarterly*, 66.

CASSESE, A., 'The Self-Determination of Peoples', in Henkin, L., (ed.) *The International Bill of Rights: The Covenant on Civil and Political Rights* (New York: Columbia University Press, 1981) 92.

—— *Human Rights in a Changing World* (Cambridge: Polity, 1990).

CHANDRA, M., *Human Rights and the New World Order* (Penang: Just World Trust, 1993).

CHAUDHRY, M. S., *Islam's Charter of Fundamental Rights and Civil Liberties* (Lahore: Al-Matbaat-ul-Arabia, 1995).

CHAUDRY, Z., 'The Myth of Misogyny: A Re-analysis of Women's Inheritance in Islamic Law' (1997) 61 *Albany Law Review*, 511.

CHEN, L., *An Introduction to Contemporary International Law* (New Haven: Yale University Press, 1989).

CHOWDHURY, N., 'What Pakistan Women Face', in Women Living Under Muslim Laws, (ed.) *Dossier No.1* (Grabels: Women Living Under Muslim Laws, 1986) 70.

CLAYTON, R., and TOMLINSON, H., *The Law of Human Rights* (Oxford: Oxford University Press, 2000) 2 Vols.

CLEVELAND, H., 'Introduction: The Chain Reaction of Human Rights', in Henkin, A. H., (ed.) *Human Dignity: The Internationalization of Human Rights* (New York: Aspen Institute for Humanistic Studies, 1979) ix.

COOK, R., 'Reservations to the Convention on the Elimination of All Forms of Discrimination Against Women', (1990) 30 *Virginia Journal of International Law*, 643.

COULSON, N. J., 'The State and the Individual in Islamic Law' (1957) 6 *International and Comparative Law Quarterly*, 49.

—— *A History of Islamic Law* (Edinburgh: Edinburgh University Press, 1964).

—— *Conflicts and Tension in Islamic Jurisprudence* (Chicago: University of Chicago Press, 1969).

CRANSTON, M., *What Are Human Rights?* (London: The Bodley Head Ltd, 1973).

CRAVEN, M. C. R., *The International Covenant on Economic, Social and Cultural Rights: A Perspective on its Development* (Oxford: Clarendon Press, 1995).

DALACOURA, K., *Islam, Liberalism and Human Rights* (London: I. B. Tauris, 1998).

D'AMATO, A. A., *Collected Papers, International Law Studies* (The Hague: Kluwer Law International, 1997) 2 Vols.

DAURA, A., 'A Brief Account of the Development of the Four Sunni Schools of Law and Some Recent Developments' (1968) 2 *Journal of Islamic and Comparative Law*, 1.

DAVID, R., and BRIERLEY, J. E. C., *Major Legal Systems of the World Today* (London: Stevens and Sons, 1985).

DETRICK, S., (ed.) *The United Nations Convention on the Right of the Child: A Guide to the Travaux Préparatoires* (Dordrecht: Martinus Nijhoff Publishers, 1992).

DICKINSON, J. C., *The Great Charter* (London: Historical Association, 1955).

DINSTEIN, Y., 'Collective Human Rights of Peoples and Minorities' (1976) 25 *International and Comparative Law Quarterly*, 102.

—— 'The Right to Life, Physical Integrity and Liberty', in Henkin, L., (ed.) *The International Bill of Rights: The Covenant on Civil and Political Rights* (New York: Columbia University Press, 1981) 114.

DOI, A. R., *Non-Muslims Under Shari'ah (Islamic Law)* (Brentwood: International Graphics, 1979).

—— *Shari'ah: The Islamic Law* (London: Ta Ha Publishers, 1984).

—— *Woman in Shari'ah* (London: Ta-Ha Publishers, 1987).

DONNELLY, J., 'Human Rights and Human Dignity: An Analytical Critique of the Non-Western Conceptions of Human Rights' (1982) 76 *American Political Science Review*, 303.

—— *The Concept of Human Rights* (London: Croom Helm, 1985).

—— *Universal Human Rights in Theory and Practice* (New York: Cornell University Press, 1989).

—— 'Human Rights and Western Liberalism', in An-Na'im, A. A., and Deng, F. M., (eds.) *Human Rights in Africa: Cultural Perspectives* (Washington DC: The Brookings Institute, 1990) 31.

DONOHUE, J. J., and ESPOSITO, J. L., *Islam in Transition: Muslim Perspectives* (Oxford: OUP, 1982).

DOUMATO, E. A., 'The Ambiguity of Shari'a and the Politics of Rights in Saudi Arabia', in Afkhami, M., (ed.) *Faith and Freedom, Women's Human Rights in the Muslim World* (New York: I. B. Tauris, 1995) 135.

DOUZINAS, C., *The End of Human Rights* (Oxford: Hart Publishing Co., 2000).

DOWRICK, F. E., (ed.) *Human Rights: Problems, Perspectives and Texts* (Farnborough, Hants: Saxon House, 1979).

DRZEWICKI, K., 'The Right to Work and Rights in Work', in Eide, A. *et al.*, (eds.) *Economic, Social and Cultural Rights: A Textbook* (Dordrecht: M. Nijhoff Publishers, 1995) 169.

DUDLEY, J., 'Human Rights Practices in the Arab States: The Modern Impact of Shari'a Values' (1982) 12 *GA Journal of International and Comparative Law*, 55.

DURANT, W., *The Story of Civilization* (New York: Simon and Schuster, 1939).

DWORKIN, G., *The Theory and Practice of Autonomy* (Cambridge: Cambridge University Press, 1988).

EATON, G., *Islam and the Destiny of Man* (Cambridge: The Islamic Texts Society, 1994).

EATON, H. G., *The Keys to the Kingdom* (London, 1977).

EIDE, A., 'The Right to an Adequate Standard of Living Including the Right to Food', in Eide, A., *et al.*, (eds.) *Economic, Social and Cultural Rights: A Textbook* (Dordrecht: M. Nijhoff, 1995) 89.

—— 'Cultural Rights as Individual Rights', in Eide, A. *et al.*, (eds.) *Economic, Social and Cultural Rights: A Textbook* (Dordrecht: M. Nijhoff, 1995) 229.

—— and ROSAS, A., 'Economic, Social and Cultural Rights: A Universal Challenge', in Eide, A. *et al.*, (eds.) *Economic, Social and Cultural Rights: A Textbook* (Dordrecht: M. Nijhoff Publishers, 1995) 27.

ENGLE, K., 'From Skepticism to Embrace: Human Rights and the American Anthropological Association from 1947–1999' (2001) 23 *Human Rights Quarterly*, No.3, 536–559.

ENTELIS, J. P., 'Tunisia', in Esposito, J.L., (ed.) *The Oxford Encyclopaedia of the Modern Islamic World* (Oxford: Oxford University Press, 1995) Vol. 4, 235.

ERMACORA, F., NOWAK, M., and TRETTER, H., (eds.) *International Human Rights: Documents and Introductory Notes* (Vienna: Law Books in Europe, 1993).

ESPOSITO, J. L., *Women in Muslim Family Law* (Syracuse: Syracuse University Press, 1982).

—— 'Contemporary Islam: Reformation or Revolution', in Esposito, J.L., (ed.) *The Oxford History of Islam* (Oxford: Oxford University Press, 1999) 643.

EZEJIOFOR, G., *Protection of Human Rights under Law* (London: Butterworth, 1964).

FARUKI, K. A., *Evolution of Islamic Constitutional Theory and Practice* (Karachi: National Publishing House, 1971).

AL-FARUQI, I. R., and AL-FARUQI, L. L., *The Cultural Atlas of Islam* (New York: Macmillan, 1986).

AL-FARUQI, L., *Women, Muslim Society and Islam* (Indianapolis: American Trust Publications, 1988).

FAZLUL-KARIM, A. A., *Al-Hadis: An English Translation and Commentary of Miskat-ul-Masabih with Arabic Text* (New Delhi: Islamic Book Service, 3rd edn, 1994) 4 Vols.

Federation of Student Islamic Societies, *Essays on Islam* (Markfield: The Islamic Foundation, 1995).

FEINBERG, R., *The Equal Rights Amendment: An Annotated Bibliography of the Issues* (Westport: Greenwood Press, 1986).

FREAMON, B.K., 'Slavery, Freedom, and the Doctrine of Consensus in Islamic Jurisprudence' (1998) 11 *Harvard Human Rights Journal*, 1.

FYZEE, A. A. A., *Outlines of Muhammadan Law* (London: Oxford University Press, 4th edn, 1974).

GAUDEFROY-DEMOMBYNES, M., *Muslim Institutions*, MacGregor, J. P., (trans.) (London: George Allen and Unwin Ltd, 1950).

GAUS, G. F., *Value and Justification: The Foundations of Liberal Theory* (Cambridge: Cambridge University Press, 1990).

GAUS, G. F., *Justificatory Liberalism: An Essay on Epistemology and Political Theory* (New York: Oxford University Press, 1996).

—— 'Liberalism', in Zalta, E. N., (ed.) *Stanford Encyclopaedia of Philosophy* (Online: http://plato.stanford.edu [1/3/2003]).

GHAI, Y., 'Human Rights and Governance: The Asia Debate', (1994) 15 *Australian Yearbook of International Law*, 11.

GHANDHI, P. R., *The Human Rights Committee and the Right of Individual Communication: Law and Practice* (Aldershot: Ashgate Publishing Ltd, 1998).

AL-GHUNAIMI, M. T., *The Muslim Conception of International Law and the Western Approach* (The Hague: Nijhoff, 1968).

GIBB, H. A. R., and BOWEN, H., *Islamic Society and the West* (London: Oxford University Press, 1957).

GORDON, C. N., 'The Islamic Legal Revolution: The Case of Sudan' (1985) 19 *International Lawyer*, 793.

GREEN, T. H., *Lectures on the Principles of Political Obligation and Other Essays*, Harris, P., and Morrow, J., (eds.) (Cambridge: Cambridge University Press, 1986).

HALLAQ, W., 'Was the Gate of Ijtihad Closed?', in Hallaq, W., (ed.) *Law and Legal Theory in Classical and Medieval Islam* (Aldershot: Variorum, 1995) Chapter V, 3.

—— *A History of Islamic Legal Theories* (Cambridge: Cambridge University Press, 1997).

HALLIDAY, F., 'Relativism and Universalism in Human Rights: The Case of the Islamic Middle East', in Beetham, D., (ed.) *Politics and Human Rights* (Oxford: Blackwell, 1995) 152.

HAMDI, M. E., *An Analysis of the History and Discourse of the Tunisian Islamic Movement, Al-Nahda* (University of London: PhD Thesis, 1996).

HAMIDULLAH, M., *The Muslim Conduct of State* (Lahore: Sh. Muhammad Ashraf, revised 7th edn, 1977).

—— *The First Written Constitution in the World* (Lahore: Ashraf Printing Press, 1981).

—— *Introduction to Islam* (Qum: Ansariyan Publication, 1982).

HANNUM, H., 'The Status of the Universal Declaration of Human Rights in National and International Law' (1995–96) 25 *Georgia Journal of International and Comparative Law*, Nos. 1&2, 287.

HARRIS, D. J., and JOSEPH, S., (eds.) *The International Covenant on Civil and Political Rights and United Kingdom Law* (Oxford: Clarendon Press, 1995).

—— O'BOYLE, M., and WARBRICK, C., *Law of the European Convention on Human Rights* (London: Butterworth, 1995).

—— *Cases and Materials on International Law* (London: Sweet and Maxwell, 5th edn, 1998).

HART, H. L. A., *The Concept of Law*. Bulloch, P. A., and Raz, J., (eds.) (Oxford: Clarendon Press, 2nd edn, 1994).

Harvard University, *Human Rights at Harvard*, Second Symposium, 5 April 1997.

HASAN, A., *Principles of Islamic Jurisprudence* (Islamabad: Islamic Research Institute, 1993).

HASHMI, S. H., 'Self-Determination and Secession in Islamic Thought', in Sellers, M., (ed.) *The New World Order: Sovereignty, Human Rights and the Self-Determination of Peoples* (Oxford: Berg, 1996) 117.

HASSAN, R., 'On Human Rights and the Qur'anic Perspective', in Swidler, A., (ed.) *Human Rights in Religious Traditions* (New York: Pilgrims Press, 1982) 51.

HAYEK, F. A., *The Mirage of Social Justice* (London: Routledge and Kegan Paul, 1976).

HAYKAL, M. H., *The Life of Muhammad* (London: Shorouk International, 1983).

HELFER, L. R., 'Consensus, Coherence and the European Convention of Human Rights' (1993) 26 *Cornell International Law Journal*, No.1, 133.

HENKIN, L., (ed.) *The International Bill of Rights: The Covenant on Civil and Political Rights* (New York: Columbia University Press, 1981).

HERSKOVITS, M., *Man and His Works* (New York: Alfred A. Knopf, 1950).

HIGGINS, R., 'Derogations under Human Rights Treaties' (1976/77) 48 *British Yearbook of International Law*, 281.

—— *Problems and Process, International Law and How We Use It* (Oxford: Clarendon Press, 1994).

—— 'The Continuing Universality of the Universal Declaration', in Baehr, P. *et al.*, (eds.) *Innovation and Inspiration: Fifty Years of the Universal Declaration of Human Rights* (Amsterdam: Royal Netherlands Academy of Arts and Sciences, 1999) 17.

HILL, E., 'Comparative and Historical Study of Modern Middle Eastern Law' (1978) 26 *The American Journal of Comparative Law*, 279.

—— 'Majlis al-Dawla: The Administrative Courts of Egypt and Administrative Law', in Mallat, C., (ed.) *Islam and Public Law: Classical and Contemporary Studies* (London: Graham and Trotman, 1993) 207.

HONARVER, N., 'Behind the Veil: Women's Rights in Islamic Societies' (1988) 6 *Journal of Law and Religion*, 355.

HOURANI, A., *Arabic Thought in the Liberal Age: 1798–1939* (Cambridge: Cambridge University Press, 1983).

Human Rights Watch, *New Islamic Penal Code Violates Basic Human Rights* (New York: Human Rights Watch, 1991).

—— *Empty Reforms, Saudi Arabia's New Basic Laws* (New York: Human Rights Watch, 1992).

—— *Sudan: 'In the name of God'* (New York: Human Rights Watch, 1994).

—— 'Forced Virginity Exams in Turkey', in Human Rights Watch, (ed.) *The Human Rights Watch Global Report on Women's Human Rights* (New York: Human Rights Watch, 1995) 418.

—— *Iran: Religious and Ethnic Minorities* (New York: Human Rights Watch, 1997).

HUMPHREY, J. P., 'The Magna Carta of Mankind', in Davies, P., (ed.) *Human Rights* (New York: Routledge, 1988) 21.

HUNTINGTON, S. P., *The Clash of Civilizations and the Remaking of World Order* (New York: Simon and Schuster, 1996).

HUREWITZ, J. C., (ed.) *The Middle East and North Africa in World Politics: A Documentary Record* (New Haven: Yale University Press, 1975) 2 Vols.

HUSSAIN, S. S., 'Human Rights in Islam: Principles and Precedents' (1983) 1 *Islamic and Contemporary Law Quarterly*, 103.

HUSSEIN, G. M., 'The Shura and Human Rights in Islamic Law', *Conference Paper at the Cairo Conference on Democracy and the Rule of Law*, 7–9 December 1997.

IBN KHALDÛN, *The Muqaddimah, An Introduction of History*. Rosenthal, F., (trans.) (London: Routledge and Kegan Paul, 1958) 3 Vols.

IBRAHIM, E., and JOHNSON-DAVIES, D., *Forty Hadith, An-Nawawi's* (Kuwait: International Islamic Federation of Students Organisations, 3rd edn, 1985).

International Commission of Jurists, *Human Rights in Islam; Report of Seminar held in Kuwait in December 1980* (Geneva: International Commission of Jurists, 1982).

IQBAL, JUSTICE J., 'The Concept of State in Islam', in Ahmad, M., (ed.) *State Politics and Islam* (Indianapolis: American Trust Publications, 1986) 37.

IQBAL, M., *The Reconstruction of Religious Thought in Islam* (Lahore: Muhammad Ashraf, 1968).

IRFANI, S., *Revolutionary Islam in Iran: Popular Liberation or Religious Dictatorship?* (London: Zed Books, 1983).

ISHAQUE, K. M., 'Human Rights in Islamic Law', (1974) 12 *Review of the International Commission of Jurists*, 30.

ISHAY, M. R., (ed.) *The Human Rights Reader: Major Political Essays, Speeches and Documents from the Bible to the Present* (London: Routledge, 1997).

ISRAEL, J., (ed.) *The State of the Union Messages of Presidents* (New York: Chelsea House, 1966) 3 Vols.

JAGERSKOILD, S., 'Freedom of Movement', in Henkin, L., (ed.) *The International Bill of Rights: The Covenant on Civil and Political Rights* (New York: Columbia University Press, 1981) 166.

JAHANGIR, A., 'How Far are Penal Laws Effective in Protecting Women', in Women Living Under Muslim Laws, (ed.) *Dossier No.3* (Grabels: Women Living Under Muslim Laws, 1988) 33.

JANIS, M. W., 'Religion and International Law' (1993) *American Society of International Law Proceedings*, 322.

JANSEN, J. G., *The Dual Nature of Islamic Fundamentalism* (London: Hurst and Co, 1997).

JEFFERY, A., 'The Family in Islam', in Anshen, R. N., (ed.) *The Family: Its Future and Destiny* (New York: Harper and Brothers, 1949) 39.

JONES, P., *Rights* (London: Macmillan, 1994).

JOSEPH, S., and LORD LESTER, 'Obligations of Non-discrimination' in Harris, D.J., and Joseph, S., (eds.) *The International Covenant on Civil and Political Rights and United Kingdom Law* (Oxford: Clarendon Press, 1995) 563.

JOSEPH, S., SCHULTZ, J., and CASTAN, M., (eds.) *The International Covenant on Civil and Political Rights: Cases, Materials and Commentary* (Oxford: Oxford University Press, 2000).

KAMALI, M. H., 'Have We Neglected the Shari'ah Law Doctrine of Maslahah?' (1988) 27 *Islamic Studies*, No. 4, 287.

—— 'Siyâsah Shar'îyah or the Policies of Islamic Government' (1989) 6 *The American Journal of Islamic Social Sciences,* No.1, 59.

—— *Principles of Islamic Jurisprudence* (Cambridge: Islamic Texts Society, 1991).

—— 'Fundamental Rights of the Individual: An Analysis of Haqq (Rights) in Islamic Law' (1993) 10 *American Journal of Islamic Social Sciences*, No.3, 340.

—— 'Appellate Review and Judicial Independence in Islamic Law', in Mallat, C., (ed.) *Islam and Public Law: Classical and Contemporary Studies* (London: Graham and Trotman, 1993) 49.

—— *Freedom of Expression in Islam* (London: Islamic Texts Society, 1997).

—— 'Law and Society: The Interplay of Revelation and Reason in the Shari'ah' in Esposito, J.L., (ed.) *The Oxford History of Islam* (Oxford: Oxford University Press, 1999) 107.

KAMEL, T., 'The Principle of Legality and its Application in Islamic Criminal Justice', in Bassiouni, M. C., (ed.) *The Islamic Criminal Justice System* (New York: Oceana Publishers, 1982) 149.

KAR, M., and HOODFAR, H., 'Personal Status Law as Defined by the Islamic Republic of Iran: An Appraisal', in Women Living Under Muslim Laws, (ed.) *Shifting Boundaries in Marriage and Divorce in Muslim Communities: Special Dossier* (Grabels: Women Living Under Muslim Laws, 1996) 7.

KEDDIE, N. R., *Iran and the Muslim World: Resistance and Revolution* (New York: New York University Press, 1995).

KELLY, P., 'Finding Common Ground: Islamic Values and Gender Equity in Tunisia's Reformed Personal Status Law', in Women Living Under Muslim Laws, (ed.) *Special Dossier: Shifting Boundaries in Marriage and Divorce in Muslim Communities* (Grabels: Women Living Under Muslim Laws, 1996) 75.

KELSEN, H., *Pure Theory of Law* (Gloucester, Mass: Peter Smith, 1967).

KERR, M., *Reform: The Political and Legal Theories of Muhammad Abduh and Rashid Rida* (Berkeley: University of California Press, 1966).

KHADDURI, M., *War and Peace in the Law of Islam* (Baltimore: Johns Hopkins University Press, 1955).

—— *The Islamic Law of Nations: Shaybani's Siyar* (Baltimore: The Johns Hopkins Press, 1966).

—— 'Marriage in Islamic Law: The Modernist Viewpoints' (1978) 26 *American Journal of Comparative Law*, 213.

KHADDURI, M., and LIESBESNY, H. J., (eds.) *Law in the Middle East* (Washington DC: Middle East Institute, 1955).

KHALIL, M. I., 'The Legal System of Sudan' (1971) 20 *International and Comparative Law Quarterly*, 626.

KHALIQ, U., 'Beyond the Veil?: An Analysis of the Provisions of the Women's Convention and the Law as Stipulated in Shari'ah' (1995) 2 *The Buffalo Journal of International Law*, 1.

KHAN, M. H., *Public Interest Litigation: Growth of the Concept and its Meaning in Pakistan* (Karachi: Pakistan Law House, 1993).

KHAN, M. M., *Sahih al-Bukhari–Arabic-English Edition* (Riyadh: Darrussalam Publishers, 1997) 9 Vols.

KIDWAI, A. R., and AHSAN, M. M., (eds.) *Sacrilege versus Civility: Muslim Perspectives on the Satanic Verses Affair* (Markfield: The Islamic Foundation, 1991).

KISS, A., 'The People's Right to Self-Determination' (1986) 7 *Human Rights Law Journal*, 165.

KUNG, H., and SCHMIDT, H., (eds.) *Global Ethic and Global Responsibility* (London: SCM Press, 1988).

KUSHALANI, Y., 'Human Rights in Asia and Africa' (1983) 4 *Human Rights Law Journal* No. 4, 404.

LAGOUTTE, A., and ARNASON, A. T., 'Article 16', in Alfredsson, G., and Eide, A., (eds.) *The Universal Declaration of Human Rights: A Common Standard of Achievement* (The Hague: M. Nijhoff Publishers, 1999) 324.

LAMBTON, A. K. S., *State and Government in Medieval Islam* (Oxford: Oxford University Press, 1981).

LAU, M., 'Islam and Judicial Activism: Public Interest Litigation and Environmental Protection in the Islamic Republic of Pakistan', in Boyle, A. E., and Anderson, M. R., (eds.) *Human Rights Approaches to Environmental Protection* (Oxford: Clarendon Press, 1996) 285.

—— 'Islamization of Laws in Pakistan and its Impact on the Independence of the Judiciary in Pakistan', *Conference Paper at The Cairo Conference on Democracy and the Rule of Law*, 7–9 December 1997.

LAUREN, P. G., *The Evolution of International Human Rights, Visions Seen* (Philadelphia: University of Pennsylvania Press, 1998).

LAURO, L. J., and SAMUELSON, P. A., 'Toward Pluralism in Sudan: A Traditional Approach' (1996) 1 *Harvard International Law Journal*, 65.

LAUTERPACHT, H., *An International Bill of Rights of Man* (New York: Columbia University Press, 1945).

Lawyers Committee for Human Rights, *Promise Unfulfilled: Human Rights in Tunisia Since 1987* (New York: Lawyers Committee for Human Rights, 1993).

—— *Beset by Contradictions: Islamization, Legal Reform and Human Rights in Sudan* (New York: Lawyers Committee for Human Rights, 1996).

—— *Islam and Justice* (New York: Lawyers Committee for Human Rights, 1997).

LEBLANC, L. J., 'Reservations to the Convention on the Rights of the Child: A Microscopic View of State Practice' (1996) 4 *International Journal of Children's Rights*, 357.

LEITES, J., 'Modernist Jurisprudence as a Vehicle for Gender Role Reform in the Islamic World' (1991) 22 *Columbia Human Rights Law Review*, 251.

LEVITT, M. A., 'The Taliban, Islam and Women's Rights in the Muslim World' (1998) 22 *The Fletcher Forum*, 113.

LIJNZAAD, L., *Reservations to UN–Human Rights Treaties: Ratify and Ruin?* (Dordrecht: M. Nijhoff, 1995).

LILLICH, R. B., 'The Growing Importance of Customary International Human Rights Law' (1995–96) 25 *Georgia Journal of International and Comparative Law*, Nos. 1 & 2, 1.

LIPPMAN, M., *et al.*, (eds.) *Islamic Criminal Law and Procedure: An Introduction* (New York: Praeger Publishers, 1988).

LITTLE, D., 'Religion: Catalyst or Impediment to International Law? The Case of Hugo Grotius' (1993) 87 *American Society of International Law Proceedings*, 322.

LITTLE, D., KELSAY, J., and SACHEDINA, A., *Human Rights and the Conflict of Cultures: Western and Islamic Perspectives of Religious Liberty* (Columbia: University of South Carolina Press, 1988).

LOCKE, J., *Two Treatises of Government*, Laslett, P., (ed.) (Cambridge: Cambridge University Press, 1967).

LONG, D. E., 'The Board of Grievances in Saudi Arabia' (1973) 27 *Middle East Journal*, 72.

LUCA, C., 'Discrimination in the Arab Middle East', in Veenhoven, W. A., (ed.) *Case Studies on Human Rights and Fundamental Freedoms: A World Survey* (The Hague: Nijhoff, 1975) Vol. 1, 113.

MACDONALD, ST. J. R., 'The Margin of Appreciation' in Macdonald, St. J. R. *et al.*, (eds.) *The European System for the Protection of Human Rights* (Dordrecht: Martinus Nijhoff, 1993) 83.

MAGNUSON, D. K., 'Islamic Reform in Contemporary Tunisia', in Zartman, I. W., (ed.) *The Political Economy of Reform* (Boulder: Lynne Rienner, 1991) 169.

MAHMOOD, T., 'The Islamic Law on Human Rights' (1984) 4 *Islamic and Comparative Law Quarterly*, 32.

—— *Statutes of Personal Law in Islamic Countries: History, Texts and Analysis* (Delhi, India: India and Islam Research Council, 2nd edn, 1995).

—— 'Freedom of Religion and Religious Minorities in Pakistan: A Study of Judicial Practice' (1995) 40 *Fordham International Law Journal*, 43.

—— 'Criminal Procedure at the Shari'ah Law as Seen by Modern Scholars: A Review', in Mahmood, T., *et al.*, (eds.) *Criminal Law in Islam and the Muslim World* (Delhi: Institute of Objective Studies, 1996) 292.

—— 'Legal System of Modern Libya: Enforcement of Islamic Penal Laws', in Mahmood, T., *et al.*, (eds.) *Criminal Law in Islam and the Muslim World* (Delhi: Institute of Objective Studies, 1996) 375.

MAHONEY, P., 'Judicial Activism and Judicial Self-Restraint in the European Court of Human Rights: Two Sides of the Same Coin' (1990) 11 *Human Rights Law Journal*, 57.

MAKDISI, G., *The Rise of Colleges: Institutions of Learning in Islam and the West* (Edinburgh: Edinburgh University Press, 1981).

MALEKIAN, F., *The Concept of Islamic International Criminal Law: A Comparative Study* (London: Graham and Trotman, 1994).

MANDELA, N., *Renewal and Renaissance: Towards a New World Order* (Oxford: Oxford Centre for Islamic Studies, 1997).

MANGLAPUS, R., 'Human Rights are not a Western Discovery' (1978) 4 *Worldview*, 4.

MANZOOR, P., 'Humanity Rights as Human Duties' (1987) *Inquiry*, July, 34.

—— 'Faith and Order: Reclaiming the Islamic Theory of Practice' (1990) 10 *The Muslim World Book Review*, No. 2, 3.

—— 'Human Rights: Secular Transcendence of Cultural Imperialism?' (1994) 15 *Muslim World Book Review*, No. 1, 3.

MARSDEN, G., *Fundamentalism and American Culture: The Shaping of Twentieth-Century Evangelicalism: 1870–1925* (Oxford: Oxford University Press, 1980).

MASUD, M. K., *Shatibi's Philosophy of Islamic Law* (Islamabad: Islamic Research Institute, 1995).

MAUDUDI, A. A., *Islamic Way of Life* (Kuwait: International Islamic Federation of Students Organizations, 1980).

—— *Human Rights in Islam* (Markfield: The Islamic Foundation, 1993).

MAUDUDI, A. A., *The Islamic Law and Constitution* (Lahore: Islamic Publications, 12th edn, 1997).

—— *Towards Understanding the Qur'an: English Version of Tafhim al-Qur'an.* Z. I. Ansari (trans.) (Markfield: The Islamic Foundation, 1998) 7 Vols.

MAYER, A. E., 'Current Muslim Thinking on Human Rights', in An-Na'im, A.A., and Deng, F. M., (eds.) *Human Rights in Africa: Cross-Cultural Perspectives: A Quest for Consensus* (Philadelphia: University of Pennsylvania Press, 1990) 131.

—— 'Islam and the State' (1991) 12 *Cardozo Law Review*, 1015.

—— 'A Critique of An-Na'im's Assessment of Islamic Criminal Justice', in Lindholm, L., (ed.) *Islamic Law Reform and Human Rights: Challenges and Rejoinders* (Oslo: Norwegian Institute of Human Rights, 1993) 37.

—— 'Universal versus Islamic Human Rights: A Clash of Cultures or a Clash with a Construct?' (1994) 15 *Michigan Journal of International Law*, 306.

—— 'Human Rights', in Esposito, J. L., (ed.) *The Oxford Encyclopaedia of the Modern Islamic World* (New York: Oxford University Press, 1995) 143.

—— 'Libyan Legislation in Defense of Arabo-Islamic Sexual Mores' in Mahmood, T., *et al.*, (eds.) *Criminal Law in Islam and the Muslim World* (Delhi: Institute of Objective Studies, 1996) 389.

—— 'Judicial Dismantling of Constitutional Protections for Religious Freedom: The Grim Legacy of Zaheeruddin v. State', *Conference Paper at the Cairo Conference on Democracy and the Rule of Law*, 7–9 December 1997.

——- *Islam and Human Rights: Tradition and Politics* (Boulder: Westview Press 3rd edn, 1999).

MCCARTHY, R., *The Theology of al-Ash'ari* (Beirut: Imprimatur Catholique, 1953).

MCCORQUODALE, R., 'Self-determination: A Human Rights Approach' (1994) 43 *International and Comparative Law Quarterly*, 857.

—— 'The Right of Self-determination' in Harris, D. J., and Joseph, S., (eds.) *The International Covenant on Civil and Political Rights and United Kingdom Law* (Oxford: Clarendon Press, 1995) 91.

MCGOLDRICK, D., *The Human Rights Committee: Its Role in the Development of the International Covenant on Civil and Political Rights* (Oxford: Clarendon Press, 1994).

MCKEAN, W., *Equality and Discrimination under International Law* (Oxford: Clarendon Press, 1983).

MEHDI, R., *The Islamization of the Law in Pakistan* (Richmond: Curzon Press, 1994).

MEHRDAD, A., 'Women in Iranian Civil Law: 1905–1995', in Women Living Under Muslim Laws, (ed.) *Dossier No.14/15* (Grabels: Women Living Under Muslim Laws, 1991) 86.

MERON, T., *Human Rights Law-Making in the United Nations: A Critique of Instruments and Process* (Oxford: Clarendon, 1986).

MILL, J. S., *J. S. Mill On Liberty: In Focus*, Gray, J., and Smith, G. W., (eds.) (London: Routledge, 1991).

MILNE, A. J. M., *Human Rights and Human Diversity* (New York: State University Press, 1986).

MIR-HOSSEINI, Z., 'The Delegated Right to Divorce: Law and Practice in Morocco and Iran', in Carroll, L., and Kapoor, H., (eds.) *Talaq-i-Tafwid: The Muslim Woman's*

Contractual Access to Divorce (Grabels: Women Living Under Muslim Laws, 1996) 121.

MOINUDDIN, H., *The Charter of the Islamic Conference and Legal Framework of Economic Co-operation among its Member States* (Oxford: Clarendon Press, 1987).

MONSHIPOURI, M., and KUKLA, C. G., 'Islam, Democracy, and Human Rights: The Continuing Debate in the West' (1994) 3 *Middle East Policy*, No.2, 22.

—— 'Islamic Thinking and the Internationalization of Human Rights' (1994) 84 *The Muslim World*, No.2–3, 217.

—— *Islamism, Secularism and Human Rights in the Middle East* (Boulder: L. Rienner Publishers, 1998).

—— 'The Muslim World Half A Century after the Universal Declaration of Human Rights: Progress and Obstacles' (1998) 16 *The Netherlands Quarterly of Human Rights*, No.3, 287.

MOORE, C. H., *Tunisia Since Independence: The Dynamics of One Party Government* (Berkeley: University of California Press, 1965).

MOORE, R. H., 'Courts, Law, Justice and Criminal Trials in Saudi Arabia' (1987) 11 *International Journal of Comparative and Applied Criminal Justice*, No.1, 61.

MORTIMER, E., 'Islam and Human Rights' (1983) 12 *Index on Censorship*, No.5, 5 October.

MOURAD, F.A., and AL-SA'ATY, H., 'Impact of Islamic Penal Law on Crime Situation in Saudi Arabia: Findings of A Research Study', in Mahmood, T., *et al.*, (eds.) *Criminal Law in Islam and the Muslim World* (Delhi: Institute of Objective Studies, 1996) 340.

MUHAMMAD, HON. JUSTICE U., 'Shari'ah and the Western Common Law: A Comparative Analysis', in Abdul-Rahman, M. O., (ed.) *Thoughts in Islamic Law and Ethics* (Ibadan: University of Ibadan Muslim Graduates Association, 1992) 16.

MUHSIN KHAN, M., and TAQI-UD-DIN AL-HILALI, M., *Interpretation of the Meanings of the Noble Qur'an in the English Language: A Summarized Version of At-Tabari, Al-Qurtubi and Ibn Kathir with Comments from Sahih Al-Bukhari* (Riyadh: Darussalam Publishers, 1996).

MUSALLAM, B. F., *Sex and Society in Islam: Birth Control Before the Nineteenth Century* (Cambridge: Cambridge University Press 1986).

MUTUA, M., 'The Ideology of Human Rights' (1996) 36 *Virginia Journal of International Law*, 589.

NANDA, V. P., 'Islam and International Human Rights Law: Selected Aspects' (1993) 87 *American Society of International Law Proceedings*, 327.

NARVESON, J., *The Libertarian Idea* (Philadelphia: Temple University Press, 1988).

NASIR, J. J., *The Islamic Law of Personal Status* (London: Graham & Trotman, 1990).

NASIR, S. V. R., 'European Colonialism and the Emergence of Modern Muslim States', in Esposito, J.L., (ed.) *The Oxford History of Islam* (Oxford: Oxford University Press, 1999) 549.

NINO, C. S., *The Ethics of Human Rights* (Oxford: Clarendon Press, 1991).

NOOR MUHAMMAD, N. A., 'Due Process of Law for Person Accused of a Crime', in Henkin, L., (ed.) *The International Bill of Rights: The Covenant on Civil and Political Rights* (New York: Columbia University Press, 1981) 155.

Nowak, M., *Commentary on the UN Covenant on Civil and Political Rights* (Strasbourg: N.P. Engel, 1993).

Nyazee, I. A. K., *Theories of Islamic Law* (Islamabad: Islamic Research Institute and International Institute of Islamic Thought, n.d.).

—— *Outlines of Islamic Jurisprudence* (Advanced Legal Study Institute, 2000).

—— (trans.) *The Distinguished Jurists Premier: Bidâyat al-Mujtahid wa Nihâyat al-Muqtasid Ibn Rushd* (Reading: Garnet Publishing Ltd, 2000) 2 Vols.

Obilade, O. A., *The Nigerian Legal System* (London: Sweet & Maxwell, 1979).

O'Boyle, M., 'Torture and Emergency Powers under the European Convention on Human Rights: Ireland v. The United Kingdom' (1977) 71 *American Journal of International Law*, 674.

Ockley, S., (trans.) *The History of Hayy ibn Yaqzan* (London: Darf, 1986).

Omran, A. R., *Family Planning in the Legacy of Islam* (London: Routledge, 1992).

Paine, T., *Rights of Man, With An Introduction by Eric Foner* (New York: Penguin Books, 1984).

Park, A. E. W., *The Sources of Nigerian Law* (Lagos: AUP Press, 1963).

Partsch, K. J., 'Freedom of Conscience and Expression, and Political Freedoms', in Henkin, L., (ed.) *The International Bill of Rights: The Covenant on Civil and Political Rights* (New York: Columbia University Press, 1981) 207.

Patel, R., *Islamization of Laws in Pakistan* (Karachi: Faiza Publishers, 1986).

Pearl, D., and Menski, W., *Muslim Family Law* (London: Sweet & Maxwell, 1998).

Pechota, V., 'The Development of the Covenant on Civil and Political Rights', in Henkin, L., (ed.) *The International Bill of Rights: The Covenant on Civil and Political Rights* (New York: Columbia University Press, 1981) 32.

Philips, A. A. B., *The Evolution of Fiqh* (Riyadh: International Islamic Publishing House, 1988).

Piscatori, J., 'Human Rights in Islamic Political Culture', in Thompson, K., (ed.) *The Moral Imperatives of Human Rights: A World Survey* (Washington: University Press of America, 1980) 139.

Popper, K., *The Open Society and Its Enemies* (London: Routledge and Kegan Paul, 1945) 2 Vols.

Pope, N., and Pope, H., *Turkey Unveiled: Ataturk and After* (London: John Murray, 1997).

Powers, D. S., 'The Islamic Inheritance System: A Socio-Historical Approach', in Mallat, C., and Connors, J., (eds.) *Islamic Family Law* (London: Graham & Trotman, 1990) 546.

Qadri, A. A., *Justice in Historical Islam* (Lahore: Sh. Muhammad Ashraf, 1968).

—— *Islamic Jurisprudence in the Modern World* (New Delhi: Taj Company, 1986).

al-Qaradawi, Y., *The Lawful and the Prohibited in Islam* (Kuwait: International Islamic Federation of Students Organisations, 1984).

—— *Non Muslims in the Islamic Society*. Hamad, K.M., and Shah, M.A., (trans.) (American Trust Publishers, 1985).

—— *Islamic Awakening Between Rejection and Extremism* (New Delhi: Qazi Publishers, 1990).

Quraishi, A., 'Book Review of Islamism, Secularism and Human Rights in the Middle East By Mahmood Monshipouri' (2000) 22 *Human Rights Quarterly*, 625.

QUTB, M., *Islam the Misunderstood Religion* (Dacca: Adhunik Prokashani, 1978).

RAHMAN, A., *Readings in Philosophy, Vol.1 Liberty* (London: Seerah Foundation, 1987).

RAHMAN, F., 'Status of Women in the Qur'an', in Nashat, G., (ed.) *Women and Revolution in Iran* (Boulder: Westview Press, 1983).

RAHMAN, S. A., *Punishment of Apostasy in Islam* (Lahore: Institute of Islamic Culture, 1972).

RAJAEE, F., *Islamic Values and World View: Khomeyni on Man, the State and International Politics* (London: University Press of America, 1983).

RAMADAN, S., *Islamic Law: Its Scope and Equity* (London: Macmillan, 1970).

RAMCHARAN, B. G., 'Equality and Non-Discrimination', in Henkin, L., (ed.) *The International Bill of Rights: The Covenant on Civil and Political Rights* (New York: Columbia University Press, 1981) 247.

—— 'The Right to Life' (1983) 30 *Netherlands International Law Review*, 297.

RAZ, J., *The Morality of Freedom* (Oxford: Clarendon Press, 1986).

RENTELN, A. D., *International Human Rights: Universalism versus Relativism* (California: SAGE Publishers Inc., 1990).

RIZVI, S. A. H., *et al.*, 'Adultery and Fornication in Islamic Criminal law: A Debate' in Mahmood, T., (ed.) *Criminal Law in Islam and the Muslim World* (Delhi: Institute of Objective Studies, 1996) 223.

ROBERTSON, A. H., 'The United Nations Covenant on Civil and Political Rights and the European Convention on Human Rights' (1968–69) 43 *British Yearbook of International Law*, 21.

ROBERTSON, B. A., 'Islam and Europe: An Enigma or a Myth?' (1994) 48 *Middle East Journal*, No.2, 288.

ROSENBAUM, A., (ed.) *The Philosophy of Human Rights, International Perspectives* (London: Aldwych Press, 1980).

ROUSSEAU, J., *The Social Contract and Discourses*, G. D. H. Cole (trans.) (London: Dent, 1913).

SACHEDINA, A. A., 'Freedom of Conscience and Religion in the Qur'an', in Little, D., Kelsay, J., and Sachedina, A., (eds.) *Human Rights and the Conflict of Cultures: Western and Islamic Perspectives on Religious Liberty* (Columbia: University of South Carolina Press, 1988) 53.

—— 'Review of Abdullahi Ahmed An-Na'im, Towards an Islamic Reformation: Civil Liberties, Human Rights and International Law' (1993) 25 *International Journal of Middle East Studies*, 155.

SAFWAT, S. M., 'Offences and Penalties in Islamic Law' (1982) 26 *Islamic Quarterly*, 169.

SAID, A. A., 'Precepts and Practice of Human Rights in Islam' (1979) 1 *Universal Human Rights*, No.1, 63.

SAID, E. W., *Orientalism, Western Conceptions of the Orient* (London: Penguin Books Ltd, 1978).

SAID, M. E., 'Islam and Human Rights' (1997) *Rowaq Arabi*, January, 11.

SALAMA, M. M., 'General Principles of Criminal Evidence in Islamic Jurisprudence', in Bassiouni, M. C., (ed.) *The Islamic Criminal Justice System* (New York: Oceana Publishers, 1982) 113.

AL-SALEH, O. A., 'The Rights of the Individual to Personal Security in Islam', in Bassiouni, M. C., (ed.) *The Islamic Criminal Justice System* (New York: Oceana Publications, 1982) 72.

SALEM, N., *Habib Bourguiba, Islam and the Creation of Tunisia* (London: Croom Helm, 1984).

SAUD, M., *Islam and Evolution of Science* (Islamabad: Islamic Research Institute, 1994).

Saudi Arabian Ministry of Foreign Affairs, *Protection of Human Rights in Criminal Procedure and in the Organization of the Judicial System* (2000). Online at: http://www.saudiembassy.net/press_release/hr-judicial-1-menu.html [1/3/2003].

Saudi Arabian Ministry of Justice, *Conference of Riyad on Moslem Doctrine and Human Rights in Islam, 23 March 1972.* Available Online at: http://www.saudiembassy.net/press_release/hr-72.html [1/3/2003].

AL-SAYYID, R., 'Contemporary Muslim Thought and Human Rights' (1995) 21 *Islamochristiana*, 27.

SCHACHT, J., 'Islamic Law and Contemporary States' (1959) 8 *American Journal of Contemporary Law*, 133.

—— *Introduction to Islamic Law* (Oxford: Clarendon Press, 1964).

SCHEININ, M., 'The Right to Social Security', in Eide, A., *et al.*, (eds.) *Economic, Social and Cultural Rights: A Textbook* (Dordrecht: M. Nijhoff, 1995) 59.

SCHMIDT, M. G., 'The Complementarity of the Covenant and the European Convention on Human Rights–Recent Developments', in Harris, D.J., and Joseph, S., (eds.) *The International Covenant of Civil and Political Rights and United Kingdom Law* (Oxford: Clarendon Press, 1995) 629.

SCIOLINO, E., 'The Many Faces of Islamic Law', *The New York Times*, 13 October 1996. Editorial, 2.

SELF, J., 'Bowers v. Hardwick: A Study of Aggression' (1988) 10 *Human Rights Quarterly*, 395.

SHAH, JUSTICE N. H., *Islamization of Law in Pakistan* (Islamabad: Shariah Academy, 1992).

—— *The Objective Resolution and its Impact on the Administration of Justice in Pakistan* (Islamabad: Shariah Academy, 1992).

SHESTACK, J. J., 'The Jurisprudence of Human Rights', in Meron, T., (ed.) *Human Rights in International Law: Legal and Policy Issues* (Oxford: Clarendon Press, 1984) 69.

SHUE, H., *Basic Rights: Subsistence, Affluence, and U.S. Foreign Policy* (Princeton, N.J: Princeton University Press, 2nd edn, 1996).

SIDDIQUI, A., (ed.) *Ismail Raji al-Faruqi, Islam and Other Faiths* (Markfield: The Islamic Foundation/IIIT, 1998).

SIEGHART, P., *The Lawful Rights of Mankind: An Introduction to the International Legal Code of Human Rights* (Oxford: Oxford University Press, 1985).

SIEGMAN, H., 'The State and the Individual in Sunni Islam' (1964) 54 *The Muslim World*, 14.

SMITH, J., (ed.) *Human Rights: Chinese and Dutch Perspectives* (The Hague: M. Nijhoff, 1996).

Sohn, L. B., 'A Short History of United Nations Documents on Human Rights' in UN, *United Nations and Human Rights* (18th Report of the Commission to Study the Organization of Peace, 1968).

—— 'The Rights of Minorities', in Henkin, L., (ed.) *The International Bill of Rights: The Covenant on Civil and Political Rights* (New York: Columbia University Press, 1981) 270.

—— 'The New International Law: Protection of the Rights of Individuals Rather than States' (1982) 32 *American University Law Journal*, 1.

Stavenhagen, R., 'Cultural Rights and Universal Human Rights' in Eide, A., *et al.*, (eds.) *Economic Social and Cultural Rights: A Textbook* (Dordrecht: M. Nijhoff, 1995) 63.

Steiner, H., 'Political Power as a Human Right' (1988) 1 *Harvard Human Rights Yearbook*, 77.

——, and Alston, P., *International Human Rights in Context: Law, Politics, Morals* (Oxford: Oxford University Press, 2nd edn, 2000).

Stowasser, B. F., *Women in the Qur'an, Traditions and Interpretations* (New York: Oxford University Press, 1994).

Strawson, J., 'Encountering Islamic Law', *University of East London Law Department Research Publication Series*, No. 1.

Szabo, I., 'Historical Foundations of Human Rights and Subsequent Developments', in Vasak, K., (ed.) *The International Dimensions of Human Rights* (Westport: Greenwood Press, 1982) Vol.1, 11.

Tabandeh, S., *Muslim Commentary on the Universal Declaration of Human Rights*, Goulding, F., (trans.) (Guildford: F.J. Goulding, 1970).

Tamimi, A., (ed.) *Power Sharing Islam?* (London: Liberty for Muslim World Publications, 1993).

Tanzil-ur-Rahman, *A Code of Muslim Personal Law* (Karachi, Pakistan: Hamdard Academy, 1978) 2 Vols.

—— *Objectives Resolution and its Impact on Pakistan Constitutional Law* (Karachi: Royal Book, 1996).

Tash, A. Q., 'Islamaphobia in the West' (1996) *Washington Report on Middle East Affairs*, November/December, 28.

Thompson, C. F., 'A Case Study from the Republic of Sudan' (1966) *Wisconsin Law Review*, 1149.

Thompson, K. W., (ed.) *The Moral Imperatives of Human Rights: A World Survey* (Washington, DC: University Press of America, 1980).

Thornton, B., 'The New International Jurisprudence on the Right to Privacy: A Head-on Collision with Bowers v. Hardwick' (1995) 58 *Albany Law Review*, 725.

Tibi, B., 'Islamic Law/Shari'a and Human Rights: International Law and International Relations', in Lindholm, T., and Vogt, K., (eds.) *Islamic Law Reform and Human Rights: Challenges and Rejoinders* (Oslo, Norway: Norwegian Institute of Human Rights, 1993) 75.

Tolley, H., *The UN Commission on Human Rights* (London: Westview Press, 1987).

Toynbee, A. J., *Survey of International Affairs* (London: Oxford University Press, 1938).

TROLL, C. W., 'Book Review of Islam and Human Rights: Traditions and Politics By Ann Elizabeth Mayer' (1992) 3 *Islam and Christian-Muslim Relations*, No.1, 131.

TYAN, E., 'Judicial Organisation', in Khadduri, M., and Liebesny, H.J., (eds.) *Law in the Middle East* (Washington DC: Middle East Institute, 1955).

UMOZURIKE, U. O., *The African Charter on Human and Peoples' Rights* (The Hague: M. Nijhoff, 1997).

UN Centre for Human Rights, *Right to Adequate Food as a Human Right* (New York: United Nations, 1989).

University of Sussex, 'Islamophobia' in *BULLETIN, University of Sussex Newsletter*, 7th November 1997, 16. Available online at: http://www.sussex.ac.uk/press_office/bulletin/07nov97/item12.html [1/3/2003].

VAN BUEREN, G., *The International Law on the Rights of the Child* (Dordrecht: M. Nijhoff Publishers, 1995).

VANHOOF, G. J. H., 'The Legal Nature of Economic, Social and Cultural Rights: A Rebuttal of Some Traditional Views', in Alston, P., and Tomasevski, K., (eds.) *The Right to Food* (Utrecht: Stichting Studie-Informatiecentrum Mensenrechten, 1984) 97.

VASAK, K., 'For the Third Generation of Human Rights; The Right of Solidarity'. Paper Delivered at the 10th Study Session of the International Institute of Human Rights, Strasbourg, France, 2–27 July, 1979.

VIERDEG, E. W., 'The Legal Nature of the Rights Granted by the ICESCR (1978) 9 *Netherlands Yearbook of International Law*, 69.

VINCENT, R. J., *Human Rights and International Relations I* (Cambridge: Cambridge University Press, 1986).

VOLIO, F., 'Legal Personality, Privacy and Family Life', in Henkin, L., (ed.) *The International Bill of Rights: The Covenant on Civil and Political Rights* (New York: Columbia University Press, 1981) 185.

WALDRON, J., *Liberal Rights: Collected Papers, 1981–1991* (Cambridge: Cambridge University Press, 1993).

WALKER, J. K., 'The Rights of the Accused in Saudi Criminal Procedure' (1993) *Loyola L.A. International and Comparative Law Journal*, 863.

WAQAR-UL-HAQ, M., *Islamic Criminal Laws (Hudood Laws and Rules) with Up-to-date Commentary* (Lahore: Nadeem Law Book House, 1994).

WATSON, J. S., *Theory and Reality in the International Protection of Human Rights* (Ardsley, NY: Transnational Publishers, 1999).

WATT, W. M., *Islamic Political Thought* (Edinburgh: Edinburgh University Press, 1980).

WEERAMANTRY, C. G., *Islamic Jurisprudence: An International Perspective* (Basingstoke: Macmillan, 1988).

—— *Justice Without Frontiers: Furthering Human Rights* (The Hague: Kluwer Law International, 1997) 2 Vols.

WESTON, B., 'Human Rights' in *New Encyclopaedia Britannica*, 15th edn, Vol. 20, 713.

WINSTON, M. E., (ed.) *The Philosophy of Human Rights* (California: Wadsworth Publishing Co., 1989).

Women Living Under Muslim Laws, 'Women Struggle Against Zia's Version of Islam', in Women Living Under Muslim Laws, (ed.) *Dossier No.1* (Grabels: Women Living Under Muslim Laws, 1986) 62.

WONG, W. M., 'The Sunday Times Case: Freedom of Expression Versus English Contempt-of-Court Law in the European Court of Human Rights' (1984) 17 *New York University Journal of International Law and Politics*, 35.

WYNN, L., 'Marriage Contracts and Women's Rights in Saudi Arabia', in Women Living Under Muslim Laws, (ed.) *Special Dossier: Shifting Boundaries in Marriage and Divorce in Muslim Communities* (Grabels: Women Living Under Muslim Laws, 1996) 106.

YAMANI, A. Z., 'The Exteral Shari'a' (1979) 12 *New York University Journal of International Law and Politics*, 205.

YAMANI, M., 'Muslim Women and Human Rights: The New Generation', Conference Paper at the Cairo Conference on Democracy and the Rule of Law, 7–9 December 1997.

YATE, A., (trans.) *al-Ahkam as-Sultaniyyah: The Laws of Islamic Governance* (London: Ta Ha Publishers, 1966).

YOUNG, M. J. L., *et al.*, (eds.) *Religion, Learning and Science in the 'Abbasid Period* (Cambridge: Cambridge University Press, 1990).

YOUROW, H. C., *The Margin of Appreciation Doctrine in the Dynamics of European Human Rights Jurisprudence* (Dordrecht: M. Nijhoff, 1996).

ZAFAR, E., *The Constitution of the Islamic Republic of Pakistan 1973 with Commentary* (Lahore: Irfan, n.d.) 2 Vols.

ZAIDAN, A. K., *Individual and the State in Islamic Law* (Kuwait: International Islamic Federation of Students Organizations, 1982).

ZAKZOUK, M., 'Cultural Relations between the West and the World of Islam: Meeting Points and Possibilities of Co-operation on the Academic Level' (1992) 3 *Islam and Christian-Muslim Relations*, No. 1, 69.

ZARABOSO, M. A., (trans.) *Islamic Fatawa Regarding Women* (Riyadh: Darussalam, 1996).

ZEARFOSS, S., 'The Convention for the Elimination of All Forms of Discrimination Against Women: Radical, Reasonable, or Reactionary?' (1991) 12 *Michigan Journal of International Law*, 905.

ZELDICH, M., 'Family, Marriage and Kinship', in Faris, R. E. L., (ed.) *Handbook of Modern Sociology* (Chicago: Rand McNally, 1964) 680.

ZULLAH, JUSTICE A., 'Human Rights in Pakistan' (1992) 3 *Commonwealth Law Bulletin*, 1343.

ARABIC LANGUAGE SOURCES

ABDUH, M., and RIDÂ, M., *Tafsîr al-Manâr* (Cairo: Dâr al-Manâr, 1947–48).

ABÛ-YÛSUF, Y., *Kitâb al-Kharâj* (Cairo: al-Matba'ah al-Salafiyyah, 1352AH).

ABÛ-ZAHRAH, M., *Tanzîm al-Islâm li al-Mujtama'a* (Cairo: Matba'ah Mukhaymar, n.d.).

ABÛ-ZAHRAH, M., *Usûl al-Fiqh* (Cairo: Dâr al-Fikr al-Arabî, 1958).

—— *al-Jarîmah wa al-Uqûbah fî al-Fiqh al-Islâmî* (Cairo: Dâr al-Fikr al-Arabî, n.d.).

ABÛ-ZAYD, M., *al-Nâsikh wa al-Mansûkh: Dirâsah Tashrî'iyyah Ta'rîkhiyyah Naqdiyyah* (Cairo: Dâr al-Fikr al-'Arabî, 1963).

AL-ALIM, Y.H., *al-Maqâsid al-Âmah li al-Sharî'ah al-Islamiyyah* (Herndon: International Institute of Islamic Thought, 1991).

AL-AMIDÎ, S., *al-Ihkâm fî Usûl al-Ahkâm* (Beirut: al-Maktabah al-Islâmî, 1402AH) 4 Vols.

AL-BALÂDHURÎ, *Futûh al-Buldân*. al-Munajjid, S., (ed.) (Cairo: Maktabah al-Nahdah al-Misriyyah, 1956–57) 3 Vols.

AL-BAYHÂQÎ, A. A., *Kitâb al-Sunan al-Kubrâ* (Hyderabad: Matba'ah Majlis Dâirah, 1925).

AL-DAWÂLÎBÎ, M.M., *Nadwah Ilmiyyah Hawl al-Sharî'ah al-Islâmiyyah wa Huqûq al-Insân fî al-Islâm* (Riyadh: Tanfîdh Matâbi' al-Asr, n.d.).

AL-DIMASHQÎ, A. A., *Rahmah al-Ummah fî Ikhtilâf al-A'immah* (Beirut: D al-Kutub al Ilmiyyah, 1995).

AL-GANÛSHÎ, R., *al-Huriyât al-Âmah fî al-Dawlah al-Islâmiyyah* (Beirut: Markaz Dirâsât al-Wahdah al-Arabiyyah, 1993).

AL-GHAZÂLÎ, A. M., *al-Mustasfâ fî Ilm al-Usûl* (Cairo: Maktabah al-Tijâriyyah, 1356AH) 2 Vols.

—— *Ihyâ' 'Ulûm al-Dîn* (Beirut: Dâr al-Qalam, n.d.) 5 Vols.

AL-GHAZÂLÎ, M., *Huqûq al-Insân Bayn T'alîm al-Islâm wa I'lân al-Umam al-Muttahidah* (Alexandria: Dâr al-Da'wah, 1993).

HUSAYN, M. H., *Naqd Kitâb al-Islâm wa Usûl al-Hukm* (Tunis: Maktabah al-Zaytûniyyah, 1925).

IBN ABIDÎN, M. A., *Radd al-Muhtar* (Beirut: Dâr al-Kutub al-Ilmiyyah, 1994) 14 Vols.

IBN AL-ARABÎ, A., *Ahkâm al-Qur'ân* (Cairo: Matba'ah Dâr al-Sa'âdah, 1330AH).

IBN FARHÛN, M., *Tabsirât al-Hukkâm* (Cairo, 1937).

IBN HAZM, A. A., *al-Muhallâ* (Beirut: Dâr al-Afâq al-Jadîdah, n.d.).

IBN KATHÎR, I., *Tafsîr Ibn Kathîr* (Riyadh: Dâr al-Salâm, 1997) (complete in 1 vol.).

IBN MALIK, I. A., *Sharh al-Manâr al-Anwâr* (Cairo: al-Matba'ah al-'Uthmâniyyah, 1308AH).

IBN NUJAYM, Z., *al-Bahr al-Râ'iq Sharh Kanz al-Daqâ'iq* (Cairo: Matba'ah al-Ilmiyyah, 1311AH).

IBN QAYYIM AL-JAWZIYYAH, *al-Turuq al-Hukmiyyah fî al-Siyâsah al-Shar'iyyah* (Cairo: al-Mu'asasah al-Arabiyyah, 1961).

—— *Kitâb Akhbâr al-Nisâ'* (Cairo: Matba'ah al-Taqaddum, 1900).

—— *I'lâm al-Muwaqqi'în 'An Rabb al-'Alamîn* (Beirut: Dâr al-Kutub al-Ilmiyyah, 1996) 4 Vols.

IBN QUDÂMAH, *al-Mugnî* (Riyadh: Maktabah al-Riyadh al-Hadîthah, 1981) 9 Vols.

IBN SA'D, ÂL DURAYB, S., *al-Tandhîm al-Qadâ'i fî al-Mamlakah al-Arabiyyah al-Sa'ûdiyyah fî Daw al-Sharî'ah al-Islâmiyyah* (Riyadh: Matâbi' Dâr al-Hilâl, 1984) 2 Vols.

IBN TAYMIYYAH, T., *al-Sarîm al-Maslûl alâ Shâtim al-Rasûl*. Abd al-Hamîd, M., (ed.) (Beirut: Dâr al-Kitâb, 1938AH).

AL-'ILÎ, A.H., *al-Huriyyah al-'Amah* (Cairo: Dâr al-Fikr, 1983).

AL-IMÂRAH, M., *Islâm Wa Huqûq al-Insân, Darûrât Lâ Huqûq* (Cairo: Dâr al-Shurûq, 1989).

AL-JAZÂ'IRî, A. J., *Minhâj al-Muslim* (Dâr al-Fikr, 1976).

AL-JAZîRî, A. R., *Kitâb al-Fiqh Alâ al-Madhâhib al-Arba'ah* (Beirut: Dâr al-Fikr, 1996) 5 Vols.

AL-KHALLÂF, A. W., *Ilm al-Usûl al-Fiqh* (Kuwait: Dâr al-Qalam, 1398AH).

—— *Masâdir al-Tashrî' al-Islâmî fîmâ lâ Nass fîh* (Cairo: Dâr al-Kitâb al-Arabî, 1955).

MAHMASSÂNî, S., *Arkân Huqûq al-Insân fî al-Islâm* (Beirut: Dâr al-'Ilm li al-Malâyîn, 1979).

AL-MAQDISî, B. A. R., *al-Uddah Sharh al-Umdah* (Beirut: Dâr al-Ma'rifah, 1997).

AL-MÂWARDî, A., *Kitâb al-Ahkâm al-Sultâniyyah* (Cairo: Mustafâ al-Bâbi al-Halabi, 1966).

AL-QARÂFî, S., *Kitâb al-Furûq* (Cairo: Matba'ah Dâr Ihyâ' al-Kutub al-Arabiyyah, 1346AH).

AL-QURTUBî, M. IBN RUSHD, *Bidâyah al-Mujtahid wa Nihâyah al Muqtasid* (Beirut: Dâr al-Kutub al-Ilmiyyah, 1988) 2 vols.

QUTUB, S., *Fî Zilâl al-Qur'ân* (Beirut, 1974).

RIDÂ, R., *Yusr al-Islâm wa Usûl al-Tashrî' al-'Amm* (Cairo: Matba'ah al-Nahdah Misr, 1956).

AL-SÂMURA'I, A. N., *Ahkâm al-Murtadd fî al-Sharî'ah al-Islâmiyyah* (Beirut: Dâr al-Arabiyyah, 1968).

SHÂFI'î, M., *al-Risâlah* (Cairo: Mustafâ al-Bâbî al-Halabî, 1983).

SHALABî, M. M., *al-Fiqh al-Islâmî Bayn al-Mithâliyyah al-Wâqi'iyyah* (Alexandria, 1960).

—— *al-Madkhal li al-Fiqh al-Islâmiyy* (Cairo, n.d.).

SHALTÛT, M., *al-Islam 'Aqîdah wa Sharî'ah* (Kuwait: Matâbi' Dâr al-Qalam, n.d.).

AL-SHA'RÂNî, A. W., *Kitâb al-Mizân* (Cairo: al-Matba'ah al-Husayniyyah, 1329AH).

AL-SHÂTIBî, A. I., *al-Muwâfaqât* (Saudi Arabia: Dâr Ibn Affân, 1997) 6 Vols.

AL-SHAWKÂNî, Y., *Nayl al-Awtâr: Sharh Muntaqâ al-Akhbâr* (Cairo: Mustafâ al-Bâbî, n.d).

AL-SHAYBANI, M. H., *Sharh Kitâb al-Siyar al-Kabîr* (Beirut: Dâr al-Kutub al-Ilmiyyah, 1997) 5 Vols.

AL-TABARî, M., *Tafsîr al-Tabarî* (Cairo: Mustafâ al-Bâbî, 1968).

TAMÛM, M., *al-Haqq fî al-Sharî'ah al-Islâmiyyah* (Cairo: Maktabah al-Mahmûdiyyah, 1978).

'UTHMÂN, M. F., *Huqûq al-Insan Bayn al-Sharî'ah al-Islâmiyyah wa al-Fikr al-Qânûnî al-Garbî* (Beirut: Dâr al-Surûq, 1982).

UWAYDAH, M. T., (ed.) *al-Fiqh al-Islâmî Asas al-Tashrî'* (Cairo: Matâbi' al-Ahrâm al-Tijâriyyah, 1391AH).

AL-ZAMAKSHARî, J., *al-Kashâf An-Haqâ'iq al-Tanzîl* (Beirut: Dâr al-Ma'rifah, n.d.).

AL-ZAYDÂN, A. K., *al-Fard wa al-Dawlah fî al-Sharî'ah al-Islamiyyah* (USA: International Islamic Federation of Students Organizations, 1970).

AL-ZAYLÂ'î, U., *Tabyîn al-Haqâ'iq:Sharh Kanz al-Daqâ'iq* (Cairo: Matba'ah al-Amîriyyah al-Kubrâ, 1313AH).

AL-ZUHAYLî, W., *Fiqh al-Islâmî wa Adillatuh* (Pittsburgh: Dâr al-Fikr, 1997) 11 Vols.

SELECTED UN DOCUMENTS

Annotation of the Draft International Covenants on Human Rights prepared by the UN Secretary General (1955). *UN Doc. A/2929* of 1/7/55.

UN General Assembly Global Strategy for Shelter to the Year 2000. *UN Doc. A/43/8/Add.1* and *UN Doc A/RES/43/181* of 20/12/1988.

Revised General Guidelines Regarding the Form and Contents of Reports to be Submitted by States Parties Under Articles 16 and 17 of the International Covenant on Economic, Social and Cultural Rights. *UN Doc. E/C.12/1991/1* of 17 June 1991.

Vienna Declaration and Programme of Action, World Conference on Human Rights, Vienna, 1993. *UN Doc. A/CONF.157/23.*

Report of the Regional Meeting for Asia on the World Conference on Human Rights (Bangkok Declaration) Bangkok, 29/03-02/04/93. *UN Doc. A/Conf.157/ASRM/8.*

Concluding Observations of the Committee on Economic, Social and Cultural Rights on Islamic Republic of Iran (1993). *UN. Doc. E/C.12/1993/7* of 09/06/93.

Human Rights Committee Summary Record of the 1251st Meeting with Islamic Republic of Iran. *UN Doc. CCPR/C/SR.1251* of 29/07/93.

Human Rights Committee Summary Record of the 1253rd Meeting with Islamic Republic of Iran. *UN Doc.CCPR/C/SR.1253* of 30/07/93.

Concluding Observations of the Human Rights Committee on Islamic Republic of Iran (1993). *UN Doc. CCPR/C/79/Add.25* of 3/08/93.

Summary Record of 8th Meeting of the Committee on Economic, Social and Cultural Rights with Islamic Republic of Iran. *UN Doc. E/C.12/1993/SR.8* of 20/12/93.

Report of the Special Rapporteur, Mr Gaspar Biro, on Situation of Human Rights in Sudan. *UN Doc. E/CN.4/1994/48* of 01/02/94.

Sudan's Response to Report of Special Rapporteur. *UN Doc. E/CN.4/1994/122* of 18/02/94.

Tunisia's Core Document Forming Part of the Report of States Parties. *UN Doc.HRI/CORE/1/Add.46* of 08/06/94.

Human Rights Committee Summary Record of the 1252nd Meeting with Islamic Republic of Iran. *UN Doc. CCPR/C/SR.1252* of 27/06/94.

Concluding Observations of the Human Rights Committee on Tunisia. *UN Doc.CCPR/C/79/Add.43* of 23/11/94.

Report of the Committee on Elimination of Discrimination Against Women, 14th Session. *UN Doc. A/50/38* of 31/05/95.

Initial Report on the Implementation of the ICCPR by Libyan Arab Jamahiriya (1996). *UN Doc. E/1990/5/Add.26* of 16/02/96.

Report of the Committee on Elimination of Discrimination Against Women (16th and 17th Sessions). *UN Doc. A/52/38/Rev.1. Supplement No. 38* of 23/01/97.

Sudan's 2nd Periodic Report on the ICCPR. *UN Doc CCPR/C/75/Add.2* of 13/03/97.

Human Rights Committee Summary Record of the 1629th Meeting with Sudan. *UN Doc. CCPR/C/SR.1629* of 31/10/97.

Concluding Observations of the Human Rights Committee on Sudan (1997). *UN. Doc. CCPR/C/79/Add.85* of 19/11/97.

Report of Special Rapporteur, Mr Gaspar Biro on Situation of Human Rights in Sudan. *UN Doc. E/CN.4/1998/66* of 30/01/98.

Initial State Party Report on the ICESCR by Egypt. *UN Doc. E/1990/5/Add.38* of 30/06/98.

Second Periodic Report on Implementation of the ICESCR by Jordan (1998). *UN Doc. E/1990/6/Add.17* of 23/07/98.

Human Rights Committee Summary Record of the 1628th Meeting with Sudan. *UN Doc. CCPR/C/SR.1628* of 02/10/98.

Summary Record of 489th Meeting of the Committee on the Rights of the Child with Kuwait. *UN Doc. CRC/C/SR.489* of 02/10/98.

Concluding Observations of the Committee on the Rights of the Child with Kuwait (1998). *UN. Doc. CRC/C/15/Add.96* of 26/10/98.

Proceedings of Seminar on Enriching the Universality of Human Rights: Islamic Perspectives on the Universal Declaration of Human Rights, Geneva, 9–10 November, 1998. *UN Doc. HR/IP/SEM/1999/1*, Part 1 and 2.

UN General Assembly Resolution on Year of Dialogue Among Civilizations. *UN Doc A/RES/53/22* of 16/11/98.

Report on the Situation of Human Rights in Islamic Republic of Iran. *UN Doc. E/CN.4/1999/32* of 28/12/98.

Second Periodic Report on Implementation of the ICESCR by Morocco. *UN Doc. E/1990/6/Add.20* of 09/01/99.

Sudan's Core Document Forming Part of the Report of States Parties. *UN Doc. HRI/CORE/1/Add.99* of 10/11/99.

3rd Periodic Report on Implementation of the ICESCR by Syrian Arab Republic. *UN Doc. E/1994/104/Add.23* of 17/11/99.

List of issues on Implementation of the ICESCR by Sudan. *UN Doc. E/C.12/Q/SUD/1* of 13/12/99.

Report on Situation of Human Rights in Islamic Republic of Iran by UN Special Representative, Maurice Danby Copithorne. *UN Doc. E/CN.4/2000/35* of 18/01/2000.

Compilation of General Comments and General Recommendations Adopted by Human Rights Treaty Bodies. *UN Doc. HRI/GEN/Rev.4* of 07/02/2000.

Replies to Written List of Issues on the Implementation of the ICESCR by Egypt. *UN Doc. HR/CESCR/NONE/2000/6* of 28/03/2000.

Saudi Arabia's Initial Report on the Convention on the Rights of the Child. *UN Doc. CRC/C/61/Add.2* of 29/03/2000.

Summary Record of the 4th Meeting at the 56th Session of the UN Commission on Human Rights. *UN Doc. E/CN.4/2000/SR.4* of 04/04/2000.

Summary Record of the 25th Meeting (56th Session) of the UN Commission on Human Rights. *UN Doc E/CN.4/2000/SR.25* of 25/04/2000.

Summary Record of 30th Meeting (56th Session) of the UN Commission on Human Rights. *UN Doc. E/CN.4/2000/SR.30* of 26/04/2000.

Statement by the Deputy Minister for Foreign Affairs of Saudi Arabia at 56th Session of UN Commission on Human Rights. *UN Doc. E/CN.4/2000/SR.30* of 26/04/2000.

Summary Record of the 11th Meeting of the Committee on Economic, Social and Cultural Rights with Egypt. *UN Doc. E/C.12/2000/SR.11* of 08/05/2000.

Summary Record of the 13th Meeting of the Committee on Economic, Social and Cultural Rights with Egypt. *UN Doc.E/C.12/2000/SR.13* of 09/05/2000.

Reply to List of Issues (E/C.12/Q/SUD/1) by Sudan. *UN Doc. HR/CESCR/NONE/2000/10* of 24/06/2000.

The UN Secretary-General's Report on Right to Development to the 55th Session of the UN General Assembly. *UN Doc. A/55/283* of 08/08/2000.

UN Secretary-General's Report on Elimination of All forms of Religious Intolerance in Turkey. *UN Doc. A/55/280/Add.1* of 11/08/2000.

UN Secretary-General's Report on Situation of Human Rights in the Islamic Republic of Iran. *UN Doc. A/55/363* of 08/09/2000.

Concluding Observations of the Committee on Economic, Social and Cultural Rights on Morocco. *UN. Doc. E/C.12/1/Add.55* of 01/12/2000.

Summary Record of the 688th Meeting of Committee on the Rights of the Child with Saudi Arabia. *UN Doc. CRC/C/SR.688 of 24/01/2001* of 24/01/2001.

Concluding Observations of the Committee on the Rights of the Child on Saudi Arabia (2001). *UN Doc. CRC/C/15/Add.148* of 26/01/2001.

SELECTED INTERNET WEB SITES

International Humanitarian Law Treaties Web Site: http://www.icrc.org/ihl.nsf/WebPRES?OpenView [1/3/2003].

International Labour Organization Conventions Web Site: http://ilolex.ilo.ch:1567/public/english/docs/convdisp.htm [1/3/2003].

International Law Association Web Site: http://www.ila-hq.org [1/3/2003].

Permanent Delegation of the Organization of Islamic Conference to the UN Web Site: http://www.oic-un.org [1/3/2003].

UN International Human Rights Instruments Web Site: http://www.unhchr.ch/html/intlinst.htm [1/3/2003].

Index